ORIENT

IN THE 70s

Tony McDonald

First Published in November, 2018 by
Football World
Tel: 01708 734 502
www.footballworld.co.uk

Copyright Football World

Designed by Jan Watts
Printed by Premier Print Group Ltd
Distributed by Football World
103 Douglas Road, Hornchurch, Essex, RM11 1AW, England
Distribution email: susie@footballworld.co.uk

ISBN 978-0-9927427-6-8

Dedicated to all Os supporters who were lucky enough to enjoy a special era in the club's history. And to all the many others too young to have seen it but wished they had.

Acknowledgements

THERE are so many people who must be thanked for their help with this book. Firstly, former Orient manager George Petchey and all the players – particularly Mickey Bullock and Peter Kitchen, who was key to the promotional launch – who kindly agreed to be interviewed and provide such an absorbing insight into life at the club during this memorable decade. And to Brian Winston, whose self-styled brand of chairmanship was years ahead of its time. Some of the forthright views of the main contributors may be contradictory but no less worthy of inclusion.

The book really is a collaborative effort by so many of the wonderfully unique 'Orient family'. Two diehard Os supporters were very helpful with the interview process, especially Paul Hiscock, while Martin Smith also deserves credit.

Many thanks to David and Clive Bloomfield, Jimmy's sons, for sharing their candid memories of a very special football man whose legacy will live on forever.

Not wishing to ignore or gloss over some of the less endearing aspects of football in the 70s, I much appreciate the honest input of Paul 'Beefy' Roberts, Trevor Simmons and others who were there at the time and don't recall everything that went on through a rose-tinted hue. Still in the fans' section, it was great to track down Mark Hodges, whose imagination helped to create the current club crest.

For their vital help with research I doff my hat to a group of fans whose acres of newspaper cuttings have been a precious reference source. Dick Richards, Martin Strong and David Jones are a cut above in this respect.

I can confidently and proudly claim that *Orient in the 70s* contains the rarest photographs ever published in any Os book and for that I owe huge thanks to Tony Furby, who sat shivering on his camera case at Brisbane Road for more years than he cares to recall while covering games for the local press and the club's match day programme. I can vouch for the rarity of most images you'll see, because Tony handed me his vast neg collection a few years back and said: 'Go on, print them all up yourself!'. I'm delighted that his efforts and endless hours of scanning have been worthwhile and that Tony's work from more than four decades ago has now seen the light of day for others to enjoy.

For the main cover images, as well as the other scarves and memorabilia items that make the collectibles section of the book drip with nostalgia, big thanks go to Martin Stern, who also helped with proof-reading and saved me – Roederesque sweeper-style – from several own-goals.

Numerous others generously gave their time by helping out with photos, scans, cuttings, programmes, advice, publicity, practical help, or answered the call on social media at all hours of the day and night, but take a bow: Keith Emmerson, Peter Law, Barry Jones, Martin Smith, David Watson, Garry Graham, John Parke, Roy Clifford, Mat Roper of Pandamonium fanzine, Lloyd Scott, Nick Sonenfield, Steve Tongue, Paul Gregory, Tom Griffiths, Simon O'Connor, Caroline Burkinshaw, George Sargent, Bill Hadgkiss, Geoff Marshall, Graham Goodall, Clive Boon and Adrian Malupa, plus my wife Susie, son Jack, designer Jan and Caroline. Special mention for Ron Hudson and Davis Watson, admins for their respective addictive Facebook groups, 'Remembering the 70's' and 'Leyton Orient FC Collectors'.

The brilliant images that adorn the preceding pages are the delicate work of John Devlin of True Colours, who also produced an Orient A3 kit poster, while his latest book, True Colours International Kits, is available from www.truecoloursfootballkits.com.

And finally, thanks, as ever, to David Dodd (chairman, Leyton Orient Supporters' Club), all the LOSC volunteers and Leyton Orient FC, and anyone else who helped.

ORIENT

Contents

Introduction

MY 10th birthday was fast approaching as the 70s dawned and, like millions of kids at that time, football already held me in a vice-like grip. I played and watched the game whenever I could, boarding buses and trains to watch live matches alone and also with school friends.

As my father Terry played most of his 171 games on the wing for Leyton Orient between 1959 and 1965, I have no recollection of watching him play during those halcyon days of the 1961-62 promotion season, so the decade that followed is the era I will always look back on with most affection.

It didn't occur to many of us adolescents that Britain was in the midst of industrial, economic and political strife. As successive prime ministers Ted Heath, Harold Wilson, Jim Callaghan and Maggie Thatcher grappled with one crisis after enough, my biggest concerns were much simpler. What provoked the miners' strikes, power cuts, petrol rationing and three-day working week was no business of ours.

What really mattered was bunking off school to see the Portsmouth FA Cup replay at 1.30 on a Tuesday afternoon (hardly worth the detention that followed); if Our Price Records would have in stock the brand new T-Rex, Bowie or Rod Stewart album for sale on its first day of release; and whether *Shoot!* had Laurie Cunningham's picture in it.

Football wise, it didn't get much better, because our beloved Os spent the entire duration of the 70s in the second tier. How unreal does that seem almost 40 years on!

Please join me in looking back at this memorable decade through a child-like rose-tinted hue . . .

Happy days, when most league games and cup ties were played on Saturday afternoon at three o'clock and we were perfectly content watching edited highlights on *Match of the Day* and *The Big Match.* Colour television was still in its infancy and only three terrestrial channels existed.

When less really was more.

Growing up with the familiar voices of David Coleman, Brian Moore, Jimmy Hill, Bob Wilson, Kenneth Wolstenholme, Barry Davies, John Motson and regional mic men Hugh Johns, Keith Macklin, Gerry Harrison and Gerald Sinstadt. The more soothing dulcet tones of radio giants Bryon Butler and Peter Jones painting vivid pictures in your father's car or from the living room.

Young boys kicked footballs over the park or in the street until dusk and bought weekly magazines, cutting out pictures of their favourite stars to decorate bedroom walls or school exercise books.

Lush, green pitches in August and September that turned to a foot of mud by November and a bobbly baked dustbowl by April. Occasionally a stray dog would enliven proceedings with a casual stroll through midfield.

Black football boots, white balls and shirts numbered from one to 11, when away strips were occasionally used to avoid the most obvious colour clash; and only match officials ever wore black.

Queuing to hand over cash at the turnstiles (or slide under them if you knew the operator) and lining up for hours on Sunday mornings for precious FA Cup tickets, clutching tokens clipped from the top corner of the previous home programme. The Cup . . . ah, yes, when winning that much coveted trophy was nearly as prestigious as lifting the league championship and everyone, players and fans, dreamed of a day out at Wembley.

When grumpy old men in caps, who'd escaped the missus for a few hours, stood shouting and hollering and smoking a fag or 10, while sneering at boisterous young lads who tied club scarves around their wrists and waist in a show of proud allegiance. Silk scarves – like those draped across this spread – were the height of football fashion years before the replica kit boom.

When our heroes were long-haired, sometimes bearded, blokes with names like Barrie, Bobby, Bill, Mickey, Peter, Tom, John, Joe and Terry, they grew sideburns longer than Pan's People's skirts and lived on the same planet as the fans who paid their wages. They wore flared trousers, ate in the same Wimpy Bars as us and drove Cortinas and Granadas home to their three-bedroomed semis.

In the pre-digital age before fans began staring incessantly at mobile phones for score updates or a WhatsApp message from someone they barely recall shagging the previous night, we were actually glued to the football action unfolding before our mince pies, while keeping half an eye on the half-time scoreboard to get a clue as to what was happening at other grounds.

And at the final whistle, for those unable to tune into Sports Report for the full classified check with the inimitable James Alexander Gordon, a visit to the newsagent's to eagerly devour the printed reports in the late Saturday editions of the *Evening Standard* and *Evening News* was part of the Saturday night ritual.

People still bought and read Sunday newspapers for more measured match reports and the latest transfer gossip; some ritually cutting them up and pasting them in scrapbooks now gathering dust in lofts.

Let's be honest, though, it wasn't all Hunky Dory and Seasons in the Sun. There was a grim, more sinister, side to some aspects of society and the game itself. Hooliganism was rife and, it's hard to believe now, but people were sometimes too scared to go to football matches.

There were 'bovver boys' in donkey jackets kicking out in Doc Marten boots, fighting running battles in towns, grounds and while being escorted to and from railway stations by harassed Old Bill.

Away venues were identified from a distance by towering steel floodlight pylons that desperate fans would sometimes clamber up to get a better view above crumbling and packed concrete terraces littered with discarded peanut shells.

Fans had to endure antiquated, uncovered toilets that stank but the stench of racism lingered much longer.

For better or worse, those were the days I remember.

Now let's go back there with the help of some of the people at Orient who created those memories . . .

Up the Os!

Tony McDonald
Hornchurch, Essex
November, 2018

CHAMPIONS IN STYLE

SEASON 1969-70

ORIENT
v
ROTHERHAM
Saturday, December 20th, 1969
Kick Off 3.09 p.m.
FOOTBALL LEAGUE - DIVISION III
Official Programme 6d.

AFTER three seasons in the third tier ensnared by crippling debts and near insolvency, Orient fought back from the brink to become champions of Football League Division Three.

Jimmy Bloomfield's Os finished two points clear of runners-up Luton Town, managed by former Leyton Orient boss Alec Stock. It was some turnaround after the previous season's brush with relegation and a scrambling 18th-place finish.

The catalyst was the decision of 35-year-old Bloomfield to hang up his boots, quit his role as player-manager and devote all his time and energies to team management.

TRANSFERS

>**IN** Dickie Plume (Millwall – free), Mark Lazarus (Crystal Palace – £10,000).
<**OUT** Jimmy Bloomfield (retired), Bert Howe (Colchester Utd – free), Roy Massey (Colchester Utd – £5,000), John Key (retired injured).

FACTS & FIGURES

* Orient dispensed with the white socks used the previous season and adopted an all-red strip.
* A new drainage system was installed to improve a playing surface that had always struggled badly to cope with the elements. To further preserve the condition of the Brisbane Road pitch, Orient's team trained at the Green and Silley Weir company sports ground at Wanstead, where their junior matches was also played.
* Catering facilities improved following the appointment of P.S. Doran & Son Ltd as new official caterers at Leyton Stadium. Pat Doran, who also held the catering rights at West Ham and Arsenal, provided licensed refreshment bars.
* The exclusive 50 Club, launched the previous season, was reorganised into a Vice-Presidents' Club.
* In December, Orient announced that licensed bars would be open one hour before and after games. The Brisbane Bar and Coronation Bar, located in the wings of the main East Stand, were named after local streets. Two further bars were under construction on the Coronation Gardens and Windsor Road terraces
* Remarkably, only 16 players were used in 46 league and four cup games (teams were permitted to name and use only one sub in those days). Of those 16, only six of were signed by Bloomfield, four were signed by Dick Graham and the rest progressed from the youth team. Such is the value of a good youth scouting and coaching system.
* Orient's total of 67 goals was the lowest by any third division table-toppers since the league was formed in 1958 and fewer than seven of the other top eight clubs. But their 36 goals conceded was the lowest of the 24 Division Three sides. Os scored more goals (24) away than they conceded (21).

DIARY: KEY MATCHES & MOMENTS

Aug 30 – Barrie Fairbrother caps his league debut at 18 with his first senior goal in the 1-0 home win v Mansfield Town. Barry Dyson's shot rebounds to Fairbrother, who sweeps the ball home from close-range in the 49th minute.

Sept 20 – Os come from behind to win 2-1 at Barnsley, where Dickie Plume – who had only just come on as second-half sub for the injured Terry Parmenter – clinched victory with his first goal for the club after Parmenter set up Fairbrother for the equaliser.

Sept 29 – At the third time of asking this season, Os finally get the better of Fulham with a classic 3-1 London derby victory to avenge their recent League Cup exit. A crowd of 18,861, Os highest since May, 1966, enjoy goals by Terry Mancini, Peter Allen and Barrie Fairbrother.

Oct 7 – Apprentice striker Bobby Moss breaks his arm the day before receiving an invitation to attend England Youth training at Lilleshall.

Oct 15 – Mark Lazarus rejoins the club from newly-promoted First Division Crystal Palace.

Dec 26 – A bumper home crowd of 17,619 receive the perfect belated Christmas present, as Allen nets the only goal v league leaders Luton Town in the 11.30am Boxing Day clash. It lifts third-placed Os to within two points of Hatters. On a sour note, Harper is stretchered off three minutes from half-time with a knee injury.

Mark Lazarus made a big impact on his return.

Feb – Jimmy Bloomfield wins the Third Division Manager of the Month award for January. Sponsors Bell's Whisky present him with a gallon of whisky. "We won't drink it until we've won promotion," he says.

Feb 16 – Os regain top spot by battering fellow promotion contenders Barnsley 4-2 – thanks to volunteer helpers. Earlier in the day 60 fans rolled and sanded the sodden pitch. The club was so convinced the evening game would be off (as was the previous game v Rochdale two days earlier), they didn't bother to print a programme. Instead, fans had to make do with a one-page team-sheet. Os stun the visitors with a three-goal first-half blast in 11 minutes through Mickey Bullock, an Eric Winstanley own-goal and Lazarus (36). Although Barnsley pull one back, stand-in skipper Dyson puts the issue beyond doubt before Dean added a late consolation. Os stay ahead of Reading on goal-average, with two matches in hand.

Feb 28 – Former Brighton centre-half Eric Whittington, 23, joins Os on a month's loan from South Africa to plug the gaps left by injuries to Harper and Mancini. Although named as 12th man at Bournemouth, he never appears for the first team.

Feb – Malcolm Slater, who declines to extend his loan to Dick Graham's Colchester, undergoes a pelvic operation.

Mar – Len Cheesewright joins the staff after the club make his position as youth team coach a full-time role.

Mar 27 – Fit again Mancini leads Os to a 4-1 home Good Friday morning win v Plymouth Argyle watched by the season's biggest crowd of 19,861 – Os' best league gate since Spurs attracted 30,987 in October, 1962. Fairbrother grabs a brace, with Dyson and Peter Brabrook also on target as Os hit three after the interval to begin their Easter programme in style.

Apr 4 – In a Saturday evening home match starting at 6.30pm to avoid clashing with the Grand National (won by Pat Taaffe on Gay Trip), relegation-doomed Barrow are beaten 2-0 by goals from Lazarus and Tommy Taylor, who cracked home a soaring 30-yard drive.

Apr 7 – In the 2-0 defeat at Walsall, Allen is sent off for the first time in his exemplary career by Sheffield-based ref Green seconds from the end of the game. He was alleged to have struck out at Mick Evans, who was also dismissed, but Bloomfield defended his wing-half afterwards: "Peter never did a thing. As far as I am concerned he was completely blameless for what happened and I was amazed he was sent-off. He was well and truly clobbered."

Apr 11 – Another Saturday night (7.30pm) home kick-off, this time to allow fans to watch David Webb's Chelsea draw 2-2 with Leeds United in the FA Cup Final before resuming their finger-biting routine at Brisbane Road. Two down to Rochdale with a quarter of an hour to go, Os show great character to force a lucky 2-2 draw. With 12 minutes to play, Brabrook back-headed home after Bullock flicks on Dyson's

Football League Division Three 1969-70

1	Aug	9	a	Rochdale	W	3-0	Rofe, Dyson, Bullock		7,114
2		16	H	HALIFAX TOWN	W	1-0	Bullock		6,027
3		23	a	Luton Town	L	2-3	Jones, Bullock		14,761
4		25	a	Barrow	D	1-1	Mancini		4,808
5		30	H	MANSFIELD TOWN	W	1-0	Fairbrother		6,018
6	Sept	6	a	Rotherham Utd	D	0-0			6,468
7		13	H	BRIGHTON & HOVE ALBION	D	1-1	Mancini		8,040
8		15	H	BRADFORD CITY	W	2-1	Bullock, Fairbrother		7,365
9		20	a	Barnsley	W	2-1	Fairbrother, Plume		11,462
10		27	H	TORQUAY UTD	D	1-1	Allen		9,176
11		29	H	FULHAM	W	3-1	Mancini, Allen, Fairbrother		18,861
12	Oct	4	a	Tranmere Rovers	D	1-1	Bullock		4,146
13		7	a	Halifax Town	D	1-1	Bullock		4,367
14		11	H	READING	L	0-1			9,809
15		18	H	DONCASTER ROVERS	W	2-0	Mancini, Bullock		9,660
16		25	a	Gillingham	W	1-0	Fairbrother		5,452
17	Nov	1	H	BOURNEMOUTH & B A	W	3-0	Dyson, Bullock 2		9,231
18		8	a	Plymouth Argyle	L	0-1			7,951
19		22	a	Shrewsbury Town	D	1-1	Bullock		4,538
20		24	H	WALSALL	W	2-0	Dyson, Bullock		6,943
21	Dec	13	a	Brighton & Hove Albion	D	0-0			9,274
22		20	H	ROTHERHAM UTD	D	1-1	Brabrook		4,593
23		26	H	LUTON TOWN	W	1-0	Allen		17,619
24		27	a	Mansfield Town	L	1-4	Lazarus		7,828
25	Jan	2	a	Fulham	D	1-1	Lazarus		12,308
26		17	a	Torquay Utd	W	1-0	Jones		5,764
27		26	H	BURY	W	3-0	Fairbrother 2, Bullock		10,616
28		31	H	TRANMERE ROVERS	W	2-0	Bullock, Rofe		11,733
29	Feb	7	a	Reading	L	2-3	Bullock 2		17,881
30		16	H	BARNSLEY	W	4-2	Bullock, Rofe, Lazarus, Dyson		10,792
31		28	a	Bournemouth & B A	W	2-0	Fairbrother, Parmenter		5,633
32	Mar	2	a	Stockport County	W	2-0	Fairbrother 2		2,850
33		9	H	BRISTOL ROVERS	D	0-0			14,324
34		14	a	Bury	W	1-0	Fairbrother		4,265
35		17	a	Southport	L	0-1			3,860
36		21	H	STOCKPORT COUNTY	W	3-0	Coddington (og), Jones, Taylor		10,905
37		27	H	PLYMOUTH ARGYLE	W	4-1	Dyson, Brabrook, Fairbrother 2		19,861
38		28	a	Bristol Rovers	L	0-1			22,005
39		30	a	Doncaster Rovers	W	1-0	Robertson (og)		5,536
40	Apr	4	H	BARROW	W	2-0	Lazarus, Taylor		11,812
41		7	a	Walsall	L	0-2			5,432
42		11	H	ROCHDALE	D	2-2	Brabrook, Lazarus		13,260
43		15	a	Bradford City	W	1-0	Bullock		5,442
44		20	H	SOUTHPORT	W	3-2	Lazarus, Bullock 2		14,216
45		25	H	SHREWSBURY TOWN	W	1-0	Lazarus		13,268
46		27	H	GILLINGHAM	L	1-2	Dyson		16,334
FA Cup									
1	Nov	15	a	Walsall	D	0-0			5,643
R		17	H	WALSALL	L	0-2			10,646
League Cup									
1	Aug	13	H	FULHAM	D	0-0			8,676
R		18	a	Fulham	L	1-3	Harper		11,424

Pos	Team	P	Home						Away						Total		
			W	D	L	F	A	W	D	L	F	A		F	A	Pts
1	ORIENT	46	16	5	2	43	15	9	7	7	24	21		67	36	62
2	Luton Town	46	13	8	2	46	15	10	6	7	31	28		77	43	60
3	Bristol Rovers	46	15	5	3	51	26	5	11	7	29	33		80	59	56
4	Fulham	46	12	9	2	43	26	8	6	9	38	29		81	55	55
5	Brighton & H A	46	16	4	3	37	16	7	5	11	20	27		57	43	55
6	Mansfield Town	46	14	4	5	46	22	7	7	9	24	27		70	49	53
7	Barnsley	46	14	6	3	43	24	5	9	9	25	35		68	59	53
8	Reading	46	16	3	4	52	29	5	8	10	35	48		87	77	53
9	Rochdale	46	11	6	6	39	24	7	4	12	30	36		69	60	46
10	Bradford City	46	11	6	6	37	22	6	6	11	20	28		57	50	46
11	Doncaster Rovers	46	13	4	6	31	19	4	8	11	21	35		52	54	46
12	Walsall	46	11	4	8	33	31	6	8	9	21	36		54	67	46
13	Torquay United	46	9	9	5	36	22	5	8	10	26	37		62	59	45
14	Rotherham United	46	10	8	5	36	19	5	6	12	26	35		62	54	44
15	Shrewsbury Town	46	10	12	1	35	17	3	6	14	27	46		62	63	44
16	Tranmere Rovers	46	10	8	5	38	29	4	8	11	18	43		56	72	44
17	Plymouth Argyle	46	10	7	6	32	23	6	4	13	24	41		56	64	43
18	Halifax Town	46	10	9	4	31	25	4	6	13	16	38		47	63	43
19	Bury	46	13	4	6	47	29	2	7	14	28	51		75	80	41
20	Gillingham	46	7	6	10	28	33	6	7	10	24	31		52	64	39
21	Bournemouth & B A	46	8	9	6	28	27	4	6	13	20	44		48	71	39
22	Southport	46	11	5	7	31	22	3	5	15	17	44		48	66	38
23	Barrow	46	7	9	7	28	27	1	5	17	18	54		46	81	30
24	Stockport County	46	4	7	12	17	30	2	4	17	10	41		27	71	23

corner. Three minutes from time Lazarus' scrambles in following another Dyson corner.

Apr 15 – Os are back in Division Two but have to wait until the 75th minute to clinch a 1-0 win at Bradford City, where Lazarus' right-wing cross is met by Bullock's diving header – his 17th goal of the season but only his first since Feb 16.

Apr 16 – Orient honour club legend Stan Charlton, now managing Southern League Weymouth, with a Thursday night testimonial game. Bloomfield's men meet a team made up of former Os, including seven of the 1961-62 promotion-winning squad captained by Stan, plus Paul Went and second-half sub David Webb.

Apr 20 – Visitors Southport boosted their hopes of avoiding relegation by leading 1-0 at half-time, before Lazarus (70) equalises with a 25-yard drive. Two headed goals by Bullock in a couple of minutes earn a memorable 3-2 victory under the lights. Os edge two points clear of Luton at the top with a game in hand.

Apr 25 – With promotion secured, Lazarus applies the icing to the cake by leaping high to head home a Bullock chip and seal a 1-0 home win v Shrewsbury Town with thunder and lightning threatening overhead.

Apr 27 – The Monday night promotion party attended by 16,000 turns into an anti-climax. Gillingham, desperate for two points to avoid relegation, provide a guard of honour as Os run out of the tunnel before kick-off and their survival hopes take a severe dent when Dyson atones for an earlier penalty miss by racing through to give lack-lustre Os the lead. But with so much more to play for than their hosts, Gills hit back with two second-half goals to win 2-1 . . . and send Bournemouth down on goal-average.

May 4 – In a hastily arranged Monday night friendly in front of 7,619, the newly-crowned Division Three champs find the Latin skills of Italy's AC Roma too hot to handle. The slick passing visitors, with Fabio Capello at inside-forward, slice open the home defence time and time again on their way to a 3-1 win laced with continental style. Dyson's last minute consolation comes via a re-taken penalty.

CHAMPIONS!

The 1969-70 Division Three champions. Back row, left to right: Ray Goddard, Barry Dyson, Peter Allen, Steve Bowtell. Middle row: Jimmy Bloomfield (manager), Charlie Simpson (physio), Peter Brabrook, Tommy Taylor, Dave Harper, Mickey Bullock, Peter Angell (assistant manager). Front row: Mick Jones, Dickie Plume, Terry Parmenter, Terry Mancini, Malcolm Slater, Barrie Fairbrother, Dennis Rofe.

THERE'S ONE BIG HAPPY FAMILY AT BRISBANE ROAD

MOST MARRIED MEN have only one set of responsibilities—the wife and kids. But Orient boss Jimmy Bloomfield is "father" to an entire squad of footballers as well.

And these days, his attractive wife

Like all fathers, Jim's very proud of his kids. David, a budding inside-forward in the same mould as his Dad, plays for Walthamstow Rangers on Sundays. And Jim watches every week, although he has never interfered with his 12-year-old son's coaching.

There is always a football handy at the Bloomfield household, though, and Jim is quick to get the boys the

And the youngsters have not let him down. Dennis Rofe, Tommy Taylor, Barrie Fairbrother and Ray Goddard have all been regulars and they have injected a wonderful playing spirit into the side.

Those who saw Tommy Taylor on ... against Stock-

ORIENT VICTORY MAKES THEM THE CHAMPIONS

THE champagne flowed down Brisbane-road way around 4.45 yesterday afternoon. Orient had just become the Third Division champions—and they celebrated in style.

mouth, who will be relegated on goal average if the Kent club can pick up those two priceless points at Brisbane Road.

Pity poor Darlington at the bottom of the Fourth Division. They lost 1—0 at Lincoln. Bobby Svare headed the winner

Peter Allen, Os' longest-serving player, started all 46 games in the Third Division title-winning season. This picture appeared in the weekly Shoot! magazine.

PETER ALLEN (Orient)

Throughout the 70s Orient prided itself on its successful youth policy that yielded a production line of talent. The first young star to emerge as the new decade dawned was teenage central defender Tommy Taylor.

Brave Brabrook earns his glory

Orient 3, Stockport 0   By SAM BARTRAM

WEMBLEY beckons for Chelsea. Jimmy Greaves has gone to West Ham. But Peter Brabrook is determined that his two former clubs will not grab all the glory.

He turned out for Orient yesterday when he should have ~~been nursing an injured back~~—and helped them keep up their

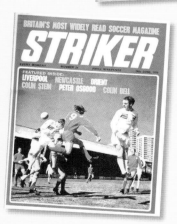

BRITAIN'S MOST WIDELY READ SOCCER MAGAZINE
STRIKER
FEATURED INSIDE:
LIVERPOOL NEWCASTLE ORIENT
COLIN STEIN PETER OSGOOD COLIN DELL

Barrie Fairbrother (9), Mickey Bullock and Terry Mancini feature in this shot, taken during the home game against Plymouth in March, 1970, that adorned the cover of Striker magazine.

Taylor clinches Orient triumph

Orient 3 Stockport 0: by ROY HOROBIN

ORIENT WON with ease as they marched on towards the Second Division. Wing-halves Peter Allen and Dickie Plume dominated the game, giving the attack superb support. Centre-forward Barrie Fairbrother and inside-forwards Mick Bullock and Barry Dyson

Well done the "Orient" & continued success for next season

from Albert of THE OLIVER TWIST

CHURCH ROAD LEYTON

O's two down, level in fighting finish

By VINCE WRIGHT
Orient 2, Rochdale 2

ORIENT, down in the dumps and woefully out of touch for most of the match, fought back magnificently in the final 20 minutes and almost snatched a sensational victory against a very capable Rochdale team at Brisbane Road on Saturday evening.

An equalising goal three minutes from time by Mark Lazarus was greeted with tumultuous cheers by Orient's faithful followers and in the remaining seconds Rochdale's goal was subjected to a barrage of shots.

Peter Brabrook and Mickey Bullock created a wonderful opening for Barry Dyson and the inside-forward's 30-yard power shot, destined for the corner of the net, was brilliantly palmed away by goalkeeper Chris Harker.

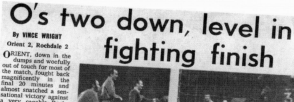

● The goal that put Orient back into the game and gave them the inspiration to snatch a last gasp equaliser, Right-back Graham Smith makes a valiant leap but fails to prevent a header by Peter Brabrook (centre of goal) from sneaking into the net. The other players are Mark Lazarus (extreme left), Terry Mancini, Rochdale centre-half Colin Parry and left-back Derek Ryder. Picture by Archie McNeice.
★ (419)

NET LOSSES MOUNT UP

DESPITE returning to the second tier after a four-year absence, Orient failed to add to their Third Division championship-winning squad during the close season – and within days of the re-start they would inevitably lose their most prized young asset.

After months of transfer speculation, with chairman Arthur Page always quick to rebuff press reports that the club would cash in on its most promising young talent, 19-year-old central defender Tommy Taylor joined East End neighbours West Ham United in a deal worth £100,000.

The board and manager Jimmy Bloomfield's faith in the men who won promotion was ultimately vindicated by their 17th-place finish – but it was a close thing. Goal-shy Os drew more than a third of their matches but still managed to end up seven points above the two relegated clubs.

TRANSFERS

>IN Peter Bennett (West Ham United – £22,000), Gordon Riddick (Charlton Athletic – £10,000).

<OUT Malcolm Slater (Folkestone Town – free), Graham Archell (Folkestone Town – free), Bill Bailey (Dartford – free), Brian Scrimshaw (Israel), Tommy Taylor (West Ham United – £78,000).

FACTS & FIGURES

* Orient adopted a new club crest. The blue/white/gold oval P&O badge, used since 1967, was replaced by a white dragon.

* Just as well that Os made a reasonable start to the campaign. They avoided going straight back down despite failing to win any of their last 10 league matches, losing seven and drawing three, although they did meet five of the top six teams in this period. That miserable finale included a barren spell of five consecutive games without scoring.

* There was an even worse 13-match winless spell between September 30 and January 9. The two victories either side of that dismal run were both against relegation-bound Bolton Wanderers.

* Along with relegated Blackburn Rovers, Os won the fewest number (five) home matches in Division Two, scoring a paltry 16 goals on home turf (and mud), while 11 draws at Brisbane Road was another unwanted record.

* With just 29 league goals scored all season, Os were the only side in their division not to exceed the 30-goal mark. Top scorer Mark Lazarus' brace in the opening day 3-0 home win against Sheffield United was the only time an Orient player scored twice in any of their 46 league and cup games.

* Even in the nine league fixtures they did win, Os lacked conviction. Seven of those victories were by the slenderest 1-0 margin. Bloomfield's men scored twice in a game on only three occasions – and one of them was a 5-2 hammering at Hull!

* Unsung heroes Barry Dyson and Gordon Riddick each earned Os five league points with vital goals over the course of a very testing season.

DIARY: KEY MATCHES & MOMENTS

Aug 7 – When pre-season friendlies actually meant something. First Division neighbours West Ham

United bring a star-studded line-up to E10 for the Brisbane Road curtain-raiser that attracts a Friday night crowd of around 13,000. Bobby Moore, fresh from a stolen bracelet accusation and spearheading England in the World Cup finals in Mexico, leads virtually a full strength Hammers side including Geoff Hurst, Jimmy Greaves, Trevor Brooking, Frank Lampard, Billy Bonds, plus Israel national skipper Mordecai Spiegler. Barry Dyson gave Os a 75th minute lead from the penalty spot before Peter Eustace – who would manage Leyton Orient from 1991 to '94 – equalised six minutes from full-time.

Aug 15 – Two goals by Mark Lazarus and one from Dave Harper give Os the best possible start to the league campaign, although the Orient board were disappointed that only 10,584 – almost 1,000 down on last season's average – turned out to see them come from behind to beat Sheffield United 3-1. "I and everyone else was expecting 15,000," commented Jimmy Bloomfield.

Sept 12 – Rain stopped play in the 33rd minute of the televised home game against Sunderland. A torrential downpour forced referee Maurice Fussey to take the teams off the field for seven minutes. When play resumed on a waterlogged surface, Os' sub Terry Parmenter (on for Peter Brabrook after 74 minutes) made a big splash by scoring a rare goal from what looked like an intended cross that swirled over keeper Jim Montgomery's head in the 81st minute.

Sept – Jimmy Bloomfield is promoted from team manager to the new role of 'general manager'. In a behind the scenes move, John Falltrick – who has been a willing helper at Orient for a number of years – is appointed club secretary in succession to long-serving George Hicks, who quit due to ill health after 13 years in the job.

Oct 10 – Clearly distracted by all the transfer talk, Tommy Taylor suffers a nightmare end to his impressive first spell with Os by gifting visitors Hull City the winner and then conceding a penalty (which Ray Goddard saved to deny Tigers' player-manager Terry Neil) four days before his big money move to West Ham United. It's the first time in 18 months that Orient have lost back-to-back games.

Oct 14 – Taylor leaves E10 to join First Division Hammers, with versatile defender/midfielder Peter Bennett, 24, moving in the opposite direction. Bloomfield uses £10k of the Taylor cash to sign forward Gordon Riddick, 26, from Second Division rivals Charlton Athletic but fails in a double bid to lure Harry Gregory from The Valley back to Leyton. Instead, the striker joins Aston Villa in a £10k deal. In his programme column for the Millwall game (Oct 24), chairman Page struck a bullish note not shared among fans when he wrote: "Take my word for it that last week's transactions were another step along the road to success." The team didn't win another game until January.

Oct – In an effort to boost crowds, Arthur Page asks Football League secretary Alan Hardaker if Os can be paired with Spurs in future fixture lists.

Nov 21 – Teenage striker Bobby Moss, 18, replacing new signing Gordon Riddick, scores with a glancing near post header from six yards, just five minutes into his league debut, to earn Os a 1-1 home draw with Watford.

Dec – Os fail in a cheeky bid to secure World Cup winner Nobby Stiles, 28, on a two-month loan from Manchester United.

Dec 19 – Terry Brisley's first league goal earns a 1-1 home draw against Blackburn Rovers. The 20-year-old midfield terrier drove home a Mickey Bullock flick-on.

Salute Moss

By DAVID KENT
Orient 1 Watford 1

A GOAL from 18-year-old debut boy Bobby Moss was not enough to end Orient's dismal home record against Watford.

Moss put Orient ahead

Jan – The club bid £10,000 for the freehold of the stadium, owned by Waltham Forest Council. "It's a very reasonable price, as we pay less than £1,000 a year rent at present," said Arthur Page.

Jan 25 – The Monday night FA Cup fourth round replay against top flight Nottingham Forest is farcically abandoned at half-time by referee Tom Reynolds due to a heavily waterlogged, pitch. Many of the 18,000 crowd were astonished that the game even started – kick-off was delayed by seven minutes – given that there were two-inch deep puddles on some parts of the Brisbane Road quagmire. The club came under

Football League Division Two 1970-71

1	Aug	15	H	SHEFFIELD UTD	W	3-1	Harper, Lazarus 2		10,584
2		22	a	Blackburn Rovers	D	0-0			9,306
3		29	H	CHARLTON ATHLETIC	D	0-0			14,746
4	Sept	2	a	Portsmouth	D	1-1	Bullock		15,218
5		5	a	Carlisle Utd	L	0-2			8,143
6		12	H	SUNDERLAND	W	1-0	Parmenter		8,919
7		19	a	Luton Town	L	0-4			16,711
8		26	H	CARDIFF CITY	D	0-0			11,992
9		30	a	Bolton Wanderers	W	1-0	Fairbrother		6,860
10	Oct	3	a	Queens Park Rangers	L	1-5	Fairbrother		14,500
11		10	H	HULL CITY	L	0-1			9,445
12		17	a	Sheffiled Utd	L	1-3	Bullock		20,205
13		19	H	SHEFFIELD WEDNESDAY	D	1-1	Dyson		10,219
14		24	H	MILLWALL	D	0-0			14,282
15		31	a	Norwich City	L	2-4	Allen, Payne (og)		11,670
16	Nov	7	H	MIDDLESBROUGH	D	0-0			6,690
17		14	a	Birmingham City	L	0-1			14,137
18		21	H	WATFORD	D	1-1	Moss		8,978
19		28	a	Leicester City	L	0-4			23,699
20	Dec	5	H	BRISTOL CITY	D	1-1	Riddick		6,250
21		12	a	Swindon Town	D	1-1	Mancini		13,863
22		19	H	BLACKBURN ROVERS	D	1-1	Brisley		5,931
23	Jan	9	H	BOLTON WANDERERS	W	3-1	Jones, Bullock, Lazarus		6,580
24		16	a	Sheffiled Wednesday	L	1-2	Lazarus		11,149
25	Feb	6	a	Bristol City	D	0-0			11,423
26		13	H	SWINDON TOWN	W	1-0	Riddick		7,797
27		20	a	Watford	D	0-0			14,336
28		26	H	NORWICH CITY	W	1-0	Dyson (pen)		8,682
29	Mar	6	a	Millwall	W	1-0	Allen, Payne (og)		7,136
30		10	a	Oxford Utd	W	1-0	Dyson		7,242
31		13	H	BIRMINGHAM CITY	L	0-2			11,167
32		20	a	Middlesbrough	W	1-0	Riddick		17,017
33		27	H	CARLISLE UTD	D	1-1	Bullock		7,998
34		29	H	LEICESTER CITY	L	0-1			12,736
35	Apr	3	a	Charlton Athletic	L	0-2			8,105
36		9	a	Sunderland	L	0-1			15,151
37		10	H	OXFORD UTD	D	0-0			6,266
38		12	H	QUEENS PARK RANGERS	L	0-1			11,949
39		17	a	Hull City	L	2-5	Bullock, Lazarus		19,320
40		24	H	LUTON TOWN	L	1-2	Brabrook		6,339
41		26	H	PORTSMOUTH	D	1-1	Lazarus		3,941
42	May	1	a	Cardiff City	L	0-1			15,772
FA Cup									
3	Jan	11	a	Sunderland	W	3-0	Fairbrother, Dyson, Lazarus		18,065
4		23	a	Nottingham Forest	D	1-1	Dyson		25,349
R	Feb	1	H	NOTTINGHAM FOREST	L	0-1			18,530
League Cup									10,975
1	Aug	19`	a	Fulham	L	0-1			10,975

Pos	Team	P	Home					Away					Total		Pts
			W	D	L	F	A	W	D	L	F	A	F	A	
1	Leicester City	42	12	7	2	30	14	11	6	4	27	16	57	30	59
2	Sheffield United	42	14	6	1	49	18	7	8	6	24	21	73	39	56
3	Cardiff City	42	12	7	2	39	16	8	6	7	25	25	64	41	53
4	Carlisle United	42	16	3	2	39	13	4	10	7	26	30	65	43	53
5	Hull City	42	11	5	5	31	16	8	8	5	23	25	54	41	51
6	Luton Town	42	12	7	2	40	18	6	6	9	22	25	62	43	49
7	Middlesbrough	42	13	6	2	37	16	4	8	9	23	27	60	43	48
8	Millwall	42	13	5	3	36	12	6	4	11	23	30	59	42	47
9	Birmingham City	42	12	7	2	30	12	5	5	11	28	36	58	48	46
10	Norwich City	42	11	8	2	34	20	4	6	11	20	32	54	52	44
11	Queens Park Rangers	42	11	5	5	39	22	5	6	10	19	31	58	53	43
12	Swindon Town	42	12	7	2	38	14	3	5	13	23	37	61	51	42
13	Sunderland	42	11	6	4	34	21	4	6	11	18	33	52	54	42
14	Oxford United	42	8	8	5	23	23	6	6	9	18	25	41	48	42
15	Sheffield Wednesday	42	10	7	4	32	27	2	5	14	19	42	51	69	36
16	Portsmouth	42	9	4	8	32	28	1	10	10	14	33	46	61	34
17	ORIENT	42	5	11	5	16	15	4	5	12	13	36	29	51	34
18	Watford	42	6	7	8	18	22	4	6	11	20	38	38	60	33
19	Bristol City	42	9	6	6	30	28	1	5	15	16	36	46	64	31
20	Charlton Athletic	42	7	6	8	28	30	1	8	12	13	35	41	65	30
21	Blackburn Rovers	42	5	8	8	20	28	1	7	13	17	41	37	69	27
22	Bolton Wanderers	42	6	5	10	22	31	1	5	15	13	43	35	74	24

attack from fans accusing them of a "money-grabbing" policy to bank the much needed gate receipts. Touts also made a killing – local *Guardian and Gazette* reporter Vince Wright revealed that 20 minutes before kick-off, 12 shilling stand tickets were going for £3 each.

Feb 1 – Despite the massive incentive of a money-spinning fifth round visit to Tottenham, unlucky Os – wearing all-white – go out of the FA Cup, losing 1-0 to a soft goal at home to Forest in the rearranged replay played on another paddyfield. Terry Brisley hit a post and Mark Lazarus had a goal disallowed.

Feb 6 – Peter Allen, the club's longest-serving player, is placed on the transfer list at his own request for "personal reasons". Papers link him with a £40,000 move to Chelsea, managed by ex-Os boss Dave Sexton who signed the midfield workhorse as a pro at Orient in 1965.

Feb – Plagued by a serious knee problem since the League Cup defeat at Fulham in August, Dave Harper announces his retirement at 32. The dedicated wing-half had sacrificed an insurance pay-out by defying medical advice to quit the game seven years earlier.

Feb 26 – Os' experiment with Friday night football proves a big flop. Instead of the hoped for 15,000 crowd, only 8,682 bothered to venture out in perfect weather conditions and without counter-attractions to see Barry Dyson's crucial 35th minute penalty send Norwich City packing, 1-0.

April 26 – Arthur Page uses the final home programme of the season – for the Monday evening visit of Portsmouth – to ask 30 supporters to chip in £500 each so that Orient can launch a "lavish" vice-presidents' club. Investors are promised two seats in the main stand for at least the next 10 years. In the same column, the chairman is anguished to admit that Os now rival Fourth Division Brentford as the worst supported club in London. As if to underline his sombre tone, the Pompey game drew the lowest crowd of the season, a meagre 3,941. Reporter Jim Gains noted that the most disgruntled among them chanted "We want football", "What a load of rubbish", "Referee blow your whistle" and even "Ar-sen-al" accompanied bursts of slow-handclapping.

May 10 – A strong West Ham side attracted a crowd of 6,921 – generating gate receipts of £2,249 – for Dave Harper's testimonial match played on a Monday night. Portsmouth striker Mike Trebilcock, one of Bloomfield's summer targets, failed to impress in a guest appearance for Os.

CUP GLORY THRILLS

NEW manager George Petchey, a surprise choice to replace Leicester City-bound Jimmy Bloomfield in the summer of 1971, oversaw one of the most exciting seasons in Orient history.

The FA Cup fifth round victory against top flight Chelsea at Brisbane Road, where Os came from two down to win 3-2 in the dying minutes, will forever rank as one of the all-time greatest games and a day all those present will never forget.

To earn the right to topple the defending Cup holders Petchey's men went to Leicester in round four and brushed aside Bloomfield's Foxes, 2-0. Significantly, the first goal was scored by Ian Bowyer – Jimmy's final buy just before he left E10 to accept the Filbert Street job. Arsenal needed huge slices of good fortune to deny Orient a place in the semi-final.

Former Manchester City forward Bowyer, 20, justified his status as Os' new club record signing by top-scoring with 15 goals in the league and two in the FA Cup, including one in the 3-0 third round victory over Wrexham. He settled in remarkably quickly and his impressive form was the main factor in consolidating their place in Division Two. Os finished 17th – four points clear of safety but also only a point short of 12th position.

TRANSFERS

>IN Ian Bowyer (Manchester City – £30,000), John Sewell (Crystal Palace – free), Len Tompkins (Crystal Palace – free), Phil Hoadley (Crystal Palace – £35,000), Tom Walley (Watford – £25,000).

<OUT Dave Harper (retired), Terry Parmenter (Gillingham – free), Terry Mancini (Queens Park Rangers – £25,000), Mick Jones (Charlton Athletic – free).

FACTS & FIGURES

* Kevin Moseley, who worked for Reg Hayter's sports agency, was appointed programme editor from the start of the new season. Moseley went on to become a leading football writer for the *Daily Mirror* and *Daily Express* in the late 80s and throughout the 90s. Strangely, though, the programme cover never carried the date of the game!

* Orient's solid home form ensured their continued stay in Division Two. Their 12 league wins at Brisbane Road was the highest number achieved by Os in the second tier since 1959-60 and has yet to be equalled.

* Orient went 10 away games from the start of the season, and had lost six on the trot outside E10, before finally winning on the road – 1-0 at Watford on December 4. Paul Harris, who replaced Mancini at centre-half, scored the 27th minute winner. During one particularly bleak spell between September and November, they conceded 22 goals in six games. Their only other away league success came at Charlton, 2-1 on March 31.

* Back-to-back league wins happened only once all season, when Orient smashed Sunderland 5-0 and then beat Burnley 1-0 in January. The victory over Sunderland was Os' biggest for 10 years and the first time they had scored five in a game since defeating Swansea Town 5-2 in September, 1964.

* Ian Bowyer's hat-trick on his home debut against Cardiff City was the first by an Orient player in the league in more than four years – since Cliff Holton bagged three (one penalty) in the 4-1 home win over Mansfield Town on May 12, 1967.

* The official attendance figure of 33,363 for the final game of the season, against Birmingham City, was

the biggest ever for a league match at Brisbane Road. It was around 1,000 short of the all-time record of 34,345 established at the FA Cup tie against West Ham United in January, 1964.

DIARY: KEY MATCHES & MOMENTS

Aug 21 – After a season-long struggle to find the net, Os get the Brisbane Road league campaign off to a flier by caning Cardiff City. It's a memorable home debut for Ian Bowyer, who scores a hat-trick in the 4-1 romp. As well as keeping the match ball, he was also rewarded with a bonus fiver from George Petchey. The other goal was Terry Mancini's last for Os before his move to QPR.

Sept – The club announces it will hold a dance and buffet at Leyton Assembly Halls in the High Road to further aid recently retired player Dave Harper, who has opened a sandwich bar near Hatton Garden. Commercial manager Brian Blower, a driving force behind the scenes in raising much needed revenue through various enterprising schemes, presented Harper with a cheque for £3,700 – the proceeds of his testimonial fund.

Sept 18 – Chairman Arthur Page is loudly banging the 'come and support us' drum again. Through his regular programme column, he writes: "To survive we should be getting average gates of about 14,000. Yet at the moment we get nowhere near that figure." After breaking his collarbone in pre-season and missing the first six games, Peter Bennett's return to first team action inspires a 2-1 home win over Carlisle United.

Oct 9 – New club record signing Phil Hoadley, 19, must have wondered what he'd let himself in for after Os were battered 4-1 on his debut at Blackpool.

Dec 11 – Two days after his mistake cost Watford a 1-0 home defeat to Orient, former Welsh U23 international midfielder Tom Walley, 26, joined Os and made his debut in the home 1-0 defeat by Swindon Town.

V-SIGN TO THE BOO BOYS..

IAN BOWYER

THE BOO-BOYS of Manchester City must be feeling pretty foolish this morning. Ian Bowyer, the kid they tried to force into obscurity, gave them a Soccer striker's version of the V-sign on Saturday.

Dec 27 – With their most exhilarating league performance of the season, Os thrilled a bank holiday morning crowd of 19,081 with a 2-0 victory over promotion-chasing Queens Park Rangers. Two first-half goals in the space of five minutes, by Barry Dyson and a spectacular half-volley by Mickey Bullock, who gave the returning Terry Mancini a torrid time, put Orient in control. But the biggest cheer came around the hour mark, when Ray Goddard dived to his right to save newly-capped England international Rodney Marsh's penalty. Ray and Marsh – who performed his familiar 'dying swan' act to gain the pen at Phil Hoadley's expense – used to be team-mates at Fulham.

Jan 8 – Os made a mockery of their lowly league position by slaughtering fourth-placed Sunderland, 5-0 at home, to record their biggest win of the season. Mickey Bullock and Ian Bowyer netted a brace each, while Tom Walley notched his first goal for the club with a long-range ripper.

Feb – Two more additions to the backroom staff. Arthur Rowe, manager of Spurs' famous 'push-and-run' champions of 1950-51, becomes general advisor to George Petchey, while Ernie Shepherd succeeds Charlie Simpson as first team physio.

Mar 11 – Petchey collects the Bell's Whisky Manager of the Month award for February, thanks to the home league win against Bristol City and shock FA Cup victories over First Division Leicester City and Chelsea.

Apr – Orient's athleticism and general fitness was underlined by their success in a special athletics meeting for pro footballers held at Crystal Palace, where they claimed three firsts, three seconds and the team award. Phil Hoadley won the long jump with a record 21 feet, four inches; Dennis Rofe the 50-yard dash in another best-ever 5.7 seconds; and these two combined with Barrie Fairbrother and Barry Dyson to win the 4 x 100 metres relay in 44.4 seconds. Fairbrother was runner-up in the 200m; Bobby Moss in the mile; and Ray Goddard and Peter Bennett in the penalty-taking competition.

Football League Division Two 1971-72

1	Aug	14	a	Oxford Utd	D	1-1	Bullock	7,884
2		21	H	CARDIFF CITY	W	4-1	Bowyer 3, Mancini	7,824
3		28	a	Sunderland	L	0-2		14,544
4	Sept	1	a	Norwich City	D	0-0		13,940
5		4	H	LUTON TOWN	D	0-0		8,703
6		11	a	Portsmouth	L	2-3	Brisley, Bowyer	10,966
7		18	H	CARLISLE UTD	W	2-1	Allen, Dyson	7,068
8		25	a	Fulham	L	1-2	Dyson (pen)	9,153
9		28	a	Burnley	L	1-6	Bowyer	12,398
10	Oct	2	H	CHARLTON ATHLETIC	W	3-2	Harris, Allen, Bullock	9,600
11		9	a	Blackpool	L	1-4	Bowyer	14,657
12		16	H	OXFORD UTD	D	1-1	Dyson (pen)	5,202
13		18	H	PRESTON NORTH END	W	3-2	Bullock 2, Bowyer	7,391
14		23	a	Bristol City	L	3-5	Brisley, Bowyer 2	17,772
15		30	H	MILLWALL	D	2-2	Dyson, Lazarus	13,074
16	Nov	6	a	Birmingham City	L	0-2		27,349
17		13	H	HULL CITY	W	1-0	Bowyer	6,614
18		20	a	Middlesbrough	L	0-1		13,288
19		27	H	SHEFFIELD WEDNESDAY	L	0-3		6,673
20	Dec	4	a	Watford	W	1-0	Harris	9,518
21		11	H	SWINDON TOWN	L	0-1		6,120
22		18	a	Luton Town	L	0-2		9,193
23		27	H	QUEENS PARK RANGERS	W	2-0	Dyson, Bullock	19,081
24	Jan	1	a	Carlisle Utd	L	0-2		11,449
25		8	H	SUNDERLAND	W	5-0	Bullock 2, Walley, Bowyer 2	6,966
26		22	H	BURNLEY	W	1-0	Bullock	9,231
27		29	a	Preston North End	D	1-1	Bullock	19,692
28	Feb	12	H	BRISTOL CITY	W	2-0	Bullock 2	13,112
29		19	a	Millwall	L	1-2	Dyson	18,986
30	Mar	4	a	Hull City	D	1-1	Allen	12,845
31		11	H	BLACKPOOL	L	0-1		11,582
32		24	H	PORTSMOUTH	W	2-1	Hand (og), Allen	9,492
33		31	a	Charlton Athletic	W	2-1	Dyson (pen), Shipperley (og)	12,375
34	Apr	1	a	Queens Park Rangers	L	0-1		12,042
35		3	H	FULHAM	W	1-0	Bowyer	16,024
36		8	H	MIDDLESBROUGH	D	1-1	Dyson (pen)	7,372
37		12	a	Cardiff City	L	0-1		16,866
38		17	a	Sheffield Wednesday	L	1-3	Dyson	15,188
39		22	H	WATFORD	W	1-0	Bowyer	7,244
40		24	H	NORWICH CITY	L	1-2	Bowyer	15,530
41		29	a	Swindon Town	D	2-2	Walley, Allen	8,564
42	May	2	H	BIRMINGHAM CITY	L	0-1		33,363

FA Cup								
3	Jan	15	H	WREXHAM	W	3-0	Dyson (pen), Fairbrother, Bowyer	8,253
4	Feb	5	a	Leicester City	W	2-0	Bowyer, Allen	31,402
5		26	H	CHELSEA	W	3-2	Hoadley, Bullock, Fairbrother	30,329
6	Mar	18	H	ARSENAL	L	0-1		31,768

League Cup								
1	Aug	17	H	NOTTS COUNTY	D	1-1	Lazarus	8,263
R		25	a	Notts County	L	1-3	Bullock	13,607

Pos	Team	P	Home					Away					Total		
			W	D	L	F	A	W	D	L	F	A	F	A	Pts
1	Norwich City	42	13	8	0	40	16	8	7	6	20	20	60	36	57
2	Birmingham City	42	15	6	0	46	14	4	12	5	14	17	60	31	56
3	Millwall	42	14	7	0	38	17	5	10	6	26	29	64	46	55
4	Queens Park Rangers	42	16	4	1	39	9	4	10	7	18	19	57	28	54
5	Sunderland	42	11	7	3	42	24	6	9	6	25	33	67	57	50
6	Blackpool	42	12	6	3	43	16	8	1	12	27	34	70	50	47
7	Burnley	42	13	4	4	43	22	7	2	12	27	33	70	55	46
8	Bristol City	42	14	3	4	43	22	4	7	10	18	27	61	49	46
9	Middlesbrough	42	16	4	1	31	11	3	4	14	19	37	50	48	46
10	Carlisle United	42	12	6	3	38	22	5	3	13	23	35	61	57	43
11	Swindon Town	42	10	6	5	29	16	5	6	10	18	31	47	47	42
12	Hull City	42	10	6	5	33	21	4	4	13	16	32	49	53	38
13	Luton Town	42	7	8	6	25	24	3	10	8	18	24	43	48	38
14	Sheffield Wednesday	42	11	7	3	33	22	2	5	14	18	36	51	58	38
15	Oxford United	42	10	8	3	28	17	2	6	13	15	38	43	55	38
16	Portsmouth	42	9	7	5	31	26	3	6	12	28	42	59	68	37
17	ORIENT	42	12	4	5	32	19	2	5	14	18	42	50	61	37
18	Preston North End	42	11	4	6	32	21	1	8	12	20	37	52	58	36
19	Cardiff City	42	9	7	5	37	25	1	7	13	19	44	56	69	34
20	Fulham	42	10	7	4	29	20	2	3	16	16	48	45	68	34
21	Charlton Athletic	42	9	7	5	33	25	3	2	16	22	52	55	77	33
22	Watford	42	5	5	11	15	25	0	4	17	9	50	24	75	19

Apr 22 – Full-back Bobby Arber, replacing the injured Rofe, makes his league debut in the 1-0 home win against Watford.

Apr – Arthur Page announces that the club will install new floodlights in the summer of 1972 and move to a new training ground at Springfield Park, Upton Clapton. Tip-up seats will be installed in the north wing of the main stand. Next season will also the introduction of a '50 Club' which entitles each £50-paying member a seat in the directors' box plus club-room facilities before and after matches.

May 2 – Tuesday night visitors Birmingham City have their sights set on promotion to the top flight along with champions Norwich City. The biggest crowd of the season crammed into every inch of Brisbane Road, with some fans climbing the floodlight pylons, to see Blues pip Millwall to the second promotion spot thanks to a solitary 58th minute goal from the head of Bob Latchford. Fifteen minutes from the end, a group of Millwall fans – who were cheering on the Os – invaded the pitch in a failed effort to get the game abandoned.

The drama continued after the final whistle. A few minutes before the end of the game the club received a phone call warning them that a bomb had been planted under the main stand, so a PA announcement urged fans to leave the ground quickly. In fact, within minutes of the stand being evacuated, one device exploded – there were no casualties – and another was dismantled by bomb experts. This was at the height of 'The Troubles' in Northern Ireland, just weeks after Bloody Sunday and the Official IRA's first bomb in England had killed seven civilians at Aldershot army barracks.

Hours before the final league game, Orient completed the £25,000 signing of winger Derrick Downing from Middlesbrough.

May 3 – Two Gordon Riddick goals earned Os a 2-1 victory over amateur neighbours Dagenham in the London Challenge Cup Final replay at Leyton. The first leg at Victoria Road in November had ended 1-1, with Mark Lazarus on target against the Athenian Leaguers. The original replay was postponed due to fog.

CONSOLIDATION

AFTER the euphoria of their thrilling FA Cup exploits the previous season, Orient used their second term back in Division Two as a period of consolidation.

Coventry City removed Os' tag as giant-killers with an easy 4-1 third round win at Brisbane Road, although George Petchey's side did at least put on a much better showing at home in the league.

It was a bad season for injuries, with the manager rarely able to name an unchanged side. Worst hit was tenacious midfielder Tom Walley, who underwent two knee operations that restricted him to just eight starts.

TRANSFERS

>IN Derrick Downing (Middlesbrough – £25,000), Ray Fulton (West Ham United – free), Gerry Queen (Crystal Palace – £50,000), Ricky Heppolette (Preston North End – £43,000).
<OUT John Sewell (USA – free), Mark Lazarus (Folkestone Town – free), Bobby Moss (Colchester United – free), Martin Binks (Colchester United – free), Johnny South (Colchester United – free), Dennis Rofe (Leicester City – £112,000).

FACTS & FIGURES

* Os lost their fewest number of home league matches – four – at Division Two level since 1923-24. The only sides to leave Brisbane Road victorious this season were Luton Town, Bristol City, Preston North End and Portsmouth. Just as well, because their away record was abysmal. Their only win on the road was at Burnley – who were crowed champions!
* The tally of 33 home goals was Orient's highest in the Second Division throughout the 70s.
* Top scorer Barrie Fairbrother netted a brace in three games but no Os player managed a hat-trick.
* Eleven matches were lost by a single goal margin.
* A strong finish saw Os win seven of their last eight home league matches, scoring 19 times in the process. Those 14 points, plus a final day draw with soon to be FA Cup winners Sunderland, would prove crucial after a dreadful start had seen Os win just one of their first 13 games.
* Finishing 15th was minor progress, a jump of two places on the previous season, but Os were only three points clear of the bottom two.
* Os negotiated with Woodford Town FC chairman Bill Larkin for Os' youth teams to play their home South-East Counties League games at the Snakes Lane ground (2.30pm kick-off). In a move to bolster their youth production line, the club extended the number of apprentice pro's on its books to 11. One of them was 15-year-old Tony Grealish, who chose Os over his local club Queens Park Rangers.
* Not to be left behind in the football fashion stakes, Os' adopt red-and-white numbered sock tags that were first introduced by Leeds United the previous season.
* For the first time, Orient start to run official coach trips and occasional rail excursions to away fixtures.
* The board gained two new members at the start of the season in Max Page, son of the chairman, and Brian Winston. The other three directors were Harry Zussman, Reg Briggs and Frank Harris.

DIARY: KEY MATCHES & MOMENTS

D. Rofe (Orient)

Aug 16 – In his programme column for the League Cup tie against Watford, George Petchey revealed that the club had failed in a bid to sign Israel international striker George Borba. He also offered his best wishes to Phil Hoadley, Barrie Fairbrother and Terry Brisley, who were all married during the close season.

Aug – After starting the first three games, Dennis Rofe finally leaves Brisbane Road once Jimmy Bloomfield's Leicester City meet Os' valuation of £112,000 – a British record for a full-back. To underline what a good piece of business this was by Orient, Queens Park Rangers paid £110,000 to Carlisle United for Stan Bowles, while Arsenal forked out an eye-watering £200,000 for Coventry City's central defender Jeff Blockley.

Sept 16 – After missing the first six games following a cartilage operation, Tom Walley comes on as sub (for the injured Peter Bennett) in the dreary 1-1 draw at Blackpool, where Mickey Bullock scores Os' first away goal of the season.

Sept – Phil Hoadley is Os' leading contender for the *Evening Standard's* 'Hottest Shot in Football' award after his most ferocious strike registered 69.8mph in the Orient round of the competition involving all London clubs. Fifteen players took part and just behind Phil were Ian Filby (68.9), Ian Bowyer (65.5), Ray Goddard (65.3) and Mickey Bullock (64.5).

Sept 23 – New club record signing Gerry Queen – according to Petchey, he cost £50,000, not the widely quoted £70k – makes his debut in the home 2-2 draw with Queens Park Rangers. It's watched by England manager Sir Alf Ramsey, who was there to open the new-look boardroom and vice-presidents' lounge. Transfer-listed Barrie Fairbrother makes another point to the manager by scoring in his second consecutive game, after moving in off the wing to a more central attacking role. With his first league goal for the club, Derrick Downing completed the four-goal first-half tally. The 'unsettled' Terry Brisley joins Fairbrother on the transfer list at his own request.

Sept 25 – A dart thrown by a Preston fan misses Ray Goddard and lands in the penalty area during the 0-0 stalemate at Deepdale.

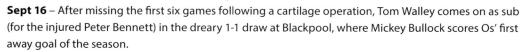

Dart from the terraces misses Orient keeper

Preston 0, Orient 0

A DART thrown from the terracing missed Orient goalkeeper Ray Goddard—and buried itself near the eight-yard line. It was a senseless attack that seemed to sum up a match that won few friends for Soccer. The two best chances went to Orient, both in the first half. First, new signing Gerry Queen streaked through Preston's defence in great style, but he looked [...]

Oct 14 – The 2-0 defeat at Millwall leaves Os second from bottom, just above Cardiff City, after 13 games.

Oct 21 – A nine-game winless run ends with a 2-1 home win over fellow strugglers Carlisle United. Gerry Queen scores his first Os goal with a header, while skipper Peter Bennett grabs the winner 16 minutes from time with a diving header. Amid increasing concerns about hooliganism, the club publishes a prominent 'Warning' notice in the match programme, stating that in its attempt to stamp out 'rowdy and violent behaviour' police will now attempt to stop groups of fans from moving around the ground and offenders will be banned.

Nov 3 – Another Friday night experiment, this time to avoid clashing with West Ham United's home game the next day. But a 1-0 win for visitors Preston North End, watched by only 5,661, proves that Os are very capable of losing on Saturday, Monday, Wednesday, Friday . . . any day! In fairness, crowds are falling throughout the country.

Nov 11 – Goals by Paul Harris and an 88th minute Gerry Queen winner earn Os a 2-1 win at Burnley, who end up champions of the Second Division. It was Clarets' first defeat of the season at Turf Moor, ending their unbeaten run of 22 matches.

Nov 18 – Ray Fulton, 18, makes his debut at left-back in the 3-1 loss at Swindon Town.

Nov 25 – Another young debutant, this time John Lewis comes on as sub to replace the injured Bobby Arber in the 3-2 home win against Sheffield Wednesday.

Dec – Tall, blond striker Dean Mooney maintains his goalscoring spree for the youth side by bagging a hat-trick in the 3-2 South-East Counties Cup semi-final victory over Crystal Palace. We're not even halfway

Football League Division Two 1972-73

1	Aug	12	H	OXFORD UTD	D	1-1	Bowyer		7,249
2		19	a	Sunderland	L	0-1			12,658
3		26	H	LUTON TOWN	L	0-1			6,494
4		28	H	MIDDLESBROUGH	W	2-0	Bullock, Allen		5,130
5	Sept	2	a	Hull City	L	0-2			7,902
6		9	H	BRISTOL CITY	L	0-2			4,482
7		16	a	Blackpool	D	1-1	Bullock		10,471
8		18	H	BURNEY	D	1-1	Fairbrother		4,924
9		23	H	QUEENS PARK RANGERS	D	2-2	Fairbrother, Downing		9,492
10		25	a	Preston North End	D	0-0			10,709
11		30	a	Fulham	D	1-1	Queen		10,991
12	Oct	7	H	CARDIFF CITY	D	0-0			6,284
13		14	a	Millwall	L	0-2			10,074
14		21	H	CARLISLE UTD	W	2-1	Queen, Bennett		4,695
15		28	a	Huddersfield Town	D	1-1	Downing		6,232
16	Nov	3	H	PRESTON NORTH END	L	1-2	Fairbrother		5,661
17		11	a	Burnley	W	2-1	Harris, Queen		12,036
18		18	a	Swindon Town	L	1-3	Brisley		7,953
19		25	H	SHEFFIELD WEDNESDAY	W	3-2	Bowyer. Hoadley, Queen		5,254
20	Dec	2	a	Nottingham Forest	L	1-2	Downing		7,959
21		9	H	BRIGHTON & HOVE ALBION	W	1-0	Downing		5,387
22		16	a	Aston Villa	L	0-1			20,572
23		23	H	PORTSMOUTH	L	0-1			4,466
24		26	a	Queens Park Rangers	L	1-3	Brisley		15,062
25	Jan	6	a	Luton Town	D	1-1	Brisley		8,344
26		20	H	HULL CITY	D	0-0			3,887
27		27	a	Bristol City	D	2-2	Allen, Queen		11,766
28	Feb	10	H	BLACKPOOL	W	2-0	Brisley, Queen		4,923
29		16	a	Oxford Utd	L	1-2	Fairbrother		7,021
30		24	H	ASTON VILLA	W	4-0	Queen, Harris, Fairbrother 2		9,085
31	Mar	3	a	Cardiff City	L	1-3	Bullock		8,463
32		10	H	MILLWALL	W	3-1	Downing, Brisley, Bowyer		10,532
33		17	a	Carlisle Utd	L	0-1			5,696
34		24	H	HUDDERSFIELD TOWN	W	3-1	Fairbrother, Allen, Hoadley		5,497
35		31	a	Sheffield Wednesday	L	0-2			10,003
36	Apr	7	H	NOTTINGHAM FOREST	W	3-0	Hoadley, Queen, Bullock		6,373
37		14	a	Brighton & Hove Albion	L	1-2	Queen		14,744
38		20	a	Portsmouth	L	0-1			8,954
39		21	H	SWINDON TOWN	W	1-0	Queen		6,386
40		23	H	FULHAM	W	3-2	Fairbrother 2, Bowyer		9,953
41		28	a	Middlesbrough	L	2-3	Fairbrother 2		7,939
42		30	H	SUNDERLAND	D	1-1	Downing		9,157
FA Cup									
3	Jan	13	H	COVENTRY CITY	L	1-4	Arber (pen)		12,272
League Cup									
1	Aug	16	H	WATFORD	W	2-0	Downing, Bowyer		5,193
2	Sep	5	a	Wolverhampton Wanderers	L	1-2	Downing		15,969

Pos	Team	P	Home						Away						Total		
			W	D	L	F	A	W	D	L	F	A		F	A	Pts
1	Burnley	42	13	6	2	44	18	11	8	2	28	17		72	35	62
2	Queens Park Rangers	42	16	4	1	54	13	8	9	4	27	24		81	37	61
3	Aston Villa	42	12	5	4	27	17	6	9	6	24	30		51	47	50
4	Middlesbrough	42	12	6	3	29	15	5	7	9	17	28		46	43	47
5	Bristol City	42	10	7	4	34	18	7	5	9	29	33		63	51	46
6	Sunderland	42	12	6	3	35	17	5	6	10	24	32		59	49	46
7	Blackpool	42	12	6	3	37	17	6	4	11	19	34		56	51	46
8	Oxford United	42	14	2	5	36	18	5	5	11	16	25		52	43	45
9	Fulham	42	11	6	4	32	16	5	6	10	26	33		58	49	44
10	Sheffield Wednesday	42	14	4	3	40	20	3	6	12	19	35		59	55	44
11	Millwall	42	12	5	4	33	18	4	5	12	22	29		55	47	42
12	Luton Town	42	6	9	6	24	23	9	2	10	20	30		44	53	41
13	Hull City	42	9	7	5	39	22	5	5	11	25	37		64	59	40
14	Nottingham Forest	42	12	5	4	32	18	2	7	12	15	34		47	52	40
15	ORIENT	42	11	6	4	33	18	1	6	14	16	35		49	53	36
16	Swindon Town	42	8	9	4	28	23	2	7	12	18	37		46	60	36
17	Portsmouth	42	7	6	8	21	22	5	5	11	21	37		42	59	35
18	Carlisle United	42	10	5	6	40	24	1	7	13	10	28		50	52	34
19	Preston North End	42	6	8	7	19	25	5	4	12	18	39		37	64	34
20	Cardiff City	42	11	4	6	32	21	0	7	14	11	37		43	58	33
21	Huddersfield Town	42	7	9	5	21	20	1	8	12	15	36		36	56	33
22	Brighton & Hove Albion	42	7	8	6	32	31	1	5	15	14	52		46	83	29

through the season and 16-year-old Mooney has already banged in 22 goals. The following day, he scored Os' goal in a 1-1 draw with England Youth.

Dec 16 – With injuries and suspensions taking their toll, full-back Peter Wall – on loan from Crystal Palace – makes his debut in the 1-0 defeat at Aston Villa.

Dec 23 – Injuries mean a debut for Malcolm Linton in the 1-0 home loss to Portsmouth.

Dec 26 – Ricky Heppolette becomes the first Asian to play for Orient's first team when he makes his debut in the 3-1 Boxing Day defeat at Queens Park Rangers. QPR went on to gain promotion with Burnley.

Jan – Tom Walley re-enters the London Hospital for his second cartilage operation in six months. Reserve team goalkeeper Steve Bowtell also undergoes cartilage surgery.

Jan 20 – The FA charges Os with a breach of ground rules after a spectator runs onto the pitch during the goalless 0-0 draw with Hull City.

Feb 10 – Arthur Page admits that letters from fans are prompting the board to give serious consideration to changing the home kit from all-red to a white shirt with red 'V' – re-adopting the colours of Clapton Orient.

Feb 25 – The day after thumping Aston Villa 4-0 at Brisbane Road, the board hosts a public meeting at the stadium, where chairman Page, fellow board members and George Petchey 'discuss club policy and future plans'. One decision taken is to stick with the all-red strip.

Mar 10 – Os record their third consecutive home win with a polished 3-1 victory over Millwall, managed by ex-Leyton Orient manager Benny Fenton. Derrick Downing, returning from a three-match ban, opens the scoring with a header. And although former Orient inside-forward Gordon Bolland scores from the rebound after Ray Goddard pushes his penalty onto the post, second-half goals for Terry Brisley and Ian Bowyer, who gleefully latched onto a gift backpass from Lions' Doug Allder, complete a fine win.

Apr – Orient are supporting a resolution at Football League level to extend the promotion/relegation battles in the Second, Third and Fourth divisions to either four-up/four down or, more likely, three up/three down from next season.

SO NEAR, SO FAR

ORIENT have never gone so close to returning to the top flight than they did in May, 1974, when they finished one agonising point short of the promoted top three, runaway champions Middlesbrough, Luton Town and late chargers Carlisle United.

From the start of this season The Football League adopted the 'three up, three down' promotion and relegation system but it wasn't enough to secure Os a place among the elite for the first time since the 1962-63 season.

Orient finished with a superior goal-average to Carlisle, so just one more draw – 18 games ended all-square – would have been enough.

TRANSFERS

>IN David Payne (Crystal Palace – £25,000), John Jackson (Crystal Palace – £25,000), Bill Roffey (Crystal Palace – £5,000), John Boyle (Chelsea – free).
<OUT Barry Dyson (Colchester United – free), Steve Bowtell (Margate – free), Ray Fulton (Folkestone Town – free), Ian Bowyer (Nottingham Forest – £40,000), Bobby Arber (South Africa – free).

FACTS & FIGURES

* Os recorded their highest number of away league wins – six – at Division Two level since 1961-62. The happiest away days were at Fulham, Sheffield Wednesday, Millwall, Notts County, Bristol City and Preston North End.
* They equalled their fewest number of Second Division defeats on the road – five, as previously set in the promotion campaign 12 years earlier. Significantly, though, three of those losses came away to the top three, Middlesbrough, Carlisle United and Luton Town, plus Nottingham Forest and West Bromwich Albion.
* The home and away defeats by Carlisle, without scoring, proved catastrophic. Os took only three points out of a possible 12 off the promoted trio.
* Os stumbled at a critical time, winning only two of their last 15 matches from early February.
* The mass exodus of management, players and staff from Crystal Palace to Brisbane Road continued. Peter Barnes replaced John Falltrick as secretary, while Terry Long became reserve and youth team coach.
* The Mayor and Mayoress of Hackney officially opens Os' new training HQ at the Spring Hill complex in Clapton, E5, where the newly-formed Orient Sportsman's Club make use of the facilities to host fund-raising social events.
* The new-look match programme, costing 10p, is extended from 12 to 16 pages and includes a regular column from *Evening Standard* journalist Jill Palmer.

DIARY: KEY MATCHES & MOMENTS

Aug 25 – New signing David Payne makes his debut in midfield, while 17-year-old right-back Bobby Fisher comes off the bench 15 minutes from time for his first league appearance in the creditable opening 1-1 draw at FA Cup holders Sunderland. Tom Walley, having recovered from another cartilage op', lined up in defence alongside Malcolm Linton, although Ricky Heppolette will miss the first couple of matches due to a leg injury and Peter Bennett is recovering from a bad groin strain.
Aug 28 – Ian Bowyer ends his two-year stay by scoring in the 2-1 League Cup win at Brentford.

Sept 15 – Chairman Arthur Page reveals in his programme notes that he and fellow directors and staff have come under hostile fire from fans over the club's controversial decision to close the Supporters' Section. Page cited "lack of activity and a substantial financial loss" as the main reasons.

Oct 6 – Youth team keeper Mike O'Shaughnessy (pictured) makes his senior debut in the 1-1 draw at Hull and earned praise from his manager as well as the press. "He made two brilliant saves from Hull centre-half Steve Deere," wrote John Dunnill of the *Daily Mail*. O'Shaughnessy, 17, brought in after Ray Goddard failed a fitness test, was only beaten by a Stuart Pearson penalty after David Payne had handled in the 34th minute.

Oct 20 – Another goalkeeping change sees John Jackson make his debut in the 2-0 home win over Luton following his arrival from Palace. Os' best crowd of the season sing "We're going to win the league" as Petchey's entertainers take second spot behind leaders Middlesbrough in front of *The Big Match* cameras.

Oct 27 – Jackson quickly proves his worth by saving Derek Clarke's penalty in the 1-1 draw at Oxford.

Nov 3 – Bill Roffey, the 19-year-old left-back signed from you know where, makes his league debut as a replacement for the injured Derrick Downing in the home 2-2 draw with Preston.

Dec 8 – Gerry Queen scores twice in the impressive 4-2 win at Notts County before being taken off with a dislocated shoulder that will keep him out for seven games. Another huge blow is the ankle injury sustained by John Jackson that will trouble him for the rest of the season.

Dec 15 – The general sense of gloom among the footballing public following England's recent shock elimination from the World Cup at the hands of Poland and their goalkeeping 'clown' (according to Brian Clough) Jan Tomaszewski has spread to east London, where mid-table Carlisle inflict what was ultimately a very costly 1-0 home defeat. Dennis Martin applied the killer touch against the run of play, shooting past Ray Goddard in the 77th minute, before Terry Brisley had a 'goal' disallowed because Peter Allen pulled the ball back from behind the goal-line.

Dec 22 – Three days before his 27th birthday John Boyle comes in for his debut in the 2-2 draw at Swindon. Os should have had both league points sewn up but home sub David Moss fired a 30-yarder through the hands of John Jackson with just four minutes to go. Jacko aggravated his injury, now diagnosed as a broken ankle, and will be sidelined again until February.

Dec 26 – a large Boxing Day morning crowd of 20,000-plus receive a perfect belated Christmas present as Os romp to a 3-0 victory over Malcolm Allison's Crystal Palace, thanks to goals by Barrie Fairbrother (2) and Mickey Bullock.

January 5 – With Bill Roffey in hospital for an appendix operation, full-back Bobby Arber makes his one and only senior appearance of the season – and his last-ever in Os' colours – in the 2-1 home FA Cup third round defeat of Third Division Bournemouth.

Jan 27 – Encouraged by Portsmouth's experiment with Sunday afternoon football, a record 45 coach-loads of Orient fans set off for the south coast to see the FA Cup fourth round clash end goal-less.

Jan 29 – Due to the Tory government's restrictions on the commercial use of electricity (effectively a ban on football floodlights) during the power crisis caused by miners' strikes, the replay against Pompey kicks-off at the highly unusual time of 1.30pm on a Tuesday. Nearly 15,000, including many boys who bunked off school, turn out to see another draw – 1-1 after extra-time. The club apologises for its drastically reduced four-page 'programme' due to the three-day working week imposed between January 1 and March 7.

Feb 5 – The Portsmouth FA Cup trilogy ends in a 2-0 second replay defeat played at Crystal Palace. Peter Allen misses all four FA Cup ties following the ankle injury he suffered in the New Year's Day win at Bristol City.

Feb 9 – The home game against Aston Villa is postponed due to a waterlogged pitch. Orient had

Football League Division Two 1973-74

1	Aug	25	a	Sunderland	D	1-1	Queen	28,211
2	Sept	1	H	BRISTOL CITY	L	0-1		7,216
3		8	a	Fulham	W	3-0	Bullock 2, Queen	10,984
4		11	a	Bolton W	D	1-1	Queen (pen)	16,761
5		15	H	BLACKPOOL	W	3-2	Bullock, Allen, Queen (pen)	7,352
6		17	H	MIDDLESBROUGH	D	0-0		9,744
7		22	a	Aston Villa	D	2-2	Bullock, Heppolette	26,685
8		29	H	SWINDON TOWN	D	0-0		7,799
9	Oct	2	a	Middlesbrough	L	2-3	Bullock, Heppolette	22,164
10		6	a	Hull City	D	1-1	Bullock	7,434
11		13	H	NOTTINGHAM FOREST	W	2-1	Fairbrother, Heppolette	8,346
12		20	H	LUTON TOWN	W	2-0	Queen, Fairbrother	11,135
13		22	H	BOLTON WANDERERS	W	3-0	Queen 2 (1 pen), Fairbrother	11,706
14		27	a	Oxford Utd	D	1-1	Bullock	8,830
15	Nov	3	H	PRESTON NORTH END	D	2-2	Fairbrother, Bullock	12,484
16		10	a	Sheffield Wednesday	W	2-1	Bullock, Fairbrother	9,961
17		17	H	WEST BROMWICH ALBION	W	2-0	Fairbrother, Heppolette	11,581
18		24	a	Millwall	W	1-0	Bullock	13,057
19	Dec	1	H	CARDIFF CITY	L	1-2	Fairbrother	9,564
20		8	a	Notts County	W	4-2	Bullock, Queen 2, Fairbrother	11,264
21		15	H	CARLISLE UTD	L	0-1		7,645
22		22	a	Swindon Town	D	2-2	Bullock, Fairbrother	5,718
23		26	H	CRYSTAL PALACE	W	3-0	Bullock, Fairbrother 2	20,611
24		29	H	FULHAM	W	1-0	Roffey	14,666
25	Jan	1	a	Bristol City	W	2-0	Walley, Downing	19,126
26		12	a	Blackpool	D	1-1	Bullock (pen)	8,760
27		19	H	SUNDERLAND	W	2-1	Queen, Fairbrother	14,533
28	Feb	2	a	Carlisle Utd	L	0-3		9,422
29		23	H	HULL CITY	D	1-1	Heppolette	9,830
30		26	a	Nottingham Forest	L	1-2	Heppolette	16,632
31	Mar	3	a	Crystal Palace	D	0-0		29,056
32		10	H	OXFORD UTD	D	1-1	Downing	10,375
33		16	a	Luton Town	L	1-3	Hoadley	17,045
34		23	H	SHEFFIELD WEDNESDAY	L	0-1		9,392
35		30	a	Preston North End	W	1-0	Downing	7,650
36	Apr	6	H	MILLWALL	D	1-1	Fairbrother	10,445
37		12	a	Portsmouth	D	0-0		10,944
38		13	a	West Bromwich Albion	L	0-1		11,291
39		15	H	PORTSMOUTH	W	2-1	Queen 2	11,540
40		20	H	NOTTS COUNTY	D	1-1	Fairbrother	11,711
41		27	a	Cardiff City	D	1-1	Bullock	11,640
42	May	3	H	ASTON VILLA	D	1-1	Bullock	29,766
FA Cup								
3	Jan	5	H	BOURNEMOUTH	W	2-1	Fairbrother 2	9,589
4		27	a	Portsmouth	D	0-0		32,838
R		29	H	PORTSMOUTH	D	1-1**	Fairbrother**	14,879
2R	Feb	5	n*	Portsmouth	L	0-2		19,595
				*Played at Selhurst Park			**After extra-time	
League Cup								
1	Aug	28	a	Brentford	W	2-1	Bowyer, Fairbrother	6,620
2	Oct	9	H	BLACKBURN ROVERS	W	2-0	Fairbrother, Bullock	7,374
3		31	H	YORK CITY	D	1-1	Queen	12,061
R	Nov	6	a	York City	L	1-2**	Bullock**	11,152
							**After extra-time	

Pos	Team	P	Home					Away					Total		Pts
			W	D	L	F	A	W	D	L	F	A	F	A	
1	Middlesbrough	42	16	4	1	40	8	11	7	3	37	22	77	30	65
2	Luton Town	42	12	5	4	42	25	7	7	7	22	26	64	51	50
3	Carlisle United	42	13	5	3	40	17	7	4	10	21	31	61	48	49
4	ORIENT	42	9	8	4	28	17	6	10	5	27	25	55	42	48
5	Blackpool	42	11	5	5	35	17	6	8	7	22	23	57	40	47
6	Sunderland	42	11	6	4	32	15	8	3	10	26	29	58	44	47
7	Nottingham Forest	42	12	6	3	40	19	3	9	9	17	24	57	43	45
8	West Bromwich Albion	42	8	9	4	28	24	6	7	8	20	21	48	45	44
9	Hull City	42	9	9	3	25	15	4	8	9	21	32	46	47	43
10	Notts County	42	8	6	7	30	35	7	7	7	25	25	55	60	43
11	Bolton Wanderers	42	12	5	4	30	17	3	7	11	14	23	44	40	42
12	Millwall	42	10	6	5	28	16	4	8	9	23	35	51	51	42
13	Fulham	42	11	4	6	26	20	5	6	10	13	23	39	43	42
14	Aston Villa	42	8	9	4	33	21	5	6	10	15	24	48	45	41
15	Portsmouth	42	9	8	4	26	16	5	4	12	19	46	45	62	40
16	Bristol City	42	9	5	7	25	20	5	5	11	22	34	47	54	38
17	Cardiff City	42	8	7	6	27	20	2	9	10	22	42	49	62	36
18	Oxford United	42	8	8	5	27	21	2	8	11	8	25	35	46	36
19	Sheffield Wednesday	42	9	6	6	33	24	3	5	13	18	39	51	63	35
20	Crystal Palace	42	6	7	8	24	24	5	5	11	19	32	43	56	34
21	Preston North End	42	7	8	6	24	23	2	6	13	16	39	40	62	31
22	Swindon Town	42	6	7	8	22	27	1	4	16	14	45	36	72	25

originally hoped to make club history by scheduling it for the following day, Sunday the 10th, but Villa refused. The fixture is now rearranged for Friday, May 3 . . .

Mar 8 – Youth team starlet Laurie Cunningham signs pro on his 18th birthday.

Mar – Bobby Arber leaves the club to go and live and play football in South Africa.

Mar – After recovering from food poisoning, Ricky Heppolette is now sidelined by a dislocated shoulder.

Mar 10 – Oxford United obliged where Villa wouldn't, by becoming Os' first-ever Sunday opponents at Brisbane Road, although only an average crowd of just over 10,000 turned up for the 3.00pm kick-off to see Derrick Downing salvage a point with an injury-time header.

Mar 30 – A terrible run of 10 weeks without victory finally ends at Preston, where Downing nets the only goal to keep Os in the promotion hunt.

Apr 2 – Centre-back Nigel Gray and keeper John Smeulders are the latest two teenagers to sign as full professionals.

Apr 6 – A highly controversial decision by Staffs-based ref Roy Capey, who disallows a perfectly legal looking Barrie Fairbrother headed goal, ruling Terry Brisley offside despite being pushed into the back of the net, in the 1-1 home draw with Millwall.

Apr 13 – With the goal at his mercy, unmarked Gerry Queen somehow manages to head the ball against the post from six yards in the 1-0 defeat at West Brom.

Apr 20 – Another dagger through the heart, inflicted this time by Don Masson, whose 30-yarder deflects off Terry Brisley's shoulder and flies past Ray Goddard to earn Notts County a point.

Apr 27 – Mickey Bullock's goal in the 1-1 draw at Cardiff, where David Payne suffers a broken leg, means Os' promotion bid will go to the wire.

May 3 – FA Cup Final eve brings Aston Villa to Leyton for the critical, rearranged final home game of the season. Orient must win to clinch the third promotion place but the dreams of 29,000-plus Orient fans – and those of Arthur Page who hoped to stand down as chairman with Os in the First Division – are shattered by Ray Graydon's penalty at the Coronation Gardens end. Mickey Bullock's equaliser is not enough to prevent Os' fans of all ages from shedding tears of misery.

BACK TO THE FUTURE

AFTER missing out on promotion by a point the previous May, there was bound to be a king-sized hangover and so it proved as Orient came crashing back to Earth with a bang. The team never got going and their lack of firepower resulted in a woeful shortage of goals.

If teams had received three points for a win, instead of two, Os would have been embroiled in a relegation battle. As it was, the bore draw specialists somehow clung on to mid-table obscurity in a season of transition.

True, they did have to contend with an horrendously long injury list that never seemed to shorten. The one shining light in a gloomy campaign was that George Petchey had little choice but to blood home-grown youngsters. Five teenagers made their league debuts, most notably the dazzling Laurie Cunningham.

TRANSFERS
>**IN** Derek Possee (Crystal Palace – £60,000).
<**OUT** Roy Cotton (Brentford – free), Malcolm Linton (Tampa Bay Rowdies, USA – free).

FACTS & FIGURES
* Os drew more away league games – 11 – in their Second Division history.
* Orient were painful to watch at times this season if all you wanted to see was the net bulging. Their miserable tally of just 11 away goals was their lowest in the second tier since they mustered a meagre 10 in 1921-22. However, by conceding only 23 at the other end, Os equalled their all-time best defensive record in Division Two (set in the 1961-62 promotion campaign and subsequently matched again in 1979-80).
* In only six of their 42 league matches did Os manage to score twice in one game, while they managed to notch three just the once – the 3-1 home win over Oldham. Seven of their 11 combined home and away victories were by 1-0.
* Their abysmal tally of 28 league goals was the worst in the entire 92-club Football League. And yet Orient still managed to finish 12th.
* Five teenagers who rose through the youth ranks were given their league debuts – Tony Grealish, Laurie Cunningham, Dean Mooney, Glenn Roeder and Nigel Gray.
* A change of kit saw plain red socks replaced by black ones with red tops and two white hoops, although the sock tags introduced last season were abandoned.
* In a move to quell rising crowd trouble throughout the country, the club announced that supporters would no longer be able to transfer from the terracing behind each goal to the main enclosure of the East Stand or the West Stand terrace.
* The programme, although still priced at 10p, was cut from 16 to 12 pages. In October, it underwent a revamp that incorporated a new front cover design making better use of pictures.
* Brian Winston succeeded the retiring Arthur Page as chairman and was immediately to the fore by contributing a regular page in the programme headed 'Supporters' Soapbox'. He set about raising Orient's profile and was always keen to engage with critical fans.

DIARY: KEY MATCHES & MOMENTS

Aug 3 – Laurie Cunningham is unleashed! Os are one of 16 invited clubs contesting the Texaco Cup, with the four English group winners going on to meet four nominated clubs from Scotland in the quarter-finals (not that this would concern us). Orient are in Group 2, along with West Ham, Luton and Southampton. It's the first game, at Upton Park, that sparks most interest for Os fans, because *The Big Match* cameras are present to capture the debut of 18-year-old youth discovery Cunningham. In a 1-0 defeat, the pacy, tricky right-winger gives Frank Lampard a torrid time.

Aug 17 – When the fixture lists came out, Orient fans must have thought they were either hallucinating or Ray Graydon's penalty was just a nightmare that didn't really happen, for the opening day league visitors to Leyton were Manchester United. No, it was true – Orient did miss promotion by a whisker and the once mighty Reds had just been relegated from the top sphere. Remarkably, for the third week in succession, Orient were on *The Big Match*.

Hours before kick-off, United's hordes caused disturbances in surrounding streets and pubs, and on Underground trains, and there's trouble inside the ground too, where several fans run on the pitch before kick-off and the embattled police make a further number of arrests. Offenders were taken to two waiting 52-seater coaches in Brisbane Road used as a holding area.

Eventually, a football match broke out and Tommy Docherty's United – in plain all-white and including three of Scotland's World Cup stars – strolled to a comfortable 2-0 win over an Orient's side wearing a new strip identical to Man U's home kit.

Os start the season with four senior players on the injured list – Peter Allen, David Payne, Terry Brisley and John Boyle.

Aug 31 – Ricky Heppolette is back on the treatment table again, this time nursing a torn Achilles tendon that ruled him out of the home draw with Portsmouth.

Sept 7 – Another injury blow, as Gerry Queen damages his wrist in the 3-1 defeat at Aston Villa.

Sept 21 – After five draws and two defeats, at last a first league success. Derrick Downing and Tom Walley find the net as Os come from behind to win 2-1 win at Oxford.

Sept 28 – Sheffield Wednesday, who are destined to finish rock bottom, are the first to lose a league game at Brisbane Road this season, courtesy of Mickey Bullock's penalty. Youth team graduate Tony Grealish comes on to replace Barrie Fairbrother for his league debut. Meanwhile, Brian Winston reveals that a board meeting will discuss calls from some fans to revert to Leyton Orient.

Oct 12 – The visit of Oldham marks Laurie Cunningham's league debut. He replaces the injured Barrie Fairbrother in a 3-1 victory.

Oct – Keeper Ray Goddard, out of the first team picture again now that John Jackson has regained full fitness, goes on loan to Greenock Morton.

Nov 6 – David Payne makes his long-awaited comeback for the reserves in the Midweek League against Peterborough, his first appearance since breaking his leg at Cardiff at the end of last season.

Nov – Os welcomed the diversion of the Daily Express-sponsored National Five-a-Side Championships at Wembley Pool. So much so, they actually won the thing, winning penalty shootouts before beating Spurs in the final. Our squad featured John Jackson, Phil Hoadley, Peter Allen, summer signing Derek Possee, Terry Brisley and Gary Hibbs.

Nov – Two youngsters are sent out on loan: Malcolm Linton to Bath City and Ian Filby to St Mirren.

Nov 30 – Tony Grealish (pictured) celebrates his first full league game by scoring Os' goal in the 1-1 home draw with Nottingham Forest.

Dec 14 – 200 travelling Os fans are denied a sensational victory in front of 41,000-plus at Old Trafford, where after a backs-to-the-wall resilience to thwart Man United, Tom

Football League Division Two 1974-75

#									
1	Aug	17	H	MANCHESTER UTD	L	0-2			17,772
2		20	a	Blackpool	D	0-0			9,314
3		24	a	Bristol City	D	0-0			10,985
4		27	H	BLACKPOOL	D	0-0			7,314
5		31	H	PORTSMOUTH	D	1-1	Bullock		6,861
6	Sept	7	a	Aston Villa	L	1-3	Downing		16,902
7		14	H	FULHAM	D	0-0			8,927
8		21	a	Oxford Utd	W	2-1	Downing, Walley		6,864
9		24	a	Notts County	D	1-1	Possee		7,883
10		28	H	SHEFFIELD WEDNESDAY	W	1-0	Bullock (pen)		7,378
11	Oct	5	a	Bolton Wanderers	L	0-2			9,769
12		12	H	OLDHAM ATHLETIC	W	3-1	Possee, Bullock, Walley		6,511
13		19	a	Southampton	L	2-4	Brisley, Possee		14,542
14		26	H	NORWICH CITY	L	0-3			8,708
15	Nov	1	a	York City	W	1-0	Possee		7,649
16		9	H	CARDIFF CITY	D	1-1	Queen		6,412
17		16	a	Bristol Rovers	D	0-0			10,526
18		23	H	WEST BROMWICH ALBION	L	0-2			6,771
19		30	H	NOTTINGHAM FOREST	D	1-1	Grealish		5,217
20	Dec	7	a	Millwall	D	1-1	Fairbrother		8,145
21		14	a	Manchester Utd	D	0-0			41,200
22		21	H	HULL CITY	D	0-0			4,679
23		26	a	Fulham	D	0-0			9,600
24		28	H	SUNDERLAND	D	1-1	Downing		10,029
25	Jan	11	H	MILLWALL	W	2-1	Possee, Grealish		9,584
26		18	a	Nottingham Forest	D	2-2	Possee, Chapman (og)		17,582
27	Feb	1	a	Cardiff City	D	0-0			8,011
28		8	H	YORK CITY	W	1-0	Heppolette		6,454
29		15	a	West Bromwich Albion	L	0-1			9,364
30		22	H	BRISTOL ROVERS	W	1-0	Hoadley		6,503
31		28	a	Portsmouth	L	0-3			11,619
32	Mar	8	H	NOTTS COUNTY	L	0-1			4,352
33		15	a	Sheffield Wednesday	W	1-0	Queen		8,492
34		22	H	ASTON VILLA	W	1-0	Heppolette		9,466
35		28	a	Sunderland	L	0-3			30,908
36		29	a	Hull City	D	0-0			5,203
37		31	H	OXFORD UTD	D	1-1	Queen		6,524
38	Apr	5	a	Norwich City	L	0-2			18,116
39		12	H	BOLTON WANDERERS	D	0-0			5,478
40		15	H	BRISTOL CITY	W	1-0	Possee		6,487
41		19	a	Oldham Athletic	D	0-0			9,688
42		26	H	SOUTHAMPTON	W	2-1	Queen, Cunningham		7,580
FA Cup									
3	Jan	4	H	DERBY COUNTY	D	2-2	Possee, Queen		12,490
R		8	a	Derby County	L	1-2	Fairbrother		26,501
League Cup									
2	Sept	10	a	Queens Park Rangers	D	1-1	Hoadley		14,304
R		17	H	QUEENS PARK RANGERS	L	0-3			11,750

32

Pos	Team	P	Home W	D	L	F	A	Away W	D	L	F	A	Total F	A	Pts
1	Manchester United	42	17	3	1	45	12	9	6	6	21	18	66	30	61
2	Aston Villa	42	16	4	1	47	6	9	4	8	32	26	79	32	58
3	Norwich City	42	14	3	4	34	17	6	10	5	24	20	58	37	53
4	Sunderland	42	14	6	1	41	8	5	7	9	24	27	65	35	51
5	Bristol City	42	14	5	2	31	10	7	3	11	16	23	47	33	50
6	West Bromwich Albion	42	13	4	4	33	15	5	5	11	21	27	54	42	45
7	Blackpool	42	12	6	3	31	17	2	11	8	7	16	38	33	45
8	Hull City	42	12	8	1	25	10	3	6	12	15	43	40	53	44
9	Fulham	42	9	8	4	29	17	4	8	9	15	22	44	39	42
10	Bolton Wanderers	42	9	7	5	27	16	6	5	10	18	25	45	41	42
11	Oxford United	42	14	3	4	30	19	1	9	11	11	32	41	51	42
12	ORIENT	42	8	9	4	17	16	3	11	7	11	23	28	39	42
13	Southampton	42	10	6	5	29	20	5	5	11	24	34	53	54	41
14	Notts County	42	7	11	3	34	26	5	5	11	15	33	49	59	40
15	York City	42	9	7	5	28	18	5	3	13	23	37	51	55	38
16	Nottingham Forest	42	7	7	7	24	23	5	7	9	19	32	43	55	38
17	Portsmouth	42	9	7	5	28	20	3	6	12	16	34	44	54	37
18	Oldham Athletic	42	10	7	4	28	16	0	8	13	12	32	40	48	35
19	Bristol Rovers	42	10	4	7	25	23	2	7	12	17	41	42	64	35
20	Millwall	42	8	9	4	31	19	2	3	16	13	37	44	56	32
21	Cardiff City	42	7	8	6	24	21	2	6	13	12	41	36	62	32
22	Sheffield Wednesday	42	3	7	11	17	29	2	4	15	12	35	29	64	21

Walley's winner 10 minutes from time is controversially ruled out. George Petchey takes consolation from the fact that his side are the first to keep a clean sheet there this season.

Jan 4 – Os take great pride in holding First Division champions-elect Derby County to a thrilling 2-2 draw at home in this pulsating third round FA Cup tie covered by *Match of the Day*. Cracking left-foot shots from Derek Possee and Gerry Queen stunned Dave Mackay's men in the first 16 minutes and Os could easily have had three or four goals before half-time had Queen's header and Barrie Fairbrother's close range effort not hit the woodwork. Derby got luckier when Colin Todd's feeble, low shot went through Derrick Downing's legs shortly before the interval and the same player broke Orient hearts eight minutes from time when his deflected effort forced a replay. Apart from Fairbrother's goal on the Baseball Ground mud, Os' only consolation from a 2-1 replay defeat was the share of gate receipts from a 26,000-plus crowd.

Jan 11 – After missing virtually half the season, Ricky Heppolette makes a welcome return following an Achilles tendon operation in the 2-1 home win over Millwall, ending a run of nine winless games.

Feb 22 – Prolific reserve and youth team striker Dean Mooney comes on for his league debut two minutes from the end of the 2-1 home win against Bristol Rovers, before being given the full second half to show his worth at Portsmouth six days later.

Mar – Derrick Downing has surgery to remove three pieces of bone from his knee.

Mar – Out of favour Terry Brisley joins Southend on a month's loan.

Mar 8 – After two appearances off the bench, Dean Mooney starts his first league game, in the 1-0 home defeat by Notts County. There's also a starting debut for another youth team product, Glenn Roeder.

Mar 22 – Too little, too late . . . almost a year after they wrecked our promotion party, Aston Villa return and this time they lose 1-0 to a Ricky Heppolette goal.

Apr 12 – A goal-less draw at home to Bolton is OK for centre-half Nigel Gray, the fifth youth discovery to make his senior debut this season.

Apr 26 – After popping over to Norway to play Viking Stavanger in a friendly, Os are back in E10 to conclude a disappointingly dull season. But at least they end it on a high. Laurie Cunningham seals a 2-1 home win over Southampton with his first league goal for the club.

THE KIDS ARE ALL RIGHT

ANOTHER season of mid-table mediocrity and no progress in either Cup competition saw the average attendance fall by around 700 on the previous season, as Os slipped one place in the final table.

Long-term injuries to Peter Allen and Derek Possee created openings for youngsters to show their potential and three, in particular, grabbed their chance. Laurie Cunningham, Tony Grealish, who earned his first Irish cap, and Glenn Roeder enjoyed extended runs in the first team, with the promise of much more to come.

TRANSFERS

>IN Doug Allder (Millwall – part exchange), Malcolm Beason (Crystal Palace – free).
<OUT Barrie Fairbrother (Millwall – part exchange), Terry Brisley (Millwall – part exchange), Derrick Downing (York City – free), Paul Harris (Swansea City – free), Mike O'Shaughnessy (free), Billy Bragg (free), Bobby Broomfield (free).

FACTS & FIGURES

* Solid Os conceded just 12 home league goals, their best defensive record at Brisbane Road in Division Two since 1923-24. Only champions Sunderland (10) let in less on their own ground.
* Inconsistent Orient failed to win back-to-back league matches all season.
* Os lost only one of their six London derbies, when Charlton won by the only goal at Brisbane Road in early March. Laurie Cunningham, Os' top scorer with eight, found the net home and away against both Chelsea and Fulham.
* Peter Bennett was the only player to score twice in the same game, in the 3-0 home win over Luton.
* Keeper John Jackson, who earned the fans' vote as Player of the Season, and Tom Walley were the only two ever-presents.
* Os were readmitted to the Football Combination but, due to an admin mix-up, their intended withdrawal from the Midweek League wasn't received in time, so the reserves faced a gruelling schedule competing in two divisions.
* There was another revamp for the 10p programme, with its 12 pages produced in landscape format.
* Pat Doran's company won the contract to supply and run all the bar and catering facilities at Leyton Stadium.

DIARY: KEY MATCHES & MOMENTS

Aug 16 – Doug Allder, the only summer signing, makes his debut in the opening 1-1 home draw against Blackburn Rovers. The former Millwall left-winger will struggle to win over Os' fans disappointed to see local favourites Barrie Fairbrother and Terry Brisley head to The Den as part of the same swap deal. Peter Allen plays the full game but a serious knee injury will keep him out of the side until March – a bleak start to his testimonial season.

Brian Winston begins his page 3 'Editorial' leader by apologising to fans for the increase in terrace admission price of 75p (inc of VAT and a programme), after The Football League raised its minimum entrance charge to 65p.

Sept 2 – Roy Cotton, a 19-year-old winger signed from Brentford and a regular for the Midweek League side that finished runners-up to Colchester last season, makes his debut in the 4-0 League Cup battering at Birmingham.

Sept – Unlucky David Payne undergoes an operation on his Achilles tendon.

Oct 27 – Not many testimonial matches end goal-less but that was the spectacle served up by Os and West Ham in Peter Allen's testimonial match on this Monday evening.

Nov 1 – Midfielder Malcolm Beason, 19, the least known of George Petchey's army of recruits from Crystal Palace, makes his one and only first team appearance of the season of his Orient 'career' as sub (for Peter Bennett) in the 2-0 home win against Oldham.

Nov 15 – When Southampton defender Peter Rodrigues put through his own net to clinch a 2-1 Orient home win, it was the third own-goal Os had benefited from this season. 'Own-Goal' went one ahead of Peter Bennett and Glenn Roeder in the scorechart.

Nov 22 – Dean Mooney sets Os on their way to a 2-1 win at Carlisle with his first league goal for the club.

Dec 6 – Club record signing Derek Possee, who underwent a knee operation in the summer, starts for the first time this season in the 1-1 draw at home to Nottingham Forest. George Petchey had previously used his programme notes to reveal the circumstances behind the striker's injury and the reasons for his long lay-off: "Derek was involved in a car crash while at Crystal Palace and played all last season suffering from the effects of an injury to his knee. He saw a specialist and had numerous X-rays, all to no avail, until he had an exploratory operation and four pieces of bone were removed from the knee during the summer. Derek worked hard, had a few reserve games and made a brief return to the first team squad before tearing ligaments in his other knee during training."

Dec 26 – Only 15,000-plus turn out on Boxing Day afternoon for the visit of Chelsea but those who did were treated to the most satisfying win of the season to date. Possee got his first of the campaign, while 'Les' Bennett and Laurie Cunningham completed the 3-1 rout.

Jan 10 – Young centre-back Nigel Gray comes in for his only appearance of the season, replacing the injured Phil Hoadley, in a 3-0 defeat at Plymouth.

Jan 17 – After disappointing attendances for previous Friday night home games against Portsmouth, Bristol Rovers and Blackpool, Orient decided to abandon their experiment and put back the visit of Hull by 24 hours.

Feb 14 – Os lose 1-0 at home to Bristol City in what is their first fixture in a month. The home match against Charlton, scheduled for the previous Saturday, was postponed after a flu epidemic swept through the Orient camp, while the away game at Notts County was twice called off due to a frozen pitch. Poor gates and postponements are taking their toll on club finances and George Petchey warned in his programme column: "Unless our home attendances improve steadily during the rest of the season we may have to sell one of our senior players to help the club pay its way."

Feb – Mickey Bullock is allowed to leave Os for a "modest" fee, so that he could accept an offer to join Fourth Division Halifax Town in a player-coach role.

Feb 24 – Our prolific old friend 'Own-Goal' got back on the scoring trail, with Os' first in the 2-0 victory at York. 'OG' is now only two behind leading marksman Laurie Cunningham.

Feb 28 – Another one-off sub appearance, this time by 17-year-old striker Mike Everett, who comes on to replace Tony Grealish in the 2-0 home victory over Fulham.

Mar – What a coup! The front cover of *Time Out* magazine (dated Mar 5-12) featured an unusual team photo of the Os, while inside Peter Ball wrote an article on the day-to-day working of the club.

Mar 13 – In a season ravaged by injury that restricted him to just seven Division Two matches, Peter Allen set a new all-time club league appearance record when he led the side out against champions-elect Sunderland. His 374th game took him past

Football League Division Two 1975-76

#	Month	Date	H/a	Opponent	Result	Score	Scorers	Attendance
1	Aug	16	H	BLACKBURN ROVERS	D	1-1	Waddington (og)	6,054
2		19	H	NOTTS COUNTY	D	1-1	Bullock	5,223
3		23	a	Blackpool	L	0-1		6,626
4		29	H	PORTSMOUTH	L	0-1		5,056
5	Sept	6	a	Hull City	L	0-1		5,194
6		13	H	PLYMOUTH ARGYLE	W	1-0	Grealish	5,010
7		20	a	Bolton Wanderers	D	1-1	Roeder	10,218
8		23	H	YORK CITY	W	1-0	Bennett	4,290
9		26	H	BRISTOL ROVERS	D	0-0		4,978
10	Oct	4	a	Oxford Utd	L	1-2	Bennett	4,569
11		11	a	Sunderland	L	1-3	Queen	28,327
12		18	H	CARLISLE UTD	W	1-0	Heppolette	4,600
13		25	a	Fulham	D	1-1	Cunningham	10,464
14	Nov	1	H	OLDHAM ATHLETIC	W	2-0	Roeder, Holt (og)	4,576
15		7	a	Bristol City	D	0-0		14,553
16		15	H	SOUTHAMPTON	W	2-1	Queen, Rodrigues (og)	6,332
17		22	a	Carlisle Utd	W	2-1	Mooney, Cunningham	6,502
18		29	a	Luton Town	L	0-1		7,897
19	Dec	6	H	NOTTINGHAM FOREST	D	1-1	Cunningham	5,629
20		12	H	BLACKPOOL	L	0-1		4,337
21		20	a	Blackburn Rovers	D	1-1	Hoadley	7,136
22		26	H	CHELSEA	W	3-1	Possee, Bennett, Cunningham	15,509
23		27	a	West Bromwich Albion	D	1-1	Possee	20,626
24	Jan	10	a	Plymouth Argyle	L	0-3		11,934
25		17	H	HULL CITY	W	1-0	Cunningham	3,876
26	Feb	14	H	BRISTOL CITY	L	0-1		5,785
27		21	a	Southampton	L	0-3		17,230
28		24	a	York City	W	2-0	Scott, Queen	2,857
29		28	H	FULHAM	W	2-0	Cunningham, Queen	7,558
30	Mar	2	H	CHARLTON ATHLETIC	L	0-1		9,754
31		6	a	Oldham Athletic	D	1-1	Walley	6,851
32		13	H	SUNDERLAND	L	0-2		7,954
33		20	H	LUTON TOWN	W	3-0	Bennett 2, Heppolette	5,544
34		23	a	Charlotn Athletic	D	1-1	Queen	10,625
35		27	a	Nottingham Forest	L	0-1		11,127
36	Apr	3	a	Bristol Rovers	D	1-1	Mooney	5,182
37		10	H	BOLTON WANDERERS	D	0-0		6,294
38		13	a	Portsmouth	L	1-2	Queen	5,069
39		17	a	Chelsea	W	2-0	Possee, Cunningham	17,679
40		20	H	WEST BROMWICH ALBION	D	0-0		10,857
41		24	H	OXFORD UTD	W	2-1	Cunningham, Mooney	5,014
42		27	a	Notts County	L	0-2		8,515
FA Cup								
3	Jan	3	H	CARDIFF CITY	L	0-1		8,031
League Cup								
2	Sept	9	a	Birmingham City	L	0-4		18,238

Pos	Team	P	Home W	D	L	F	A	Away W	D	L	F	A	Total F	A	Pts
1	Sunderland	42	19	2	0	48	10	5	6	10	19	26	67	36	56
2	Bristol City	42	11	7	3	34	14	8	8	5	25	21	59	35	53
3	West Bromwich Albion	42	10	9	2	29	12	10	4	7	21	21	50	33	53
4	Bolton Wanderers	42	12	5	4	36	14	8	7	6	28	24	64	38	52
5	Notts County	42	11	6	4	33	13	8	5	8	27	28	60	41	49
6	Southampton	42	18	2	1	49	16	3	5	13	17	34	66	50	49
7	Luton Town	42	13	6	2	38	15	6	4	11	23	36	61	51	48
8	Nottingham Forest	42	13	1	7	34	18	4	11	6	21	22	55	40	46
9	Charlton Athletic	42	11	5	5	40	34	4	7	10	21	38	61	72	42
10	Blackpool	42	9	9	3	26	22	5	5	11	14	27	40	49	42
11	Chelsea	42	7	9	5	25	20	5	7	9	28	34	53	54	40
12	Fulham	42	9	8	4	27	14	4	6	11	18	33	45	47	40
13	ORIENT	42	10	6	5	21	12	3	8	10	16	27	37	39	40
14	Hull City	42	9	5	7	29	23	5	6	10	16	26	45	49	39
15	Blackburn Rovers	42	8	6	7	27	22	4	8	9	18	28	45	50	38
16	Plymouth Argyle	42	13	4	4	36	20	0	8	13	12	34	48	54	38
17	Oldham Athletic	42	11	8	2	37	24	2	4	15	20	44	57	68	38
18	Bristol Rovers	42	7	9	5	20	15	4	7	10	18	35	38	50	38
19	Carlisle United	42	9	8	4	29	22	3	5	13	16	37	45	59	37
20	Oxford United	42	7	7	7	23	25	4	4	13	16	34	39	59	33
21	York City	42	8	3	10	28	34	2	5	14	11	37	39	71	28
22	Portsmouth	42	4	6	11	15	23	5	1	15	17	38	32	61	25

Arthur Wood's haul of 373 achieved in 1931.

Mar 24 – At the age of just 19, Grealish makes his full international debut for Republic of Ireland in a 3-0 friendly win against Norway at Dalymount Park, Dublin. The first Irishman to be capped by his country while playing for Os, 'Paddy' also joined a very select group of eight Orient players who appeared in senior internationals during their time at Brisbane Road. Grealish went on to win 45 caps (eight goals) between 1976 and November, 1985.

Apr 10 – To boost their precarious financial position, Orient reorganised the share capital structure of the club by offering new shareholders the chance to buy at least 100 shares at 25p per share. Under the programme heading 'Thanks for your Help', Brian Winston admitted: "It must be realised that the investment is purely one relating to support of the club and as chairman I could not possibly suggest that it was one that offers a financial return in any way."

Apr 17 – Os complete a hugely satisfying league double over London rivals Chelsea. Derek Possee and Laurie Cunningham, who both netted in the Boxing Day victory over Blues, were on target again in the 2-1 win. Cunningham scored from a stunning solo effort.

Apr 27 – Youth team prospect Gary Hibbs' patience is finally rewarded when he's given his debut in the number 10 shirt in the last game of the season. He'll probably remember it better than the Orient diehards who witnessed a 2-0 defeat at Notts County. Hibbs, 19, never played for the first team again before George Petchey cancelled his contract.

Apr 28 – For the second time in 18 months, we're crowned five-a-side kings. This time the ITV cameras captured victory in the all-London Evening Standard Five-a-Side Championships at Wembley Pool, where Orient benefited from a first round bye before hammering Brentford 5-1, then Chelsea 2-1 in the semi-final before smashing QPR 6-1 in the final. Orient were leading scorers on the night, with Doug Allder – who failed to register a league goal all season – netting five, while the outstanding Laurie Cunningham collected the Player of the Tournament award. The rest of the winning squad was made up of John Jackson, Phil Hoadley, Tom Walley and Gary Hibbs.

HATS OFF TO GLOVER

ONLY goal-difference – the first time it was used to separate teams finishing level on points – saved Orient from tumbling back to Division Three at the end of another largely joyless season in which the club's fate hung in the balance right up to the final whistle of the last game.

With Laurie Cunningham having been sold to West Bromwich Albion, Os desperately needed to take at least a point from the home decider against Hull City – and did so thanks to a goal from new signing Allan Glover. Fortunately, it didn't ultimately matter that John Jackson's uncharacteristic howler gifted the Tigers an equaliser.

After seeing Carlisle United cruelly snatch promotion from our grasp three years earlier, many Os fans viewed the Cumbrians' demotion as sweet revenge. Although Carlisle bettered Os' goals-for total by 12, they conceded 20 more, so went down by eight on goal-difference.

TRANSFERS

>IN Derek Clarke (Oxford United – £10,000), Alan Whittle (Crystal Palace – free), Joe Mayo (West Bromwich Albion – £7,500), Allan Glover (West Bromwich Albion – £7,500).
<OUT Dean Mooney (Dulwich Hamlet – free), Ricky Heppolette (Crystal Palace – £15,000), Gerry Queen (Arcadia Shepherds, South Africa – £5,000), Laurie Cunningham (West Bromwich Albion – £110,000).

FACTS & FIGURES

* Os' woeful tally of four home league wins is their worst since being relegated in May, 1966.
* Southport, second bottom of Division Four, were the only club to score fewer home goals (17) than the 18 Orient mustered.
* The total of 23 home league goals conceded was the most in any season during George Petchey's six-year reign. Nine defeats at Brisbane Road was also an unwanted record for the manager.
* Orient flirted with relegation by failing to win any of their last 11 matches. And for the second consecutive season, they didn't manage any back-to-back league victories.
* Even with squad rotation, clubs grumble today about a heavy schedule of games. Well, in 1976-77, due to our involvement in the Anglo-Scottish Cup, Orient played 59 senior matches. John Jackson and Glenn Roeder played in every one.

DIARY: KEY MATCHES & MOMENTS

Aug 14 – Three days after opening the Brisbane Road campaign with a 2-1 Anglo-Scottish Cup (ASC) win against Fulham, their noisy west London neighbours returned to E10 and, as Blues fans piled on to the pitch at the end of their side's 2-1 defeat in the same competition, a 30-foot section of concrete fencing at the front of the West Stand collapsed. Thankfully, with Os having booked their place in the quarter-final, the only damage was to Orient's bank overdraft.
One national press reporter noted that Orient fielded four 'coloured' players for the first time in a senior game: Laurie Cunningham, Ricky Heppolette, Bobby Fisher and 16-year-old debutant Kevin Godfrey.
Aug 24 – Summer signing Derek Clarke makes his debut, subbing for Derek Possee, in the 1-0 defeat at Bolton.
Sept 15 – Clarke opens his account by scoring the only goal at Aberdeen in the first leg of the ASC quarter-final.

Sept 18 – Alan Whittle enjoys a scoring debut in the 3-0 home win over Cardiff, with Laurie Cunningham grabbing a brace.

Sept 25 – Phil Hoadley misses a 17th minute penalty and then has a late headed 'goal' disallowed in the 0-0 draw at Oldham. "Peter Bennett is our best penalty-taker," says George Petchey, "but he's injured."

Sept 29 – The return leg against Aberdeen is postponed by 24 hours after the Scottish side were prevented from travelling to London on the Tuesday. They were unable to take off from Aberdeen airport, were diverted by road to Edinburgh and then faced further delays due to a bomb scare. Some fans arrived at the ground, unaware that it had been called off at 4.45pm. The following night, Gerry Queen's goal secures a 2-0 aggregate win.

Oct 2 – After playing in the 1-0 home defeat by Blackburn Rovers, Ricky Heppolette gets his wish to join Crystal Palace, where manager Terry Venables finally reverses the one-way traffic trend at George Petchey's expense.

Oct 9 – After failing to find the target in their first four away league games, two Derek Clarke goals and a strike from Phil Hoadley's free-kick saw Os come from 3-1 down to draw 3-3 at Burnley.

Oct 19 – After two 0-0 League Cup stalemates with Millwall, the second replay of the third round tie is played at neutral Highbury, where ex-Os' Barrie Fairbrother scores in a 3-0 Lions victory.

Nov 6 – Peter Bennett is sent-off in our 2-2 draw at Southampton and, having already clocked up six bookings for the season, faces a two-game ban.

Nov 24 – We're through to the ASC Final after beating Partick Thistle 3-2 at home in the semi-final, second leg, with goals by Gerry Queen (2) and Alan Whittle. Laurie Cunningham scored the only goal of the first leg in Glasgow.

Nov 27 – Os concede four goals at home for the first time since 1968, when champions-elect Wolves romp to a 4-2 win. Queen scored one penalty and missed another.

Dec 11 – Terry Glynn, 18, becomes the latest youth team graduate to make his first team debut, in the goal-less draw at home to Fulham. Derek Clarke suffers a torn medial ligament in his right leg that requires surgery and puts him out for the season.

Dec – Os fail in a bid to sign Peter Osgood on loan from Southampton, while Phil Hoadley turns down the chance to join Charlton, who offered £50k for him.

Dec 15 – Nottingham Forest shatter Os' hopes of silverware by winning the ASC Final by 4-0 at the City Ground. The first leg, postponed for six days due to yet another waterlogged pitch, had ended 1-1 at Leyton two nights earlier, when home fans expressed their displeasure by chanting "Petchey Out". Brian Winston called the abuse "diabolical".

Dec 18 – Orient bounce back to win 3-2 on their first-ever visit to Hereford United, where goals from Alan Whittle (2) and Peter Bennett's 84th minute winner on an icy, slippery top lift us off the bottom of the table.

Jan – The club's finances suffer a double blow, as consecutive home games against Bolton and Blackpool are postponed, despite recent drainage improvements. In the absence of any club matching Os' minimum £100,000 valuation of Laurie Cunningham, they are inviting offers for Derek Possee and Phil Hoadley.

Jan 17 – After a 2-2 draw at Darlington and neither side managing to score despite extra-time in the Brisbane Road replay, Os make the short trip to neutral Tottenham to try and settle this irksome FA Cup third round tie. A brace from spiky Scouser Alan Whittle and a Bill Roffey slammer finally send 'Darlo' packing in front of 4,000-plus fans.

Feb 19 – Gerry Queen plays his final game, as sub in the 2-0 home win against Bristol Rovers, before emigrating to Pretoria, South Africa. Nigel Gray nets his first for the club.

Mar 6 – The day Os' fans had been dreading and hoped would never come. Laurie Cunningham, the

Football League Division Two 1976-77

#	Month	Day	H/a	Opponent	Result	Score	Scorers	Attendance
1	Aug	21	H	CHELSEA	L	0-1		11,456
2		24	a	Bolton Wanderers	L	0-2		11,600
3		28	a	Blackpool	L	0-3		7,928
4	Sept	4	H	PLYMOUTH ARGYLE	D	2-2	Hoadley 2	4,808
5		11	a	Bristol Rovers	L	0-1		5,494
6		18	H	CARDIFF CITY	W	3-0	Cunningham 2, Whittle	5,743
7		25	a	Oldham Athletic	D	0-0		7,938
8	Oct	2	H	BLACKBURN ROVERS	L	0-1		5,082
9		9	a	Burnley	D	3-3	Hoadley, Clarke 2	9,943
10		16	a	Notts County	W	1-0	Roffey	8,129
11	Nov	6	a	Southampton	D	2-2	Cunningham. Queen	16,974
12		13	H	NOTTINGHAM FOREST	L	0-1		5,921
13		20	a	Sheffield Utd	D	1-1	Allen	14,745
14		27	H	WOLVERHAMPTON WANDERERS	L	2-4	Queen (pen), Cunningham	6,888
15	Dec	4	a	Carlisle Utd	L	0-1		5,294
16		11	H	FULHAM	D	0-0		11,237
17		18	a	Hereford Utd	W	3-2	Whittle 2, Bennett	5,640
18		27	H	LUTON TOWN	W	1-0	Bennett	8,356
19	Jan	22	a	Chelsea	D	1-1	Whittle	25,744
20	Feb	12	a	Plymouth Arglye	W	2-1	Possee, Cunningham,	9,551
21		15	a	Charlton Athletic	L	0-2		10,562
22		19	H	BRISTOL ROVERS	W	2-0	Gray, Whittle (pen)	4,062
23	Mar	2	a	Cardiff City	W	1-0	Cunningham	9,357
24		5	H	OLDHAM ATHLETIC	L	0-2		5,206
25		8	H	MILLWALL	D	1-1	Bennett	7,431
26		12	a	Blackburn Rovers	D	2-2	Mayo, Glover	7,707
27		15	H	BOLTON WANDERERS	D	2-2	Grealish, Roeder	5,413
28		19	H	BURNLEY	L	0-1		5,610
29		26	H	NOTTS COUNTY	W	1-0	Stubbs (og)	4,635
30		29	a	Nottingham Forest	L	0-3		16,267
31	Apr	2	a	Millwall	W	1-0	Bennett	6,702
32		9	H	CHARLTON ATHLETIC	D	0-0		6,623
33		11	a	Luton Town	D	0-0		11,066
34		16	H	SHEFFIELD UTD	L	0-2		4,795
35		19	a	Hull City	D	1-1	Roeder	4,495
36		23	a	Wolverhampton Wanderers	L	0-1		19,877
37		26	H	SOUTHAMPTON	L	2-3	Gray, Bennett	5,226
38		30	H	CARLISLE UTD	D	0-0		4,183
39	May	7	a	Fulham	L	1-6	Grealish	11,822
40		10	H	BLACKPOOL	L	0-1		4,730
41		14	H	HEREFORD UTD	D	1-1	Roffey	4,956
42		17	H	HULL CITY	D	1-1	Glover	8,400
FA Cup								
3	Jan	8	a	Darlington	D	2-2	Possee, Hoadley	8,161
R		11	H	DARLINGTON	D	0-0**		5,620
2R		17	n*	Darlington	W	3-0	Whittle 2, Roffey	4,342
4		29	a	Blackburn Rovers	L	0-3		12,367
				*Played at White Hart Lane			**After extra-time	
League Cup								
2	Aug	31	H	HULL CITY	W	1-0	Cunningham	3,578
3	Sep	21	a	Millwall	D	0-0		11,636
R	Oct	12	H	MILLWALL	D	0-0**		9,201
2R		19	n*	Millwall	L	0-3		8,844
				*Played at Highbury			**After extra-time	

Pos	Team	P	Home					Away					Total		Pts
			W	D	L	F	A	W	D	L	F	A	F	A	
1	Wolverhampton W.	42	15	3	3	48	21	7	10	4	36	24	84	45	57
2	Chelsea	42	15	6	0	51	22	6	7	8	22	31	73	53	55
3	Nottingham Forest	42	14	3	4	53	22	7	7	7	24	21	77	43	52
4	Bolton Wanderers	42	15	2	4	46	21	5	9	7	29	33	75	54	51
5	Blackpool	42	11	7	3	29	17	6	10	5	29	25	58	42	51
6	Luton Town	42	13	5	3	39	17	8	1	12	28	31	67	48	48
7	Charlton Athletic	42	14	5	2	52	27	2	11	8	19	31	71	58	48
8	Notts County	42	11	5	5	29	20	8	5	8	36	40	65	60	48
9	Southampton	42	12	6	3	40	24	5	4	12	32	43	72	67	44
10	Millwall	42	9	6	6	31	22	6	7	8	26	31	57	53	43
11	Sheffield United	42	9	8	4	32	25	5	4	12	22	38	54	63	40
12	Blackburn Rovers	42	12	4	5	31	18	3	5	13	11	36	42	54	39
13	Oldham Athletic	42	11	6	4	37	23	3	4	14	15	41	52	64	38
14	Hull City	42	9	8	4	31	17	1	9	11	14	36	45	53	37
15	Bristol Rovers	42	8	9	4	32	27	4	4	13	21	41	53	68	37
16	Burnley	42	8	9	4	27	20	3	5	13	19	44	46	64	36
17	Fulham	42	9	7	5	39	25	2	6	13	15	36	54	61	35
18	Cardiff City	42	7	6	8	30	30	5	4	12	26	37	56	67	34
19	ORIENT	42	4	8	9	18	23	5	8	8	19	32	37	55	34
20	Carlisle United	42	7	7	7	31	33	4	5	12	18	42	49	75	34
21	Plymouth Argyle	42	5	9	7	27	25	3	7	11	19	40	46	65	32
22	Hereford United	42	6	9	6	28	30	2	6	13	29	48	57	78	31

club's jewel in the crown, is sold to West Bromwich Albion for £110,000 two days before his 21st birthday. Orient may never discover another player as good as him again. Watford reject a bid for striker Keith Mercer.

Mar 8 – John Chiedozie – 10 days short of his 17th birthday – takes over Laurie's number seven shirt for his debut at home to Millwall. There's also a first start for Terry Glynn in the 1-1 draw, although it turns out to be his last in an Os first team shirt.

Mar 12 –Winger Allan Glover and striker Joe Mayo mark their debuts by scoring in our 2-2 draw at Blackburn Rovers.

Mar 15 – But three days later, Mayo tears knee ligaments on his first home appearance, in the 2-2 draw with Bolton.

Apr 19 – Striker Billy Hurley, 17, makes his debut in the 1-1 draw at Hull.

Apr 26 – Peter Allen becomes the first Os player to make 400 league appearances but there's nothing to celebrate for the team after a 3-2 home defeat by FA Cup holders Southampton leaves us in deep trouble.

Apr 30 – In retrospective, the point gained from the goal-less draw at home to Carlisle was all that was required. At the time, it felt like another priceless point dropped to a relegation rival.

May 7 – Fears deepen as Os are thrashed 6-1 at Fulham, our worst league defeat since losing by the same score at Burnley in September, 1971.

May 10 – As a cost-cutting measure, the club issues a one-page, double-sided, black-and-white team-sheet for the Tuesday night rearranged game against Blackpool. This ninth home league defeat of the season leaves us perilously close to the drop zone.

May 14 – It's back to the standard eight-page (10p) prog for the visit of Hereford, whose relegation fate is sealed by a 1-1 draw. Meanwhile, the same result between Cardiff and Carlisle at Ninian Park means the Welsh club are safe while the Cumbrians need Hull to win at Brisbane Road in three days' time.

May 17 – A four-page prog (along with the optional original from the postponed game) is produced for the critical, final game at home to Hull, a fixture that was twice postponed. Os kick-off occupying the third relegation place but Allan Glover's first-half goal preserves Os' Second Division status.

KITCHEN ON A ROLL

IT is easy to reflect on the magical few months at the start of 1978, when 'little Orient' slayed a few giants on the way to the FA Cup semi-final, and forget that for the second time in 12 months we desperately needed a result from the last league game of the season to ensure survival Division Two survival.

Inevitably, it was Peter Kitchen, that insatiable masterchef of goal feasts, who served up the winning ingredients yet again to grab the winner at Cardiff which kept Os safe and sent Blackpool down. The 14th-place finish shouldn't hide the fact that we were the highest of SIX clubs to finish on 38 points – just one ahead of the Tangerines, who had the league's top scorer in Bob Hatton (22 goals), one more than our own Kitch.

TRANSFERS
>IN Peter Kitchen (Doncaster Rovers – £40,000).
<OUT Derek Possee (Vancouver Whitecaps, Canada – free), Doug Allder (Brentford – free), Alan Whittle (Persepolis, Iran – free), Peter Allen (Millwall – free).

FACTS & FIGURES
* A big improvement in home form saw just two visiting teams – Blackpool, who ended up relegated, and promotion-chasing Brighton – leave E10 with the maximum two points.
* Five players – John Jackson, Bobby Fisher, Bill Roffey, Glenn Roeder and Peter Kitchen – were all ever-present in the Second Division. Fisher, Roeder and Kitchen also played in all 11 Cup games.
* Os had a major new-look. The home shirt – manufactured by Admiral – was predominantly white, with wide red collars and two red vertical strips that also ran down the white shorts. The socks were also white but with red tops. The first choice away strip was the same design but with the white and red reversed, while a similarly styled sky/navy blue away combo was produced as a third option for use against teams who usually wore red. The 'Braces Kit' was born! A re-designed club crest, positioned in the centre panel of the shirt, added a classy touch to what quickly became the most popular strip in the club's modern history.
* After the previous season's spate of expensive postponements, the club reinvested a chunk of the Cunningham money in substantial improvements to the pitch, which included improved drainage and re-turfing overseen by head groundsman Maurice Reed.
* Orient's 700 or so season ticket-holders have never had such a great deal. The cost of an ST included a guaranteed main East Stand seat for three home Cup ties.
* Cost of the new squarer-shaped, 12-page programme has gone up by 5p, to 15p.
* For the first time, youth team games were played at Truman's Sports Ground, Highams Park.
* Adrian Harding and Ronnie Russ are the latest two board members.

DIARY: KEY MATCHES & MOMENTS
Aug 13 – Summer signing Peter Kitchen immediately proves his worth by scoring in the 2-0 League Cup, first round victory at Fulham and a 2-1 defeat in the return clash three days later doesn't stop Os from progressing to a second round tie with Derby. The two matches against Fulham – both played at Craven Cottage – also marked the only first team appearances ever made by goalkeeper John Smeulders, yet another youth product.

Aug 23 – After losing their first league game, 1-0 at Luton, Os are battered 4-1 in the Brisbane Road opener by Blackpool. The Orient board reacts decisively by terminating George Petchey's turbulent six-year reign as manager. In addition to the two league losses, the directors were also mindful of previous Anglo-Scottish Cup defeats in early August by Fulham (1-0) and Chelsea (2-0), plus a goal-less draw with Norwich.

Aug 27 – In the meantime, assistant manager Peter Angell, supported by coaches Terry Long and Alan Stephenson, takes temporary charge of team affairs and picks up a creditable 1-1 draw at Sunderland, where Peter Kitchen opens his league account.

Sept 3 – The midweek League Cup exit at Derby is swiftly forgotten, as 'Kitch' nets his first brace at Orient and further goals by Allan Glover, Derek Clarke and Peter Bennett earn Angell his first league points in a 5-3 victory over Oldham.

Sept 17 – After six years with Leicester City, Jimmy Bloomfield returns to begin his second spell as Orient boss. He resumes in style with a 2-1 home win over Bristol Rovers and then announces that Peter Angell has the new title of assistant manager.

Dec 3 – Peter Kitchen becomes the first Os' player to score a league hat-trick since Ian Bowyer in August, 1971. John Chiedozie completed the 4-2 home rout of Mansfield with his first senior goal.

Dec 10 – Two down at half-time, Os fight back to draw 2-2 at Hull with goals from Kitchen and Joe Mayo.

Dec 27 – Allan Glover, last season's final game hero, makes his final appearance for the club in the 2-0

Classy sweeper Glenn Roeder, architect of the 'Roeder Shuffle', was one of three players to appear in all 53 league and Cup games long before the term 'squad rotation' had been invented.

Football League Division Two 1977-78

1	Aug	20	a	Luton Town	L	0-1			8,061
2		23	H	BLACKPOOL	L	1-4	Glover		5,328
3		27	a	Sunderland	D	1-1	Kitchen		28,261
4	Sept	3	H	OLDHAM ATHLETIC	W	5-3	Kitchen 2, Glover, Clarke, Bennett		4,704
5		10	a	Charlton Athletic	L	1-2	Glover		8,751
6		17	H	BRISTOL ROVERS	W	2-1	Fisher. Kitchen (pen)		5,104
7		24	a	Blackburn Rovers	L	0-1			6,326
8	Oct	1	H	TOTTENHAM HOTSPUR	D	1-1	Mayo		24,131
9		4	a	Southampton	L	0-1			15,789
10		8	a	Notts County	D	1-1	Kitchen		7,482
11		15	H	CARDIFF CITY	W	2-1	Kitchen 2		5,444
12		22	a	Fulham	W	2-1	Kitchen, Mayo		9,126
13		29	H	MILLWALL	D	0-0			8,791
14	Nov	5	H	BOLTON WANDERERS	D	1-1	Roffey		7,547
15		12	a	Brighton & Hove Albion	L	0-1			20,830
16		19	H	CRYSTAL PALACE	D	0-0			10,037
17		26	a	Burnley	D	0-0			8,506
18	Dec	3	H	MANSFIELD TOWN	W	4-2	Chiedozie, Kitchen 3		4,426
19		10	a	Hull City	D	2-2	Mayo, Kitchen		4,279
20		17	H	BRIGHTON & HOVE ALBION	L	0-1			9,374
21		26	a	Sheffield Utd	L	0-2			18,370
22		27	H	STOKE CITY	W	2-0	Kitchen 2		6,192
23		31	a	Blackpool	D	0-0			6,911
24	Jan	2	H	LUTON TOWN	D	0-0			9,270
25		14	H	SUNDERLAND	D	2-2	Kitchen, Chiedozie		6,737
26		21	a	Oldham Athletic	L	1-2	Mayo		8,206
27	Feb	11	a	Bristol Rovers	L	1-2	Mayo		9,416
28		25	a	Tottenham Hotspur	D	1-1	Mayo		32,869
29	Mar	4	H	NOTTS COUNTY	D	0-0			5,828
30		17	H	FULHAM	D	1-1	Kitchen		7,928
31		21	a	Millwall	L	0-2			6,833
32		25	a	Stoke City	L	1-5	Mayo		14,595
33		27	H	SHEFFIELD UTD	W	3-1	Kitchen 3 (1 pen)		6,725
34	Apr	1	a	Bolton Wanderers	L	0-2			17,957
35		4	H	BLACKBURN ROVERS	D	0-0			7,072
36		15	a	Crystal Palace	L	0-1			15,414
37		18	H	BURNLEY	W	3-0	Bennett, Clarke 2		5,795
38		22	H	HULL CITY	W	2-1	Kitchen Clarke		5,776
39		25	H	SOUTHAMPTON	D	1-1	Mayo		19,248
40		29	a	Mansfield Town	D	1-1	Mayo		6,336
41	May	3	H	CHARLTON ATHLETIC	D	0-0			10,217
42		9	a	Cardiff City	W	1-0	Kitchen		8,270

home win over Stoke.

Jan 6 – Norwich snatch an equaliser two minutes into injury-time of this Friday night third round FA Cup tie after Peter Kitchen had given us a 27th minute lead.

Jan 14 – John Jackson removes a stray mongrel from the pitch and Sunderland's Gary Rowell is in the doghouse for missing a penalty in the home 2-2 draw with Sunderland.

Jan 16 – Kitch settles the third round replay at Norwich three minutes from time, slotting home John Chiedozie's cross from close range.

Jan 17 – John Chiedozie suffers a broken leg while playing in the Southern Junior Floodlit Cup semi-final at Ipswich. Os lose 2-0 but the biggest blow is losing the lively winger for the rest of the season.

Pos	Team	P	Home W	D	L	F	A	Away W	D	L	F	A	Total F	A	Pts
1	Bolton Wanderers	42	16	4	1	39	14	8	6	7	24	19	63	33	58
2	Southampton	42	15	4	2	44	16	7	9	5	26	23	70	39	57
3	Tottenham Hotspur	42	13	7	1	50	19	7	9	5	33	30	83	49	56
4	Brighton & Hove Albion	42	15	5	1	43	21	7	7	7	20	17	63	38	56
5	Blackburn Rovers	42	12	4	5	33	16	4	9	8	23	44	56	60	45
6	Sunderland	42	11	6	4	36	17	3	10	8	31	42	67	59	44
7	Stoke City	42	13	5	3	38	16	3	5	13	15	33	53	49	42
8	Oldham Athletic	42	9	10	2	32	20	4	6	11	22	38	54	58	42
9	Crystal Palace	42	9	7	5	31	20	4	8	9	19	27	50	47	41
10	Fulham	42	9	8	4	32	19	5	5	11	17	30	49	49	41
11	Burnley	42	11	6	4	35	20	4	4	13	21	44	56	64	40
12	Sheffield United	42	13	4	4	38	22	3	4	14	24	51	62	73	40
13	Luton Town	42	11	4	6	35	20	3	6	12	19	32	54	52	38
14	ORIENT	42	8	11	2	30	20	2	7	12	13	29	43	49	38
15	Notts County	42	10	9	2	36	22	1	7	13	18	40	54	62	38
16	Millwall	42	8	8	5	23	20	4	6	11	26	37	49	57	38
17	Charlton Athletic	42	11	6	4	38	27	2	6	13	17	41	55	68	38
18	Bristol Rovers	42	10	7	4	40	26	3	5	13	21	51	61	77	38
19	Cardiff City	42	12	6	3	32	23	1	6	14	19	48	51	71	38
20	Blackpool	42	7	8	6	35	25	5	5	11	24	35	59	60	37
21	Mansfield Town	42	6	6	9	30	34	4	5	12	19	35	49	69	31
22	Hull City	42	6	6	9	23	25	2	6	13	11	27	34	52	28

FA Cup								
3	Jan	6	H	NORWICH CITY	D	1-1	Kitchen	14,538
R		16	a	Norwich City	W	1-0	Kitchen	20,421
4		28	H	BLACKBURN ROVERS	W	3-1	Kitchen 2, Mayo	9,547
5	Feb	18	H	CHELSEA	D	0-0		25,123
R		27	a	Chelsea	W	2-1	Kitchen 2	36,379
6	Mar	11	a	Middlesbrough	D	0-0		33,426
R		14	H	MIDDLESBROUGH	W	2-1	Kitchen, Mayo	18,051
SF	Apr	8	n*	Arsenal	L	0-3		49,698
				*Played at Stamford Bridge				

League Cup								
1	Aug	13	n**	Fulham	W	2-0	Kitchen, Lacy (og)	4,704
		16	a	Fulham	L	1-2	Allen	4,372
2		31	a	Derby County	L	1-3	Bennett	16,948
				**Home tie played at Craven Cottage				

Jan 21 – Chiedozie's injury paves the way for Kevin Godfrey to make his league debut in the 2-1 defeat at Oldham.

Jan 28 – Blackburn Rovers, among the Second Division front-runners, dominate the first hour of the FA Cup fourth round tie in treacherous conditions at Brisbane Road (which required a 2.00pm pitch inspection) and they look set to progress further after Stuart Metcalfe puts them ahead in the 68th minute. John Jackson made a couple of important saves before centre-half Nigel Gray was pushed upfront as Os lay siege to the Rovers' goal. Within five minutes of Rovers taking the lead, Peter Kitchen latches onto Phil Hoadley's long pass to equalise. Then Kitch notches his 20th goal of the season, tucking away a rebound, to put Orient ahead before Joe Mayo seals an unlikely 3-1 victory from Kevin Godfrey's cross.

Feb 18 – After a few days spent bonding and relaxing at the Queens Hotel, Eastbourne, where John Jackson and Peter Bennett beat David Payne and Peter Angell in the table tennis doubles tournament and

'Jacko' and Joe Mayo combined to win the snooker event against Allan Glover and John Smeulders, Os get back down to serious business in the fourth round of the FA Cup at home to Chelsea. With neither side able to break the deadlock, thanks largely to Jacko's full-stretch dive to deny Ian Britton, all the post-match focus is on the trouble that occurred at the Coronation Gardens end, where the front wall collapsed under pressure from surging visiting fans. Although no serious injuries were reported, a number of supporters were taken to hospital for treatment to minor cuts and shock.

Feb 25 – A Joe Mayo header from Kevin Godfrey's cross earns impudent Os' a deserved 1-1 draw at neighbourly league leaders Tottenham.

Feb 26 – Manager Jimmy Bloomfield is admitted to hospital for tests.

Feb 27 – Assistant manager Peter Angell is in charge for the fourth round replay at Stamford Bridge, where Os produce one of the most memorable performances and results in their history. It looked curtains when Bill Roffey hooked the ball over Jacko to gift Blues the lead but Kitch stole the show with his well-chronicled second-half goals to clinch a superb 2-1 victory. 'GLORIENT!' boomed the *Daily Express* as Os reached the quarter-final for only the fourth time in their history.

Mar 4 – Only three sides of the ground are open – the South Terrace is closed pending repairs – as Peter Allen plays his 481st, and final, first team game for the club in the goal-less home draw with Notts County.

Mar 11 – With Jimmy Bloomfield still in hospital recovering from abdominal surgery, Peter Angell leads the team to First Division Middlesbrough for the FA Cup quarter-final. Against all odds,

Mar 14 – Two goals in the first 12 minutes, by Peter Kitchen – a spectacular volley – and Joe Mayo, stunned Middlesbrough in the replay at windswept Brisbane Road. Previously unbeaten in nine games, Boro's

Jubilant dressing room scene after the sensational 2-1 FA Cup fourth round replay victory at Chelsea.

Jimmy Bloomfield is greeted on his return by happy fans and a lucky mascot.

response from David Armstrong four minutes before time came too late to deny history-making Os their first-ever FA Cup semi-final experience.

Mar 27 – Jimmy Bloomfield returns to the dug-out for the Bank Holiday Monday morning clash with Sheffield United and is feeling even better after seeing that man Kitch hit a hat-trick in the 3-1 victory after Blades took a 10th minute lead.

Apr 1 – Winger Tunji Banjo makes his first senior appearance, coming off the bench to replace Kevin Godfrey, in Os' 2-0 defeat at Bolton.

Apr 8 – All good things must come to an end . . . although worthy winners of the semi-final, 11/10 FA Cup favourites Arsenal enjoyed huge slices of good fortune with two deflected killer goals in the opening 20 minutes to set up a comfortable 3-0 win against underperforming Os.

Apr 22 – With vulnerable Os just one place clear of the relegation zone and Hull second from bottom, Os take a vital 2-1 home victory courtesy of goals from Kitch and Derek Clarke's lobbed winner.

Apr 29 – Sub Tunji Banjo catches the eye as Joe Mayo's equalising goal – his second in two games – earns a precious point at Mansfield.

May 5 – Spurs are Friday night visitors for a testimonial match to jointly honour Peter Angell and Brian Blower.

May 9 – Peter Kitchen nets his 29th, and most important, goal of a brilliant personal campaign in the 34th minute at Cardiff. Phil Hoadley nodded down a Tony Grealish throw-in and there was Kitch to hook home the only goal in the victory that prolongs Orient's stay in Division Two.

SITTING COMFORTABLY

AFTER nervous endings to the previous two seasons, Orient were eyeing up a top six finish before stumbling in the final stages and having to settle for mid-table stability despite the loss of a few big-name players from the famous Cup side of '78.

They were sitting more comfortably off the field, too, with the old West Side terrace making way for seats.

TRANSFERS

>IN Paul Went (Cardiff City – £20,000), Ian Moores (Tottenham Hotspur – £55,000), Ralph Coates (Tottenham Hotspur – free), Alan Whittle (Retained by Orient – free), Mark Gray (Fulham – part-exchange).

<OUT Glenn Roeder (Queens Park Rangers – £250,000*), Phil Hoadley (Norwich City – £110,000*), Allan Glover (Brentford – free), Peter Kitchen (Fulham – £150,000), David Payne (Millwall – free). *Fees fixed by tribunal.*

FACTS & FIGURES

* For the first time, Orient were forced to release two star players under the new freedom of contract rules introduced by The Football League prior to the 1978-79 season. Skipper Phil Hoadley and fellow defender Glenn Roeder both exercised their right to decline new contract offers from the Os in order to negotiate their own terms with new clubs. The size of their respective transfer fees paid by First Division Norwich City and QPR was determined by a league tribunal.

* The final position of 11th was Os' highest since 1973-74.

* By conceding only 23 away league goals, it equalled their best defensive record of the 70s, achieved in 1974-75.

* During the summer of 1978 the old West Stand enclosure became all-seater. The club installed plastic seats where battles were once fought between rival fans on concrete terraces. "This is probably one of the biggest steps forward that the club has made for many years," enthused Brian Winston, confirming seating capacity had been increased to in excess of 7,200.

* Len Cheesewright rejoined the club as chief scout following Arthur Rowe's decision to join George Petchey at Millwall.

* At the start of the season director Frank Harris resigned after 28 years on the board, while long-serving club doctor Mr D. Dodds decided to hang up his stethoscope. Three months into the season, Ronnie Russ resigned his short-lived directorship.

DIARY: KEY MATCHES & MOMENTS

Aug 5 – After the Cup heroics of the previous season, an opening day Anglo-Scottish Cup (ASC) tie at home to Mansfield was never going to set pulses racing. There was certainly no Argentina-style World Cup 'ticker tape' welcome for the teams from a 3,385 gathering unenthused by the visitors' 1-0 win. A 3-2 home defeat by Notts County three days later, followed by a goal-less draw at Norwich spelt the end of Os' ASC involvement, which at least spared the pitch – now under the supervision of Charlie Hasler – any extra punishment.

Aug 19 – Joe Mayo and Peter Kitchen notched the goals that inspired Os to recover from a third minute deficit to win their opening league game, 2-1, at Sheffield United, where midfielder Henry Hughton made his Second Division debut in the number six shirt.

Aug 22 – Bill Roffey showed lots of fighting spirit, too, in the 3-0 home win over Sunderland. With a retaliatory right-hook that would have graced the nearby York Hall, Roffey floored Wayne Entwistle – an incident that prompted ref Ron Challis to send off both players before half-time.

Aug 26 – Mark Smith, 16, makes his only first team appearance against Wrexham, who snatch a 1-0 win thanks to a dubious penalty awarded against John Chiedozie for handball. Os begin a dreadful run of six league games without scoring.

Sept 2 – There's an unhappy senior debut, too, for John Kane, who subs for the injured Peter Bennett after 29 minutes of our 3-0 defeat at Blackburn.

Sept 9 – Paul Went, 29, who became the youngest-ever Os player when he made his original debut at the age of 15 years and 327 days in 1965, returns to the back four but 1-0 winners Stoke spoil his homecoming party.

Oct 6 – The day after his 24th birthday, tall, lean striker Ian Moores celebrates his debut by scoring both goals in the 2-0 Friday victory at Charlton, our first defeat of the Addicks since 1972. Balding former England international midfielder Ralph Coates – signed from Spurs in the same deal with Moores – is equally impressive on his first appearance,

Nov 11 – Brian Winston tackled the issue of racist chanting by Orient fans in his programme column for the Sheffield United game. Under the heading 'Please Stop This Now!', he wrote: "The chanting of bad language will not be tolerated at the Orient, and the use of animal noises in response to the efforts of coloured members of visiting teams is as upsetting to our own players as it is to the rest of the spectators. I am taking this opportunity to advise any future offenders that they will be escorted from the ground and banned for life should this practice recur among supporters." He also pointed out that visiting fans will be directed to the North Terrace at the Windsor Road end.

Nov 14 – IFK Gothenburg become the first foreign visitors to Orient since Roma in 1970. The Swedes, won the hastily arranged Tuesday night friendly, 2-0. Os gave rare first team outings to striker Nigel Meeking and American sub Chris Carenza.

Nov 21 – Frustrated Peter Kitchen, replaced by John Chiedozie at half-time in the 2-0 home win over Blackburn, goes on the transfer list at his own request.

Nov 22 – Unlucky Peter Bennett, whose Orient career was blighted by injuries, suffered a broken leg in the Combination League game away to Reading reserves.

Dec 16 – Injury to Paul Went just before the game at Oldham meant striker Joe Mayo filling in at centre-back throughout the goal-less draw. Oddly, it was Kitch, a late inclusion in the side, who took over Went's number six shirt. Jimmy Bloomfield faced press criticism for deploying defensive tactics.

Dec 23 – Went recovered in time to score in our 2-1 home win against Millwall.

Dec 26 – Our most satisfying away win of the season. Relegated at the end of the previous season, West Ham were the league's leading scorers by the time Os made the short Boxing Day trip to Upton Park. Hammers forced 18 corners but met with stubborn resistance and were chasing the game from the moment Joe Mayo gave Os an 18th minute lead following a knock-down from Ian Moores. With five minutes left, John Chiedozie ran from halfway to clinch a 2-0 victory that he celebrated with undisguised glee.

Jan 9 – Third Division Bury made Os work hard for the 3-2 win at Brisbane Road before Cup legend Kitch did the business with a couple of goals, while John Chiedozie netted his first in the competition he largely missed out on through injury the previous year.

Jan 27 – Os' reward for beating Bury was a trip up the A12 to Ipswich, who paraded the trophy they won by beating Arsenal in last year's final. The First Division side threw everything at Orient on a tricky,

Football League Division Two 1978-79

#	Month	Date	H/a	Opponent	Result	Score	Scorers	Attendance
1	Aug	19	a	Sheffield Utd	W	2-1	Mayo, Kitchen	19,012
2		22	H	SUNDERLAND	W	3-0	Hughton, Mayo, Grealish	7,373
3		26	H	WREXHAM	L	0-1		6,416
4	Sept	2	a	Blackburn Rovers	L	0-3		6,781
5		9	H	STOKE CITY	L	0-1		6,587
6		16	a	Notts County	L	0-1		8,094
7		23	a	Newcastle Utd	D	0-0		26,356
8		30	H	LEICESTER CITY	L	0-1		5,430
9	Oct	6	a	Charlton Athletic	W	2-0	Moores 2	11,024
10		14	H	CARDIFF CITY	D	2-2	Mayo, Grealish	6,064
11		21	a	Bristol Rovers	L	1-2	Moores	7,234
12		28	H	LUTON TOWN	W	3-2	Coates, Kitchen 2	7,035
13	Nov	4	a	Cambridge Utd	L	1-3	Grealish	6,655
14		11	H	SHEFFIELD UTD	D	1-1	Kitchen (pen)	5,540
15		18	a	Wrexham	L	1-3	Moores	9,122
16		21	H	BLACKBURN ROVERS	W	2-0	Mayo, Moores	4,415
17		25	H	PRESTON NORTH END	W	2-0	Hughton, Moores	4,702
18	Dec	2	a	Brighton & Hove Albion	L	0-2		16,691
19		9	H	BURNLEY	W	2-1	Grealish, Kitchen	4,764
20		16	a	Oldham Athletic	D	0-0		5,169
21		23	H	MILLWALL	W	2-1	Went, Chiedozie	6,185
22		26	a	West Ham Utd	W	2-0	Mayo, Chiedozie	29,220
23		30	a	Crystal Palace	D	1-1	Mayo	20,100
24	Jan	20	H	NOTTS COUNTY	W	3-0	Moores 2, Chiedozie	4,803
25	Feb	3	H	NEWCASTLE UTD	W	2-0	Mayo, Kitchen (pen)	7,251
26		10	a	Leicester City	L	3-5	Chiedozie 2, Kitchen	12,050
27		24	a	Cardiff City	L	0-1		8,256
28	Mar	3	H	BRISTOL ROVERS	D	1-1	Moores (pen)	5,078
29		10	a	Luton Town	L	1-2	Moores	6,003
30		14	a	Stoke City	L	1-3	Mayo	16,183
31		17	H	CAMBRIDGE UTD	W	3-0	Grealish, Mayo, Coates	4,577
32		20	H	CHARLTON ATHLETIC	W	2-1	Chiedozie, Whittle	6,457
33		24	a	Sunderland	L	0-1		21,189
34		27	H	FULHAM	W	1-0	Went (pen)	6,645
35		31	a	Preston North End	D	1-1	Moores	9,494
36	Apr	7	H	BRIGHTON & HOVE ALBION	D	3-3	Mayo, Coates, Moores	11,567
37		10	a	Millwall	L	0-2		6,117
38		14	H	WEST HAM UTD	L	0-2		17,517
39		16	a	Fulham	D	2-2	Moores, Banjo	6,956
40		21	H	OLDHAM ATHLETIC	D	0-0		4,340
41		28	a	Burnley	W	1-0	Mayo	7,162
42	May	5	H	CRYSTAL PALACE	L	0-1		19,945
FA Cup								
3	Jan	9	H	BURY	W	3-2	Kitchen 2, Chiedozie	6,192
4		27	a	Ipswich Town	D	0-0		23,337
R		30	H	IPSWICH TOWN	L	0-2		18,672
League Cup								
2	Aug	30	H	CHESTERFIELD	L	1-2	Fisher	4,667

Pos	Team	P	Home					Away					Total		Pts
			W	D	L	F	A	W	D	L	F	A	F	A	
1	Crystal Palace	42	12	7	2	30	11	7	12	2	21	13	51	24	57
2	Brighton & Hove Albion	42	16	3	2	44	11	7	7	7	28	28	72	39	56
3	Stoke City	42	11	7	3	35	15	9	9	3	23	16	58	31	56
4	Sunderland	42	13	3	5	39	19	9	8	4	31	25	70	44	55
5	West Ham United	42	12	7	2	46	15	6	7	8	24	24	70	39	50
6	Notts County	42	8	10	3	23	15	6	6	9	25	45	48	60	44
7	Preston North End	42	7	11	3	36	23	5	7	9	23	34	59	57	42
8	Newcastle United	42	13	3	5	35	24	4	5	12	16	31	51	55	42
9	Cardiff City	42	12	5	4	34	23	4	5	12	22	47	56	70	42
10	Fulham	42	10	7	4	35	19	3	8	10	15	28	50	47	41
11	ORIENT	42	11	5	5	32	18	4	5	12	19	33	51	51	40
12	Cambridge United	42	7	10	4	22	15	5	6	10	22	37	44	52	40
13	Burnley	42	11	6	4	31	22	3	6	12	20	40	51	62	40
14	Oldham Athletic	42	10	7	4	36	23	3	6	12	16	38	52	61	39
15	Wrexham	42	10	6	5	31	16	2	8	11	14	26	45	42	38
16	Bristol Rovers	42	10	6	5	34	23	4	4	13	14	37	48	60	38
17	Leicester City	42	7	8	6	28	23	3	9	9	15	29	43	52	37
18	Luton Town	42	11	5	5	46	24	2	5	14	14	33	60	57	36
19	Charlton Athletic	42	6	8	7	28	28	5	5	11	32	41	60	69	35
20	Sheffield United	42	9	6	6	34	24	2	6	13	18	45	52	69	34
21	Millwall	42	7	4	10	22	29	4	6	11	20	32	42	61	32
22	Blackburn Rovers	42	5	8	8	24	29	5	2	14	17	43	41	72	30

snow-covered surface but wave after wave of attack was repelled by solid defence underpinned by the goalkeeping heroics of 'Stonewall' John Jackson.

Jan 30 – Ipswich were worthy 2-0 replay winners thanks to a Paul Mariner brace, although Joe Mayo shot against the post in the 31st minute.

Feb 10 – Peter Kitchen ends his first spell with the club by scoring in the 5-3 defeat at Leicester, where Jimmy Bloomfield made an unhappy return to the club he left to rejoin Os 18 months earlier.

Feb 24 – After 18 months playing in war-torn Iran, Alan Whittle returns and has an opening goal ruled out. Joe Mayo also had a goal inexplicably disallowed as Cardiff somehow sneak a 1-0 win. Derek Clarke, recalled from his loan spell with Carlisle, came on as sub.

Mar 3 – Bristol Rovers end Os' run of six consecutive home league wins with a 1-1 draw, despite having Frankie Prince sent-off before the break. Ian Moores put us ahead four minutes from the end from the penalty spot but Steve White snatched the equaliser 60 seconds from time.

Mar – Leicester City's former Orient left-back Dennis Rofe turns down an offer to link up with Jimmy Bloomfield for the third time.

Mar 27 – Welsh forward Mark Gray, 19, who came from Fulham reserves as part of the Kitchen deal, appears as sub on his first team debut in the 1-0 home win over his former club. Paul Went, another ex-Fulham man, settled it from the penalty spot.

Apr 7 – Os and table-topping Brighton served up a six-goal thriller for *The Big Match* cameras. Ralph Coates, with a 25-yard cracker on the half-hour, won most plaudits in this classic 3-3 draw.

Apr 16 – Tunji Banjo thought he'd netted the winner eight minutes from time at Fulham on Easter Monday . . . only to concede a penalty and then watch Kevin Lock make it 2-2 in the dying minutes.

Apr 28 – Mark Gray starts for the first time but goes off injured in the 1-0 win at Burnley, where Joe Mayo was gifted the only goal soon after half-time.

May 5 – Crystal Palace attract the biggest crowd of the season to Leyton and their happy fans leave celebrating a 1-0 win that left them needing a point from their final game to clinch promotion.

MIDDLE CLASS

CONSIDERING they lost to bottom club Shrewsbury Town and dropped to the foot of the table at the end of September, Orient were relieved to begin the 80s as a Second Division club.

They did so largely thanks to a much-improved mid-season spell before a poor end to the campaign that produced just 29 home goals.

But wasn't it good to be an average team in the Second Division – for 10 whole years?

TRANSFERS

>IN Mervyn Day (West Ham United – £100,000), Tommy Taylor (West Ham United – £70,000), Billy Jennings (West Ham United – £75,000), Margerrison (Fulham – £70,000), Steve Parsons (£42,000 – Wimbledon), Steve Hamberger (Walthamstow Avenue – free), Sean Rafter (Leicester City – free), Mark Penfold (Charlton Athletic – free).
<OUT Tony Grealish (Luton Town – £150,000), John Jackson (Millwall – £7,500), Derek Clarke (Crewe Alexandra – free), John Smeulders (AFC Bournemouth – free).

FACTS & FIGURES

* Despite failing to win any of their first nine or last 10 matches of the season, Os still managed to finish 14th.
* Four players were ever-present in the league: Bobby Fisher, Tommy Taylor, Ralph Coates and Mervyn Day.
* Full colour was used in the 16-page programme (25p) for the first time.

DIARY: KEY MATCHES & MOMENTS

July 18 – Everyone at Orient is devastated by the sudden death of assistant manager Peter Angell, who suffered a heart attack, aged 47, during a training session at Epping Forest.

Aug – Bullish Brian Winston is talking up Os' promotion chances: "I've been chairman for five years and for the first time we are ready to go to the very top."

Aug – Paul Went and Ian Moores missed the early weeks of the season following cartilage operations.

Aug 18 – Despite twice going ahead, Os have to settle for a 2-2 draw in the league curtain-raiser against Burnley. Ralph Coates (pictured), the oldest player on the pitch, scores both Orient goals.

Aug 25 – John Margerrison's first goal for the club is too late to avoid a 2-1 defeat to Tony Grealish's Luton at Kenilworth Road.

Sept 1 – Billy Jennings opens his goal account with the equaliser in the 1-1 home draw with Charlton.

Sept 8 – Jennings finds the net again but Newcastle stun Os with a 4-1 victory despite managing only one corner to Orient's 19. Magpies were three up by half-time.

Sept 4 – Ray Goddard came back to haunt Os. After both legs of the League Cup second round tie against Third Division Wimbledon end 2-2, the former keeper is the star of the penalty shootout at Plough Lane. Goddard saves Joe Mayo's spot-kick and then, with the scores locked at 4-4, steps up himself to slot the winner.

Sept 22 – Two second-half goals by Joe Mayo, the second in injury-time, earned Os a last-gasp draw against Birmingham at Brisbane Road. Orient remain second from bottom.

Sept 29 – PE teacher Steve Biggins scores the goal that sees Shrewsbury leapfrog Os and send Jimmy Bloomfield's men to the foot of the table.

Oct 9 – After nine league games without a win, Os move off the bottom. Ralph Coates, in his new role as player-coach, nets the 10th minute winner in the 1-0 home victory against Fulham that was more convincing than the result suggested. Fulham striker Peter Kitchen came on for Peter Marinello in the 47th minute.

Oct 15 – Brisbane Road stages the England B v New Zealand international.

Nov 3 – Former Burnley midfield star Ralph Coates inspires Os' 2-1 victory over his old club at Turf Moor. Joe Mayo headed the visitors ahead on 13 minutes and Coates added a second soon after half-time. Clarets' late goal by Tony Arins was mere consolation.

Nov 10 – Shell-shocked Orient slumped to a very heavy 7-3 home defeat by Chelsea, who scored seven away goals in the league for the first time in Geoff Hurst's first official game as manager. Lee Frost bagged his first hat-trick and Clive Walker, whom Bloomfield revealed he'd tried to sign, got two. "I tried to buy Walker two years ago, when he was in the reserves," said Os' boss.

Dec 1 – Tommy Taylor's best moment since returning. Ralph Coates taps a short free-kick to the centre-back, who slams the winner into the roof of the net from 25 yards with eight minutes left against Ken Knighton's Sunderland. "It was a goal in a million," said Knighton. Billy Jennings had headed Os in front from John Chiedozie's pinpoint deep cross in first-half injury-time.

Dec 8 – Chiedozie gave Dennis Rofe a roasting as Os claimed a deserved 2-2 draw at Leicester, where Bloomfield reckoned both goals by his former club should have been ruled out. After Joe Mayo had put the visitors ahead, Bloomfield thought Bobby Fisher had cleared Martin Henderson's goal-bound header off the line, while two minutes after John Margerrison had restored Os' lead, Mark Goodwin looked offside for Foxes' second equaliser.

Dec 21 – Os make it nine points from 11 away games thanks to another Coates-Taylor free-kick combination. Defender Tommy unleashed a 25-yard drive that took a slight deflection off Swansea's wall on its way in as the visitors seized control on the half-hour.

Dec 26 – The Boxing Day game at QPR is postponed.

Dec 29 – Sub Kevin Godfrey, sent on for the injured John Chiedozie in the 81st minute, rescues a point for Os three minutes from time in the 2-2 draw against Luton. Billy Jennings began the fightback after David Moss had given Hatters a two-goal lead before half-time.

Ralph Coates scored both goals in the opening day win against his former club Burnley.

Jan 1 – Keeper Mervyn Day endured a New Year's nightmare against his former club West Ham, who enjoyed a 4-0 romp.

Jan 5 – Billy Jennings spared Orient blushes with the equaliser 13 minutes from time at Alliance League leaders Altrincham in the third round of the FA Cup. Kevin Godfrey beat two defenders before deceiving keeper Alex Stepney, to set up Jennings.

Jan 9 – The non-leaguers made Os work hard for victory in the replay. It took second-half goals by Joe Mayo and Billy Jennings to earn a lucrative fourth round home tie with West Ham, although Jeff Johnson provoked a nervy finish by scoring with eight minutes to go.

Jan 12 – Ralph Coates scores a memorable 20-yard volley through a crowded area in the 70th minute to deepen Charlton's relegation fears and warm the hearts of freezing Os fans among the 6,000 crowd at The Valley.

Jan 26 – Despite showing a big improvement on their recent league drubbing by West Ham, Os couldn't capitalise upon Tommy Taylor's opening goal from the penalty spot in this frenetic fourth round FA Cup tie at Leyton. Orient had Sean Rafter deputising for Mervyn Day in goal but the youngster was unable to stop a headed own-goal by Nigel Gray, a penalty from Ray Stewart or Stewart's winner after John Chiedozie had scored the best goal of the game.

Feb 2 – Orient romp to their biggest win of the season to walloping Wrexham 4-0 at home. Another Billy Jennings header and further strikes by Joe Mayo and Tommy Taylor (pen) had Os comfortably three up by

Football League Division Two 1979-80

#									
1	Aug	18	H	BURNLEY	D	2-2	Coates 2		6,151
2		22	a	Fulham	D	0-0			9,174
3		25	a	Luton Town	L	1-2	Margerrison		6,705
4	Sept	1	H	CHARLTON ATHLETIC	D	1-1	Jennings		6,052
5		8	H	NEWCASTLE UTD	L	1-4	Jennings		5,700
6		15	a	Wrexham	L	1-2	Mayo		8,195
7		22	H	BIRMINGHAM CITY	D	2-2	Mayo 2		5,550
8		29	a	Shrewsbury Town	L	0-1			6,176
9	Oct	6	a	Oldham Athletic	L	0-1			6,700
10		9	H	FULHAM	W	1-0	Coates 2		5,090
11		13	H	WATFORD	W	1-0	Mayo		7,506
12		20	a	Cambridge Utd	D	1-1	Chiedozie		5,151
13		27	H	BRISTOL ROVERS	W	2-1	Coates, Went (pen)		4,645
14	Nov	3	a	Burnley	W	2-1	Mayo, Coates		6,534
15		10	H	CHELSEA	L	3-7	Jennings 2, Fisher		13,005
16		17	a	Cardiff City	D	0-0			8,119
17		24	a	Preston North End	D	2-2	Penfold, Taylor		7,835
18	Dec	1	H	SUNDERLAND	W	2-1	Jennings, Taylor		6,582
19		8	a	Leicester City	D	2-2	Mayo, Margerrison		16,303
20		15	H	NOTTS COUNTY	W	1-0	Jennings		4,115
21		21	a	Swansea City	W	1-0	Taylor		10,342
22		29	H	LUTON TOWN	D	2-2	Jennings, Godfrey		9,292
23	Jan	1	H	WEST HAM UTD	L	0-4			23,885
24		12	a	Charlton Athletic	W	1-0	Coates		6,357
25		19	a	Newcastle Utd	L	0-2			20,881
26	Feb	2	H	WREXHAM	W	4-0	Jennings 2, Mayo, Taylor (pen)		4,469
27		9	a	Birmingham City	L	1-3	Mayo		17,474
28		12	a	Queens Park Rangers	D	0-0			11,361
29		16	H	SHREWSBURY TOWN	L	0-1			4,326
30		23	a	Watford	W	3-0	Jennings, Chiedozie, Coates		15,144
31	Mar	1	H	CAMBRIDGE UTD	W	2-0	Coates, Mayo		5,150
32		8	a	Bristol Rovers	W	2-1	Mayo, Jennings		5,798
33		14	H	OLDHAM ATHLETIC	D	1-1	Mayo		4,953
34		22	a	Chelsea	L	0-1			19,706
35		29	H	CARDIFF CITY	D	1-1	Roffey		4,081
36	Apr	5	a	West Ham Utd	L	0-2			22,066
37		8	H	QUEENS PARK RANGERS	D	1-1	Fisher		9,389
38		12	a	Sunderland	D	1-1	Coates		33,279
39		19	H	PRESTON NORTH END	D	2-2	Fisher, Taylor (pen)		4,509
40		26	a	Notts County	D	1-1	Chiedozie		5,505
41		30	H	SWANSEA CITY	D	0-0			3,779
42	May	3	H	LEICESTER CITY	L	0-1			13,828
FA Cup									
3	Jan	5	a	Altrincham	D	1-1	Jennings		7,844
R		9	H	ALTRINCHAM	W	2-1	Mayo, Jennings		8,841
4		26	H	WEST HAM UTD	L	2-3	Taylor (pen), Chiedozie		21,521
League Cup									
2	Aug	29	H	WIMBLEDON	D	2-2	Chiedozie, Hughton		4,964
	Sept	4	a	Wimbledon	D	2-2*	Mayo, Margerrison		3,510
							*Wimbledon won 5-4 on penalties		

Pos	Team	P	Home W	D	L	F	A	Away W	D	L	F	A	Total F	A	Pts
1	Leicester City	42	12	5	4	32	19	9	8	4	26	19	58	38	55
2	Sunderland	42	16	5	0	47	13	5	7	9	22	29	69	42	54
3	Birmingham City	42	14	5	2	37	16	7	6	8	21	22	58	38	53
4	Chelsea	42	14	3	4	34	16	9	4	8	32	36	66	52	53
5	Queens Park Rangers	42	10	9	2	46	25	8	4	9	29	28	75	53	49
6	Luton Town	42	9	10	2	36	17	7	7	7	30	28	66	45	49
7	West Ham United	42	13	2	6	37	21	7	5	9	17	22	54	43	47
8	Cambridge United	42	11	6	4	40	23	3	10	8	21	30	61	53	44
9	Newcastle United	42	13	6	2	35	19	2	8	11	18	30	53	49	44
10	Preston North End	42	8	10	3	30	23	4	9	8	26	29	56	52	43
11	Oldham Athletic	42	12	5	4	30	21	4	6	11	19	32	49	53	43
12	Swansea City	42	13	1	7	31	20	4	8	9	17	33	48	53	43
13	Shrewsbury Town	42	12	3	6	41	23	6	2	13	19	30	60	53	41
14	ORIENT	42	7	9	5	29	31	5	8	8	19	23	48	54	41
15	Cardiff City	42	11	4	6	21	16	5	4	12	20	32	41	48	40
16	Wrexham	42	13	2	6	26	15	3	4	14	14	34	40	49	38
17	Notts County	42	4	11	6	24	22	7	4	10	27	30	51	52	37
18	Watford	42	9	6	6	27	18	3	7	11	12	28	39	46	37
19	Bristol Rovers	42	9	8	4	33	23	2	5	14	17	41	50	64	35
20	Fulham	42	6	4	11	19	28	5	3	13	23	46	42	74	29
21	Burnley	42	5	9	7	19	23	1	6	14	20	50	39	73	27
22	Charlton Athletic	42	6	6	9	25	31	0	4	17	14	47	39	78	22

half-time, before Jennings capped a fine afternoon with his second. "Don't blame the Wrexham defence. We owe it all to one-touch football and movement off the ball," purred Jimmy Bloomfield.

Feb 23 – Billy Jennings set Os on their way to a 3-0 win at his former club Watford with a 24th minute header. John Chiedozie added the second from Mervyn Day's long kick, before Ralph Coates sealed a convincing away win by converting a Jennings header three minutes from the end.

Mar 1 – Os notched what proved to be their last home win of the season to end Cambridge United's nine-match unbeaten run. The tireless Ralph Coates put Orient ahead a minute into the second-half with a shot from the edge of the box and then the midfield general laid on the other goal for Joe Mayo five minutes from time.

Mar 4 – Jimmy Bloomfield is appointed managing director designate, a role he will take up at the end of the season pending a change to FA rules that will allow him to continue as manager.

Mar 8 – Despite conceding a second-minute penalty from Stewart Barrowclough, Os hit back within a minute through Joe Mayo, who headed home Bill Roffey's corner. Billy Jennings netted the winner on half-time.

Apr 8 – Steve Parsons, who impressed for Wimbledon against Os in the League Cup early in the season, is signed for £42,000 and does well on his debut in the home 1-1 Easter draw at Glenn Roeder's QPR, where Bobby Fisher gave Orient the lead with a neat drive. Clive Allen snatched a controversial equaliser 18 minutes from time – Os reckoned his shot hadn't crossed the line after hitting the underside of the bar.

Apr 12 – Dropped for the 1-1 home draw with Sunderland, Billy Jennings is transfer-listed at his own request.

Apr 26 – John Chiedozie reminds Notts County of his class by eluding two defenders before scoring with a driven shot in the 1-1 draw at Meadow Lane. Magpies will see a lot more of the winger in due course . . .

May 3 – Leicester City clinched promotion and the Second Division title after Larry May bundled in their 12th minute winner following a free-kick, much to the delight of the visiting fans who outnumbered the home contingent. Sadly, their celebrations turned sour as they proceeded to smash up the ground, including the goalposts and crossbar at the Coronation Gardens end. An irate Brian Winston condemned their riotous behaviour, saying: "They were a disgrace to a fine club. I estimate the damage to our ground and surrounding houses to be between £7,000 and £10,000."

From gloom to glory

Born: Notting Hill, London, February 15, 1934
Orient Management Career: Mar 1968-May 1971 & Sept 1977-Aug 1981
Matches in Charge: League 315, FA Cup 22, League Cup 12
LEAGUE – P 315 W 102 D 105 L 108 GF 349 GA 368 Pts 311
CUP – P 34 W 9 D 12 L 13 GF 37 GA 43

WHEN Jimmy Bloomfield arrived at Orient in March, 1968, he joined a lower league club in financial crisis. There were no funds to buy new players and the injury list was as long as Leyton High Road. His predecessor Dick Graham had grown so frustrated and weary that he jumped ship after 18 months in the job. In fact, it was Colchester-bound Graham who suggested to the club's board of directors that they appoint a player-manager to save them money.

Enter Bloomfield, a cultured, dark-haired midfielder who left school at 15 to become a trainee pencil liner in a bike factory in Park Royal and began his long playing career with non-league Hayes before joining Second Division Brentford in 1952. After 42 league appearances and a stint of National Service (he starred for the British Army team), he was signed by Arsenal for £10,000 in July, 1954. Over the next six years Jimmy blossomed as a classy, elegant playmaker who scored 54 goals in 210 First Division league matches for the Gunners, played twice for England Under-23s and represented A Football League XI.

In November, 1960 he was transferred to Birmingham City (123 apps) for a Blues' club record £30,000, scoring in the League Cup Final victory over arch rivals Aston Villa in 1963. The previous year he'd been chosen for the initial 40-man England World Cup squad but suffered a broken arm and was among the 18 omitted from the final 22 who travelled to Chile for the 1962 tournament.

A fee of £30,000 brought the 5ft 10ins midfield general back to Brentford (44 apps) in 1964. He had a season with West Ham United (10), appearing in the European Cup Winners' Cup semi-final, and then spent a couple of years with Plymouth Argyle (25) before returning to the capital with the Os. There's a delightful line from Bobby Moore, who walked in to training one morning and handed Bloomfield one of his England shirts, saying: 'Here you go, Jim, you should've had one of these'.

From the moment he arrived at Brisbane Road and vowed "we'll stay in the Third", Jimmy set about transforming Orient, making them more professional both on and off the field. He appointed a full-time physio in Charlie Simpson, recruited from Whipps Cross Hospital, because the treatment of injured players was inadequate, and he brought in a full-time groundsman to try and get to grips with one of the worst pitches in the country.

Dick Graham had already laid the foundations for a

Jimmy helping groundstaff to get the notorious Brisbane Road pitch in a playable state.

successful youth production system, giving Tommy Taylor his first team debut, converting Dennis Rofe from inside-forward to left-back and signing Barrie Fairbrother as a trainee apprentice, and Bloomfield underlined his eagerness to continue developing local talent by appointing Len Cheesewright as Os' first full-time youth team manager.

But his biggest challenge over the next 15 months was keeping Orient in Division Three. Jimmy oversaw the team's first away win of the season, 3-2 at Gillingham on March 9, before making his debut three days later as substitute in a 4-0 defeat at Swindon Town, which still left them languishing third from bottom. They won his first home game in charge – 2-1 against fellow strugglers Scunthorpe United – but just three more victories from the last 15 games meant Os survived by the skin of their teeth, in 18th position, four points above the four relegated teams.

If Os had dropped into the fourth tier for the first time in its history, would Bloomfield have stayed at the club?

> **"Basically, our style is 4-2-4 and this is because I believe in using more or less orthodox wingers. In my view, this is still the best way to overcome modern defences and you will find that most successful clubs have wingers prepared to go past their opponents."**

They were asking the same question a year later, when Orient again flirted with disaster. Os repeated their 18th-place finish but this time only two points separated them from the relegated quartet. Victories at Bournemouth and at home to Shrewsbury Town – Jimmy was outstanding in what was his final game as a player – in the last two matches kept the club from falling through the trap door and into potential oblivion.

However, people who understood the game knew that Bloomfield had the right credentials to become a top manager. In March, 1969, just a year after taking over the helm, he turned down a very tempting offer to manage fellow Third Division club Reading, a club he respected who were willing to double his salary.

To his credit, Bloomfield never compromised his footballing principles to drag cash-strapped Orient out of the mire. At the start of his first full season holding the reins, 1968-69, he said: "That we have transformed the playing style and attitude so completely in such a short time is a tribute to the willingness and ability of my players. Playing our new, open type of game, we are liable to concede one or two goals but I am confident we will score a lot more than we let in and provide the sort of entertainment that will bring back the crowds our club deserves."

Unlike many lower divisions teams who attempt to kick their way to safety, Orient clawed their way from the brink by playing in an attacking style as often as possible. Interviewed by Jim Gaughan in 1970, decades before billion pound television deals transformed the game and the pursuit of money became the be all and end all for most and pragmatism replaced panache, Jimmy said: "As a player, I always tried to be creative and I still believe football should be entertaining. Though a 1-0 win is better for the goal-average than a 4-3, I prefer the big score because it means entertainment for the fans. I would rather it be said that Orient win by playing attractive football than that we gain points through dull, defensive stuff.

"Basically, our style is 4-2-4 and this is because I believe in using more or less orthodox wingers. In my view, this is still the best way to overcome modern defences and you will find that most successful clubs have wingers prepared to go past their opponents," added Jimmy, speaking four years after Alf Ramsey won the World Cup by largely abandoning wingers in favour of midfield supremacy and many English managers followed suit.

From talking to a number of those who played under the level-headed Bloomfield, it's clear that he didn't burden them with rigid tactical plans or complicate things. He put his trust in them and was happy to give some of his more creative men licence to express themselves. He encouraged intelligent use of the ball, in an off the cuff manner reminiscent of the policy that brought Sir Matt Busby the highest domestic and European honours at Manchester United. Bloomfield, like Busby, detested foul play.

It spoke volumes for Jimmy's persuasive powers that he managed to sign two vastly experienced, street-wise wingers, Peter Brabrook and Mark Lazarus, from First Division West Ham United and Crystal Palace respectively. In doing so, he also demonstrated that he wasn't afraid to introduce big personalities into the dressing room. On the contrary, he blended their Cockney nous with youthful exuberance to create a swashbuckling team and, off the field, a family vibe that resonated throughout the club. Gloom and doom no longer existed at Orient under Jim, the quietly spoken, smiling gent whom *Evening Standard* writer Peter Blackman once described as the "Val Doonican of soccer".

From day one, Bloomfield told his players and staff: 'Call me Jim, or whatever you're comfortable with'. He earned their respect rather than demanded it. And when the Brisbane Road pitch became a quagmire, as it always did back then, Jimmy was there, shovel in hand and wearing wellies, helping his band of volunteers to get the notorious surface playable.

Bloomfield proved himself a shrewd judge of players, too. As well as Brabrook and Lazarus, he saw enough of Mickey Bullock in their time together at Birmingham to know he would lead the line with strength and honesty and score the goals required to mount a serious promotion challenge. Barry Dyson, from Watford, was another forward who did a good job for Orient.

He also got the best out of himself. One of his smartest decisions was to call time on his playing career at the age of 35 and devote all his energies to management from the start of the 1969-70 season. "We have stopped the slide and now we start the climb," Jimmy said.

It's unthinkable today that a Football League club would expect a man to combine playing with management duties, especially a hands-on, tracksuit manager like Bloomfield who had to

juggle daily training sessions with managing the side and then get behind his office desk, looking every inch the debonair executive, to negotiate transfer deals. And yet even at the start of the 70s there were still half a dozen player-managers struggling to cope with dual roles: Terry Neill (Hull City), Len Ashurst (Hartlepool), Johnny Newman (Exeter City), Jim Iley (Peterborough United), Jimmy Melia (Aldershot) and Jimmy Armfield (Bolton Wanderers).

Even once he'd hung up his boots after 47 league and Cup starts, two sub appearances and four goals, Bloomfield still devoted almost all of his energies to football, leaving little time to spend at home with his family – wife Sue, his childhood sweetheart, and young sons David and Clive – or play golf, although his wife and the boys attended the majority of games.

The remarkable thing is, Bloomfield turned near disaster into triumph in 1969-70 despite bringing in only one new player – Lazarus from Palace two months into the campaign. He was deservedly named Third Division Manager of the Year not only for steering them to

Midfield general, running the show on and off the field.

promotion, but for trebling Os' gates and making them a profit in the transfer market.

Days before the Third Division title had been clinched and the champagne corks popped, Bloomfield spoke of his ambitious plans to take Os up to the second tier. Interviewed by Tex Hennessey of the *Guardian and Gazette* at the family's Epping home in April, 1970, Bloomfield said: "When I played I wanted to be the best in the land. I wasn't, of course, but at least it gave me something to aim at. And it's the same with managing. I want to be the tops and will do everything to get there."

As well as politely declining Reading's advances, Bloomfield also turned down a very lucrative offer to manage Ethnikos, a Greek club based in Piraeus who would have paid him £20,000 a year – more than any British manager was earning at the time. "Dad and Mum did give it a lot of serious thought . . . I've seen a hand-written contract offer and it included things like paid schooling for Clive and I," said David Bloomfield. "There was also a good offer to manage in America but in those days everywhere overseas seemed so far away."

Debonair Jim, the 'Val Doonican of soccer'.

Although he enjoyed the support of chairman Arthur Page and the board who rewarded him for delivering promotion with a new five-year contract reportedly worth almost £5,000 a year, Bloomfield never expected the club to break the bank for a player. Most clubs would have strengthened after gaining promotion but as Orient prepared for their first season back in Division Two after an absence of four years, they didn't make even one new signing. In fact, before the clocks went back, Bloomfield was forced to sell one of his best players and brightest young prospect, Tommy Taylor, to West Ham in a £100,000 deal that brought Peter Bennett to Brisbane Road in October 1970. The only other newcomer during that season was Gordon Riddick, a £10,000 buy from Charlton Athletic.

"Even if I had wanted to spend I could not have done. This isn't a rich club – we even rent our ground from the local council," Jim told interviewer Terry Poskitt.

Given the lack of investment, no-one should have been surprised that Orient just about kept their head above water at the higher level. Finishing 17th was not to be sniffed at, despite press criticism of "uninspired" performances and a miserably poor league goal tally of 29 that caused crowds to dwindle.

But Jimmy knew he was ready for the challenge of managing at the top level. And so did Leicester City, looking to replace Frank O'Farrell, who was heading for Manchester United with his assistant, ex-Os winger Malcolm Musgrove.

LEICESTER City were so convinced of Jim's ability to manage in the First Division that they made him the highest paid manager in the country on about £7,000 a year and also agreed to pay Orient £5,000 in compensation. In truth, it was a derisory amount which caused indignant hand-wringing in the Os' boardroom.

The East Midlands club had timed their cunning approach to perfection, catching Os with their pants down. In the absence of chairman Arthur Page, who was on a three-week holiday abroad,

Orient's driving force. Jim at the wheel of the team bus, surrounded by members of the 1968-69 squad.

Leicester's surprise offer was accepted by vice-chairman Neville Ovenden. Page was reportedly furious, words were exchanged and Ovenden resigned his position after five years on the board.

Orient had clearly expected Bloomfield to lead them again from the start of 1971-72. Why else would they back him with £30,000 to make Ian Bowyer, from Manchester City, their new record signing, in June, just days before Jimmy left the club?

Page vehemently refuted supporters' criticism of the club that it should have done more to keep Bloomfield – who still had two years on his contract to run – but Orient were in no position to resist once a First Division club came knocking. Page said: "This is nonsense. When Jimmy was with us he was better paid than some First Division managers. I thought it was obvious we weren't prepared to let him go easily when we demanded compensation from Leicester. A club of our financial standing could hardly have done more than this."

> **"David Bloomfield revealed that Harry Zussman, the longest-serving Orient director, actually advised Jimmy to accept Leicester's offer. 'You should take it,' he urged."**

David Bloomfield revealed that Harry Zussman, the longest-serving Orient director, actually advised Jimmy to accept Leicester's offer. 'You should take it,' he urged.

So, in mid-summer, Bloomfield was on his way to Leicester, declaring: "I have been extremely happy with Orient in the last three years but this is an opportunity not to be missed. The challenge attracts me greatly."

The Express newspaper wrote: "Bloomfield is considered one of the most intelligent and promising of the game's younger generation of managers and at Brisbane Road managed to build a successful side on a shoestring budget."

He guided Leicester – newly-promoted as Second Divisions champions – to a very respectable 12th-place finish at the end of his first season at Filbert Street, although his hopes of leading them to their second FA Cup Final in two years were wrecked by his former club.

After seeing his weakened Leicester side lose 2-0 at home to George Petchey's Orient in the fourth round, Jimmy was typically magnanimous. He told the press: "Orient outplayed us in the first-half and we've got no excuses."

In his six seasons at Leicester, Oadby-based Bloomfield guided them to three top-half finishes and an FA Cup semi-final. Seventh place in 1975-76 was their highest in 10 years. He was also short-listed for the England job – "I recall a series of calls from FA people to our home," says David – before Ron Greenwood, who had coached Jimmy at Arsenal and signed him for West Ham, was appointed to succeed Don Revie in 1977. "Leicester City's chairman Len Shipman was also president of The Football League and he put some obstacles in the way," David added.

After reportedly making the club a £285,000 profit on transfers, Bloomfield resigned in May, 1977 when a club director started telling him his job. He briefly became a marketing consultant for Admiral, the Leicester-based sportswear firm, but when Orient decided to call time on Petchey's six-year reign, there was only one man on their wanted list.

Ironically, the director who advised him to leave for Leicester was largely instrumental in bringing him back. David Bloomfield revealed: "It was Harry Zussman who made the initial call from Orient to ask Dad if he wanted his old job back. He also had an offer to go to West Brom."

THE second coming of Jimmy Bloomfield at Brisbane Road heralded some of the most memorable and exciting times in Os' history.

After Petchey's team lost by the only goal at Luton and were battered 4-1 at home by Blackpool, a hangover from the terrible end to the previous season in which they managed to win just one of their last 13 league matches and finished 19th, Bloomfield resumed as manager for the 2-1 victory against Bristol Rovers at Leyton on September 17, 1977.

Early the following year, soon after Os embarked upon their greatest-ever FA Cup run that began with wins over Norwich City and Blackburn Rovers, Jimmy required long spells in and out of hospital due to the illness that would eventually claim his life five years later.

His very able and trusty assistant Peter Angell was in temporary charge on the night Peter Kitchen – Petchey's last signing – scored the two goals that dumped Chelsea out of the competition, while Jimmy was glued to the radio in his hospital bed. "Dad had tried to entice Peter Angell to Leicester but his wife Wilma had a very good job at the *Daily Mail* and they didn't want to uproot," said Jimmy's eldest son.

Although he was back in the dug-out for the quarter-final replay win over Middlesbrough and the semi-final against Arsenal played at Chelsea's ground, the fairytale ended there. It had been a remarkable journey, though, which Orient fans still recall with great affection.

League finishes of 14th, 11th, 14th and 17th ensured Orient retained their Second Division status under Bloomfield, who paid a club record £150,000 fee to sign Tottenham winger Peter Taylor and around £100,000 for maverick playmaker Stan Bowles shortly before he resigned in the club's centenary year.

But just like George Petchey before him, Bloomfield had to face the harsh realities of managing a club on the breadline, where the best

Jimmy and Peter Angell at training with players Phil Hoadley, John Jackson, Peter Bennett and Bill Roffey.

Second coming. Jim on a much better looking Brisbane Road pitch during the FA Cup run in 1978.

home-grown players progressed until inevitably being snapped up by wealthier clubs. He'd experienced this frustration in his first spell with the sale of Tommy Taylor and he was on the other side of the coin when he signed Dennis Rofe for Leicester. But Laurie Cunningham had been sold six months before his return, while Glenn Roeder, Phil Hoadley and Tony Grealish were all allowed to leave from under his nose before the decade was out.

As the 1981-82 season got underway, the impending £600,000 sale of winger John Chiedozie to Notts County felt like the final straw for Bloomfield, although Brian Winston told me: "Jimmy didn't quit because we sold Chiedozie – we used the money to buy other players, like Peter Taylor and Stan Bowles. He left for health reasons – he had cancer and, sadly, he eventually died from it. Jimmy was incredibly brave and did a tremendous job."

David Bloomfield says there was more to it, though. "It was more the timing of Chiedozie's sale that disappointed Dad. He thought that Notts County wasn't the right club for John and, had Orient been more patient, they would have received a bigger and better offer from a London club within two or three months of the season starting – Tottenham did eventually sign him. I think he felt undermined by some of the board's decisions but he was reluctant to go.

"It was a tough decision for him to leave, because my brother Clive had just signed for Orient as an apprentice. We're all inside-forwards – I played for Walthamstow Rangers as a kid and had a couple of games for Leicester City reserves, although the fact that Dad was manager probably got me in the team! Orient didn't offer Clive professional terms – neither of us were good enough – but the fact that they were both at the club at the same time made Dad's decision to quit even harder."

Orient's elevation of former player Paul Went from reserve team coach to first team manager lasted no more than a month before he was relieved of his duties. Orient experienced the same fate Leicester did in the season immediately after Jimmy left: they were relegated.

What will surprise many is David's revelation that Orient tried to recruit Jimmy for a THIRD time. Before the end of Ken Knighton's reign in 1983, chairman Neville Ovenden approached his father to ask if he'd take up the reins again. "But by then Dad was too poorly and couldn't accept. He had bowel cancer, which we thought was under control, but then it spread to his lungs," he said.

Jimmy died at his North Chingford home, surrounded by his loving family, on April 3, 1983. He was just 49. His final resting place is Kensington & Chelsea Cemetery.

Sadly, David and Clive lost their mother Sue – "a real football woman" – last year (2017) but they still treasure various mementoes of their father's two spells at Orient, including his Third Division winner's medal, club blazer and ties.

Jimmy Bloomfield will forever remain an Orient legend and arguably their greatest-ever manager.

By Tony McDonald

Os' Guardian Angell

THROUGHOUT the 70s, players, managers and directors came and went at Orient but there remained one pillar of stability: Peter Angell.

Slough-born Peter was a man of many talents – trainer, assistant manager, coach, confidant and, when he needed to be tough, an old school voice of authority in the dressing room and on the training ground always urging players to give a little more.

A left-half who played more than 500 games for Queens Park Rangers between 1953 and 1965, four seasons as skipper, Angell then joined Charlton, where he progressed from assistant trainer to coach.

He was brought to Orient by manager Dick Graham in 1967. So Peter had been at Brisbane Road a year before Jimmy Bloomfield came.

When Bloomfield left to go to Leicester in 1971, Angell turned down Jim's offer to join him and remained with his family in London. Assisting Petchey – Bloomfield's successor – was no problem for Angell because they already knew each other well from their playing days together as half-backs at QPR.

And when Jimmy was enticed back to Orient six years later, the rock was still there waiting for him. Angell and Peter Bennett being the only survivors from Bloomfield first spell.

While Os enjoyed their greatest-ever FA Cup run to the semi-finals in 1978, Bloomfield knew that from his hospital bed he could count on his own guardian Angell to help him through it. He told the *Evening Standard's* Michael Hart at the time: "When I was in hospital recently, he worked non-stop to keep things ticking over. He deserves all the praise for our Cup run. He did a wonderful job. But for Peter, none of this would have been possible."

A number of the players interviewed over the following pages talk fondly and respectfully of 'Gunner'. They appreciate how much of his working life he devoted to the club right up to that sad day, July 18, 1979, in Epping Forest, where he suffered the heart attack that killed him, aged 47, during a training run.

Make no mistake, for 12 years Peter Angell was the superglue that held Orient FC together.

Jimmy Bloomfield and his trusty ally Peter Angell.

'Henry' hit the right notes

Born: Camden Town, London, October 4, 1942
Usual position: Centre-half Orient Career: **1967-71**
Orient Appearances: League 167, FA Cup 12, League Cup 9
Orient Goals: League 16, FA Cup 1, League Cup 0

TERRY MANCINI is one of only five players in the club's history to have led the Os to promotion. He made a total of 188 appearances, scoring 17 goals, including one on debut in a 4-2 home win against Barrow on November 11, 1967.

Eventually, and having spent a decade plying his trade as a good, honest professional around in the lower leagues, he experienced an unexpected upturn that saw him play at the very highest level for club and country.

This circuitous route took this most genial of centre-halves from Watford to Arsenal via stop-off points in South Africa, the Orient – the Leyton version – and Queens Park Rangers. He also won five caps for the Republic of Ireland and enjoyed a spell playing for Los Angeles Aztecs with George Best and against another legend, Pele.

Yet the international stage seemed a distant dream when, as a youngster, he was told on two occasions that he would be better off looking elsewhere to make a living. But Terry's determination and character prevailed to ensure that, despite doubts from some quarters, he was good enough to enjoy a memorable career.

One of those rejections came when his first club, Watford, decided not to offer him another professional contract. As one door closed, another opened that was to lead to windows of

Proud Terry lifts the Third Division championship trophy, accompanied by Tommy Taylor and Peter Allen, on a special night marred slightly by the bitter words of the Bournemouth manager.

opportunity over the years ahead and would subsequently see this most engaging of characters appear alongside, and against the world's finest players including George Best and Pele.

Terry – affectionately nicknamed 'Henry' by the Os faithful after famous American composer, conductor and arranger Henry Mancini – recalled: "After 80-plus games for Watford, they gave me a free transfer. A few other British-born players were playing in South Africa and I was offered the opportunity to join them out there. I signed for Port Elizabeth and in my second season there we won the South African championship."

As Terry explained, it was former Orient centre-forward, big Cliff Holton, who lured him to east London: "I decided I wanted to return home in the autumn of 1967 to start a business in Battersea. I had a letter of recommendation from ex-Watford colleague Cliff and, having heard that Orient were looking for players, I arrived on their doorstep and asked for a trial. Dick Graham was manager at the time. He played me in a practice match and then offered me terms to play for Orient.

"Dick was old school, a tough guy in terms of training methods, it was run, run, run and hard-tackling, kick, shove and push. It was all physical work under him. He was manager at the time when we probably only had one training ball at the club – in stark contrast to my days at Arsenal where each player had his own ball at training. So they were tough times at the Os and Dick was a hard taskmaster. But I have to say that he was a very fair man – he was good to me."

It was under Graham's successor, Jimmy Bloomfield – the manager who made him club captain – that Mancini hit all the right notes for Orient.

"Jimmy was a lovely man, truly wonderful," Terry continued. "We did our hard, physical work but nowhere near as much as we did under Dick's regime. With Jimmy, he preferred working with the ball and playing five-a-side football.

"The season we went up we had a super team and everybody knew their roles and played for each other. People talk about playing as a team when you're all mates but that was how we developed over a couple of years under Jimmy at the Os.

"There was genuine team spirit and that goes a long way towards getting results. When things go against the side, you all pull together and get out of trouble, and this attitude certainly worked well for us.

"Jimmy came to the club as player-manager in March, 1968, when we were involved in a relegation battle and we had another struggle the next season. So throughout my first two years at Orient we were fighting to retain our Division Three status. In fact, I was never relegated at any time in my career anywhere, so that's something that pleases me.

"Then before the start of the 1969-70 season, Jimmy decided to hang up his boots and concentrate on management and we got immediate success. We won the league playing good football and in an entertaining way.

"One thing that really surprised me during the promotion-winning season was the size of the attendances. We'd had the odd decent sized crowd for a cup-tie but in that promotion campaign we were getting regular gates of well over 12,000 and, on occasions, a lot more. We'd started the season and only expected about 6,000 at Brisbane Road in those days but then, all of a sudden, gates rocketed up to 10, 12 and 14,000. They were wonderful times and it was a great atmosphere to play in."

Mancini's influential role was endorsed by Jimmy Bloomfield. He said of the Os legend: "He is one of the most popular players at the Orient and who I rate an ideal skipper and the best centre-half in the Third Division. Terry is dominant in the air and a lot better player on the ground than he is often given credit for."

"I was happy to be skipper," said Terry, who also took on the added role and responsibility of penalty-taker. "Frankly, I only took penalties because nobody else wanted the job and as captain, I felt I should show some responsibility.

"I scored a couple of pens and that was OK but then we got a penalty in one particular game at home – I can't remember who it was against. There was a photographer sitting by the side of the goal and the opposition goalkeeper asked him if he knew which side of the goal I hit my kicks. He told him: 'In this corner, here'. I hit the ball in the usual place, the keeper saved it and that was it for me – I vowed not to take any more and I gave up on them."

The task then fell to Barry Dyson, a player Mancini identified as a key component in the late 60s. "Barry had a terrific impact," says Terry. "His goals (10 in 25 games) helped us stave off relegation in 1968-69 and then he became an influential part of the promotion-winning side. His role was as a link-man between the forwards and midfield and, for me, he made the difference between us being a relegation-threatened side and promotion contenders. But it wasn't only Barry. We had a super team the year we went up.

"Everyone played their part. We only used 16 players throughout the entire promotion season and one of those, reserve goalkeeper Steve Bowtell, only played twice. We had a terrific defence. Ray Goddard was the first-choice keeper. He was very underrated and didn't get the amount of praise he should have done. He was brave, he would dive fearlessly at people's feet, and was a super lad.

"I lay down on the bench in the dressing room afterwards and cried my eyes out. It was a culmination of Orient getting promoted, plus the amount of pain I'd put myself through and knowing that I could now relax in the knowledge that we would be playing Second Division football the following season."

"Micky Jones played right-back. He was a good striker of the ball and got up and down the pitch tirelessly. Dennis Rofe, our left-back, was the same. He got into our side when he was just 18-years-old and, after his first season of battling relegation, he really developed and was flying. He was a good, quick and dependable defender.

"Then we had Tommy Taylor, who came through the youth team with Dennis. He was quick and read the game very well for a young boy in the centre-half position. He went on to do very well for himself elsewhere in the game. Throughout the team we had a great rapport. Our motto was: 'If they don't score, we've come away with a point and got a result'. That was our approach defensively.

"In front of the defence, we had people like Barrie Fairbrother, who had also come through the youth team, Terry Brisley, Mickey Bullock and Peter Allen – all terrific players. How Peter never got picked up by another club, I will never know. He had a terrific engine and would continually go up and down the field, getting stuck in and winning the ball. What a terrific defensive midfield player he was.

"The fact that he went largely unnoticed by other clubs never ceased to amaze me but we loved him. He made more appearances for the Os than any other player and that's a record that is never likely to be beaten. As I say, it remains a mystery why a bigger club never came in for him, because he was quality.

"Then we had two outstanding wingers in Peter Brabrook and Mark Lazarus. They were two vastly experienced players in terms of having played at a higher level and in some games, particularly away from home, their experience proved invaluable. Mark was a good goalscorer, while Peter could beat players and hold the ball up but he also had a terrific knowledge regarding

Leading the way . . . Terry followed by underrated keeper Ray Goddard and Dennis Rofe.

all aspects of the game.

"I remember playing at Torquay, where we were winning 1-0 but were on the back foot and battling to hold on. With about 10 minutes to go, we managed to win a corner. Peter went over to take it and as he ran up to kick the ball, he deliberately clicked his heels together, went down like a ton of bricks and rolled over and over. Our physio must have been on the pitch treating him for three or four minutes, which took the whole sting out of the game.

"I was really worried about him and thought he must have done his Achilles or whatever, so I ran over to where Peter lay. But as I looked down at him, he just glanced up and winked at me. In those days, we played for 90 minutes, no added time, and so he'd used up valuable time and we held onto our lead for the win. Both Mark and Peter were terrific for us."

Mancini's run of 105 consecutive league appearances, stretching back to his debut, ended when he suffered a broken right leg, just above his ankle, midway through the first-half of the 2-0 home win against Tranmere Rovers on January 31, 1970.

"I was out for two months. But, in fact, I missed only eight games. We had a helluva lot of snow around that time, so quite a few matches got postponed.

"Jimmy (Bloomfield) wanted me back as quickly as possible and although I played, I was struggling because the leg ached badly.

"I remember we got promoted after winning 1-0 at Bradford City and I lay down on the bench in the dressing room afterwards and cried my eyes out. It was a culmination of Orient getting promoted, although we hadn't won the title at that stage, plus the amount of pain I'd put myself through and knowing that I could now relax in the knowledge that we would be playing Second Division football the following season. We clinched promotion with three matches still to play and in the second of those we beat Shrewsbury at home to lift the title. Winning the Third Division was something special and a great feeling that was shared equally by the players and the fans. We were truly one happy club."

But Terry can reveal that the championship celebrations were slightly soured for him personally.

"Our last match of the season was against Gillingham at Brisbane Road and they were battling against relegation. We were to collect the Third Division trophy that night and, regardless of the result, we were champions. So it was going to be a great night and the pressure was off.

"My leg still ached but I was determined to play – the place was packed out and it was a wonderful atmosphere. We went one-up, despite Barry Dyson missing a penalty, and, unbeknown to me, sitting in the stand was the Bournemouth manager Freddie Cox. His side were facing the possibility of relegation and, although they had a slightly better goal-average than Gillingham, if the match finished a draw or we beat Gillingham, then Bournemouth would have stayed up. Anyway, we lost 2-1 (Os' first home defeat since Oct 11), Gillingham stayed up on goal-average, the result sent Bournemouth down to Division Four and Cox lost his job. But that's football.

"As we came off the pitch that night, Cox came down out of the directors' box and into the

Mancini to the rescue

ORIENT'S defence, brilliantly marshalled by Tom Taylor and Terry

| Blackburn | 0 |
| Orient | 0 |

settle for a point from the start.

They have their position to consolidate now that they are back in the Second Division.

Magnificent Mancini

CARDIFF ought to know better how to deal with teams of Orient's modest status if they fancy themselves for a First Division place.

A draw was all the Second Division leaders get out

Orient 0, Cardiff 0
By JACK WELLING

one dangerous effort—a header cleared off the line by Taylor in the early part

Cardiff defence, was brought down from behind by Murphy

football, as Bell fouled Lazarus, Lazarus fouled Bell, and Bell fouled Lazarus again, all under the referee's nose. Little wonder the book came out for Bell.

Lazarus, enjoying his moments of melodrama, almost turned the ball in

players' tunnel, headed straight for me and swore at me. As I said, we were presented with the Third Division trophy after the game but as I went up to receive it, I was still annoyed and upset to think that someone had thought we'd lost on purpose."

With his baldpate, tall, lean physique and cheery disposition, Mancini was not the archetypal rugged centre-half who thundered into opposing strikers. He wasn't a ball-playing centre-back either but he was a good, strong leader who knew his strengths and limitations.

"I enjoyed the tough, physical battles with centre-forwards and there were a few tough opponents in our division. You'd give them a whack and immediately get one in return. They were tough days, physically, but I relished the battles and always preferred to play against the big man up front, because the little, nippy small guys, who zipped around and knocked the ball between your legs, weren't my cup of tea. I left them to Tommy Taylor to look after. But give me the tough nut up front and I was happy. People like Andy Lockhead (Burnley, Leicester City and Aston Villa) and Alex Dawson (Preston North End, Bury and Brighton & Hove Albion) were real hard men."

Having gained promotion, Os survived the following season despite a paucity of goals. "We only scored 29 in 42 league matches, yet we stayed up," recalls Terry. "What sort of testimony is that to our defence? We conceded 51 goals and finished sixth from bottom. To only score 29 goals in a season and survive was incredible."

In 1970-71, our first season back in the second tier, Orient won just nine matches but drew 16 and kept 15 clean sheets. Throughout February and early March, Os kept six clean sheets in succession during which time we won four matches, all by the most slender 1-0 margin.

"We were still a work in progress under Jimmy but we'll never know how things might have panned out, because he moved on. Like all good managers, if they have a good season or two, other clubs come chasing them.

"Jimmy went to Leicester City and George Petchey took control. After a dozen games or so, he decided that I was past it. I was still only 29 but because I had little hair by then, I genuinely think he thought that I was older and was just playing out time in my career. Unfortunately, there was little I could do to convince him otherwise. In truth, I just don't think I was his type of player."

Mancini made way for Phil Hoadley, signed by Petchey from Crystal Palace, and local youngster Paul Harris, who emerged from the club's youth ranks.

"So when an offer came from Fulham, it seemed a good move for everybody. They were my local club and Orient would receive a £25,000 transfer fee. But the deal broke down because one or two of the Fulham directors thought I was too old.

"Then, within a few days, I got a call from Gordon Jago at Queens Park Rangers asking me to go to Loftus Road to discuss a transfer. Within 48 hours, I'd signed for them. That was in October, 1971 and everyone was now happy again. I'd got a move to a higher sphere (QPR were promoted to the top flight in his second season at Loftus Road) and Orient had picked up £25,000 from the transfer deal.

"Obviously, you always have ambitions and like to think you can do better. I was Orient captain and a regular in the side and I suppose I was in a comfort zone. I never felt I was going to be left out the team. Until Fulham and QPR came in for me, no other club had shown any interest in me and I never dreamed that I might move into a higher level of football."

It's an irrefutable fact that Terry Mancini left Orient in a much healthier state than the ailing club he'd joined four years earlier.

"When I signed for the Os, the directors paid us on a Monday out of the gate takings from Saturday's game. I remember that a blanket would be carried around the pitch at half-time and supporters would throw money in – the club was so hard-up.

"Yet they were lovely days and I have so many happy memories of my time there. It was always a pleasure to get up and go to work and I have to say they were the happiest days of my career. I did enjoy a special empathy with the fans, they were marvellous towards me and it was not long after I arrived that they gave me the nickname 'Henry' after the famous music composer.

"That was before what I'd call my 'entertaining days', with QPR and Arsenal, when I was looking for ways to amuse the crowd and got the reputation as a bit of a character. But when I was at the Os, it was strictly business.

"But I always enjoyed playing, gave 100 per cent and I suppose the Orient crowd could appreciate that. It was later in my career, when I was more experienced and relaxed, that I became a 'character'. I thought that I was one of the luckiest people in the world to be doing something I really loved, so why wouldn't I play with a smile on my face?"

As well as playing the game in a great spirit, likeable Mancini earned a reputation as an entertaining television pundit, making regular appearances as a studio guest on, and occasional host of, ITV's Sunday afternoon highlights show, *The Big Match*.

After leaving E10, Mancini went on to make 111 senior appearances for an upwardly mobile QPR before a shock £20,000 move to Arsenal in October, 1974. It was, however, a lowly period in Gunners' history, Bertie Mee's side finishing 16th and 17th respectively in Mancini's two seasons back near his north London birthplace, before he joined Fourth Division Aldershot on a free transfer in 1975-76.

"I then went to the States and played for Los Angeles Aztecs for five months before I decided that at the age of 35 or 36, enough was enough and so I decided to retire," added Terry, who – thanks to qualifying through his Irish father – gained five Republic of Ireland caps between 1973-74.

"I did do some coaching at Fulham and was appointed assistant manager at Luton in 1989 but I then got involved in business interests outside football. I ran the family pub in Hammersmith. My dad wanted to get out of the business and sold me his share but I really didn't enjoy it. I sold up in 1991 and had a bit of a break before running a car hire business for a while. Then, about 14 years ago, I joined Barwood Leisure, a sports travel firm, as a sports events director."

When that folded, Terry started his own company, Mancini Events (www.mancinievents.co.uk), specialising in celebrity golf events and lunches, in the UK and Spain.

He reflects on his playing days with genuine gratitude. Being a late starter in the pro game, he admitted: "I never dreamed of actually becoming a footballer. I saw kids who desperately wanted to become professional footballers and they would work their way through apprenticeships before, at the age of 18 or so, being told that they weren't going to be taken on as pro's.

"Football was all they thought about, whereas I had no real plans to become a footballer and it happened almost as an after-thought – I always planned to do other things. Then as my career progressed and I started playing at a high level and won international caps, I'm thinking, 'how lucky am I to be doing all this? I'm one of the luckiest people in the world'.

Interview: Paul Hiscock

Overlapping crowd favourite

Born: Berkhamsted, Hertfordshire, January 8, 1945
Usual position: Right-back   Orient Career: 1966-71
Orient Appearances: League 223/5, FA Cup 15, League Cup 10
Orient Goals: League 16, FA Cup 0, League Cup 0

SIGNED by acting manager Les Gore in February, 1966, Mick Jones spent a further six seasons at Brisbane Road during which he saw the club re-emerge from the brink of extinction to regain its Second Division status.

"Although I was a permanent fixture in the reserves at Chelsea, it was clear that I wasn't going to get any first team opportunities," explained Mick, who made just two league appearances for The Pensioners since joining them from near-neighbours Fulham in December, 1964. "I desperately wanted to play first team football and wasn't concerned if I had to drop a division to do so.

"A few clubs showed interest, including Watford and Charlton, but a close family friend, who had played football with Les Gore earlier in his career, suggested I go to Orient. He said Les was a fair and straightforward person who would give me a chance, and I never regretted the move for one moment."

With David Webb having been sold to top flight Southampton to ease the club's worsening financial plight, Jones proved an ideal replacement. The attacking right-back immediately became a crowd favourite thanks to his wholehearted attitude and overlapping runs.

However, he was unable to prevent Orient being relegated at the end of the season and even bigger storm clouds were gathering over E10.

Mick recalls that the players remained united, although the off-field problems that prompted the infamous 'pass the bucket' routine before the end of '66 did affect them. "It was strange, because I had been at Fulham where they were talking about increasing wages and having the first £100 per week player (Johnny Haynes) and now here I was at Orient wondering if I'd even be paid at all! But, thankfully, the club came through its financial plight."

Mick loved to join the attack and at one stage, with goals a rare commodity, manager Dick Graham briefly tried him as a centre-forward with instant success. He scored a hat-trick against Doncaster in April, 1967 but soon returned to his more customary defensive position.

He readily recalls the appalling state of the Orient pitch in those days: "It was dreadful. I can remember a cup replay against Nottingham Forest when the pitch was waterlogged before the game started but, somehow, the referee was persuaded to start the match and he kept it going until he finally abandoned it at half-time. Apparently, at that time, the club kept all the gate takings if a match was called off, so, given their financial situation, it was perhaps no real surprise that the game started in farcical conditions.

"Mind you, there were a few other bad pitches around but you still had a lot of classy players who could pass the ball well and produce plenty of skill.

"I think I played under five different managers at Orient and they all had their own characteristics. Jimmy Bloomfield did well for the club but he was a totally different personality to his predecessor, Dick Graham.

"Dick had us working on the physical side of the game and, in training, we'd run and run until we dropped. That was his permanent regime and we ran out of energy well before the end of the season. With Jimmy, once the hard graft was done pre-season and in the early weeks of the campaign, we spent a lot of time playing small-sided games.

"We underwent a dramatic transformation in fortunes under Jimmy. One year we were fighting to avoid relegation and needed to win our last two games to stay up. We won at Bournemouth, who had Ted MacDougall and Phil Boyer scoring goals for fun. But we beat them at their place 1-0 and then did Shrewsbury 4-0 in our final home game.

"The next season we won the Third Division. Jimmy brought in a bit of experience in Mark Lazarus and Peter Brabrook to bolster the side and it worked a treat. But we also had a terrific team spirit and I think that was a very important factor in our success. Also, we had a very settled side – I was one of four players (along with Ray Goddard, Tommy Taylor and Barry Dyson) who played every game and three others only missed two or three matches.

"A couple of games in particular from that season stick in my mind. Firstly, the match at Torquay in mid-January, when I scored the only goal of the game that sent us to the top of the league; then the match at Bradford City when we won 1-0 to ensure promotion."

Although Orient scored only 29 goals in their first season back in Division Two, the defence leaked just 51 goals and the club comfortably retained its newly achieved status with nine wins and 16 draws.

"We were a difficult side to beat," Mick recalls. "I think Jimmy just wanted to establish the club before taking us onto the next level but he was tempted away to Leicester before the next season and George Petchey took over.

> **"I had to move on because the manager didn't rate me. But it was hard for me to take, because I genuinely loved it at Orient."**

"He immediately started bringing in his own players from his former club Crystal Palace. He brought in full-back John Sewell, who was about 35, and he struggled. And then further defenders followed from Palace, players like Phil Hoadley, David Payne and Bill Roffey. It seemed that the manager wanted to work with all the players he'd known and coached at Palace but it didn't give me much opportunity.

He also brought in forward Gerry Queen and goalkeeper John Jackson, which meant that the side Jimmy Bloomfield had built was being broken up.

"It was inevitable that I had to move on because the manager didn't rate me. But it was hard for me to take, because I genuinely loved it at Orient. I'd made some great mates at the club, people like Peter Allen who I used to room with on away trips, and later Ian Bowyer became a good friend. Director Harry Zussman desperately tried to persuade me stay but my mind was made up, although it was a difficult decision.

"By now Les Gore was assistant to Theo Foley at Charlton and he suggested I went there. I was delighted to work with him again."

Mick left Brisbane Road in December, 1971 and played 66 senior matches for the Addicks before a serious knee injury forced him to quit the professional game and he went to Burnham, firstly as a player, then player-manager, before assuming the manager's role with notable success.

Mick still looks forward to his occasional return visits to the Os, a club that still holds fond memories for him. "It was lovely to go back to Orient for a reunion a short time ago and see so many lovely people, it's still a great club," he concluded.

Interview: Paul Hiscock

Local boy Den good

Born: Epping, Essex, June 1, 1950
Usual position: Left-back Orient Career: 1968-72
Orient Appearances: League 170/1, FA Cup 11, League Cup 7
Orient Goals: League 6, FA Cup 0, League Cup 0

GROWING up in Essex, Dennis Rofe was an ardent Orient supporter who went on to live the dream by playing for the club he loved. A pacy, tough-tackling left-back, he soon caught the attention of scouts after making his Football League debut as a goalscoring substitute for the Os at Bristol Rovers late in the 1967-68 season.

Diminutive Dennis became an integral member of Orient's promotion-winning side in 1969-70 and remained a virtual ever-present in the team until moving to Leicester City in September, 1972 for £112,000 – a then British record fee for a full-back.

He explained: "I was a local boy born in Epping, who lived in Loughton and went to Davenent Foundation School, Whitechapel. I signed forms for the Orient in 1964 with another lad, Terry Brisley, who was in the same class as me at school. I believe that we were the first two lads in the country to sign associate schoolboy forms with a professional club.

"We were invited to join Orient by youth team manager and scout Len Cheesewright after we both played in a match for East London Boys against South London Boys at Brisbane Road. Paul Went and a lad called Micky Vanconverden were also in that match and the four of us went along to train with Orient a couple of evenings each week. That opportunity was something I've always been grateful for."

Dennis signed as an apprentice professional in September, 1965 before turning full pro in February, 1968.

"Although Micky didn't make it, the other three of us went on to have decent professional

careers. I'd always wanted to be a footballer right from my early days at Davenant School. Realising how genuinely keen I was, my parents allowed me to leave school a year early instead of staying on to take my GCEs. Coming through the youth system, I always felt a lot of pride in representing the club because it meant such a lot to me. And that passion is something that's never left me.

"Dick Graham was the first manager that I really got to know at Orient, although I was around when Benny Fenton and Dave Sexton were there. But neither of them stayed long and because I was still in the youth set-up, I didn't have anything to do with them."

It was Jimmy Bloomfield who gave the 5ft 8ins Rofe his league bow at Bristol Rovers at Eastville on April 30, 1967. "I travelled down

Dennis closes down Birmingham City's Bob Latchford in March, 1971.

there thinking that I was just going to be in charge of the kit. In those days, only one substitute was allowed and, being a kid of 17, I was expecting to be doing all the menial tasks and just getting a taste of what first team life was about.

"But when we arrived at the ground, Jimmy told me I was going to be sub. Just after half-time, winger John Key got injured, so our left-back Owen Simpson, who had scored our first goal, switched to the wing and I came on at left-back. I'd been on about 20 minutes when I collected the ball inside our own half, took it upfield and after playing a one-two with Dave Harper, I sent in a shot which found the net. We won 2-0 – a perfect evening for me.

"Being a night match, we must have arrived back at Leyton in the early hours of the morning. When I got home, I went in to say 'good night' to my parents and my dad asked how we got on. When I told him we'd won and I scored, he jumped out of bed and hugged me. That was a really nice, special moment. I don't think he went back to bed – he couldn't wait to go down the paper shop and read all the match reports."

After sitting out the first eight games of the 1968-69 season, Jimmy Bloomfield decided the 18-year-old rookie Rofe was more than capable of replacing 30-year-old Bert Howe, who switched to the right where he vied for the No.2 shirt with Mick Jones. Bloomfield once said of Rofe: "The first thing that impressed me was Dennis' love of the game and the desire to do well."

"Jimmy was a lovely man, probably the smartest I've ever seen," says Dennis. "He always wore a suit and was an absolute gentleman who knew the game inside out. He turned the fortunes of the team around by making some shrewd signings and blooding some of the younger players.

"Two key signings he made were bringing wingers Peter Brabrook and Mark Lazarus to the club. They were hardened professionals and although there were other good signings, those two were significant players and did so much to help us win promotion from the Third Division.

"There were a lot of characters in our promotion-winning side. There was a terrific spirit and camaraderie among the squad, although we did have a little shout at one another from time to time. And the underlying reason for that was because we all wanted the club to be heading in an upward direction. For people like Tommy Taylor, me and other youngsters, to be able to learn the game and play off the experience of older players was invaluable.

"For example, I would pass the ball to our left-winger Peter. He'd take it 10 yards infield and while still in possession of the ball, he'd be waving me to go down the wing before placing the ball in my path. I learned so much about the game, positional play and such like, from players like him. You can't buy experience.

"Many a time, someone in our team would step forward just when we needed a spark to change the game around. Mark Lazarus, for example, scored some really important goals. We'd be drawing a game we expected to win but then he'd pop up with the vital goal.

"Mark and Peter were leading characters, they had both been in the game for a long while and knew all the tricks of the trade. 'Marky' had a habit that, whenever he scored, he would go on a lap of honour. He'd run along the outside of the pitch exchanging handshakes with the fans. When he got to our goalkeeper Ray Goddard, Ray would go to high-five him and Mark would shape to return the gesture . . . but, much to everyone's amusement, would dodge around him.

"Peter was another joker and he'd pull some really funny pranks that had us all in stitches. He was a master of time-wasting. He'd feign an injury that would hold up play for ages when we needed to buy a bit of time. He got away with it time and again.

"But so many others played their part, it was a team effort and we had a good bunch of players. Jimmy got the mix right. He brought in some experienced old heads, combined them with solid and dependable players and blooded some youngsters. It worked very well."

Although Bloomfield was very influential in shaping his progress, Dennis credits Dick Graham as the manager who identified his best position.

"I actually started my career as a forward because I had a bit of pace but Dick believed I'd be better served further back down the pitch," he reveals. "I think I must have played in every forward and wing half-back position as a youngster but Dick thought I would make an ideal full-back. His judgement proved sound and I have a lot to thank him for."

In Rofe, Graham recognised a tenacious tackler who could use his speed and natural sense of adventure to turn defence into attack in the blink of an eye.

"The biggest influence on my career was probably Jimmy, because I played under him at two clubs and at an important stage in my career. But firstly Dick Graham and then George Petchey, who took over from Jimmy, taught me good things about the game and important values.

"Dick always made sure you believed in yourself but Jimmy was the key figure. As a former top player himself, he understood the frustrations and emotions every player experiences and that made him a fine man-manager. Personally, he improved my game and made me a better player."

Bloomfield recommended Rofe for international honours. England manager Alf Ramsey was at Brisbane Road in November, 1970 to watch Dennis play against Middlesbrough, although he had to wait another three years until receiving his first well-earned Under-23 cap.

"Jimmy was the key figure. As a former top player himself, he understood the frustrations and emotions every player experiences and that made him a fine man-manager. He improved my game and made me a better player."

"It was a shame for Orient when Jimmy left to join Leicester. He could have taken the club a bit further but then he was followed by a very capable manager in George Petchey. I didn't really get to know him too well, because I only played for a season under him before Jimmy signed me for Leicester."

Once established in the team, blond-haired Dennis was rarely out of the No.3 jersey. The 1-0 home defeat by Reading was the only one game he missed in the promotion campaign. He was ever-present in 1970-71 and looked set to repeat the feat until an injury at Sheffield Wednesday kept him out a couple of matches in April, 1972.

Dennis is reluctant to single out the best player he played with at Orient.

"It's difficult to pick out one particular player and say he was the best, because we had a number who made vital contributions to the success of the team. Mark and Peter, as I said earlier, were decent players. Terry Mancini did a tremendous job for us at centre-half and as captain and he also got some useful goals going up for corners.

"In terms of ability, I suppose I would have to say that Tommy Taylor was the most talented player in the squad. He possessed so much potential and it was no surprise when West Ham signed him to play alongside Bobby Moore. For such a young player, Tommy always showed a lot of maturity in his game. He was always able to deal with every situation that occurred in a match. He was still only a 15 year-old when he made his debut for the club and he learned the game so quickly.

"It's easier to select my 'unsung hero'. Peter Allen is the stand-out choice. He could play a number of positions and his overall contribution from wherever he was on the pitch was superb. He should have got recognition at a higher level. He merited it and certainly deserved consideration for an England Under-23 cap."

For fans at every club, there's nothing quite like a home-grown hero to call one of their own. Dennis wore Orient red in 189 official first team matches and you can bet that those watching from the stands and terraces were full of pride and admiration for the kid from Epping who lived the dream.

"I think that there was a lot of empathy with supporters back in my day," Dennis reflected. "We mixed quite freely with fans in those days. When I was at the Os, the players would go for a drink in the supporters' club or the Coach and Horses pub and we'd chat to the fans over a beer. I used to travel in on the Central Line and often found myself sitting next to and chatting to fans on the train."

Even when Os were still challenging for promotion from Division Three, a posse of senior league scouts regularly flocked to Brisbane Road to run covetous eyes over their precocious teenagers.

Barely a week passed without press speculation linking both Taylor and Rofe, their two hottest properties, with big money moves. West Ham, Spurs, Manchester United, Chelsea, Crystal Palace, Leicester City and others all dispatched their trusted representatives to Leyton Stadium.

Orient didn't want to let them go but every talented young star has his price, especially at smaller clubs where balancing the books was paramount to survival.

"There were so many scouts around that we expected to see Baden-Powell turning up!" Dennis laughed. "I've still got a lot of press cuttings at home from that time linking me and some of the other youngsters to all manner of clubs. We were aware that scouts were watching us but, personally, that only served to spur me on and I became more determined than ever to succeed in the game. Once we were on the pitch. I'd just concentrate on doing my best for the Os and I can honestly say that I never played to impress the scouts – only to try and help Orient win.

"There were no agents in those days, you negotiated with clubs on your own. Orient were happy with the fee Leicester were offering, so I went to Filbert Street to talk terms with them. I had a figure in my mind concerning the wages I wanted and when they offered what I hoped for, the deal was done."

Leicester, where Jimmy Bloomfield was appointed manager in the summer of 1971, paid Orient £112,000 – a record fee for a full-back in those days – so it was good business for all concerned.

"It was a good move for me, I was earning a decent amount, enjoyed a good lifestyle and Leicester was a good club. The size of the transfer fee never bothered me – I just wanted to play and do well.

Dennis appeared 290 times for Leicester City spanning eight years (in 1973 he earned his only England U23 cap) before moves to Chelsea and then Southampton.

After calling time on his playing career, he spent many years in various coaching capacities, most notably at Southampton, where he progressed from academy manager to first team coach, but also with Bristol Rovers, Stoke City, AFC Bournemouth, Fulham and Kingstonian before retiring.

Dennis remains eternally grateful to Orient for the pivotal role the club and its key figures played in his formative football years.

"Of all the clubs I've been associated with during my career in football, the first two results I always look for are those of Orient and Leicester."

Interview: Paul Hiscock

ORIENT ON TOUR

(1)

LOYAL supporter Keith Emmerson sent in these rare offbeat photos of the squad which he captured on three end-of-season tours in the early 70s.

(1) The first shot shows a large group pictured with the Dutch travel rep Jeannet Marius at the Orange Park Hotel, Benidorm in May, 1971. Unfortunately, keeper Ray Goddard's face is obscured by the trophy Os won but the others in view are (standing, left to right) physio Charlie Simpson (behind Jeannet), Peter Angell, Peter Brabrook, Barry Dyson, Dennis Rofe, Mickey Bullock and Peter Bennett. Seated: Terry Mancini, Dave Harper and Gordon Riddick.

During a 15-day mini tour of Spain's Alicante region they won all three low-key friendly matches – against Villena (2-0), Eida (3-1) and a combined Santa Pola/Hercules side (2-0).

Keith recalls: "I went on the Benidorm trip with fellow supporters Dick Richards and Ray Bruce. There is a picture of the three of us in the Bar Melodia (then owned by Londoner Harry Maney) in the *Brisbane Road Memories* book. Ray and I were on both the other trips. He had the contacts to find out when and where the players were going."

(2) The players and staff are more formally attired in this picture taken in Jersey in May, 1972. Those we recognise are Gordon Riddick, Paul Harris, Barrie Fairbrother, Phil Hoadley, Peter Angell, Dennis Rofe, Terry Brisley, Peter Allen, Barry Dyson and Mickey Bullock.

Os thrashed a team called Oaklands 8-0, with goals from Dyson (2), John Lewis (2), Bullock, Fairbrother, Derrick Downing and an O.G.

Keith continues: "In Jersey we found ourselves in the same club as the players. Phil Hoadley had been newly-signed but that did not

GOLDEN JUBILEE
FOOTBALL MATCH

SPRINGFIELD STADIUM | OAKLANDS F.C.
INCLUDING GUEST PLAYERS

TUES. 16TH MAY
K.O. 7.30 p.m. | v ORIENT F.C.
Tickets available at
WHEWAYS - G. LE MAISTRE
P. DREUX, BAGOT INN

DOORS OPEN
6.30 p.m. | Admission: Adults 30p Juniors 15p
Covered Stand 75p (Inc Adm)
Open Stand 50p (Inc Adm)
Ringside 40p (Inc Adm)

ROTHMANS
KING SIZE

stop Ray Bruce chatting away to him. Finally, Phil asked: 'Do I know you?'. He was dumbfounded to find that it was no coincidence that we were on the same island as him.

"Ray died in early 1980. People like Brian Blower would remember him, because he sold many of his pontoon tickets on behalf of the club. He was nicknamed 'Radio Ray', as he always had a transistor radio with him. I seem to remember Tom Walley in Spain listening to it for some result or other.

"Ray died on a Monday night after attending a West Ham match and he never woke up. Must be a moral there somewhere. In the Sardinia group photo he is on the far left clutching a bag."

3 The Orient party on the runway before departing Sardinia, where the players and their wives were treated to a Pontinental summer holiday by the club – no football matches were played this time – in June, 1973. Players alongside the aforementioned Ray Bruce are (left to right) Phil Hoadley, Mickey Bullock, Gerry Queen, Ian Bowyer, Malcolm Linton, Paul Harris, Tom Walley and Derrick Downing.

3b Ray Goddard plays with David Payne's crutches, to the amusement of fellow injury victim Peter Allen, during a break in a promo for Berger Paints while holidaying on the Italian island.

Skilful flicks & party tricks

Born: Greenwich, London, November 8, 1937
Usual position: Winger Orient Career: 1968-71
Orient Appearances: League 70/2, FA Cup 2/1, League Cup 6
Orient Goals: League 6, FA Cup 0, League Cup 0

TO many former England internationals who had played in the World Cup finals, won the First Division championship and an FA Cup winners' medal, the Third Division would have seemed a far from appealing option when Orient came calling.

But for tricky winger Peter Brabrook, approaching the veteran stage of an illustrious career that included glory days with Chelsea and West Ham United, a few seasons in another part of east London didn't seem such a bad idea.

There were several good reasons why Brabrook agreed to drop two divisions when he left Upton Park in the summer of 1968: he didn't have to move from his home in Hyland Close, Hornchurch, where he lived with wife Doreen and young children Wayne and Donna; and he could continue to combine playing with running his butcher's shop in East Ham.

But the biggest factor in luring him to Brisbane Road was his old pal, Jimmy Bloomfield, Orient's player-manager and a former team-mate during Jim's 12-game spell as an inside-forward for West Ham in 1965-66.

"Jimmy was the main reason I went to Orient," Peter confirmed when I interviewed him at his Laindon, Essex home in March, 2014.

"Jimmy was a really good friend of mine. He was a great footballer, I admired and liked the way he played the game, and he was also a really nice man. He said to me: 'Even if you come for only one or two seasons, you could get us promoted. You'll give us a better balance'.

"His words gave me a lift, he made me feel wanted again. A couple of other little clubs came in for me but I wanted to play for Jimmy."

Given cash-strapped Orient's well chronicled perennial struggle for survival in the mid-to-late 60s, it may surprise you to know that a hefty financial inducement also helped to secure the player's services. In addition to their modest transfer fee of £5,000 to West Ham, Orient also forked out a generous signing-on fee to keep 'Braaders' close to home. He revealed: "Jimmy gave me five grand to sign on, which was a lot of money in 1968."

Can you imagine how much arm-wrestling Bloomfield had to do in the boardroom to persuade the directors to loosen the purse strings to that extent, for a player pushing 31, but Jimmy knew it was a shrewd investment that would help propel the club towards the Second Division. It's fair to say that in recruiting Brabrook, he acquired one of the most experienced and decorated players in the club's history.

Within weeks of making his debut for Chelsea in March, 1955, Peter had collected a much coveted First Division championship winners' medal – the club's first – and soon he would be supplying hatfuls of goals for the young prodigy Jimmy Greaves, as well as gaining England youth and under-23 honours.

In the summer of 1958 he was part of Walter Winterbottom's England squad for the World Cup finals in Sweden and, aged 20, made his full international debut in a group play-off defeat against the Soviet Union. He gained two more senior caps, against Northern Ireland (1958) and Spain

78

(1960), and clocked up 271 first team appearances (51 goals) for the blue-shirted Pensioners before Tommy Docherty sold him to West Ham for £35,000 in October, 1962.

The highlight of his 214 appearances (43 goals) in the claret-and-blue was his pinpoint right-wing cross for Ronnie Boyce to head the dramatic injury-time winner against Preston North End in the 1964 FA Cup Final. Typical of the accurate delivery that Mickey Bullock, Barrie Fairbrother and co. would later come to appreciate from the crafty Cockney.

After gracing the hallowed turf of Wembley and other famous grounds including Old Trafford, Anfield, Goodison Park, Stamford Bridge, White Hart Lane and Highbury, Brabrook was in for a culture shock when the 1968-69 fixture list was published. The likes of Barrow, Stockport, Hartlepool and Mansfield suddenly appeared on his radar for the first time.

"Hartlepool . . . HART-LEE-POOL!" he repeated as he raised his voice. "I didn't even know where it was! I remember going to one ground – can't remember which one – and, inevitably, you always ended up going to the loo before the game. Well, I was standing there having a pee when, all of a sudden, I felt water dripping from the ceiling onto my head. I thought, 'what's this all about?'. It was horrendous."

Not that he visited any of the above far-flung football outposts. Just seven league games into his Os career, he limped off during the 3-0 home win over Oldham Athletic on September 21 and didn't play again that season. One can only speculate what chairman Arthur Page and his fellow directors must have been thinking . . .

"I tore the Achilles tendon in my left leg, although the injury actually happened while we were training on the Redgra pitch opposite the ground. The medical people reckoned that because I'd trained on grass all my career, it was the hard, sandy-like surface that caused the injury. I kept having cortisone injections before games but I'd have to come off at half-time. I struggled on for a while but I needed surgery.

"I was standing there having a pee when, all of a sudden, I felt water dripping from the ceiling onto my head. I thought, 'what's this all about?'. It was horrendous."

"I had the heel wired up and by that stage of my career, I thought it might be the end. It's a bad enough injury to suffer today, with all the medical help and top class facilities clubs have at their disposal and the experts they call upon, but in those days I don't think they really knew how to treat it properly. To be fair, though, the surgeon who operated on me at West Ham Hospital in Stratford did a fantastic job."

Brabrook not only reclaimed the number 11 shirt, he repaid the faith Bloomfield invested in him. After undergoing a successful operation to repair his left Achilles, he played in 37 of the 46 league matches on the way to the Third Division title, netting three times but setting up plenty of chances and goals for his more youthful colleagues.

"I worked hard all that summer, really pushed myself to get fit, and I had good treatment," added Peter, rising from his armchair to reveal scarring on both lower legs. "I did both of my Achilles – the second one after I left the Orient, in a charity game at Thurrock!"

After six years developing his technique under the watchful gaze of the cerebral Ron Greenwood, Peter – deceptively tall for a winger at 5ft 11ins – was delighted to be linking up with another kindred spirit in Bloomfield, saying: "Jimmy's training was much the same as Ron's – a lot of work with the ball, passing, skills and little drills, which was quite unusual at that time.

"Jimmy was in Arsenal's first team for quite a while, a really good midfield player and all the Orient players respected him as our manager.

"Jimmy's assistant, Peter Angell, was a lot harder but they worked well together and complemented each other. Peter was a nice guy, too, but an out and out winner."

With Orient, Brabrook enjoyed a new lease of life. Instead of going through the motions, as many old-stagers tend to do as they see out their twilight days, he relished the opportunity to turn back the clock.

"I knew I was nearing the end of my playing career. I'd relied on my pace, ability to beat the full-back and skills in running with the ball and I knew they were dropping off a bit. But I felt that I still had a lot to offer playing two divisions below what I'd been used to.

"It wasn't the money that motivated us to win the Third Division, because there wasn't much money about in those days. It comes from within – you just want to play well and win matches.

"Obviously, I did take a bit of a drop in wages going from Division One to Division Three but, no, I can't complain. Orient looked after me."

As well as bringing to Orient a bit of street-wise East End nous (although born in Greenwich, he grew up in Forest Gate) and light hearted dressing room banter, he lit up the Third Division scene with his dazzling feints, flicks and tricks, which entertained the fans and bamboozled opponents in equal measure.

And when Mark Lazarus arrived from Crystal Palace in the autumn of 1969, Os had a couple of wing wonders who had been around the block more than a few times. They went together like pie and mash, their combined knowledge and experience bringing out the best in their team-mates.

"I think I started off on the right-wing but when Mark came I played more on the left, although Jimmy would often switch us around and, during games, he would just leave us both to it. We did it off the cuff," Peter recalled, smiling at the memory of his wing partner.

"I liked Mark. He was as straight as a die, a funny fella, but on the field he was a very hard player. Generally speaking, full-backs were hard and wingers soft but when you went to a game and saw Mark in action, it was a vastly different ball game. He was really powerful but he could also play and, for a winger, he scored goals for fun. He was a very good team player as well. I suppose the two of us were a bit of a handful for defences at that level.

Peter scoring in the 4-1 victory against Plymouth to set Os a step closer to the Third Division title.

"Everyone played 4-4-2 in those days – they didn't have all the different systems they have now. There weren't many attacking full-backs around either. Most of them stayed in their own half, very rarely ventured forward. And if they got a chance to kick you, they would. They were strong, hard-tackling defenders lacking finesse.

"A winger will never beat a full-back physically, so you had to beat them with pace or skill and embarrass them that way. I had to be wary of them and be a bit of a high-jumper at times to stay out of their way."

Brabrook said he enjoyed playing in front of both full-backs, Mick Jones and Dennis Rofe: "Jonesy was a good, steady player and very quick. Dennis was only a kid but he looked a good prospect, quite strong for a youngster, with a good attitude."

It's clear that Peter enjoyed the camaraderie at Orient as much as playing and training. But he and Lazarus weren't the only two dressing room jokers.

"Terry Mancini was a good character too. Even Tommy Taylor was quite forward for a young lad and said what he thought. You could see he was going to be a top player. He had an old head on young shoulders but he was far advanced in whatever he did. He was a good guy.

"It was a happy time. I was doing all sorts of fancy tricks and gawd knows what. I remember scoring a goal where I went past three or four players and side-footed the ball in the net. The crowd were all singing and it was like winning the league. I thought, 'Christ almighty!' but it was great. We were getting some terrific crowds too.

"The difference between now and then is that the players enjoyed playing, enjoyed life and they had a bit of character about them as well."

On Orient's return to Division Two, Brabrook played in just over half of their 1970-71 league campaign (28 appearances, one goal) before leaving at the end of the season, days before Bloomfield moved on to Leicester City. Peter decided to have a season playing part-time for nearby Southern League Romford but wished he hadn't.

"I should have packed up when I finished at Orient," he said. "I wasn't doing anything but then Harry Clarke, the old Tottenham centre-half who was managing Romford, persuaded me to keep going for another season. But it was a disaster, I shouldn't have done it. The standard was poor but it was the training that really did me. We never stopped running round the speedway track at Romford's stadium. We only trained on Tuesdays and Thursdays but I thought, 'Cor, dear, oh dear – no, no, I've had enough of this', so I just did the one season for them and that was it."

But Peter hadn't quite severed all of his Orient connections. Some years after he quit playing, he was employed by Ovenden Papers, the company owned by Neville Ovenden, who was Orient chairman at the time having been vice-chairman during Brabrook's three seasons with the club.

"When I finished playing, Neville said that if I ever needed a job I could go and work for him, so I phoned him up. I was still doing a bit of scouting for West Ham but he didn't mind what hours I worked. He was a lovely man.

"I worked there for about five or six years, loading reams and boxes of papers onto the lorries ready for distribution all over London and East Anglia."

After hanging up his boots in 1972, Brabrook went into coaching and management with Essex-based non-league clubs Ford United and then Billericay Town. He rejoined West Ham as a youth coach, helping to develop the careers of Frank Lampard, Joe Cole (who covered the cost of Peter's knee replacement surgery), Michael Carrick and Jermain Defoe and was still scouting for Hammers on a part-time basis right up until his death.

I'll always remember him as a very popular and sociable character, well liked and respected by his peers. He was a straightforward, down-to-earth bloke, who would always make you laugh with tales from his playing days.

Peter died of liver cancer at St Luke's Hospice, Basildon on December 10, 2016, a month after his 79th birthday. His funeral at Holy Cross Church, Hornchurch was attended by a number of his former West Ham team-mates and others associated with our east London neighbours but Mark Lazarus and my father Terry were also present to keep the Orient flag flying.

Interview: Tony McDonald

East End mark of distinction

Born: Stepney, London, December 5, 1938
Usual position: Right-winger Orient Career: 1957-61 & 1969-72
Orient Appearances: League 101/1, FA Cup 6, League Cup 3
Orient Goals: League 18, FA Cup 1, League Cup 1

MARK LAZARUS will always be remembered affectionately by Os supporters as the hero who scored the goal that clinched the Third Division championship and then netted Orient's first two upon their return to the Second Division.

Fans idolised Lazarus for his skilful endeavour, combative style and flamboyant reputation as one of the game's great showmen who ignited the crowd with his wing play. But like his teenage battles in the boxing rings of his native East End, he had to fight hard to win over his critics in his second spell at Brisbane Road.

In between two stints with the Os at opposite ends of a 15-season pro career spanning from 1957 until 1972 and almost 500 games, he had three spells with Queens Park Rangers, a couple of years each with Brentford and Crystal Palace, plus an unhappy five months at first division Wolves.

His first two-year period at Brisbane Road ended in 1961, when Alec Stock – the man who gave him his Leyton Orient debut in the club's old blue and white colours – transferred him to QPR. By the time Jimmy Bloomfield persuaded Lazarus to leave top flight Palace to reinforce our promotion bid in October, 1969, Mark II was a 31-year-old player of distinction.

Speaking at the start of the 1970-71 season, Os' £8,000 capture said: "When I first came back to the club the fans got on my back a bit. It wasn't my fault I was transferred in the first place but I got the impression some of them resented the fact that I'd left.

"And also a lot of them seemed to be expecting miracles. It was the first time a home crowd had been against me. I've never been a Stanley Matthews but it seemed that was what they expected and I got no credit from them for doing the job I was bought to do.

"A crowd means a lot to me. I like to play on the wing and have them near to me, breathing down my neck. I like to hear them rooting for me and I've never been much of a player at grounds like Chelsea and White City (QPR's temporary home), where the crowd are a long way away.

"I accept you have to take abuse away from home but it is making a difference to me now that our own fans are getting behind me. I'm 31 now and I know there are still one or two who are writing me off. But with the help of the majority of fans, I'll make them eat their words."

He did exactly that, turning back the years to finish the season as Orient's leading scorer, albeit with only six league goals.

Speaking from his immaculate Romford bungalow in 2017, Mark recalled: "I liked to play football with a smile on my face and wanted the fans to enjoy the game, too. I've read that I used to do a lap of honour around the ground each time I scored but that wasn't really the case. I celebrated by running along the touchline, shaking hands with the fans, or bowing and waving to them. It was my way of showing appreciation. I enjoyed the adulation and still do when I go back to my old clubs and receive a great reception from the crowd.

"Before I joined Crystal Palace, their fans used to boo me coming out of the tunnel before kick-off. But now when (ex-Orient full-back) David Payne organises reunions and invites me back to Selhurst Park, their supporters treat me like a superstar."

Stepney-born Lazarus came from a large family of eight brothers and five sisters and they were steeped in boxing. His grandfather on his mother's side was a bare-fisted champion of the East End. In the 50s, Mark's elder brothers, Lew and Harry, fought for British welterweight and middleweight titles under the name of 'Lazar'.

Mark turned out for Fulham and Chelsea's youth teams and the same Hainault-based Sunday side as Jimmy Greaves but it was while appearing

Mark Lazarus pictured in his two spells with Os.

for non-league Barking that the then Leyton Orient boss Alec Stock spotted the uncompromising winger's talent. That's when Mark was forced to quit as an undefeated amateur boxer and concentrate on football for a living.

His combination of quick feet and fist movement, allied to a fiery temperament, earned him a 'bad boy' tag in his younger playing days and would land him in trouble with the football authorities on numerous occasions throughout his career. But then he was fighting more battles than most. As the most successful and high-profile Jewish player of his era, he found himself targeted for abuse by opponents and rival fans.

Although Mark, whose grandparents were eastern European immigrants, didn't have a Jewish upbringing, nor was he barmitzvah, he remains proud of his heritage. As his faith demanded every season, he was missing from the side when games coincided with Yom Kippur, the Jewish Day of Atonement. He talks with typical honesty about the impact being Jewish had on him as a footballer.

"I'm sure certain managers encouraged their left-backs to try and wind me up but I only retaliated twice – and was sent-off both times," he said.

"I tried to ignore derogatory comments from the crowd, too, although I did snap once while playing for QPR at Halifax. I went to the barrier and was having a go back at an abusive fan when Alec Stock dragged me away. And as he did so, he gave me a clip round the ear and told me to get back on the pitch."

Typically pulling no punches, Mark gave an insight into the shameful extent of the anti-semitic provocation he endured from opponents on the football field. "They would make comments like: 'You stinking Jew bastard' and 'you shouldn't be here – your parents should've suffered with all the others in the ovens', and things like that.

"I mean, today it wouldn't be allowed. But referees used to let it to go on. And when Alec appealed on my behalf to the FA, they also did nothing about it except fine me and ban me for a couple of games.

"There weren't many Jewish footballers around back then. The only other one I came across was David Pleat. Dave Metchick and Barry Silkman played for Orient at different times to me."

Lazarus looks back on the first two seasons of his second coming at Orient as a happy time playing with freedom and joy under his old pal Bloomfield. He recalls his third, and last, campaign under George Petchey as acrimonious and unhappy. And he is convinced their mutual antipathy was a legacy of their time at Crystal Palace, where Petchey was first team coach.

Although a key figure in Palace's 1968-69 Second Division promotion success and in the starting line-up for their early First Division encounters the following season, a succession of substitutions – he admits he wasn't fully fit – convinced him his Selhurst Park days were numbered. "I got on all right with manager Bert Head, he liked me as a player, but I don't think Petchey wanted me in the team and he had quite a lot of influence over Bert.

"I didn't enjoy training under Petchey at Palace. I'd come from QPR, where we'd always trained with a ball, we had a lot of success and it was enjoyable. But under him at Palace, there was too much running, which was OK for all the youngsters but me and 'Budgie' Byrne hated it. As we lapped the pitch – he'd be shouting at me to 'hurry up', basically humiliating me in front of the younger players, so I had a word with him about it. Then we'd be training with a skipping rope and sprinting in running shoes with spikes, so training was crap.

"Over the years I've often thought about our constant personality clashes and the possible reasons behind it. Maybe it goes back to the days when I always used to give him a terrible time while playing for QPR against him, when he was Palace's left-half.

"They would make comments like: 'You stinking Jew b*****d' and 'you shouldn't be here, your parents should've suffered with all the others in the ovens' and things like that. I mean, today it wouldn't be allowed."

"When I joined Palace in '68 he took an instant dislike to me. Whether it was because he thought I was his guv'nor on the pitch and he didn't like what I used to do to him and Palace as a player, I don't know, but he never opened up to me.

"I know we never got on. At Palace, I used to 'offer him out' three times a week," added Mark, still physically strong, dressed – as ever – very smartly and, though he's pushing 80 with silver hair, still looking as if he could land a prime role in a re-make of *The Sopranos*.

For Lazarus, Jimmy Bloomfield was different gravy. "I knew Jimmy from when we played together at Brentford (1964-65). He came over for a chat and he said: 'We're going for promotion and we're desperate for you to join us'. Jim was a nice man, I really liked him a lot, and he talked me into going back to my first club. He knew how to handle and treat players properly.

"He had a look at my Palace contract and it just blew his mind but it wasn't a case of money, fame or anything like that. The fact is, I wasn't happy at Palace at the time, I didn't like the travelling to and from south London and I'd always loved the Orient. I took a huge drop in wages by going from the First Division to the Third – I'd been on a basic of £80 per week, plus £20 appearance money and a £20 win bonus – but that didn't matter. I knew I could just get in my car and more or less drive round the corner to the ground."

Lazarus made his second Os debut in our 2-0 home victory against Doncaster Rovers on October 18, 1969. His seven goals in 29 league matches included four in the last seven matches. It was from his cross that Mickey Bullock headed the winner that clinched promotion at Bradford City on April 15. Ten days later, in front of 13,268 jubilant fans at Brisbane Road, it was a case of role reversal: Mark nodded home Bullock's 55th minute centre for the only goal in the win against Shrewsbury Town that sealed the title.

Lazarus had a natural taste for dramatic Roy of the Rovers-style finales, having etched his name in QPR folklore by scoring the late winner in their historic 3-2 League Cup Final triumph over West Bromwich Albion in 1967 – the first played at Wembley.

And when the champagne flowed in the dressing room at Brisbane Road in April, 1970, he was celebrating his fourth promotion in consecutive years, having starred for Rangers in their surge through divisions three (1966-67) and two (1967-68) and also helped Crystal Palace into the top flight for the first time in their history (1968-69).

He made the best possible start to life back in Division Two with the Os, stunning Sheffield United with two goals in the space of four ecstatic second-half minutes, having set up the other goal for Dave Harper in our 3-1 victory.

In January, 1971, to the relief of Bloomfield, he emerged from another FA tribunal with a £75 fine and a suspended six-week ban after incurring five bookings (in the days when you virtually had to flatten your opponent with a right hook to force the ref into scribbling your name in his little black book).

Built like a boxer and very bullish, Lazarus said: "I used to frighten full-backs. If they kicked me, I'd kick them back – I didn't give a shit. I wouldn't shirk a challenge. The hardest I played against was Don Megson of Sheffield Wednesday. I could beat him easily enough but to get past him you virtually had to run off the pitch – he was a dangerous player. A f*****g nutcase. I'm sure they used to cage him up during the week and tease him with a football."

There was more trouble in store in March, when Orient crossed the river and, thanks to Peter Allen's tame effort timed at anything between 32 and 40 seconds, depending on which newspaper you read, took a 1-0 win from The Den. Fifteen minutes from the end, 5ft 9ins, 11-stone Lazarus inflamed the crowd with a robust challenge on Millwall favourite Harry Cripps – too robustly according to one irate Lions fan, who took exception by running onto the pitch and trying to assault the Orient number seven. Only the quick actions of the home skipper, who coaxed the trespasser back to the terraces, averted an ugly flashpoint. "I don't remember that happening but I know it had nothing to do with anti-semitism," Mark said. Cripps was quoted as saying: "I pulled him away from Lazarus, or he would have punched him. I remember him running on brandishing an umbrella during a match with Plymouth four or five years ago!"

"I think Harry was one of those left-backs who was frightened of me. He couldn't kick me to save his life – he never got near enough! – but he was a great fella and a tremendously loyal servant to Millwall. I went to his funeral.

"I don't think I played my best football for Orient – far from it – but I enjoyed my first couple of years back there – until George Petchey arrived.

"In fact, I decided to quit professional football the day I played for Orient reserves at Millwall. Before this, I'd had good memories of playing at the old Den – Millwall tried to sign me from Leyton Orient when I was a youngster but Watford, who were also going for promotion that year, got the move blocked – but on this occasion I hit a new low.

"I pulled up outside the ground, got out of my car and as I walked towards the little gated

---

"He offered us a nice few quid to beat Birmingham and I told all the players that we were all on an extra £100 per man to win the game. But he didn't have to pay out, because we lost 1-0."

---

players' entrance, a kid came along on a push-bike and nearly knocked me over. He got off his bike and apologised, so I said: 'That's all right' and continued making my way to the changing rooms.

"But when I got out on the pitch, I saw the kid who'd been on the bike – he was playing against me! I thought to myself, 'I've got to f****** turn it in'. I don't know his name but he couldn't have been more than 15 or 16. And I was only playing at Millwall that day *because* of Petchey.

"I'm not that religious – I always have to be told the date on which Yom Kippur falls each year – but when it clashed with a football match, I never made myself available to play that day – regardless of what club I happened to be with at the time.

"I was doing OK in the first half of Petchey's first season as manager but it just so happened that, in 1971, Yom Kippur was on a Tuesday (Sept 28) – the same day Orient were playing at Burnley. They lost 6-1 there without me but he decided to name the same team for the following Saturday's home game (v Charlton Athletic). When I walked in the dressing room and saw I wasn't in the side, I asked: 'What's going on, George?'

"He replied: 'I don't want to blame an individual for our defeat at Burnley'. I said: 'I'm not asking you to blame any individual. My position is right-wing, not left-wing, right-back, centre-forward or wherever. 6-1 is 6-1'.

"I said: 'Do me a favour' and walked out. Anyway, we beat Charlton (3-2) that day but I was also left out of the following game (a 4-1 bashing at Blackpool). When I questioned him again in his office before the match, Petchey said: 'I don't think we need you anymore. In fact, I don't even want you at the club'.

"If anyone was standing outside his little office at the stadium, they would have heard me call him every name under the sun. I said: 'If you were any sort of man, you would get up off that seat and chin me'. So that was basically it for me, although I didn't take any notice of him. I would still go to the club and hang about, just to needle him.

The record books prove that Lazarus' first team days weren't quite finished. After missing those three autumn games, he was recalled to the side in mid-October and started the next 10 league matches. But with Barrie Fairbrother given an extended run, Lazarus was left out from December 11 until returning for the last three games of the season.

His final first team appearance was a crucial promotion decider on the evening of Tuesday, May 2, 1972, when 33,363 crammed into Brisbane Road. Visitors Birmingham City needed a win to clinch their place in the top flight. A draw or an Orient victory would have sent Millwall – who had quite a number of their own fans in the sell-out crowd – up instead. There was nothing on the game except pride for 17th-placed Os but, as Lazarus revealed, a bonus incentive offered by a third party shortly before the decisive game ensured an honest performance from the home team.

He said: "A wealthy Millwall supporter called Gover, who was in textiles – I'd done a bit of business with him the past – came to the game and we met outside the ground beforehand. He offered us a nice few quid to beat Birmingham and I told all the players that we were all on an extra £100 per man to win the game. But he didn't have to pay out, because we lost 1-0 – I missed a good chance – and Birmingham went up (as runners-up to Norwich City, a point ahead of Millwall).

"But it wasn't about doing favours; it was about doing your best. I couldn't try any harder than I did anyway, it was just a case of a bigger reward."

After leaving Orient Lazarus turned down the chance to join former Os manager Dick Walker at Colchester United but he played on for another few years at non-league level.

"I got a nice few quid playing part-time for Folkestone and enjoyed it. I took Tony Nicholas, the former Orient wing-half, with me and they said that I didn't even need to train with them.

"I ended up playing for Ilford and then Wingate – a Jewish club, where I'd played as a teenager – with Cliff Jones, who was on the opposite wing."

Orient had Lazarus to thank for the legacy of his nephew Bobby Fisher, who made 353 appearances for Os over a 10-year period between 1973-83. Mark explained: "Bobby was adopted by my late eldest sister, Rose, when he was around six weeks old. She brought him up and doted on him – there was nothing she wouldn't do for him and she was at every game he played for Orient.

"I had an influence on his early days in football. I put QPR in touch with him as a kid and he spent a while training with them. But when they didn't sign him, by which time I'd joined Orient,

Os are the champions thanks to idol Mark

ORIENT ... 1, SHREWSBURY ... 0

Headline grabber Mark nets the title-clinching winner against Shrewsbury.

I asked Jimmy Bloomfield to take a look."

Lazarus began planning his future outside football while still at Orient. He got into the waste paper and haulage business by chance through his youngest brother Joe – "Mickey Bullock worked for me for a while" – before, in 1970, starting a successful storage and removals company that still bears his name today.

In addition to football and boxing, Mark's other main sporting interest is snooker. He became a big friend of Barry Hearn's well before the former Leyton Orient chairman began building his Matchroom empire at Romford Snooker Club in the early 80s.

Mark and his wife Fay were married in 1959 and the couple have two grown up children – son Nicky (the former snooker star who runs the family business, Mark Lazarus & Son Removals & Storage, following his dad's retirement some 12 years ago) and daughter Dena. There are five grandchildren: Remy, Tyler, Louis, Ryan and Blair.

It was a measure of his wholehearted endeavour, as well as his skill and showmanship qualities, that Mark remains a popular character with fans of all his former London clubs. Puffing on another chunky cigar, let's end with some final reflections on an eventful career: "I wouldn't be able to play in the modern game – they wouldn't have me! I wasn't the type to run back into my own half to help out my full-back, like wingers do today. I wasn't a good defender at all. My ability was going forward, giving full-backs a chasing, not backwards. You never saw me defending in our penalty area. I couldn't defend anyway.

"Scoring a simple goal at Wembley (his League Cup winner), which is what it was, obviously meant a lot to thousands of QPR supporters but I couldn't really put it down as one of my personal highlights. Goals are single moments of elation and my best one for Orient was at Sheffield Wednesday (Jan 16, 1971) – that was a cracker. For me, though, it was more about all the fun and pleasure I got out of the game.

"I hope fans remember me as a player who had a lot of heart, someone who would never back out of a challenge and would get in there where it hurts.

"For being exciting and uplifting, someone who would get them roaring when I had the ball at my feet. I wasn't the greatest player – and I'm not boasting – but I'll tell you what, I was exciting to watch.

"Peter Brabrook would murder me in terms of ability, he was a great winger, but if he'd had my heart, or if I'd had his ability, I'd have been the first name on the England team-sheet.

"Above all, I would most like them to remember me as an entertainer."
Interview: Tony McDonald

Bradford triumph & tragedy

Born: Stoke-on-Trent, Staffordshire, October 2, 1946
Usual position: Centre-forward Orient Career: 1968-76
Orient Appearances: League 267/10, FA Cup 16, League Cup 14
Orient Goals: League 65, FA Cup 1, League Cup 3

OF all the 69 goals Mickey Bullock scored for Orient in his 307 matches spanning eight seasons with the club, none were more important than his headed winner at Bradford City's Valley Parade that confirmed Orient were going back to Division Two.

It was the night of Wednesday, May 15 and only around a quarter-of-an-hour remained of the vital Third Division game when Mark Lazarus found Bullock with a right-wing cross and the burly number nine did what he did best. His 19th goal of the triumphant 1969-70 season sealed promotion with three matches, all at home, still to play.

Fifteen years later, in May 1985, Bullock returned to Valley Parade on one of the most tragic days in football history. He was lucky to escape the fire that killed 56 supporters and left around 300 injured. Mercifully, he suffered no physical injuries but the mental scars ran deep for a number of years.

He's since had another close brush with death but before recounting his health issues, let's rewind to much happier times that followed Bullock's £10,000 transfer from newly-promoted Third Division champions Oxford United to Orient in October, 1968, as a replacement for Fulham-bound Vic Halom.

"I wasn't unhappy at Oxford – I'd been their top scorer the previous season – but Jimmy Bloomfield 'sold' Orient to me. I knew him from our days playing together for Birmingham City," explained Mickey, who got his Blues career off to a flier by scoring the winner on his debut against Manchester United at Old Trafford as a 16-year-old in January, 1964.

"Although Jimmy didn't offer me an increase on my basic pay, I earned more at Orient through bonuses. Players were paid extra according to our number of appearances but he also had this unusual incentive scheme whereby we were targeted to achieve certain blocks of points over periods of, say, four or six games. It worked really well – if we lost, we didn't receive any extra. The most I earned was something like £140-150 a week. I was never on a goal bonus at Orient – those kind of deals weren't thought of in our day."

Newly-weds Mick and Brenda moved into club digs in Ewellhurst Road, Clayhall, near Barkingside, which they rented for a meagre 50p per week. He said: "We didn't get our first mortgage until we moved up here to Yorkshire when I was about 32-33. In fact, when I left Orient in 1976, chairman Brian Winston offered us the opportunity to buy the three bedroom semi-detached house where we lived from the club for £3,000 but I said 'no' because we couldn't afford it at the time. Then, about six months after we left, I heard that they sold it for about £118,000! I realised that Brian had more or less tried to give us the property and set us up for life."

Bullock recalls how close Os came to dropping in to the bottom, fourth tier for the first time in their history at the end of his first season in east London. "We needed to win our final game, at home to Shrewsbury, to guarantee staying in Division Three. We were under a lot of pressure but played them off the park that night," said Mickey, who opened the floodgates with a 20-yard volley after five minutes before further goals from Barry Dyson, Terry Mancini and Dave Harper completed a 4-0 rout. In his match report for the *Waltham Forest Guardian,* Jeff Powell awarded every Orient player a perfect 10/10 rating.

After taking a while to settle in his new surroundings, scoring just six goals from 33 league games in 1968-69, former England Schoolboy international Bullock averaged nearly a goal every other game in the title-winning campaign. His ability to almost hang in the air, shield the ball and hold it up, before sweeping accurate right or left-footed passes out to either wing, formed the basis of many Orient counter-attacks; with wingers Mark Lazarus and Peter Brabrook also prospering from his prime strengths as a target man with thighs like tree trunks. For defenders, he posed a threat in the air and on the deck.

By then Bloomfield had packed up playing and was fully focused on management. "By distancing himself from the players, he became more authoritative," Mickey observed.

Bullock recalls his first home goal of the championship campaign – a late winner against Halifax Town, the West Yorkshire club he would go on to play for, coach and manage after he left Orient. "There were about seven minutes left when we got a corner on the left-hand side. Peter Brabrook took it and it went past me at around head-height and, somehow or other, I managed an overhead kick into the top corner. Their manager, Alan Ball senior, came up to me afterwards and called me all the names under the sun!"

Eight of his 19 goals came away from Brisbane Road. As well as the points he helped to secure by hitting the target, both home and away, against Halifax and Bradford, he was also the only Os player on the scoresheet in a couple of other 1-1 draws – at Tranmere and Shrewsbury. Those key goals, worth nine points (still in the days of two points for a win), made all the difference in the final analysis. For Os pipped Luton Town to the title by a two-point margin, with Bristol Rovers a further six back from the champions.

Match-winning hero Mickey now reveals that he was very doubtful for the final away game at Valley Parade that effectively clinched promotion (Bristol Rovers needed to score 30 from their last three matches to pip Orient!). "I shouldn't really have played after getting injured in training on the Monday (two days before the game). My ankle swelled up like a balloon, so I laid on top of the bed all night with ice wrapped around it and I was still icing it all the way up to Bradford on the train. I had a fitness test and though I still wasn't really 100 per cent fit, Jim said: 'I want you to play'.

"We partied all the way back to London and by the time our train got back in to King's Cross at about half-past six on the Thursday morning, we were all a bit worse for wear. If I remember rightly, I got the tube home with Dennis Rofe and Paul Harris."

"We came back on the overnight sleeper train and had an absolutely fabulous night. We partied all the way back to London and by the time our train got back in to King's Cross station at about half-past six on the Thursday morning, we were all a bit worse for wear. If I remember rightly, I got the tube home with Dennis Rofe and Paul Harris.

"I remember beating QPR 2-0 around Christmas (1971) and after I scored our second goal, Mark Lazarus – who was out injured at the time – came onto the pitch on crutches, wearing his normal day clothes, to celebrate with the rest of us. He was so pleased we'd beaten his former club."

Bullock and Lazarus worked well together on and off the field. Mickey explains: "While we were both players at Orient, Mark got me a job in the waste paper business. We'd hire a lorry in the afternoons and drive to a printer at Southend to collect their waste. To further supplement my earnings, I also coached football three days a week in a school near the Blackwall Tunnel for five years."

We asked Mickey to open a window on a number of his Os team-mates . . .

"Goalkeeper Ray Goddard was a typical 'Jack the Lad' Londoner. He was brilliant on tour – a good looking lad who could talk to any bird. Him and Steve Bowtell, our reserve team keeper, were very similar. They were both good keepers and Steve was unfortunate that he didn't get more first team chances when Ray was there and, likewise, Ray was unlucky to be left out when John Jackson joined us.

"Jacko came into a good team and he was so big and dominant in the penalty box that he was difficult to beat. He was a better keeper than Ray.

"Mick Jones was a good lad. He was a little bit carefree – to him, football was important but not the end of the world.

"Dave Harper was a good pro who always gave 100 per cent. He was the type of lad who would always help the club and play when he was injured. It was a knee injury that finished his career and he played a lot of games when he wasn't fit. He was well respected.

"Everybody used to hate playing against Terry Mancini in training. When I met up with him again at the 2014 Play-off final at Wembley I reminded him of the time we thrashed his QPR side, which included Phil Parkes, Terry Venables, Gerry Francis and Rodney Marsh, the day after Boxing Day (1971), when I 'rolled him' before scoring our second in a 2-0 win (Barry Dyson got the first). Terry was our captain, very vocal on the field and a good motivator, although he wasn't a fantastic trainer.

"Off the pitch, he would stand up for other players and the team as a whole if anything needed to be said or asked. He did a lot to help the development of Tommy Taylor and Dennis Rofe, who were raw youngsters when I arrived. Terry was good in the air and attacked the ball well.

"Tommy was a joker, another Jack the Lad. He liked a laugh but in saying that, he was a good player – you could see that he and Dennis would go on and play at the highest level. I used to get on very well with Dennis – him and his wife Sue used to come over to our place and she got on well with Brenda. Dennis had a good attitude, he really wanted it, although he didn't have total belief in himself as a youngster.

"Peter Allen was a more vocal captain than Terry and had a nastier streak on the field. He had a lot of passion for the game and really didn't need to say too much because of the way he played – always leading by example. If there was a tackle to be made, he'd go for balls others would shy away from. He'd take the ball and the man – everything went. His bravery earned him the respect of all the players. He'd gee up everyone and always trained hard.

"Peter, Jacko and George Petchey used to travel up together on the train from Brighton every day, so it's fair to assume that Peter had a better working relationship with George than he did Jimmy Bloomfield.

"Apart from Peter, Laurie Cunningham and Tony Grealish were also particularly good trainers. Laurie was a lovely lad, shy and ever so polite. But a very private person – he never spoke about his home life, girlfriends or whatever. I didn't know anything about what he did away from the club. Always immaculately dressed, even when he turned up for training. He wasn't flash, he was a quiet lad, but he clearly had a very good upbringing.

"Although he was naturally fit, it used to rankle him that he couldn't beat me over the first five yards when we did short sprints. But after 50 yards, he'd be seven or eight yards ahead of me!

Come rain or snow . . . Mickey fires Os in front against Barnsley on the way to the title in February, 1970.

"There were times when we needed to lift his spirits in the dressing room if he got down about his game. Not have a go at him, but gently coach him. I don't think he believed he was as good as he really was at that early stage of his career.

"But I never heard any opposing players having a go at Laurie because he was black. And as far as I was aware, he never complained to any of us about being subjected to racism on the field.

"Bobby Fisher was also very well-mannered, although sometimes you got the feeling that his mind was maybe elsewhere. He was good mates with Tony Grealish. Those two and Laurie stuck together.

"Tony was a salt of the earth guy who appreciated everybody and everything and he really loved life. He enjoyed having a good time. He always came in to training with a smile on his face. He was our Dave Mackay – a real warrior.

"Malcolm Slater was a good Scottish lad who lived at Southend. He was a bit of a comedian and had a weird sense of humour. He was as fit as a fiddle but he had a horrible habit of being sick after his meals. It was unbelievable. After training at the ground, we'd all go up to Pete's fish shop in the High Road, where he'd have rock eel and chips and then go straight in the Coach and Horses and bring it all up. There wasn't an ounce of fat on Malcolm.

"Terry Parmenter was a quiet lad who kept himself to himself. I remember him scoring a great goal against Sunderland, although we didn't play together much.

"Barrie Fairbrother was a goalscorer who scored a lot of goals at youth and reserve level, and he adapted really well in the first team when he went from centre-forward to right-wing. I thought he lacked confidence and would take it to heart if he wasn't in the side. It didn't take a lot to upset him. But he was a good lad and did very well for Orient. We had a good understanding on the field.

"I got on all right with Ian Bowyer – probably because we were both northerners.

"Phil Hoadley joined us from Crystal Palace but within two days he was Orient. He had no side to him – you couldn't help but take to him straight away. He's a good lad, very sincere and always told it like it was. He was a bit of a comedian in the dressing room, always having a laugh and a joke.

"Gerry Queen had pace and movement, with a good left peg and he could finish. We appreciated and respected each other's strengths and he could adapt his game. He had a good brain. If he had a weakness, it was that he wouldn't always put his head where it might get hurt.

"Gerry and Barry Dyson were the only two forwards who played up alongside me – the others, like Barrie and Ian, tended to play off me. Gerry was a Scottish comedian – although a bit tight!

"Ricky Heppolette was a good player with vision and he scored some good goals with his head too. He wasn't the fastest but, like Gerry, he had a good left foot. He brought enthusiasm to the dressing room.

"John Boyle was a good club man and motivator of other players. He'd come from the big-time at Chelsea but he wasn't a Jack the Lad-type character.

"Bill Roffey did well for Orient, especially considering he hadn't played many first team games for Palace before he joined us. He had a cracking shot on him and was a good worker. Off the field, 'Jaffa' had a nice sense of humour and a wry smile.

"We had a good set of lads at Orient – no cliques."

IN those far off days, long before footballers' wives sipped Chardonnay in their luxury gated mansions with the 4x4s in the driveway and spent their days indulging themselves while flouncing around spas, nail bars and beauty salons, Brenda Bullock always went out to work. As she served up a delicious lamb roast dinner with all the trimmings to the delight of Dave Dodd (Leyton Orient Supporters' Club chairman) and myself when we visited their home at High Burton, near Huddersfield, in 2014, she said: "I wasn't a WAG, as they're called today, and never wanted to be one. While Mike was playing for Orient, I had a job with a Gants Hill company handling microfiche film. When our two children, Wenda – "a Welsh name" – and Mark, were at school, I worked at our local school in Clayhall as a cleaner and dinner lady. And on my days off, I also worked part-time as a child minder."

What did she cook for her husband on match days? Mickey said: "My routine for a Saturday home game kicking-off at three o'clock would be to eat nothing more than scrambled eggs for breakfast. Then I'd read the paper and put a bet on, either with my local bookie or in a shop near the ground. Occasionally, me and Tom Walley would go to Hackney dogs, which started at 11.00am, where we'd have a cup of coffee or tea before getting to the ground at around 1.30-2.00, when it was time to start psyching myself up for the game. On a good day, we'd play, get a result and then I'd pick up my winnings from the betting shop on my way home!

"One day, a trainer at Hackney called Jim Annets gave Tom and me a greyhound for nothing. The first time it ran, we had a few bob on it and it looked like it was going to catch the race leader as they came off the last bend. But just as it hit the front, it spun round and bit the dog it had just passed. Not only was it disqualified from the race, it was banned for several meetings! But going to the dogs helped us to relax on the day of a home game."

Recalling the separate factions – drinkers, gamblers and 'the quiet ones' – that existed within every top club back in the day before dieticians, fitness coaches and an army of other non-football employees were brought in to pamper the players, Mickey said: "The main drinkers were myself, Dennis Rofe, Paul Harris, Tom Walley and occasionally Tommy Taylor."

Brenda laughed as she recalled one particularly boozy session that followed a Tuesday night game at Leyton, when Mickey didn't arrive home until the early hours and she decided to lock him out of their home. He said: "A few of us had been in the Coach and Horses until gone midnight and Jimmy, the owner, went to bed and just told us to leave the money for our drinks on the bar when we left.

"Apart from enjoying a Bacardi, Tom Walley was the biggest punter in my time at Orient – he knew the Newmarket-based trainer Robert Armstrong whose son-in-law was Lester Piggott. Tom was on the phone to Armstrong every day. Anyway, in the 1973-74 season, we had to play a couple of games up north, at Middlesbrough and Hull, in the space of four days, so we stayed in a hotel at Whitby. Tom had a very reliable tip that Piggott was going to win two of his races at York, so he went into a little betting shop in Whitby to place his wagers.

"I don't know how much he had on – he wouldn't tell us – but both bets won and on the way home I remember him he sitting at the back of our coach guarding a carrier bag stuffed full of fivers, tenners and £20 notes. I think the poor bookie had to close down in the end!

"Dave Harper also liked a bet and Glenn Roeder came in every morning holding a copy of the

Sporting Life. He was always studying form before training.

"Glenn surprised me how well he did as a player, coach and manager (In his first season as manager of West Ham United and Newcastle United he guided both clubs to top seven Premier League finishes), because when he first came into the team as a young centre-back he was a shy, quiet lad and you doubted if he possessed the necessary characteristics to go on and achieve what he did."

TO celebrate promotion to Division Two, the players went on an end-of-season tour to Benidorm, Spain. "We had a good time – it was players only, so great for camaraderie – but the Orange Park Hotel we stayed at was an absolute disgrace. The food was terrible, so we went out every night to a place where we ate fried squid off saucers.

"We played one game in about 90 degrees heat but no-one took the football too seriously. I remember Jimmy and Peter Angell had us training on the beach, where the locals took the mickey

With son Mark and 'Blackie', the family's Cross Lab.

His most famous Os goal, against Chelsea in the FA Cup. David Webb and Peter Bonetti look to be stuck in the mud.

out of us something shocking."

If his winner at Bradford in 1970 will forever be remembered as his most important for the club, his equaliser in the epic 3-2 FA Cup fifth round victory against Chelsea almost two years later probably rates as his most famous and memorable in the eyes of jubilant Os supporters among the 30,329 crowd on that unforgettable February afternoon.

Mickey said: "I'm grateful to David (Dodd) for sending me a 20-minute video recording of the game. I showed it to my family and friends and they were absolutely amazed by the quality of football we played, the pace we used to play at and the honesty of the players. The pitch was a mudbath that day – although not the worst I've ever played on – but that didn't stop either Chelsea or ourselves playing good football.

"Phil Hoadley's goal just before half-time was just what we needed, although from looking at the *Match of the Day* coverage again now you can see that we hadn't played that badly in the first half. In the first 10 minutes we could have gone two up. In the first five or six minutes I put Barrie Fairbrother through on his own and I think it should have been a penalty. They didn't have close-up action replays in those days but it still looked a penalty to me. It wasn't awarded, though – we weren't even given a free-kick.

"My goal came from a terrible mix-up between David Webb and their keeper Peter Bonetti, who I think should have stayed on his line and let 'Webby' deal with it. When the ball came down the middle, I didn't expect to get on the end of it. It was an unusual goal for me – probably the easiest I've ever scored – but it was very important because we were then back to 2-2 and had the bit between our teeth.

"It was the type of goal that Barrie would have got and, indeed, his winner came from a similar type of mistake in the Chelsea defence."

Bullock revealed a scary postscript to the Chelsea thriller which also underlined Orient's reputation as a caring family club. "Prior to the Saturday home cup tie, we spent the week training down on the coast at Eastbourne, from Monday to Friday. Unbeknown to me, on the Monday, my son Mark, who was two-years-old, had a nasty accident at home. He pulled a rubber hosepipe out of the back of our washing machine and the hot water that poured out of it left his arms and chest badly scolded.

"Brenda informed George Petchey what had happened but asked him not to mention the accident to me because she didn't want to upset or distract me before our big game. I didn't find out about Mark's injuries until after the Saturday night.

"It was a very emotional time but Orient were brilliant to us. The following Monday, my wife received a surprise delivery at home – the biggest bunch of flowers you've ever seen plus a new washing machine, paid for by the club. They were sent courtesy of George and Orient director Brian Winston."

The '72 Cup dream was finally shattered in the next round by Arsenal, whom many believe stole a 1-0 quarter-final victory from E10. "I'm not saying we deserved to win that day but we didn't deserve to lose either," Mickey recalls. "After the game, their captain Frank McLintock offered me his commiserations and said: 'What are you doing playing in Division Two?'. He was a real gentleman and he knew Arsenal had been in a game. Fulham's Bobby Moore and Alan Mullery paid me similar compliments after I twice scored against them at Craven Cottage (Sept '73). They didn't need to flatter me but it was nice coming from players of their class."

Reflecting on his role during that exciting period between 1971 and '74, Mickey continued: "Our forward formation was arrow-shaped, with myself down the middle and two players wide in

'Hang man' Mickey rises above Arsenal's Frank McLintock, with Barrie Fairbrother (7) and Gunners' Pat Rice (2) and their white-booted cup tie-winner Alan Ball looking on.

a 4-3-3 set-up. Barrie Fairbrother liked to run in behind their defence and I also had Ian Bowyer up alongside me for a while – but then he went back into midfield, so we didn't usually play with two strikers for long.

"Coming to Orient did Ian a lot of good, because he hadn't been getting a look-in at Manchester City. Although not a prolific goalscorer, he was a workhorse and look how far he went in his career. He won the European Cup twice under Brian Clough at Nottingham Forest."

The flame-haired Bowyer had scored Orient's first in their 2-0 FA Cup fourth round victory at Leicester City (Peter Allen also netted), who were then managed by Jimmy Bloomfield. "I think Jimmy was very much aware that we were capable of beating them and that's what happened. We were tremendous. To be fair to him, though, he came in our dressing room afterwards and, before we'd even sat down, he told us: 'You were absolutely fantastic and deserved it. If my team had to lose, I'm glad it was to the Orient'."

Bullock thrived under both Bloomfield and his successor Petchey, who arrived from Crystal Palace in the summer of '71. As his seven-and-half years at Orient were split fairly equally between the respective reigns of the two managers, Mickey is well placed to make accurate comparisons.

He said: "They both earned the players' respect in different ways. Jimmy was a gentleman. But he also had a ruthless streak, although he didn't need to show it very often. If you weren't doing your job, he wouldn't hold back in the dressing room at either half-time or after the game.

"He would always ask Peter Angell if he had anything to say. And Peter would be typically blunt and to the point – he always called a spade a spade. He was more of a disciplinarian than Jimmy. For instance, the kit room was his domain and he didn't like players going in there.

"People said he would be under more pressure in his job once other coaches, like Terry Long, were brought in by George but he stayed and went on to work well with the new manager. But Peter had no inclination to become a manager himself – he was happy to remain a number two.

"Coaching wise, Jimmy was more about getting the ball down and using it. He concentrated on our skills and focused on improving our quality. He was a complete football man.

"I was shocked and disappointed when he left us to go to Leicester, although I thought the higher up he went the better he'd become.

"The Orient players didn't even know who George Petchey was when it was announced he would be replacing Jimmy. Then we heard that he'd been assistant to Bert Head at Palace.

"Orient changed completely once George arrived. He made it very plain that it wasn't going to be an easy ride and training would be a different ball game altogether. He believed in the mantra of 'train hard, play hard'.

"He definitely made us a fitter, more physical and 'nastier' side. We started going on big cross-country runs at Chigwell and he would also take us to the National Sports Centre at Crystal Palace, where he had good contacts from his days as a player and coach at Selhurst Park. We'd do physical work on the athletics track there and then go indoors to use weights, do circuit training and play five-a-sides. Under George, pre-season training became very concentrated.

"When I left school at 15, I weighed 14 stone but in George's first season as manager at Orient my weight went down to 11st 7lbs. I didn't have pace but his training methods made me sharper over short distances.

"George took us to Arnhem, Holland twice for pre-season friendlies, which did us a lot of good. We trained three times a day: at seven o'clock in the morning, two in the afternoon and seven at night. It was hard work but enabled the players to bond. Having said that, he never accompanied us on end-of-season tours. We went to Sardinia twice but I don't believe he came with us.

"One year we were in Arnhem at the same time as Barcelona and we played against them in friendly five-a-side games. They noticed and commented on how fit and competitive we all were. There was a collective will to do well, which is why it was so disappointing to miss out on promotion in 1974.

"But I can't ever remember Tom Walley going to Arnhem – he hated all the pre-season work. Besides, he didn't want to miss out on the horseracing back home!

"George wasn't as close as Jimmy had been to the players and, at times, he had a strange sense of humour. Some of the things that he thought were funny, the players might have felt were a bit insulting, even though that wasn't his intention.

"If he had a problem with a player, he dealt with it privately, face to face, although I never had any rows with either him or Jimmy. The Palace lads, who knew him a lot better, told the rest of us not to mess with him. He signed a lot of players from his former club but they were good blokes and there were no dressing room cliques.

"Although George and Peter Angell operated well together (they were wing-half team-mates at QPR), it was a different relationship to the one Peter had with Jimmy. He and Jimmy were a lot friendlier with each other, whereas with Peter and George it was more businesslike."

Bullock confirmed that training under Petchey wasn't all work and no play. "He did technical work too. One of the best things he ever did . . . and it was so simple, it was untrue. Every morning when we trained at Springhill, he'd get the first team to stand in their usual positions on the field while he stood on the halfway line with a bag of footballs.

"He'd kick a ball to John Jackson and 'Jacko' would then throw it to an outfield player but, for example, George would go: 'Stop! Jacko, that's no way to throw the ball to a defender', and he'd make him do it properly. We'd practice passing the ball into different areas, with players holding the ball up and laying it off. But there was no-one marking us – it was shadow play and I'd never done it before. He was a bit of a perfectionist.

"Tactically, George liked me to play as the target man down the middle. They say we played route one football but we didn't simply hoof long balls to the front or over the top. It was usually a controlled long pass. Because I was good at being the target man, it gave other players the confidence to run off me, knowing they were usually going to receive a lay-off or flick-on. Barrie Fairbrother made lots of runs in behind and we also had midfielders, the likes of Peter Allen and Terry Brisley, who would get forward.

"But once we got the ball into our opponent's defensive third, that's when George's push-and-run style came into full effect. He was very much influenced by his mentor, Arthur Rowe, who made push-and-run famous during his time at Spurs in the 50s. I don't know whether Arthur was ever paid by Orient but he was always at training and up in the stand watching our matches."

Bullock's most prolific season in the Second Division was 1973-74, when his 16 goals from 40 matches propelled Os to within a whisker of the top flight. But, as he explained, he might not even have been an Orient player that season after spending the summer weeks on the transfer list at his own request. Having started only 25 league games and made six appearances from the bench the previous season, he explained: "I wasn't getting the opportunities but I also blame myself because I wasn't fit enough. From 1969 to 1973 I didn't have a summer off, I even trained by myself. I trained twice a day, every day, doing cross-country runs and sprinting up hills in my spikes.

"When I first came to Orient, I couldn't manage the cross-country runs Jimmy and Peter had us doing at Epping Forest. We had to run up and down the last hill three times and I always trailed in the back three group. That's when I decided I needed to keep training throughout the close season.

"I was always a good trainer but I carried weight. I was overweight at Oxford, even though I was their top scorer when we gained promotion in '68, and Peter Angell told me so. They used to check the players' weight three times a week at Orient. So if we'd had a good result, I'd have a good drink on the Saturday night and then go to the ground on Sunday morning and spend two hours sweating off weight in the sauna . . . because I knew there would be another weight check on Monday morning. It was George Petchey who had the sauna installed in our dressing room."

In the summer of '73 Bullock heard whispers that Newcastle United were interested in buying him for £100,000. "A reporter phoned up and told me that Newcastle boss Joe Harvey was looking at me but nothing came of it. But then Bolton Wanderers agreed a deal with Orient to buy both Gerry Queen and myself for £100,000. We arranged to meet Bolton manager Jimmy Armfield at the Keele services on the M6 to talk terms and drove up together in my car.

"We discussed personal terms with Jimmy in turn before he spoke to us together. He came across very well. Gerry was keen to sign but I wanted more time to think it over and Jimmy was quite happy to give us a few days to consider everything.

"But before we even had a chance to get back to him, Jimmy phoned to say the deal was off – he was leaving Bolton to join Leeds United! He was very apologetic about it. I don't know if I would have left Orient for Bolton at the time, though."

Bullock came off the list and proceeded to enjoy a fine season in 1973-74, leading the line as Os maintained their promotion bid until the final game. Victory against Aston Villa at home on Friday, May 3 would have sent Orient into the top flight for only the second time in their history but it just wasn't to be.

"We were all very disappointed. It's not often you see every player crying in the dressing room after a game but we all shed a tear or two that night. Everybody was so traumatised by the result. I look back now, remember the quality football we played and think the team we had then would have graced the Premier League today."

Reliving the heartbreak of that decisive encounter that some supporters who were there still struggle to come to terms with today, Mickey said: "Ray Graydon scored the first goal of the game from a penalty (51 mins) and I got one back in the second-half (66 mins) to make it 1-1. Then, with about seven minutes to go . . . I'll never forget it . . . the ball came to me on the edge of the penalty box. It bounced up lovely, I hit it on the volley and it was going straight in at the top corner – it had 'goal' written all over it – but their keeper, Jimmy Cumbes, made a fantastic save, pushing my shot over the bar.

"We were all very disappointed. It's not often you see every player crying in the dressing room after a game but we all shed a tear or two that night. Everybody was so traumatised by the result.

"Up until Christmas we'd looked certainties to finish in the top three (the first season of three up/three down). I'd scored 13 of my 16 league goals that season by Boxing Day. I look back now, remember the quality football we played and think the team we had then would have graced the Premier League today.

"But in the second half of the season we suffered a few injuries. I tore my hamstring in an FA Cup (second) replay against Portsmouth at Crystal Palace's ground and had to come off after about 10 minutes. It felt like a sniper had shot me in the back of my left leg.

"They got me playing again within two or three weeks but I was only 60-to-75 per cent fit in the closing weeks of the season. The hamstring wasn't fully right after that and I was never quite the same player again. I'd become fatigued from around the 60th minute of games, unable to run flat out, which was very frustrating," Mickey admits.

Even in the depths of despair, their promotion dream cruelly snatched from their grasp, the human side of Orient FC showed itself again. "The day after the Villa game, Brian Winston called a team meeting. He said that in three days' time he'd be sending all the players, along with our wives, girlfriends and kids, to Sardinia for a fortnight's holiday – at HIS expense. Brian actually organised for us all to visit Sardinia twice and he showed his gratitude to my family many times. He really was fantastic to us, I can't say a bad word about him."

But there's not a lot of sentiment in professional football. After a disappointing 1974-75 season that yielded only three league goals and was punctuated by a 14-game mid-season absence, Bullock started just 16 league matches the following season and by February, 1976 his Os playing days were over.

"It was a sad day when I left Orient. That's when Brian asked if I wanted to buy

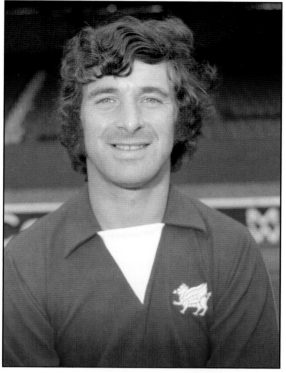

The pre-season photo call in August 1974.

our rented house off the club but Alan Ball (senior) offered me a player/coaching role at Halifax Town and I accepted."

After 106 games (19 goals) for Halifax in the Fourth Division between 1976-81, he was appointed manager at The Shay. "I spent three tough years there as manager, having to cut costs to the bone, before they sacked me (in 1984). I took it very badly.

"I went downhill after that, became quite ill with stress and for a while I behaved like an alcoholic. During the day I worked for Allied Dunbar selling mortgages and pensions, which I hated, and at night I was drinking six bloody cans of Special Brew and a bottle of whiskey. I'd lay on the floor with my head leaning on the settee until half-past two in the morning.

"In the end, I had a breakdown. I was scouting at Lincoln and after the game I collapsed outside the ground. They took me to hospital, where I spent three days in intensive care. At first they thought I'd had a heart attack but, thankfully, that wasn't the case. It was simply a build up of stress – I've been on medication for high blood pressure ever since.

"But I got a grip of myself and turned my life around. I don't touch any spirits now but I still enjoy the occasional beer and glass of red wine."

And he has much to live for too. As well as Mark and Wenda, Brenda and Mickey have five grandchildren: Emily, Mollie, Thomas, Hollie and Daniel.

After recovering from the bitter blow of losing his job at Halifax, Mickey returned to management at non-league level in the late 80s, firstly at Goole Town and then Ossett Town.

He also stayed in touch with the game as an interviewer and co-commentator for Pennine Radio, covering matches in the Yorkshire region. But there is one infamous game he wishes he'd never been asked to attend. On Saturday, May 11, 1985, he and his presenter colleague Tony Delahunty were covering Bradford City coronation as Third Division champions before the Bantams faced

Lincoln City . . . and they were working from the main stand when it caught fire, killing 56 fans among a terrified crowd of 11,000.

Reliving the horror of that tragic afternoon, Mickey lowers his voice and says: "It was a terrible experience, it really was. I saw an old man die as he tried to make his way out of the burning stand. I wanted to try and help him but the police wouldn't allow me to enter that section – they said it was too dangerous.

"Tony had just bought a new car, worth about 10 or 12 grand, so Bradford City gave him special permission to park it just outside the main stand. The fire spread along that stand and the mains wires we were using had actually started to melt while Tony and I were still on air – it was a scoop for him and he didn't want to pack up and get out of there until the last possible moment.

"In fact, at first he wanted to go towards the back of the stand, to the exit that led out onto the road where his car was parked, to see if it was all right. But I said: 'No way, we're not going up there – we're going down THERE', pointing towards the pitch, which was the safest place to be as the flames roared all around us. I pushed a couple of women and kids, who were trying to get out of the paddock, over the high wall and onto the pitch. Then Tony and I followed them. I was wearing a sheepskin jacket or coat and there were big lumps of black tar attached to it. It was shocking.

"The fire started shortly before half-time but my memory of events from then on is largely a blank. I suppose I was in shock. I remember walking around the ground for two hours afterwards and everywhere I looked the people looked completely stunned.

"I know I went back to the radio station's office in Bradford at one stage but I didn't get home until about half-past nine that night and I don't know where I'd been or what I did. I've never been able to account for all my movements that day. It broke my heart and I just buried it – never spoke about what happened to anybody.

"I was still working for Halifax Town at the time and they had given me a membership card for the Booker cash and carry warehouse in Bradford – it used to be in Halifax but they moved – where I could go and buy cheaper food and what have you. I'd drive into the city but then find myself going miles out of my way, along the wrong road, simply because I couldn't bear to go anywhere near Valley Parade after the disaster.

"Bradford City FC got in touch and asked if I would come to a memorial anniversary but I said 'no'. I just couldn't face it.

"As a result of what I witnessed that day, I suffered post traumatic stress disorder (PTSD), although I didn't know it until four years later. I went to see Paul Hunt, a psychologist at St Luke's Hospital in Huddersfield, and really opened up to him. He said that, in his experience, my case was the longest anyone had suffered PTSD before it was finally diagnosed.

"I went to him twice a week for 15 months. I told him everything about what I saw that day at Bradford and he had me sobbing my eyes out. It was Paul who got me to go back to the ground years later. I drove there, sat in my car in the car park and just cried, which Paul thought was a good thing. He wanted me to go back there again but this time go inside the ground. But I couldn't.

"It wasn't until Terry Venables asked me to do some scouting for him – watch Portsmouth play at Bradford – that I was finally able to step foot inside Valley Parade again. It was a horrible sensation but by then the ground had been revamped and was unrecognisable from how it was on the day of the fire."

In March, 2015, Mickey suffered another major health scare when Brenda awoke at 4.00am to find him slumped on the floor of their lounge. "I'd been sitting in the armchair and then I suddenly collapsed with a pulmonary embolism," he recalls. "I actually 'died' for about nine minutes but

Brenda performed CPR on me and brought me back to life by the time the ambulance arrived, although I don't have any memory of what happened that night – I had a blank half-hour.

"When I got to hospital, I needed an injection to smash all the blood clots around my heart. I remained in intensive care for two weeks. Now I have to take 11 tablets a day, including four of warfarin, but the medical staff told me that I was a very lucky lad.

"I'd put on a lot of weight at the time. When they measured my weight on my last visit to the doctor (in Sept, 2018), I was 14st 9lbs . . . but when I collapsed three years ago I was up to 19 stones. Now I've cut out alcohol completely – I don't touch a drop – and I'm speed-walking for 20 minutes every morning.

Being able to cherish the many happy memories from his eight years with the Os has helped him to overcome such health scares and ease those painful psychological scars inflicted at Bradford, the West Yorkshire city where Mickey was touched by both triumph and tragedy 15 years apart.

"I still often wonder what might have been had I stayed at Orient," he mused. "It really used to give me a great boost when the fans chanted 'my song' (to the tune of The Beatles' 1968 hit *Hey Jude*):

Nah-nah-nah-nah
Nah-nah-nah-nah
Hey, Mickey Bullock

"Hearing those words made me feel emotional. My two kids were only young at the time but they still remember it too.

"At times our crowd would generate a great atmosphere, especially at the Boxing Day morning games. I mentioned the QPR game earlier and then there was the time when we beat Malcolm Allison's Crystal Palace 3-0 (1973). The fans were absolutely brilliant.

"My family and I remember my time at Orient with great affection. I can only say what a great club it was and how much of a privilege it was to spend eight years playing for them. And I consider myself lucky to have played at the time I did. The 70s was a special decade."

"After leaving Orient, I received quite a lot of letters from fans thanking me for my efforts. They were always brilliant for me. And when I went down for the supporters' club Star Man Dinner (2014), the reception I got that night just blew me away. It made me appreciate what we had and how lucky we were. There are not many clubs like Leyton Orient.

"My family and I remember my time at Orient with great affection. I can only say what a great club it was and how much of a privilege it was to spend eight years playing for them. And I consider myself lucky to have played at the time I did. The 70s was a special decade."

It was not until the autumn of 2014 that Mickey made his first return visit to Brisbane Road but he and Brenda have been back in E10 a couple of times since and in September 2018 – shortly before this book came out – the Bullocks kindly invited Dave Dodd and his wife Maureen up to stay the weekend, and all four were thrilled to watch Justin Edinburgh's new-look Leyton Orient hammer league leaders Harrogate Town 3-0 in their quest for promotion from the National League.

Humble, unassuming and approachable, Mickey Bullock very much enjoys meeting up with supporters who remember him fondly as one of the club's greatest ever strikers – statistically the most prolific marksman of the 70s decade and fifth in the overall top scorers' list – and 12th highest all-time appearance-maker.

Interview: Tony McDonald

AT THE RACES

To help them relax the day before the FA Cup sixth round tie against Arsenal in March, 1972, the Orient players headed for Lingfield Park racecourse. From left: Barrie Fairbrother, Ray Goddard, Dennis Rofe, Mickey Bullock, Barry Dyson, Terry Brisley, Ian Bowyer, Peter Allen and Phil Hoadley.

Boys' Own Barrie

Born: Hackney, London, December 30, 1950
Usual position: Forward/Right-winger   Orient Career: 1969-75
Orient Appearances: League 171/17, FA Cup 15, League Cup 7/1
Orient Goals: League 41, FA Cup 7, League Cup 2

IT will never be considered one of the finest goals ever scored at Brisbane Road, but Barrie Fairbrother's last minute Cup winner against Chelsea in 1972 is unsurpassed for sheer drama and the enduring feeling of exhilaration it still evokes in those of us lucky enough to have witnessed it.

Tom Walley controls a pass from Mickey Bullock on his chest and volleys a hopeful punt from the centre spot spreading panic in the Chelsea penalty box, where Os' forward Ian Bowyer gallops after the bouncing ball and nips in between hesitant goalkeeper Peter Bonetti and defender Ron Harris.

The ball rebounds off Bonetti and plops into the path of the onrushing Fairbrother, who calmly passes it over a sea of mud and sand into the net from six yards, beyond the despairing lunge of David Webb.

Phil Hoadley's rocket at the end of the first period had halved Chelsea's lead and given Os a glimmer of hope; Bullock made it 2-2 by capitalising on more indecision in the visitors' box. But Fairbrother provided the killer blow to knock the First Division aristocrats, a classy Chelsea side it has to be said, off their lofty perch and put Os into the quarter-finals.

As the number seven turned away and began sprinting at full pelt towards the West Stand, left arm raised in triumphant salute, the ground erupted into a cacophony of East End roars that would have been heard on the farthest pitch on Hackney Marshes.

There was only a minute or two of this typically pulsating English Cup tie left, barely time for Ray Goddard to pull off a stupendous save from a 20-yard John Hollins piledriver and for Webb – Blues' Cup-winning hero of 1970 – to somehow scoop a gold-plated sitter over the bar from six

His greatest Orient moment . . . Barrie after scoring the winner against Chelsea, Peter Allen and Ian Bowyer can't get near him while John Dempsey (5), Ron Harris (3) and Peter Bonetti can't quite believe what has just happened.

yards, before the final whistle sounded just as Goddard's goal-kick dropped into the arms of Fairbrother on the right-wing. He caught it with two hands on the run, like a cricketer patrolling the deep mid-wicket boundary, and proceeded to sprint across the halfway line towards the players' tunnel with the ball tucked under his right arm and a smile as wide as Stratford Broadway, while hundreds of jubilant Orient fans ruined their footwear by running onto the mud to congratulate their heroes in all-red.

There is a delightfully evocative black and white photo – it filled a spread in *Brisbane Road Memories* – of Barrie just ahead of the others players as the match officials wait by the touchline for him to lead everyone off the field.

Mercifully, because the BBC *Match of the Day* cameras were present to record the highlights of this epic encounter, we can all continue to re-live

The bearded wonder at the pre-season photo call in July, 1974.

the magical experience time and again thanks to the online video channel YouTube.

Not that Barrie needs to be reminded of this most special of all his 50 league and Cup goals for Orient. For the purpose of this interview, I phoned him at his home on Australia's Gold Coast, where he has lived since emigrating in 1977. There's no longer any trace of a Cockney accent but being 10,000-plus miles away can't stop him from reminiscing about his six seasons at Brisbane Road and the greatest day of his career.

"It was a good, old fashioned, end-to-end Cup tie in the mud and you could really feel the atmosphere building. When Tom Walley put the ball through, Ian Bowyer and Bonetti collided and the ball just dropped kindly for me to tap it in. You have to keep going all day just for that one chance. The roar that went up from the crowd was just incredible."

Barry, 18, is Orient hero

Orient 1 Mansfield 0

BARRY FAIRBROTHER, 18, who collected 110 goals with the youth side in two and a half seasons, made his debut in Orient's League team — and scored.

Fairbrother had shown some bright touches in the first half, but his big moment came four minutes after the interval.

FAIRBROTHER IS GREAT
Rotherham 0, Orient 0

Fairbrother fires Orient back to top

Stockport County 0   Orient 2

Running man puts the Oxford United defence under pressure in March, 1974, the first Sunday league game played at Brisbane Road.

"We took the Central Line tube from Leyton to Liverpool Street station, where we went to a bar for a quick drink before getting the overground to Harlow. While we were in there, a group of Chelsea fans came in and this young kid looked at me and said: 'You're the guy who scored that goal?'"

Barrie recalls a "scary" situation within seconds of scoring when a number of Chelsea fans came onto the pitch from that (Coronation Gardens) end, in a vain attempt to persuade referee Ray Tinkler to abandon the match.

"I was surrounded by young Chelsea lads aged about 14, 15, 16 – bovver boys in their big boots who were making all sorts of threats. I was just standing there waiting for the police to come on and get them off the pitch. It was a bit scary. And because it was on TV as well, I didn't want to create a scene by getting involved with the Chelsea fans.

"But as soon as they did get them all off, I think we only played for another minute before the final whistle went."

And what happened to the match ball? If Orient had a museum, it would be among prize exhibits. Or perhaps he has it encased and displayed somewhere at home? "I don't know what happened to the ball," Barrie says, disappointingly. "I passed it to the ref, as we are supposed to do, and it was probably put back into the kit room to be used next by the reserves, then passed down to the youth team and colts before finishing up as a training ball."

Barrie recalls that the Orient players knew a short while after beating Chelsea 3-2 that they would be facing another mouth-watering London derby in the sixth round.

"The country was having power cuts around that time, so instead of the FA doing the Cup draw as usual on the following Monday lunch-time, the quarter-final draw was done very soon after the Chelsea match. We were still in the dressing room, hadn't even got in the bath, when the news came through that we'd be meeting Arsenal at home."

Fairbrother revealed a bizarre and previously untold postscript to this most momentous of Orient occasions: "Because we'd been away all week down near Brighton for special training before the Chelsea game, I didn't have my car at the ground. So after the game, my wife Sian and I had to get home to Harlow by train.

"We took the Central Line tube from Leyton to Liverpool Street station, where we went to a bar (now called Hamilton Hall) for a quick drink before getting the overground to Harlow. While we were in there, a group of Chelsea fans came in and this young kid looked at me and said: 'You're the guy who scored that goal?'

"I said: 'Yeah'.

"So he said: 'You were lucky'. I wasn't going to argue with him, so I agreed: 'Yeah . . .'

"And then he added: 'Good game, though?'

"Again, I nodded politely, took the drinks back to the missus and said: 'Drink up, we're going'."

ORIENT have over many years picked up countless players who were overlooked or rejected by bigger London clubs. In Barrie's case, Tottenham Hotspur's loss was Os' gain.

He explained: "Although born in Hackney, I grew up in Harlow New Town, so Tottenham was regarded as our local team and Dad supported them.

"I'd only had a couple of training sessions with Spurs at their old Cheshunt training ground and played in one trial game. Then Dad got a phone call inviting me to go down to the Os, where I trained on Tuesday and Thursday nights. Len Cheesewright looked after all the schoolboy amateurs and put me in the youth team. Len was great.

"If I remember rightly, my first game for Orient Youth was against Chelsea and although we lost 4-2, I scored both goals, and that was it . . . I just kept my place and worked my way right through.

"There was another game, against Colchester, which we won 3-1. Again, I scored two goals and the next day Dad received a phone call from the club saying that they wanted to sign me as an apprentice professional.

"As I was in the process of leaving Burnt Mill Comprehensive School, I had to tell the headmaster what was happening. He tried to talk me out of taking up football as a career, saying it was 'dodgy and anything can happen', but a few years later he let his daughter marry Glenn Hoddle! Glenn and I went to the same school, although not at the same time – he's six or seven years younger than me."

As a teenager, Fairbrother earned a reputation as a pacy, prolific goalscorer. He netted more than 100 times for the youth and reserve teams before Jimmy Bloomfield awarded him his first team debut five matches into the 1969-70 promotion-winning season. It was against Mansfield Town at home on August 30 and 19-year-old Barrie scored the only goal.

"On the Friday, after training with the reserves, I was called into the boss's office. I thought, 'Oh Christ, what have I done wrong now?' Anyway, Jimmy just said: 'Mickey Bullock has rolled his ankle, so you're playing tomorrow'.

"The first-half was a bit of a blur, I just remember the pace of the game being so much faster than what I'd been used to. Then the ball went up and I chased after it. I stretched and got to it just before their keeper. I saw the ball hit the back of the net and everything went a bit blurry again . . . I think there must have been a few tears in my eyes."

A sad epitaph to Barrie's football highlights, his most famous match-winner that sank Chelsea

Sending Portsmouth defender, ex-Os Paul Went, the wrong way in April, 1974.

and the dream debut against Mansfield, was that his father Edward wasn't there to celebrate and share those special moments with the son whose career he had helped to shape and follow so closely.

"That was hard," Barrie admits. "Dad watched all my games up until when he passed away in about 1967. My mum (Hazel) was on holiday with my sister June in Yarmouth when I made my debut, so I couldn't let her know that I would be playing. They only found out I'd scored when they heard the classified football results and reports on the radio on the bus journey back from the coast. Apparently, Mum said: 'That's my boy!'."

Barrie's winning strike against Mansfield was his first 'Boy's Own stuff' experience. He kept his place for the rest of the season, missing only three matches and coming on as a sub in four others, while playing a key role in winning Division Three. After Bullock's tally of 19 league goals, Fairbrother (13) was the only other scorer in double figures.

For a forward who wasn't the biggest at 5ft 8ins, he had a tremendous zest for the game. Many of his goals were the result of honest endeavour and selfless running, both on and off the ball. This was best typified by his pursuit of the through-ball that preceded his classic FA Cup winner.

He would chase lost causes and turn nothing into something. Qualities appreciated by fellow strikers like Mickey Bullock, who profited from Barrie's lightning pace and willingness to chase everything.

"The first thing Tom would do when he came in was pick up the phone and call his mate at Newmarket stables. Trouble was, he always spoke Welsh, so none of us could understand what he was saying or which horses he was backing!"

I think Os' fan Michael Kasler summed up Barrie's football ethos perfectly in a Facebook post he made while a group of us were recently discussing the bearded wonder's merits and tireless contribution to the side. He wrote: "You have heard the expression 'ran his socks off'. Well, Barrie Fairbrother must have spent a fortune on socks. Forget his talent, he was worth his place for his work-rate alone."

But Fairbrother didn't just get plenty of goals, he scored important league goals that aren't remembered with the same affection as *that* one in the FA Cup in '72. Consider the facts: when Os finally topped Division Three, just two points clear of Luton Town, he'd bagged four winners. In addition to his Mansfield debut strike, he scored the only goals in three vital away victories – at Gillingham, Stockport County, where he netted twice, and Bury. He was also on target in consecutive wins by the odd goal against Bradford City (home) and Barnsley (away). We won every game in which he scored in 1969-70.

"I played my best football under Jimmy Bloomfield, because he allowed me to play up front with Mickey Bullock, our big striker, and it worked really well. Jimmy kept me in the side until the final game of the season, when he left me out purely because he wanted Dave Harper to play his final game before his intended retirement (Harper actually started the first game of the 1970-71 season but his chronic knee problem ended his career).

"I had to stand down for Dave that night but Jimmy took me aside beforehand to explain the situation to me and I fully understood his reasoning. Jimmy was the type of guy you could approach and chat to.

"When I first joined the club as an apprentice, I had more to do with Jimmy's assistant, Peter Angell. He became like a father figure to me, he was such a nice guy. The biggest thing he gave me was encouragement. He was the go-to guy. I remember Peter taking charge of the reserve team one day and everyone gave 100 percent because they respected him so much."

Barrie is undoubtedly one of the best young, local discoveries the club has ever produced and he was big mates with another in Terry Brisley.

"I moved out to Braintree in Essex and Terry lived quite near me, so we used to drive to training together each morning. And when the team played away, our wives would stay together. Terry, Peter Allen, Ray Goddard and myself made up a group of four friends."

Barrie was asked to shine a light on the different friendly cliques that inevitably exist in almost every football dressing room.

"The gambling group was led by Tom Walley. Obviously, no mobiles in those days but we had a phone in the dressing room at the ground and the first thing Tom would do when he came in was pick up the phone and call his mate at Newmarket stables. Trouble was, he always spoke Welsh, so none of us could understand what he was saying or which horses he was backing that day! Mickey Bullock and Ian Bowyer also liked to have a bet.

"I was in the group who enjoyed a drink. I think we all did – Phil Hoadley could certainly knock a few back. Perhaps the only exception was 'Queenie' – Gerry Queen. He was always there with us but, being Scottish, he didn't want to buy a round!

"Then we had the Crystal Palace group, who all knew each other from their previous club, that George Petchey brought in. They seemed to get a little bit more favouritism, which upset the camp a little bit. Those lads did join in with the rest of us but you could tell that George actually favoured them.

"When I had my problems with the manager and was trying to get away, I was only on half the money the Palace boys were getting. The guys who came up through the ranks, like Terry Brisley and myself, were on a poor deal really. Over time, you found out what others were earning and you feel a bit aggrieved.

"The most I ever earned at Orient was a basic of £30 per week. although we did get extra appearance and win money, etc. There was a sliding scale where pay was based on our points tally, so in the season where we nearly went up we all did quite well.

"The average working wage at that time was £20 per week, so I was doing all right. Then again, a footballer's career is only short."

Barrie is congratulated after scoring in the 1-1 draw with Notts County in the penultimate home game of the oh-so-close season. Derrick Downing and David Payne embrace in front of the West Stand while Phil Hoadley (5), Terry Brisley, Gerry Queen (10) and Peter Allen are the other Os in view.

BARRIE enjoyed playing at a time when, although many teams used physical intimidation to try and suppress more creative opponents, players would still occasionally see the funny side of the game and didn't always take themselves as seriously as modern players appear to. When was the last time you saw a player from a Premier League or Championship club enjoy a laugh and a joke with a rival during an important game? Barrie recalls an incident from his playing days that encapsulates the era.

"It was a home game against Sunderland the season after they had won the FA Cup (Jan, 1974). You remember how our pitch used to be just a mudbath? Anyway, the ball came through and I went after it. At the same time, the Sunderland keeper Jim Montgomery came rushing out and as I went to knock the ball past him, we both slipped. I just about connected with the ball, which then hit him on the hip, popped up in the air and landed about two feet from the goal-line. It just about rolled over the line for a goal.

"As our fans celebrated the goal, we were both sitting there in the mud, looking at each other and smiling. But the thing was, a photographer just happened to capture the moment when Jim and I smiled at each other and on the Monday morning his photo was published on Page 3 of *The Sun* newspaper – it was what they called 'Smile Week', so they had used this picture of Jim and me covered in mud and smiling. My son Samuel came home and said: 'Look, Dad, you've kept the topless girls off Page 3!'.

"There were a lot more characters around in the game back then," Barry agrees, before sharing a few tales about a few of them whose personalities livened up the Orient dressing room.

"I was sub at Birmingham one bitterly cold day (Nov, 1970) and Peter Brabrook didn't fancy playing. I was sub when, only about a minute or so into the game, Peter went on a run and then stopped sharply. He looked over to Jimmy Bloomfield and Peter Angell and said: 'I've pulled a Jane', which was Cockney rhyming slang . . . as in (American film actress) Jane Russell equals muscle. So the boss told me to get warmed up, I was going on

"At half-time, we came back in the dressing room, freezing cold and covered in mud, and there was Peter sitting in a lovely hot bath. There was nothing wrong with him, he just didn't want to play!

"Terry Mancini was another character. You had to be careful what you wore and make sure your clothes looked good – you couldn't go in the dressing room with holes in your socks or a button missing off your shirt, otherwise he'd notice it and not let you forget it.

"We used to wear flared trousers, big collars on our shirts and kipper ties. I liked wearing a grey, three-piece, hand-made suit.

"I remember one year the club arranged for a tailor to come in and measure us up at the end of the season. The problem was, by the time he came back to do the fitting, we'd done four weeks of intense pre-season training, built up muscles and put on a bit of weight, so not one suit fitted. There he was, this poor little fella, ripping sleeves off jackets and having to re-make them to different sizes!

"The flares on Laurie Cunningham's trousers were about three foot wide. Now there was a snappy dresser."

AFTER a brilliant debut season, the goals dried up for Barrie in his second season – only two in 31 Second Division starts – and he became even more marginalised once George Petchey succeeded Bloomfield in the summer of 1971.

What is easily overlooked is that even during the season in which he reached the pinnacle with his sensational Cup winner, he featured in less than half – just 17 starts – in the 1971-72 league campaign and didn't score at all.

Barrie admits: "George Petchey didn't rate me. I'd had a great partnership up front with Mickey Bullock – he was the big guy who held the ball up and would lay it off, and I was quicker and could play off him. But Petchey kept changing formation and wanted me to play out wide and track back. Basically, to be an extra full-back."

The fans were never slow to let the manager know their views by chanting 'We Want Barrie!' as Orient struggled to create chances.

His goal return improved considerably in 1972-73, when he notched 11 from 24 starts, before his most productive spell, goals-wise, when he regained a regular place in 1973-74. He was slow to get off the mark but when he and midfielder Ricky Heppolette scored in the 2-1 home win against Nottingham Forest on October 13, the goals started flowing again for Fairbrother, who found the net 11 times in a sizzling hot spell of 13 matches stretching to Boxing Day.

As well as the soft winner against Sunderland, he also scored the only Orient goals in 1-1 draws at home to Millwall and Notts County late on in the season when the wins dried up.

The interchangeable movement between main striker Mickey Bullock (16 goals), Barrie (14) and Gerry Queen (12), who amassed 42 league goals between them, confused opposing defences but it still wasn't quite enough in their quest for promotion.

"We all felt very low afterwards. At three o'clock in the morning there was still a few of us sitting up in the directors' box in a daze. A bottle of champagne remained unopened."

Recalling the drawn final game with Aston Villa at Brisbane Road, Barrie says: "We didn't perform that night. There was so much riding on it and we didn't start playing until about 10 minutes from the end. Nothing went right for us.

"Naturally, we all felt very low afterwards. At three o'clock in the morning there was still a few of us sitting up in the directors' box in a daze. A bottle of champagne remained unopened.

"We played on the Friday night and I remember getting home at about six o'clock in the morning, feeling depressed. The FA Cup Final (Liverpool 3 Newcastle United 0) was played later that day but I didn't really take it in."

Some small consolation to Barry is that Os' supporters named him as their Player of the Year for 1973-74. Apart from the fact that he was a local lad made good, his relentless effort and commitment earned him crowd favouritism throughout his Orient career.

"The club had actually paid for the players and wives to go on holiday to Sardinia, so Tom Walley and myself were the only two players present at the awards dinner in London. I'd stayed behind to see my sister off to New Zealand but Sian and I joined up with the others in Sardinia the following week.

"I still have the Player of the Season trophy here in my study – it means a lot to me.

"Right from my first game I always tried to give 100 percent and I think the fans appreciated that. I had a great rapport with them. I just didn't want to let them down."

The trademark long hair and beard – he was the first in the team to sport the hirsute look – endeared him to male and female supporters alike, although there were odd occasions when it rebounded on him. "I remember once going down after a heavy challenge from a keeper who stuck his knee in my ribs. I was down on the ground writhing in pain and then I heard a guy – an Orient fan – in the crowd shout: 'Get up, you poofter!' It was all good fun.

"The fans had a great song for Mickey Bullock but because my name was so long, they couldn't come up with one for me."

IF ever there was a case of after the Lord Mayor's show, then Orient's 1974-75 season was definitely it. The exciting promise of Laurie Cunningham helped to lift the gloom but the team slipped eight places down the table and Barrie, with just one goal from 23 starts and three sub outings, knew his Brisbane Road days were numbered. If anything, Cunningham's sudden emergence on the wing only hastened his departure.

"It was hard the following season after just missing out on promotion by a point," he admits. "George Petchey wanted to play a 4-3-3 system but he had the two wide guys – Derrick Downing and me – pulled right back, really to help out the defence. I remember him having a go at me once because I was 10 yards behind the ball – I just couldn't get there from full-back.

"The system also isolated Mickey. He was great at laying the ball off but he had no-one to lay it off to.

"George was always trying different tactics. He'd go from a 4-3-3 to 4-4-2 to 4-2-4. Basically, I didn't fit into his plan and I wasn't enjoying it anymore. The games became really hard because all I was doing was running, running, running."

With the 1973-74 Player of the Year award at the Europe Hotel, Park Lane. Barrie still has the trophy at his home in Australia.

The last of Barrie's 193 first team appearances came on February 22, 1975, when he went off (Dean Mooney came on for his league debut) reportedly nursing a groin strain in the 1-0 home win over Bristol Rovers. Fairbrother saw out the rest of the season in the reserves, playing Midweek League football in front of a few hundred diehards. How quickly things can change in this game. A year earlier, his 14 goals had nearly catapulted Os into the Promised Land and he was voted the fans' best player.

In the summer of '75 he and his friend Terry Brisley were destined for Millwall, who had just been relegated out of Orient's division, in an exchange deal that brought Doug Allder – probably the least popular of all Petchey's signings – the other way.

Barry says: "When George wanted me to go to Millwall, I didn't want to leave but I could see the writing on the wall.

"Chairman Brian Winston, whom I liked and respected because he wanted to take Orient forward as a club, came to my house in Braintree – I remember his Bentley filling my driveway – and explained the situation to me, face to face. He said that although he didn't want me to go, the club had to back its manager. I understood and respected what he meant. That's business. The next day I went over to Millwall and signed.

"Brian was very good and well liked by the players. He was really involved. He used to leave us little gifts. Because he ran a chain of airport gift shops, we would come in before a game and find things like a bottle of perfume – a present for the wife – waiting for us by our kit.

"I also have fond memories of Harry Zussman. I was an apprentice when they held that famous Sunday meeting at the ground when the club had to pass the bucket round so that fans could donate money to help keep Orient going. I was only on £8 a week but despite all the financial struggles the club was going through at the time, my money was always in the bank – never any problem.

"Harry did more than anyone to keep the club alive. After away games, he was always first in the dressing room to buy the boys a drink and hand out his big cigars. I reckon he was Orient's number one supporter.

"I didn't have so much to do with Arthur Page, the chairman before Brian Winston. He was more aloof than Harry. It was always 'Mr Page' and you had to mind your Ps and Qs with him, whereas you could have a bit of a laugh with Harry and Brian.

"But I look back and think, 'didn't we have some good players?'. You go back to Tommy Taylor and Dennis Rofe, then around the time I left we had Paddy Grealish and Laurie Cunningham coming through."

The move to Millwall was doomed more or less from the start. In only his second game, Barrie turned sharply and caused the tendon to come away from his hip joint. "I had two operations and missed the whole season. I came back the following season but I'd lost a bit of speed, so that injury more or less finished my career in England."

But Orient hadn't quite seen the last of one of its most celebrated former heroes. In October, 1976 Barry scored in Millwall's 3-0 League Cup, third round, second replay victory against Os at Arsenal's Highbury Stadium.

Fairbrother recalls the contrasts he experienced playing in the hostile Lions' den. "I was playing there for Orient and went in for a tackle with Millwall full-back David Donaldson. His foot caught my studs and as he went down injured, the abuse aimed at me came raining down from the terraces. As I walked off at the end where they had the cage to stop their fans getting at the players, they were spitting at me.

"Of course, two years later, I was playing for them. I remember before a home game against Chelsea where the two rival groups of fans met on the halfway line – two hours before kick-off – and fought running battles. There were bodies strewn everywhere, with medics coming on to treat the injured. It was absolute madness.

"Although I was now playing for Millwall, their fans – mostly dockers or dockers' sons – still scared me!"

While Britain basked in endless days of sunshine and the hottest temperatures recorded in more than 350 years, Barrie spent a few weeks in mid-1976 considering options that would take him to even sunnier climes. Among five clubs who wanted him were Pietermaritzburg, near Durban, in South Africa, where he'd played previously in the English close season for them and Durban Celtic.

He was also offered short-term contracts to play in the USA, Belgium and France but the one that appealed most was the two-year deal from a successful Australian club called Mooroolbark United, based on the eastern outskirts of Melbourne in the state of Victoria, who rose rapidly through the leagues and are officially recognised as the first members of the Australian Soccer League formed in 1977.

"Forty years ago, I thought I'll never get to Australia, the other side of the world, but I thought I'd take it and two weeks later we were on a plane," Barrie recalls of that life-changing decision.

WHERE Barrie lives now and the idyllic lifestyle he leads couldn't be further removed from the hustle and bustle of London. Now retired, he lives happily alone in a house at Forest Lake, about 20 kms from Brisbane city centre and an hour's drive from the Sunshine Coast.

His son Sam, daughter Rhiannon and her son – Barrie's grandson – Emlyn live close by, while brother Bob is only 10kms away. Although now divorced from Sian, Barrie says the couple remain "good mates".

By quirk, the number seven has also remained a constant in his life. "I arrived in Australia on the 7th day of the 7th month in 1977 and my daughter was born at seven minutes past seven o'clock.

"I returned to England three times in my first 10 years in Australia but I've not been back there for 31 years until this year (2018).

Reflecting on his life Down Under over the past four decades and more, he says: "After about half a dozen games for Mooroolbark I was asked if I wanted to play for Australia. I didn't because it would have meant becoming an Australian citizen and, to my mind, I was going back to England after two years – I didn't really settle much in those early days here. But after about six months we transferred up to Brisbane . . . from Brisbane Road to Brisbane, eh!" he laughed.

"We got into a good crowd up here, the Queensland weather is lovely and after four years we decided to stay. I originally came over on a sportsman's visa but got a job as a sales rep, selling stationery supplies, and my boss sponsored me. I became an Australia citizen on January 8, 1981, although I have dual nationality.

"I worked my way up to sales manager and then joined another company, as a part-owner, importing fine art materials. We sold that in '87, when I got into real estate, specialising in investment property by selling houses and units that took advantage of tax breaks. I ran my own company, Hooker Investor, until retiring two years ago.

"I might live here because the weather's nice but I'm still English through and through – a Pommie. As well as what is happening in football, I always keep a close eye on the England cricket scores. From the time I arrived, we didn't beat Australia in an Ashes series played here for many years and it was an absolute nightmare.

"I regularly visited The Gabba to watch Test matches. I was there one day when Bob Willis had Australia at about 29 or something for 6 by lunch. Cor, did the Aussie fans give their team some stick that day! I just sat there with a smile on my face. I wasn't going to say anything – I might have had a can thrown at me!"

Barrie explained that an old football injury came back to haunt him. "They told me when I got injured playing for Millwall that in 40 years' time I would have hip problems. Well, as soon as I get back from my (2018) trip to America, Europe and Asia, I'll be having hip replacement surgery.

"Before the hip started playing me up again, I used to keep fit by cycling about 180kms a week. But since I stopped riding three months ago, I've put on about 10 or 11 kilos.

"What I have lost, though, is my hair – I'm bald now!"

Beating a Derby County defender to the ball in the FA Cup tie in January, 1975.

EVEN from such a distance, Barrie has kept a watchful eye on events at Leyton Orient and was dismayed by the rapid decline since 2014.

"Every Monday I log on to the internet and read the match reports and see what's going on and it was unbelievable. I felt for the whole club. When I was there Orient was one happy family . . . all the backroom people, like Alice the tea lady, who made you a drink when you arrived for a game, and Jack and Charlie, the old groundsmen. Mrs Lewis, who washed the kit . . . we were a big family.

Barrie lets fly against Millwall in January, 1975, one of his last games in a red shirt before joining the Lions in the summer.

"To see from afar what happened to the club after going so close to promotion to the Championship was criminal. The Football League should have stepped in and taken it away from the owner (Francesco Becchetti)," he said without concealing his annoyance.

When Barrie returned to Leyton in September, 2018 to watch Os play Sutton United, it was no surprise that he received such a warm, affectionate East End welcome from many who idolised him and his team-mates some 40-to-50 years earlier. Supporters Bryan E. Goulding and Anthony Ruffy commented on Facebook just prior to his return: "Barrie is my favourite Orient player of all-time."

I caught up with him after the game in the Supporters' Club bar, where footage of his FA Cup goal had earlier been replayed on screens countless times and he was besieged non-stop by well-wishers wanting autographs and selfies. He obliged them all wholeheartedly with a smile and kind words even though he was supported by crutches and must have felt in some discomfort due to his hip.

'What do you reckon to that pitch, then?' I ventured. "That's not a pitch, it's a carpet," he grinned.

After a whirlwind three-week tour that began with a helicopter ride over America's Grand Canyon, then took in a trip to Las Vegas, a school reunion in Harlow, a catch-up with his sister in Hastings, then over to Russia for some sightseeing in St Petersburg, followed by a ride on the bullet train to Moscow and five days in Bangkok, Thailand, the first email he sent on his return home was to David Dodd, chairman of LOSC. It read:

I wanted to thank you for organising such a special day back at the Os. It was the highlight of my trip. The reception I received when I went on to the pitch was overwhelming and I must admit I had tears in my eyes. Please thank everyone for making it such a special day. I can't thank you enough.

With my very best regards and best of luck to the Os!
Barrie Fairbrother
The pleasure was all ours, Barrie.
Interview: Tony McDonald

Mr Professional

Born: Hove, Sussex, November 1, 1946
Usual position: Midfield Orient Career: 1965-78
Orient Appearances: League 424/8, FA Cup 25, League Cup 24
Orient Goals: League 27, FA Cup 1, League Cup 1

GOAL

PETER ALLEN Orient

GOAL magazine gave Peter the full-page treatment.

MARCH 13, 1976 was a landmark day in the career of Peter Allen who set an Orient club record for most League appearances when he led the team out against Sunderland, thus breaking the previous figure of 373 by goalkeeper Arthur Wood that had stood for almost 45 years.

By the time he left the Os in 1978, Peter had advanced the total to 424 (plus eight as sub) matches spanning 13 seasons. And when you include FA and League Cup ties, his staggering haul soars to 481 (that's without nine Anglo-Scottish Cup outings) – a remarkable achievement by a superb professional and loyal servant that will surely never be emulated.

Allen's record looked under potential threat until the departure of Matt Lockwood to Nottingham Forest in 2007, after the left-back had played 328 league games, but Peter's proud milestone remains unsurpassed.

"When you're playing, you don't really think about things like that," he said. "From time to time it would be mentioned that a certain record had been achieved, such as when I made 100 consecutive league appearances – I was given the match ball afterwards.

"I never thought about a record number of appearances but it's something I'm delighted to have recorded."

A cultured player, who combined skill and awareness with a combative attitude, Allen joined Orient from Tottenham Hotspur, where he had been on associated schoolboy terms and was perhaps a little awestruck being surrounded by half-back greats such as Danny Blanchflower and Dave Mackay.

He was an outstanding academic but managed to combine studies with football to ultimately forge successful careers in both fields, having become a solicitor since retiring from the game. However, let's rewind to those early days of his first profession, when he first wore Leyton Orient blue before we turned red.

"Rather than leave school at 15, I was persuaded by my parents to stay on until I was 18 and I've not regretted it. When you are 15, you just want to play but I didn't have a problem with continuing my education," said Peter, who achieved three 'A' levels and seven 'O' levels at Hove Grammar School.

Allen was still at school when Leyton Orient manager Dave Sexton persuaded him to try his luck in football rather than pursue a course at University. After a short period playing as an amateur, Peter opted to take up the offer of a professional contract.

"I was only 18 when I came to Orient and didn't really worry about what was happening off the pitch. I was a young lad who was enjoying the opportunity to be with a professional club," he reflected. "One positive aspect of joining Orient was that they could offer young players like myself opportunities to play first team football at an earlier age than would have been expected elsewhere. I had only played schoolboy and youth football, so to be playing league football was an exciting experience and although we went down from the Second Division, the standard of football was good."

Allen made his league debut in a 4-1 defeat at Portsmouth on September 25, 1965, three days after his senior bow in a home 3-0 League Cup loss to Coventry City.

Peter recalled a chastening experience after his home debut: "There I was, a very green and innocent recruit to the ranks of professional football, feeling on top of the world at making what I felt was a fairly successful debut, when a long-time fan began to talk to me.

"Not knowing me from Adam, he ran the team down terribly as I nodded and shook my head in all the appropriate places but it was not long before he got round to Peter Allen. Needless to say, I took more than my fair share of stick, he wondered what I was even doing at the club, and I left the ground that evening feeling rather disillusioned."

After a disastrous start and lack of transfer funds, Sexton resigned after just a year in charge and the team was relegated at the end of the season.

"Dave Sexton signed me but he left in December, 1965 and then we had Les Gore (caretaker) for a brief time, Dick Graham, Jimmy Bloomfield and George Petchey," Peter continued.

"I learned a lot from so many people and Dave was certainly one person that had an influence on me, yet I don't think I appreciated how much he knew until he'd gone.

"Of the players that I initially worked with at Orient, Malcolm Musgrove and John Smith guided me. Malcolm was the players' union rep and after I'd been at the club about a month he asked me if I'd received the usual £25 signing-on fee. When I said 'no' he went to try and sort it out for me. But then he came back and said that this club rule had just been changed before I signed! My basic weekly wage was £18 during the season and £14 in the summer months. From memory, according to my first contract, I think I got £25 for playing in the first team, plus £5 win bonus or £2 for a

A photo of some of the lovely Orient WAGS of 1973-74 that sums up the family spirit at Orient during this special era. From left: Patricia Queen, Karen Payne, Jill Allen, Sian Fairbrother, Cathrine Jackson, Lynn Goddard, Mandy Hoadley and Jill Brisley. When Lynn and Ray Goddard were married in June, '74, Sian Fairbrother and Jill Brisley were bridesmaids.

draw. When Dick Graham came my first team wage increased to £30.

"Someone once said to me that you don't understand the game until you can't run anymore. Some of the older players that were in the Orient side at the start of my time there didn't have the legs to run everywhere, so they would talk you through the game and let you do *their* running."

At the start of his time at Brisbane Road, Peter was considered more as an attacking player but his powerful tackling prowess and defensive qualities saw him soon converted to a ball-winning and constructive midfielder role, although he did make a number of appearances at full-back and even in the heart of defence on one occasion.

Bloomfield was appointed player-manager in March, 1968 and the man he immediately replaced was . . . Peter Allen. Bloomfield, an inside-forward, subbed himself on for Allen on his debut at Gillingham and then replaced him from the start of the next five matches before injury to Roy Massey saw Allen briefly recalled to the side.

It was an unsettling period for Allen, who admitted in an exclusive (previously unpublished) 1996 interview with long-time Os' fan Martin Smith: "People have different views. Jimmy and I never really hit it off. I was the first player to be dropped when he came – we were competing for the same position – and in fact he was the first manager I had a really serious disagreement with."

Peter explodes any mythical romantic notions that he and Orient were wedded in holy matrimony when he reveals: "I put in a transfer request because I thought my days at Orient were numbered. And did so again later on when Jimmy was also in charge. I don't think I was his sort of player.

"But one of Jimmy's strengths was that he was good with the press and handling that side of management."

Bloomfield must have changed his view of Allen, or how he wanted to construct his team, because after being left out of the first two games of the 1968-69 campaign, the fearless grafter hardly missed another over the next seven seasons until injury intervened. With Bloomfield having quit playing to focus fully on management, Allen started all 46 games of the 1969-70 Division Three title-winning season.

His impeccable disciplinary record remained unblemished even though he was actually sent off (along with Walsall's Mick Evans) a minute from the end of Os' 2-0 defeat at Fellows Park as the championship chase suffered a temporary setback. But it was such a poor decision by the referee that the Football League took no action against Orient's left-half.

Even so, Allen remained unsettled under Bloomfield. He sought a move in the summer weeks prior to Os resuming in Division Two and was transfer listed again at his own request – Bloomfield citing "personal reasons" – after Os had been knocked out of the FA Cup by Nottingham Forest in February, 1971. Local newspaper reporter Vince Wright, valuing Peter at around the £50,000 mark, wrote: "It is ironical that Allen's transfer request should come at a time when the fans are at last appreciating his sophisticated brand of football."

After the home win over Swindon on February 13, reporter Bernard Josephs wrote that scouts from Chelsea – managed by Dave Sexton – were at the game eyeing up Allen's midfield talents. He quoted Orient chairman Arthur Page: "Naturally, we will be sorry to see Peter go, and we can only do so for a high enough cash return to enable us to strengthen our side still further."

Later, there was talk of a strong bid from Everton but Merseyside must have seemed a world away from his permanent base on the Sussex coast.

When checking back through the press cuttings and reading of these repeated transfer requests and speculation about an impending move, it makes Allen's place in Orient folklore all the more remarkable.

But to his great credit, he put any thoughts of getting away from Bloomfield aside once the games were underway. With doubts about his future still swirling all around him, Allen popped up with what proved to be a vital winner at Millwall.

"We had some characters in the side around that time, none more so than Peter Brabrook and Mark Lazarus who would make you laugh on and off the field," recalls Peter. "If Mark didn't like someone, he'd just hit them, knowing he'd probably get away with a booking.

"Peter had played for England and was a wonderful player, while Mark added that bit of aggression that perhaps we didn't have before he came back to the club. Terry Mancini had just arrived back from South Africa and the way we played suited him down to the ground. If any high balls came into our box, he headed them away."

IT is no secret that Peter played his best football and enjoyed his happiest times under George Petchey, who replaced Leicester City-bound Bloomfield in the summer of 1971.

"George was the biggest influence on my career because he wanted us to play the style of football that I wanted to play and he knew a huge amount about the game," Peter says.

"I remember a couple of matches at Fulham that had two very different outcomes. We went to Craven Cottage under Jimmy and they slaughtered us. It was a chaotic performance, no-one seemed to know what they were doing but we somehow managed to get a goal and win. To read the press reports afterwards you'd have thought we were an attack-minded side who had played exceptionally well and it was all part of some master plan.

"Then we played at Fulham under George and although we played them off the park, I think we were well and truly stuffed. But we'd played the right way and lost to some cracking goals that we could do nothing about.

"What this showed was that perhaps George suffered a bit because he didn't always get his thoughts across to the press as well as Jimmy did.

"George made Orient a good, family club and deserves a lot of credit for the way he brought through a very talented group of youngsters – Laurie Cunningham, Tony Grealish, Glenn Roeder and Nigel Gray – and if they had stayed together the club could have really taken off."

Allen netted 27 league goals for Os and one that gave him particular satisfaction was the one that killed off Leicester in the FA Cup fourth round in February, 1972. Ian Bowyer gave Os a shock 32nd minute lead after controlling a pass from Allen – "It was a cracking goal, he definitely meant it," recalls Peter.

The visitors rubbed Leicester noses in the Filbert Street mud – home from home for the visitors who were used to the Brisbane Road pudding – in the 64th minute, when Allen embarrassed Foxes' 17-year-old debutant keeper Carl Jayes, deputising for the

Programme cover for Peter's testimonial match against West Ham that attracted a crowd of 7,500. The game ended goalless but Orient reported that the gate revenue boosted the skipper's testimonial fund by £4,000.

injured Peter Shilton.

One or two tabloid pressmen lost all perspective by describing Jayes' error as "a tragedy", while reporter Kevin Moseley, who awarded Allen a mark of nine out of 10, praised the Orient engine room: "Allen and (Tom) Walley were giants in midfield." Pat Gibson added: "With Barry Dyson snapping at their heels, Keith Weller and Jon Sammels were never in the game and Peter Allen and Tom Walley were in emphatic control of the middle."

"My goal was a cross-cum-shot," Peter acknowledged. "Their young keeper didn't know whether to come off his line or stay but did neither and ended up fumbling the ball into the net.

"Leicester were a good First Division side, managed by Jimmy Bloomfield, so it was a sweet victory for me, because I didn't think he did me any favours at the Orient."

The most extensive report of the 2-0 victory at Leicester was penned by Brian Glanville in the following Monday's *Daily Telegraph*. He observed how much Allen had blossomed under Petchey and quoted them both. "When I came here," said Petchey, "he was just an ordinary marker, he just wanted to mark people. I rucked him up and down hill to run square and get the ball."

Allen responded: "Before, I'd have thought always to give it to somebody and support them, and George keeps pushing me to give it to someone and go again, rather than drop back. It seems to be easier. We went from one manager who more or less said 'go out and play', to George, who gets the side very well organised. It's a big jump."

Asked to select one outstanding recollection from his Os' career, Allen responded without hesitation: "Beating Chelsea in the FA Cup in 1972 is the favourite memory of my time at Orient," he declared.

"They had won the European Cup Winners' Cup the previous season and had so many wonderful players. I was still quite young and I just thought, 'That was good' and you'd just go out and play the next week and get on with your game. I wish now that we'd had time to sit down as a team and enjoy those wonderful moments. I look back and probably savour them more now recalling that we had beaten a calibre side that included such gifted players as Peter Osgood, Alan Hudson, Charlie Cooke and Peter Houseman.

"If I remember correctly, we went into the players' bar at the club, the champagne was cracked open, we had a few drinks and then I got on the train back to Brighton – and that was it. I don't remember sitting down and thinking what a wonderful achievement it was, it all seems a bit of a blur now. The following day we started looking towards the next game but that Chelsea game is probably the highlight of my career."

On the day he set a new club league appearance record, Peter drives forward into the Sunderland penalty area.

Os were handed another plum draw when they came out of the hat alongside Arsenal. "We had played well against Chelsea, so we thought that if we could beat them, we could beat anybody. We went into the game full of confidence," Peter continued.

"But Arsenal's 'lucky' tag saved them that day. I had a shot that hit the post and Tom Walley and Barry Dyson also struck the woodwork. And just before Alan Ball scored their winner, I'm sure there was a foul (by Ray Kennedy on Ray Goddard) that should have been awarded against us. We were robbed."

The Sun reporter Ken Montgomery agreed when he added: "It was a pity that players like Dennis Rofe, Peter Bennett, Peter Allen and Barry Dyson will not be allowed to parade their talents under the spotlight of an FA Cup semi-final. They matched anything their opposite numbers in the Arsenal side achieved."

But Jeff Powell, a self-confessed Orient supporter from his early days as a rookie hack on the *Walthamstow Guardian,* cleared Kennedy and referee Bill Matthewson of any wrongdoing in allowing Ball's controversial 49th minute winner when he filed his report for the *Daily Mail.* He said that Ray Goddard "carried the can" for not making a "stronger challenge or crisp punch" to clear Charlie George's header that fell at Ball's white boots. Powell, fully aware of Os' perilous financial state in the late 60s, also made the valid point that the only goal of the game had denied Orient a share of the Highbury replay gate with an estimated worth of "£12,000".

Back down to earth, in Orient's next home game Allen sliced a soft winner against Portsmouth to ease relegation fears.

WHILE Peter enjoyed many good times with Orient, there was a particular moment of discontent that still lingers long in the mind – after more than 40 years.

"The most disappointing moment was missing out on promotion at the end of the 1973-74 season when we needed to beat Aston Villa to go into the First Division," he admitted. "The 1-1 draw settled our fate and I think all the players in our dressing room were in tears afterwards.

"I usually trained very hard in pre-season but, because I had a calf injury, I did less work and therefore went into the season feeling more refreshed.

"The whole side had been flying up until Christmas, we were playing out of our skins, and we had a terrific team spirit. The players mixed very well socially and our wives all got on well too."

Allen reflects that his personal contribution to the promotion bid was severely hampered by a bad injury to his left ankle suffered in an over-the-top tackle in the 2-0 New Year's Day victory at Bristol City.

"I thought I'd broken my leg," he said. "They put me on the stretcher and strapped my legs together. Funnily enough, I remember the medical people didn't position me well because my head was left dangling over one end of the stretcher as they carried me off the field and it felt very uncomfortable!

"I really ought to have stopped playing at that point. I was out for about six weeks and when I did come back into the side, I was having pain-killing injections and played with my ankle strapped up.

"We didn't seem to get much luck in the latter part of the season," he added, before recalling a horror moment that denied Os a priceless victory in their penultimate home drawn league match against Notts County. "There was nothing we could do about Don Masson's 30-yard shot that hit Terry Brisley and looped over Ray Goddard into the top corner of the net.

"Ray was my best friend at the club at that stage – we socialised together and shared hotel rooms on away trips – and everything was going well until John Jackson – who was probably a better keeper than Ray and went on to give the club great service – was introduced in the wrong way and at the wrong time by an otherwise good manager. Ray was a very nice chap and he probably didn't get the best of treatment from Orient but that happens at football clubs and it's a fact of life in general.

"Towards the end of the season we had a perfectly good goal against Millwall disallowed. The ball came back off the bar, Barrie Fairbrother headed it in but Terry Brisley was given offside . . . even though he had been pushed into the back of the net and was clearly not interfering with play. Frank Saul, who I think had the same thing happen to him, reminded the referee of it and so he ruled out the goal and we drew 1-1 again.

"Also, I don't think it helped that we needed three matches to settle an FA Cup (fourth round) tie with Portsmouth, which possibly affected us.

"We missed out on promotion by one point in the end and you do look back at individual matches and incidents that had an effect on the final outcome. The nearly season . . . it just wasn't to be."

AFTER undergoing an ankle operation performed by the club's consultant surgeon Mr A. Lettin in the summer of '74, Allen missed the first six league games of the following season, when his tally of 32 appearances was his lowest in a decade with the Os. He admits that he was never quite the same player after the ankle problem.

But worse was to follow. A knee injury one game into the 1975-76 campaign restricted him to just seven senior appearances in a season that should have been cause for personal celebration. Because he'd begun a long period of rehabilitation when the club staged his richly deserved testimonial match against FA Cup holders West Ham United on Monday, October 27.

In his programme notes, George Petchey paid a fulsome tribute to his absent skipper: "A player who stays at a Football League club for 10 years has to have several exceptional qualities. A certain standard of ability, professional value to that club, loyalty, being able to adapt to most positions on the field, particularly when a club cannot afford a big staff and especially when they have injuries. He has to be a good person, a good advert for the club and conscientious in his thinking as a professional. We are lucky because we have one such player who fits all the above qualities and you (the supporters) are lucky to have seen his ability and loyalty for the past 10 years."

Allen appreciated the kind words of not only his manager, but numerous others who rallied round at a difficult time. He said: "My testimonial season showed me just how many friends I had. I was struggling with a bad knee injury at the time – I'm a bit of a fatalist; I believe you have seven good years and seven bad years and I was just starting the bad years. But so many supporters and people directly involved with the club helped make the testimonial a success."

He did recover to make 29 starts the following term but the sudden dismissal of Petchey just days into the 1977-78 season, which precipitated Bloomfield's return as boss, only hastened Allen's departure. He started only 18 league games, while his involvement in the famous FA Cup run was confined to just a solitary appearance, albeit a memorable one, in the 2-0 fifth round win at Chelsea. Significantly, Bloomfield was hospitalised at this stage and Peter Angell briefly took over as team manager. Peter had been recalled for the previous away league game, the 1-1 draw against his boyhood club Tottenham at

TOP LEAGUE APPEARANCES		
300-plus appearances (subs in brackets)		
1	**PETER ALLEN**	424 (8)
2	Arthur Wood	373
3	Stan Charlton	367
4	Fred Parker	336
5	Terry Howard	327 (5)
6	Bill Roffey	324 (4)
7	Matt Lockwood	328
8	Bobby Fisher	308 (6)
9	Stan Aldous	302
10	Ken Facey	301

Peter Allen (473 + 8) and Stan Charlton (408) are the only two players to appear in more than 400 Football League, FA Cup and League Cup games.

White Hart Lane, but he had been looking to terminate his 13-year stay with the club for some weeks.

He revealed: "Brian Winston, who was very good at getting all the players together for social events, came and had a chat with me. He asked if Jim and I would ever hit it off and I said: 'No, we won't'.

"I had talks with Jimmy, too, and to be fair, he always said that he would let me go if he could sign a replacement with the money he had at his disposal. On the other side of the coin, I was saying to him: 'Look, I'm coming up for 32, I've had injuries, I didn't cost the club a transfer fee, so how about letting me finish my career off by having a move and earning a few bob?'

Peter receiving a cheque for his testimonial fund from George Petchey at the end-of-season awards dinner in May, 1976.

The final act of Allen's record-breaking Orient career came on March 4, 1978, in a goalless draw with Notts County at Brisbane Road. There was no tearful farewell for the man whose appearance record will almost certainly never come close to being beaten.

"Leaving wasn't really a wrench, it was surprisingly easy," Peter admits. "I just came in for training one morning and they said that there was someone from Millwall who wanted to speak to me. So I drove over to Millwall, agreed terms and came back and collected my boots. That was it."

Although never the most alluring destination for player or supporter, The Den held a certain pull for Allen, because by then the south London club was managed by George Petchey. But this reunion of two men who regularly shared train journeys from Brighton to London didn't go to plan.

"I picked up an injury soon after joining them," Peter explained. "My knees were beginning to go – one tackle too many really – and I decided to end my playing days and continue my studies towards becoming a solicitor."

HAVING qualified as a solicitor in 1984, four years later Peter set up his own law firm partnership, Deibel & Allen, based on the East Sussex coast at Portslade, on the border of Brighton and Hove, specialising in conveyancing, wills and probate. His wife Jill was a legal executive in Brighton when they married in 1967.

Asked if he would have preferred to play in the modern era, Peter is unhesitant in his response. "I had a great time in football, thoroughly enjoyed it and met so many wonderful people, so I wouldn't want to change anything. Besides, I think I'd get sent-off every other week if I'd tackled now in the same way I did then.

"I look at matches now and think, 'that was a good tackle' and the next thing the referee is brandishing a yellow or red card. I played in very different times, on very different pitches and relished every moment."

Peter still follows Os' fortunes and has attended several important player reunions at Brisbane Road as well as the LOSC's Star Man dinner. "I don't get back to the club that often, just once or twice a season to what is an exceptionally nice stadium now," he added.

"What amazes me is that although it's 40 years since I played for them, I still get a wonderful welcome. That makes me realise that I was so lucky to have played for Orient for so long. They were a smashing little club."

Interview: Martin Smith & Paul Hiscock

...THAMSTOW
WALTHAM FOREST
Guardian
and Gazette

5323   Week ending, Friday, March 17, 1972   4p

FA CU...

COLO...

SPEC...

ORIENT v GUNNERS

...971-72—Back row (l to r): Dennis Rofe, Tom Walley, Paul Harris, Ray Goddard,
...ck, Phil Hoadley, Peter Bennett. Front: Bobby Arber, Peter Allen, Barry Dyson,
...ck, Terry Brisley, Barrie Fairbrother, Ian Bowyer.   ★ (1211)

at full strength for big
match

...CHAMPIONS and
...ers Arsenal are
...e barrier Second
...t killers Orient
...me if they are to
...emi-finals of the
...for the first time
...ry. Arsenal's sud-
...to form against
...Monday   makes

Arsenal and their recent
achievements. They are a good
strong all-round side who give
little away but I think we will
be lifted by the atmosphere
and occasion just as we were

wing wizardry of the impish
George Armstrong, who fre-
quently   switches   flanks ?

Will Ray Goddard outshine
Bob Wilson in goal and can
Peter Allen, Tom Walley and
Barry Dyson wrest mid-field
initiative from Alan Ball, Peter
Storey and George Graham?
Finally will Ian Bowyer and
Co. find a way past Arsenal's

IT'S THE HUNDREDS OF
LITTLE THINGS THAT PUT TH...

CUP SEMI-FINAL SPECIAL

WALTHAM FOREST Guardian
AND Independent

8p

ding Friday, April 7, 1978

Vol. CIX No. 5639

★ ★

Orient v Arsenal

FULL OF EAST END PROMISE

THE hopes and dreams of thousands of Cockney fans will be with Orient as they take the field against mighty Arsenal at Stamford Bridge, Chelsea tomorrow.

Can the little club with the big heart overcome the giants from Highbury who have won the Cup four times and the first division championship eight times?

Orient have never in their 97-year history reached the semi-finals of the FA Cup. Arsenal have won the Cup four times. Orient have a team which cost thousands, Arsenal a team which cost millions. Orient have a loyal following of 5,000 fans, Arsenal can boast 30,000. It is a typical David v Goliath fairytale.

It would be a cockney miracle if Orient could overcome the Gunners and become the fourth second division side in six years to reach Wembley but when you step into the homely atmosphere of Brisbane Road you honestly believe something sensational is about to happen. Nobody talks about losing. Everybody is saying . . . " when we get to the final we'll do such and such . . . confidence is sky high.

Bubbling enthusiasm oozes through the tiny corridors from the Pools Office through to the dressing room and everybody from the groundsman to the Chairman have been working their hearts out as Orient prepare for their biggest day ever.

HELP

The players' wives have been in to help so have the wives of Secretary Peter Barnes, Manager Jimmy Bloomfield and Chairman Brian Winston—even injured player John Chiedozie has been helping to cope with a flood of continual telephone calls by manning the switchboard.

Messages of good luck have been flooding into Brisbane Road not only from close to home but from all over the world. Assistant secretary Mike Blake said: " We have had letters from Australia, Canada—all over the world. There is a girl in Albuquerque who has been

Snap-shot bonanza

Support has grown enormously since the O's qualified for the semi-finals. This was underlined last Thursday when hundreds of people queued for anything up to three hours to have their youngster's pictures taken with the cup team.

One man said: " I've been standing here all afternoon with my two kids. But it's been worth it. They can't wait to get on to the pitch and stand next to Peter Kitchen for their photograph."

Hundreds of pounds was collected for the Orient players' pool and the sun shone all day allowing the photographers to snap nearly 400 pictures.

" No way did we expect such a fantastic response said John Jackson who is pool chairman. All the players were over the moon about how many people actually turned up and we would like to thank everybody for being so patient and understanding."

Goalkeeper John who has done so much to help Orient reach the semi-final had a special message for the loyal fans who will have to be in good voice at Stamford Bridge tomorrow: " The more you roar the better we play. You

Can 'Sup

THE hopes of Orient will pinned on this man at Sta ford Bridge tomorrow — Br bane Road's goal ace Peter K chen.

Hot shot Peter will be ai ing to sink the Gunners much the same way as he h seen off Norwich, Blackbu Rovers, Chelsea and Middle brough—by scoring one those magical goals whic have given the O's fans much delight this season.

Peter, who lives in Eppin has scored a goal in ever round of the cup—seven a told—and has netted no fewe than 20 league goals this yea

It was a Kitchen goal whic felled Norwich at Carrow Roa in the first round, two Kitche beauties set Orient on the roa to victory over Blackbur another two crackers at Stan

ever stops . . .

once told by his manager that he didn't run the next few months, under the guidance of mentally tuned himself to run and keep me big Joe was at West Bromwich A

Orient's most loyal supporter

A very special Orient fan this week set off on a 24,000-mile trip to watch his club play their historic semi-final against Arsenal.

Mr Mark Lansdowne, aged 39—who now lives in Adelaide, Australia—has been in contact with Orient Commercial

Cool, classy trailblazer

Born: Wembley, London, August 3, 1956
Usual position: Right-back/Midfield Orient Career: 1973-82
Orient Appearances: League 308/6, FA Cup 26, League Cup 19/1
Orient Goals: League 4, FA Cup 0, League Cup 1

BOBBY FISHER was one of Orient's longest-serving players. A versatile defender or midfielder, he racked up 360 first team games spanning a decade at Brisbane Road. His achievements are all the more impressive because he made his mark at a time when the scourge of racism haunted the game and black footballers were very much a minority but very conspicuous target for the abusers, both on and off the field.

By the late-70s Orient had more black players in their first team than any other club in The Football League. Bobby, of mixed-race, was the first non-white youngster to graduate from Os' youth ranks and make the big breakthrough – Indian-born Ricky Heppolette had been signed the previous season from Preston North End – and over the coming years he was followed along that upward path by Laurie Cunningham, John Chiedozie, Kevin Godfrey, Tunji Banjo and Henry Hughton.

So when it comes to racism in football, trailblazer Fisher talks with admirable authority, although Orient wasn't free of its own internal ethnic prejudices.

> **"With some of the players there was a bit of a racial undertone going on, which was horrible. I'll not name names here but one of the black players had to swap shirts with a white guy during a training game and the white fella said: 'I'm not going near that shirt, it stinks'. That's sad."**

Bobby reveals: "With some of the players there was a bit of a racial undertone going on, which was horrible. I'll not name names here but one of the black players had to swap shirts with a white guy during a training game and the white fella said: 'I'm not going near that shirt, it stinks'. That's sad.

"There was another time when one of our players was having a go at a linesman who was Asian. The player came in the dressing room at half-time and, in front of everybody, said: 'What chance have you got when you get a spear-chucker as a linesman'. You'd look around and there's three or four younger players looking and wondering 'where that's come from?'.

"To be fair to George Petchey, he wanted to address it but he knew the reality was that he couldn't fight against it straight away; you would have to gradually try and educate people and change the problem from within.

"I remember on a Friday, we would have five-a-sides and it would be blacks versus whites. But it could be fun and we had a laugh, although there was probably one or two (white) players who thought, 'it's my chance to do one of those'.

"Most of our guys, though, were OK, although there was the same joke every week. George would say: 'It's black versus white – and Bobby, you can play for who you want'. Mind you, I took advantage of it and usually ended up on the winning side. But I don't believe there were any really bad racists in our dressing room. I think George sussed them out early on and got them out. He did his due diligence, because he stopped those guys from joining the club. If someone did come in with the wrong attitude, he was straight out again. George was very good about that and

so was Jimmy. I can't really remember any wrong 'uns."

Fans who have only been attending professional football matches a relatively short while may struggle to comprehend that the game – mirroring society – was blighted by racism when Fisher was trying to make the grade at Orient.

Bobby continued: "In matches, racial comments were everywhere and in every game. As soon as you walked out on the pitch, the opposition fans would call you every name under the sun but you'd somehow get used to it, because you couldn't battle against it. So you played as well as you could and maybe give them a 'V' sign at the end of the game before getting down the tunnel as quickly as possible.

"We got it everywhere we went and remember, there were often 10,000-to-15,000 people in the crowd. I think a lot of them would probably be quite ashamed of themselves and embarrassed if they looked back now on how they behaved.

"But we also received racial abuse from opposing players, who would call you every name under the sun just to try and find you out.

"And also from referees as well. Even they would give you verbal."

As well as being encouraged by managers Petchey and Jimmy Bloomfield, Bobby pointed out that the black and mixed-race playing contingent had a strong ally in the boardroom in chairman Brian Winston.

"I remember coming back with Laurie (Cunningham) from a trip to Amsterdam. When we arrived at Heathrow we were going to jump on a train into London but Brian said: 'No, boys, come in with me' – so we travelled back from the airport in his Bentley. Just imagine it: a 17-year-old mixed-race kid – me – and Laurie – a black kid – in the back of this car. As we went through London, people were staring in amazement whenever we stopped at traffic lights. It was almost as if Brian was the chauffeur, with us two in the back. Lovely.

"There was no cultural or racial issues with Brian; we were all in it together. At the time, his attitude was pretty unique.

Bobby was the elder statesman in this Colts team before facing Fulham in May, 1974. Standing, left to right: Harry Spinner, Bobby Broomfield, Glenn Roeder, Ian Woodward, John Smeulders, Dean Mooney, Nigel Gray, Trevor Spicer Terry Long (coach). Kneeling: Tony Grealish, Laurie Cunningham, Gary Hibbs, Billy Bragg, Steve Viner and Bobby. Eight of this youth side went on to play for the first team.

"He was superb, so enthusiastic, and always wanted to help me. But being young and naive, I didn't realise it so much at the time, otherwise I would have nurtured that relationship even more."

Another friendly face at the club was director Harry Zussman, an ebullient, little East End shoe manufacturer with a penchant for fat cigars who had been chairman of Leyton Orient when they were promoted to Division One in 1962.

"Because of the Jewish connection, I got on very well with Harry," Bobby recalls. "His daughter Delia used to come to all the games and there was a real connection with the pair of them. There was always going to be soft spot for me, being the youngster in the team at 17 and Jewish, and they wanted to look after me, which was lovely."

IN our interview with Mark Lazarus earlier in the book, the former crowd favourite enlightens readers with his candid accounts of personal battles to overcome anti-semitism in the 60s. As a young baby, Bobby Fisher was adopted by Mark's sister, Rose, who brought him up where they lived in Wembley.

"My Uncle Mark introduced me to Orient in about 1970, just before I signed on as an apprentice at 15 years of age. I had six months or so down there training with the youth team, under Len Cheesewright, on a Thursday night. I'd been at Queens Park Rangers before then for six months but there wasn't a lot of interest from either side, to be honest, and when they let me go it worked out well.

"A few other clubs were interested but it was Orient where I thought that I'd have the best chance of gaining a first team place if I was good enough. And that proved to be right, because I was 16-and-a-half when I was named on the subs' bench. I've got a feeling I made my first team debut, ironically, in a friendly against QPR before my 17th birthday."

Fisher made his league debut in the opening game of the 1973-74 season, when he came off the bench (replacing Gerry Queen) in the 1-1 draw at Sunderland just after his 17th birthday. He made his first start at Bolton the following month.

Despite having to commute from his home in Wembley, Bobby said: "Mark really sold Orient to me initially and I loved the club. I liked all the guys there and that East End camaraderie."

Fisher thrived under George Petchey's management. He continued: "I got on really well with him. I think Jimmy Bloomfield was just leaving when I came to Orient and then George arrived. He was really ahead of his time in his thinking. He wanted to bring a lot of the black and mixed race players into the club, which was obviously something quite stark in the early 70s. I think George always saw this as a bit of a challenge because of the old school thinking among the (white) players and the East End feel about it.

"He was always keen to encourage the development of younger players. I think he believed he would have a greater influence over them rather than the older players who were set in their ways.

"George started to introduce two or three sessions of training a day and meals between sessions, which we'd never had before. He took us away to a place called Pappendale in Holland, where we trained with the likes of Barcelona and Bayern Munich, so we had that international, cosmopolitan feel to our training.

"George was into using the ball as much as possible, whereas before it had usually been run, run, run. It was a totally different culture. We'd just come off the back of the 60s and early 70s kick-and-run era – hitting the front man, like Mickey Bullock, using him as the target man and playing off them. George introduced push-and-run – they'd probably call it 'tippy-tappy' now. It was based on the old Spurs style of the 50s and 60s. 'Give it and go' and 'keep it moving' – they were George's routine phrases. And that suited me anyway, because I was that sort of player.

Bobby tussling with Luton Town's Jimmy Husband in December, 1976.

"As a coach and in terms of his tactical awareness, I'd put him in the top-drawer, without doubt. I think he became frustrated that he didn't have the players he wanted to push his philosophy on as much as he could. He had probably 50 per cent who wanted to play that way, and were really open to it, but the other 50 per cent were reticent about it."

Fisher's versatility had its downside. He explained: "Initially, I was a midfield player but George converted me to full-back when David Payne broke his leg. I look back on it now as a bit of a double-edged sword. I'd been known as a kind of a marauding midfielder – which is what I liked to consider myself as, although I probably wasn't – and the type of player who was going to float around and be creative.

"Obviously, when I got the chance to play as a full-back, I still wanted to carry on in the same style. But I always felt a bit restricted at full-back. It was great that I got my chance to play first team football at 17 but, at the same time, I was a bit fed up that I hadn't got the chance as a midfielder.

"I didn't have too much pace as a full-back, I was under pressure whenever I came up against pacy wingers. I always wondered what could have been, because I'd been prevented from playing in my favoured position.

"Looking back, I was very shy when I first got in the senior side and nowadays I would have an agent to deal with all my contract negotiations, because I was never one to sing my own praises. All I wanted to do was play football and whatever the club offered me each season as a pay rise, I accepted.

"Nowadays, it would be totally different. But having said that, I never had contract problems with George and to be fair to him, I think he always wanted to do the best for me, which was kind of nice. I'm sure the club offered so much by way of a rise and, unbeknown to me, George went back and got a bit more for me."

Fisher can't recall falling out with Petchey over anything before the manager was sacked in August, 1977. "He was always fair. If I did well, he'd tell me. If I didn't do so well he'd encourage me and he was always looking to nurture me. I had a really great relationship with him; he gave me my chance and really helped develop me both on and off the pitch. He had a great view of life and he wanted people to be well rounded as footballers. There isn't one single bad thing I could say about George and I couldn't say that for any other managers I played under.

"The presence of George's adviser, Arthur Rowe, contributed to our push-and-run style of play and as soon as Arthur came in, we started to play in that manner. It seemed a strange fit at the time, because it was the 70s era of outlandish clothes and the glam-rock thing that the young guys had then. But Arthur was a throwback to the 40s and 50s, if you like.

"We didn't really have much idea of his history and what he'd achieved before, particularly with Tottenham. When he first came in, we were asking ourselves, 'who's this old bloke and what's he talking about?', because all he used to say was 'give-and-go, push-and-run' and he'd always end the instructions with the word 'taxi'. No-one ever knew what he meant then and we still don't know now. But he'd say 'Taxi' just before leaving the room."

Bobby admits he preferred playing under Petchey compared to Jimmy Bloomfield. He explained: "Jimmy was another lovely man, although, to be honest, he wasn't my favourite. I got the impression that I wasn't one of his favourite players either and there was always something that stayed in my mind with Jimmy.

"Arsenal made a firm offer for me at one stage but he didn't tell me about it for some while and by the time he did actually mention it to me, Arsenal had moved in for someone else. So, as far as I was concerned, that was always going to be a bit of a problem between us.

"We had a different style of playing under Jimmy compared to George. He also had a different way of motivating people and I don't think I really bought into Jimmy's methods. That was more than likely down to me as much as him – I was probably spoilt playing for George. So I tended to match Jimmy against George, which was wrong of me.

"I didn't really have any fall-outs with Jimmy apart from that Arsenal business. I did threaten to go on the transfer list afterwards, so he just kept out of my way for two or three weeks until it all blew over.

"But for all that, Jimmy was a nice guy."

Bobby has kind words to say about key members of the backroom staff, starting with assistant manager Peter Angell.

"We called him 'Gunner' and he was a good guy, too. If any of us youth players didn't clean the dressing room properly or we did anything wrong, he would punish us by making us cut the pitch with a pair of scissors! I was boot-boy for a while and if I didn't clean them properly, I would be out on the pitch on my hands and knees cutting the grass with scissors.

"Peter was a real sergeant-major type with a 'this wouldn't have happened back in my day' attitude. He would have had you painting coal white if he could but, having said that, he was a really nice man who looked after and nurtured the youngsters to become better individuals."

What about the three physiotherapists, Charlie Simpson, Ernie Shepherd and Bill Songhurst?

"Luckily, I didn't suffer too many injuries and there was a reason for that – I didn't want to see either of the physios we had in my time at Orient. In truth, I was probably put off physios by Charlie's style. I'd just got into the first team and I got a knock on my ankle and it became badly swollen. So Peter Angell said: 'Let's go and see Charlie'.

"Everyone was quite scared of him. He used to wear a white coat and was one of those guys who I think imagined himself as a doctor. I remember going into the medical room and he told me he was going to have to put a cortisone injection into the ankle. I'd never been in a physio's room before and became very nervous as he proceeded to take a needle out of his bag before fumbling around for about 15 minutes trying to find a suitable spot around my ankle bone – he was jabbing me everywhere in my foot. It was horrendous but he finally

On the ball at Tottenham in February, 1978.

Battling against pre-match nerves in the momentous 1977-78 season.

administered the injection and told me I could play the next day.

"The next day, I came into the dressing room and the ankle was the size of a balloon, I could hardly walk. I vowed there and then that I'd never have another cortisone injection – and I never did. At the same time, I promised myself to avoid physios if at all possible!

"Charlie was old school – a bucket of cold water and a sponge – but, listen, he was still a great guy.

"After he left, we had a guy called Ernie Shepherd. I never worked out what Ernie was really about. He was a coach that just became a physio but if you did get injured, you always looked forward to going in to see Ernie. Charlie would put you on a bike or make you do upper body work and by the time he'd finished, you were knackered anyway.

"But with Ernie, we'd take a sandwich and a newspaper into the treatment room. And whenever Ernie wanted to get players out on the track or on a bike, someone would say to him: 'Wall-of-death, Ernie, wall-of-death?'. He would put a coin in his bucket and flick the bucket around and around. The coin used to go around the top of the bucket like a bike in the wall-of-death. He'd do this for half-an-hour and all the boys loved it. We kept telling him how great it was and he always took the bait. But the players only egged him on to get out of any training. He'd then look at his watch and say: 'OK, lads, lunch' and that was it. It was like being part of a pub team and very funny.

"It's strange how things like that stay in your mind 40-plus years on but it underlines the fun and camaraderie we had at the club at the time.

"Bill Songhurst came in after Ernie. He was unbelievably different, another who was before his time. He wanted to initiate all these different ideas he was getting from America. He had ideas about nutrition, the way we trained, about resting and getting over injuries, and he wanted to bring all these ideas into the club. He was incredible.

"I was lucky not to suffer too many injuries but the feedback I got from the other players was that they really loved Bill's ideas and initiatives. Before him, it would be a case of put your foot in ice and then go out and play through the pain barrier. Then you'd have a week off, have a cortisone injection on the Friday and play the next day through the pain.

"But Bill knew that was not the way to do things. He realised that players who were being treated in that way wouldn't be able to walk by the time they were 40 or 50-years-old.

"I really got on well with him. We used to call him 'Skippy' because of the way he ran onto the pitch – he skipped when he was running – but he was a good fella. He wanted to be one of the boys and used to join us on a few of our nights out."

BOBBY says that his best mate at Orient was "probably Tony Grealish". Their unlikely alliance was forged despite a heated – and racist – exchange as schoolboy rivals.

"I knew 'Paddy' as a 14-year-old, when he used to play in the same area in London as I did. I think he played for Paddington Boys, which was a top team in London, while I played for another leading side, Kilburn Boys' Club. One of my everlasting memories of him was playing against him in a big cup game at the age of 14. He gave me a wallop in the last couple of minutes and then, standing over me, called me every racial name you could think of! And I was lying there calling him every Irish insult I knew.

"Moving on six months, I'd signed for Orient and was boot-boy. Peter Angell came in and said: 'Bobby, I've got someone here you are going to have to look after, he's going to be your number two boot-boy. And there was Paddy. We looked at each other and said: 'No!'. But we really hit it off and became great mates.

Physio Bill Songhurst was "ahead of his time".

"On the pitch, we looked after each other. And off the pitch, we were always out together. The other players used to call us the 'Laughing Hyenas' because we never took anything seriously. Even when we had a bad game and were getting slagged off, we'd end up laughing.

"We roomed together; in fact, we roomed together before the Cup semi-final. The team was staying in a hotel around Hyde Park – our old stomping ground really. We couldn't sleep and although there was a curfew, we went out and had a pint in a pub we knew well and ended up eating a couple of ham rolls at one o'clock in the morning around Paddington and walking back to the hotel. We only did it because we were nervous – the adrenalin was going ahead of the big game.

"Paddy and I had a great relationship and were always getting up to tricks. I had to look after him off the pitch, because he did like a drink. I was his protector. I was always in with George Petchey trying to explain why Paddy hadn't arrived for training. He'd ask: 'Where were you last night? Paddy's not in, where was he?' As I say, I was like his minder.

"I was really good friends with Laurie as well and the three of us would go around together. I'd been there longer than both of them, so I knew the club and the ropes and, again, George wanted me to protect Laurie. I was asked to look after him on and off the pitch and to make sure he came in for training in the mornings. That was the hardest thing – Laurie's time-keeping wasn't always the best. I think his watch must have kept stopping! That was a complete nightmare."

Although team spirit was invariably very good, like all families, there were the occasional inevitable fall-outs.

"You know what, there was conflict virtually every day," reveals Bobby. "Not involving me, because I was easy-going and relaxed but others were always having arguments – both verbal and sometimes physical.

"There were always people in the dressing room having a go at each other. I remember Derrick Downing and Ian Bowyer having a real set-to. It was pre-season and we were having a friendly match between ourselves when George blew the whistle. Ian went up to Derrick and grabbed him by the neck. He lifted him off the floor and said to him: 'If you kick any of these young lads today, I'll break your leg'. He put him down and the game carried on. It really happened."

But there were plenty of laughs, too. Bobby says: "There were always a few boys who would play jokes and pranks. When we stayed in hotels we'd go into players' rooms and get up to a few pranks. We went up to Scotland and stayed in a castle beside a loch which we thought was haunted. Someone got the key to Gerry Queen's room. There was a statue – the head and shoulders of some famous person. Anyway, Gerry – who happened to be Scottish – was on the top floor in what was probably the creakiest room, and I remember a few of the boys got this statue and put it in his bed one night.

"After he'd had a couple of drinks and went back up to his room, a few of us who were waiting at the bottom of the stairs heard this big scream, quickly followed by Gerry coming running down the stairs in just a pair of Y-fronts, swearing and claiming that there was someone in his room!

"Silly, I know, but this sort of thing went on a lot when we went away. There were the usual pranks: Deep Heat cream in your jockstrap, holes cut into your socks. If we went away, one player would be reading a paper and another player would set light to it. You'd be in a five-star hotel and all of a sudden, someone was holding a burning newspaper.

"So many antics . . . but I've seen players crying on occasions because they couldn't handle all the jokes at their expense. Some ended up being tainted for life because they weren't able to simply laugh it off. Of course, when the boys found someone vulnerable like that, they'd just wind them up even more."

MORE defensive players are naturally unlikely to have many outstanding individual moments to store away in the memory bank and Bobby admits: "I don't know whether this is a defence mechanism inside me, but I only clearly remember just a handful of the 350-plus games I played for Orient.

"I don't know whether that was because I was always of a nervous disposition and never really enjoyed playing as much as I should have. Every game for me was always like going over the trenches, worrying about what was going to happen. Once that whistle went, it was head down and go.

"It's strange, because I talk to other players from my era and they tell me about all the games

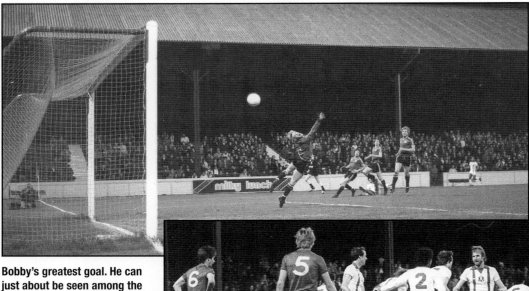

Bobby's greatest goal. He can just about be seen among the QPR defenders as his shot flies into the top corner from . . . er, not quite 80 yards! Inset: Team-mates congratulate the No.2 but Rangers' No.6 Glenn Roeder doesn't look so impressed.

they played. Maybe with me, it became all too easy a job of work and I did become cosseted. I had a well-rounded view of the game and life outside Orient because it was too easy.

"I probably needed to be transfer-listed when I was 19 or 20-years-old and be told by the club that I was going to be sold whether I liked it or not. With hindsight, that might have served me better but it wouldn't have been perfect because I would have missed out on so many good years at Orient.

"I remember a few matches better than others. We played Blackpool at home and I think that was when I scored my first own-goal. I'll never forget the look on George Petchey's face. He was always trying to nurture me along but he spoke to my mum afterwards and said: 'Can you tell Bob, he can also put it in at the other end as well!'. But we lost the game because of my own-goal.

"I scored a great goal against QPR (Apr, 1980). The distance from which I shot 'goes back' another five or 10 yards every time I talk about it, so now it's become an 80-yard strike! It was probably only a 10-yard effort really but it flew into the top corner.

"All the games in those great Cup runs we enjoyed are always going to be there. I remember the Chelsea game at Brisbane Road (Feb, 1972). The apprentices used to have to stand by the players' tunnel and I clearly remember watching Phil Hoadley's goal.

"When we drew with Villa (May, 1974) and just missed out on promotion. I was sat in the stands and it was very emotional watching it. I suppose if we had won that match my career might have taken a different path. One more goal and it would have all been so different for the club and the players. For me, I would have been at the start of my career and playing in the First Division.

"I recall all the matches in the '78 Cup run. We got drawn against Norwich and I remember thinking, 'we're not going to get anything from this', and I felt the same before facing both Chelsea and Middlesbrough but, somehow, we got results. When you talk about team spirit, the bunch of players we had in the 1977-78 squad encapsulated all of that.

"Fair play to Jimmy, he had a technique that frustrated our opponents. At times we were playing five across the back and teams didn't know how to break us down. Then, going forward, Bill Roffey and I would push forward, so we'd have five across midfield. We're talking about 1978 but there was definitely no team in this country – and you'd be hard pressed to find one in Europe – playing this way. At the time, I'm not sure even our own players understood it, so I don't know what anyone else made of it.

"Because teams found it so difficult to break down our resilient defence, and we had 'Kitch' up front, we felt that we only needed to score one goal and we'd fancy ourselves to hold out by just bringing everyone back. A lot of people missed Jimmy's perception and tactical nous of that time."

History records that Os' greatest Cup run was extinguished at the semi-final stage, four years after top flight football had agonisingly eluded them by a single point. Fisher more than hints that the club suffered from an inferiority complex and lacked a winning mentality.

"I look back and think that it was a great era but for all that, it could have panned out in two different ways. We could have been a really good team and challenged for promotion again. I remember the season after the Villa game (1974-75), there was a genuine feeling that we were going to push on. George and the coaching staff were working on things and even the way we travelled to away games improved. For example, the coaches we used had big leather seats. It's not a big deal now but in the 70s it was something special.

"And we had our own chefs. After the game we'd eat smoked salmon and scrambled eggs. We were treated like a top team and all that sort of stuff left the players with the feeling that we would do really well and get promotion but we just didn't push on. If we had, we'd have had a really good team because the better players – like Paddy, Glenn (Roeder) and Laurie – wouldn't have left. Or, then again, we could have gone the other way, got relegated and fell through the leagues. It's always been fine lines with Orient.

"Even as a young player, I always had the feeling that failure was ingrained in the walls around the place and that was a strange feeling to have at that early stage of my career. I always felt that we were never going to achieve anything really big as a club. We didn't seem to have that ruthless winning attitude that would take us that extra yard. When it came to the crunch, we just didn't push on.

"I was one of the guys out there playing but it seemed we didn't have that win at all costs attitude you need. I don't think we ever had that feeling as players.

"But it's not all down to players. There were times when the manager would go to the directors to ask for money to buy a player who would help us to kick-on but the board were reluctant to put their hands in their pockets."

You can't blame Bobby for reflecting on that enquiry from Arsenal and wondering what might have been. Not being even given the opportunity to go to Arsenal is a massive regret," he admits. "Having said that, no-one knows how things would have worked out. Life might have been better but it could have been a lot worse – I might not have played as many games as I did by staying at Orient.

"There were a few others clubs interested in signing me, including a couple from Holland, which would have been interesting. The Dutch league might have suited my style of play," added Bobby, who read the game well and was a neat, classy, laid-back type of player. He was a good passer and had a sense of timing that often enabled him to make slide tackles, get back on his feet and come away with the ball. Slenderly built for a defender, he certainly wasn't prone to dive rashly into physical challenges. But the deep thinking self-analyst in him insists he could have done more.

"I also have regrets regarding myself. I could have pushed a lot harder than I actually did to make it a better career. Looking back now, I should have played for England because, on reflection, I believe that I was probably good enough if only I'd had the right mindset. I was naive. I should have trained harder, my preparation should have been better and maybe at times the set-up at Orient could have been more professional too. All these factors could have taken my career to another level.

"I'll give you a small example. One Tuesday afternoon after training four of us youngsters went to a pub in Leyton. We didn't have training the next day, although we obviously still shouldn't have gone there. It got to about 5.00pm and by now we were at the station. George Petchey arrived and saw us. I'm sure he knew what we'd been up to but he didn't say anything.

"If he'd said: 'Right, you lot are all in for training tomorrow, I'm going to fine you and you're not playing on Saturday because of your behaviour', something like that could have changed everything and I would have thought, 'now I've really got to take this seriously'. I needed a really hard manager who would keep having a dig at me. I would have hated it but it was what I needed to become a better player."

ORIENT fans appreciated Bobby's efforts as a technically assured shield for the defence. He may have been one of the unsung heroes but he was a dependable one.

"I always felt I was in touch with the fans," he says. "If we were travelling back from an away game on the train, we would have a drink with the supporters and when we played at home, I'd travel on the Underground to and from matches, so I'd be chatting to supporters before and after the game. Today's players don't have that close affinity with their fans.

"I remember a lovely person called Linda Thorn, who suffered from some sort of disability but she loved Orient. She was always there wherever we were playing and even as a young player, I knew how much Orient meant to her. She loved meeting the players and having a chat but, unfortunately, sad to say, there were one or two individuals who ignored her. But I was always happy to spend a few minutes chatting to her, even just to say 'Hi', because it meant so much to her."

As someone who has worked as a sports psychologist and life coach in recent times, Bobby is perhaps well qualified to understand the psyche of a typical Orient fan. He says: "You see the real character of the supporters who follow Orient. Everyone remains loyal to the club despite all the setbacks and disappointments they experience watching the team. I'm sure they all have it in the back of their minds that better times lie ahead and that's great. With the bigger clubs, you don't tend to get that same level of passion because what does success mean to their supporters? They are used to it. For Orient fans, they just learn to appreciate and enjoy each and every one of the better moments."

No-one was ever in any doubt as to who Fisher's number one fan was. And if anyone dared criticise her son from the stands, proud Rose would be up and at 'em in a flash.

"My mum was always there watching me play and she was a bit of a character. In my younger days, she would chase referees. She'd often be wielding her umbrella and, now and again, she would have to be pulled off them! I also had two really good friends who lived in the same block of flats as me, and they were always supporting me."

After 10 seasons at Brisbane Road, Fisher joined Cambridge United in November, 1982 at the age of 26. By then, the Us were a mid-table Second Division side, while Os had been relegated from the second tier the previous May and were struggling to avoid dropping into Division Four. As departures go, he got out at the right time.

"I went to Cambridge because Ken Knighton wasn't going to play me. I wasn't his style of player. He probably thought I was jaded after 10 years with Orient, that I was part of the furniture and I think he wanted to make a bit of a statement. He might have been right, though – I wasn't playing as well as I could have, so it was time for me to move on.

"I left Orient on a Tuesday and started at Cambridge the next day, which meant I didn't have much chance to say goodbye to the players, directors and staff, so that was a bit unfortunate and sad. Also, I didn't have a chance to say farewell to the fans but that's just how things worked out."

After 42 league games for Cambridge, 45 for Third Division Brentford and a spell in non-league with Maidstone United, this loyal Os servant has enjoyed an interesting life as a football agent – alongside fellow ex-Orient player Barry Silkman – and also dabbled as an actor on the small screen, appearing in television commercials and series *Space Precinct, Starhunter, Forensic Factor* and *The Manageress*.

But he has never severed his ties with the club that gave him his chance to shine in league football. Bobby very actively supported initiatives that resulted in a blue plaque and statue erected in memory of Laurie Cunningham, the old pal he helped to keep on the straight and narrow during their formative years with Os.

Quite rightly, years after his tragic death, Laurie still receives widespread acclaim for his achievements that inspired the black community and others from ethnic backgrounds. But never forget the part trailblazer Bobby Fisher played too, especially at Orient. Summing up his time with the club, he said: "It's all a question of what might have been. What Orient, as a club, could have achieved. But it was a great time in my life and it kind of moulded me into the person I am now."
Interview: Paul Hiscock

Not exactly Band Aid, but the Orient players got together on a couple of occasions in the 70s in search of an elusive hit record. Here, in 1974, we see players (left to right) Bill Roffey, Malcolm Linton, Barrie Fairbrother, Ricky Heppolette, Paul Harris, Peter Allen, John Boyle, Ray Goddard, John Jackson, Derrick Downing, Terry Brisley, David Payne, Gerry Queen, Peter Bennett, Phil Hoadley and assistant manager Peter Angell. Pye Records initially released *Football, Football* with *We The Kings of Orient* on the B-side. But there were two versions of the 45rpm vinyl single, both written, arranged and produced by Alan Tew (pictured far left). In 1978 they re-released it, but with the A and B sides swapped.

In April, 1978, Os went back in the studio to record *Fantastic'o* as their 'Cup Final' song on the Lightning Records label during the epic run to the semi-finals.

Herb Alpert & the Tijuana Brass
TIJUANA TAXI
TIJUANA TAXI • A WALK IN THE BLACK FOREST • WALK DON'T RUN • FELICIA

Of course, one tune that will forever be associated with Orient is the enduring 60s Herb Albert hit, *Tijuana Taxi*. First introduced as the team's anthem by Os' PA announcer Keith Simpson in August, 1968, it still reverberates around the stadium when Leyton Orient run out today.

Harris among heroes

Born: Hackney, London, May 19, 1953
Usual position: Centre-half   Orient Career: 1971-75
Orient Appearances: League 96, FA Cup 7, League Cup 7/2
Orient Goals: League 4, FA Cup 0, League Cup 0

A PUPIL at Leyton County High School, Paul Harris was an outstanding schoolboy footballer and cricketer and at one stage, he had to decide which of the two sports to choose for a career.

As a cricketer, he represented England Schools and had the opportunity to turn professional with Essex or join the MCC groundstaff at Lord's. During the time he was playing representative cricket, he captained Graham Gooch well before 'Goochie' became an Essex and England legend.

However, Paul's football talents playing for Waltham Forest Schools were also attracting the attention of a number of clubs but when he was offered the opportunity to join Orient as an apprentice upon leaving school in 1969, there were no second thoughts.

"I'd been an Os supporter since I was 10-years-old and my mind was made up," he said. "My heart was in football and also my father, who played at a high level, wanted me to become a professional.

"We had a strong schools district side, getting to the national finals, and about six of our side came down to Orient for trials when we were about 14. One was Brendon Batson, who went on to the Arsenal, but it was Len Cheesewright that asked me to sign for the Os as a schoolboy.

"Dick Graham was first team manager then but he had a reputation as a strict disciplinarian and, as a 14-year-old, you just kept out of his way. Jimmy Bloomfield had taken over by the time I signed as a pro and he was great, a lovely man. Jim was the best manager I ever played for."

Having progressed to full pro status in July, 1970, teenage centre-half Paul made his debut at Cardiff City 10 months later, in the final game of the 1970-71 season. "I was marking John Toshack, so it was no easy introduction," he recalls.

Paul became a first team regular for the next two seasons. As one of the Cup heroes of 1972, Harris obviously views that exciting period as the highlight of his Orient career. Blond-haired Paul partnered Phil Hoadley at the heart of the back four, two Londoners manning the barricades against the likes of Peter Osgood and Charlie George, but nothing surpassed that epic, last-gasp victory over Chelsea, who came unstuck on the Brisbane Road pudding.

"The atmosphere building up to the game was something really special. We had a dressing room full of characters and it was great to be part of it.

"I don't think we were overawed by the occasion in any way. They were just Chelsea and we were Orient. We had belief in our own ability. One of the features of that '72 side was the team spirit. Everyone got on well.

"It was a great goal by Phil and he was good enough to be able to do that.

"The best moment was when the final whistle blew and we were through to the quarter-finals.

"If Chelsea was my high, my low was losing to Arsenal in the next round. We'd had a good few days away down in Eastbourne and our preparations were excellent. Personally, I never went into a game fearing anyone and after beating Chelsea we certainly weren't afraid of Arsenal or anyone else.

"We more than held our own against one of the best sides in the country."

"I think it was during that Cup run that we went away to Santa Ponsa in Spain for a few days' break. On the first day, as was the norm, the players were encouraged, to a minor degree, to go out and have a few drinks to boost team spirit, so a group of five or six of us, one of whom was Phil Hoadley, thought that was quite a good idea.

"But when we got up the next morning for training he was feeling a bit worse for wear. We had to walk about half-a-mile to the training pitch and on the way Phil kept moaning and mumbling that his head was hurting and he couldn't go on any longer.

"We'd just about kicked-off and all of a sudden someone said: 'Where's Phil?'. No-one had a clue where he'd gone, so we started hunting everywhere for him. Then someone spotted him by the clifftop, rolled up in a ball, fast asleep and snoring away!"

One of Paul's best mates at the club was another local lad made good. He said: "I roomed with Dennis Rofe, who was another character. He was loud in the dressing room but on the pitch he was a very good player. I thought he should have played for England and was very unfortunate not to do so."

Harris doesn't have to scratch his head long to recall the best of his four goals for Orient. "My best one was away to Burnley (Nov 11, 1972), which flew into the top corner from about 30 yards – I'd been booked in the previous minute."

With versatile Welshman Tom Walley able to slot in alongside Hoadley in the centre of defence or provide a forceful presence in midfield, plus the emergence of home-grown centre-backs Nigel Gray and Glenn Roeder, Harris' found himself shuffled to the fringes of the first team scene under manager George Petchey, as Os embarked upon their most successful season of the 70s.

And Harris felt for another long-time team-mate who was also marginalised as the 1973-74

Paul (right) and Phil Hoadley combine in the air during the famous 1972 Cup run.

HARRIS SPARKS ORIENT

By Kevin Moseley

ORIENT 3, CHARLTON 2

Kid Harris tops the Orient bill

"I remember it very clearly. We were all sitting on the coach waiting to go to training, there was a little delay and we're thinking, 'what's going on?'. Then, all of a sudden, the door opens and in walks John Jackson. Everyone on the bus, including Ray, went quiet. No-one said a word."

season gathered momentum and dreams of promotion to the top flight faded early in the New Year.

No-one can doubt John Jackson's immense contribution to the club over a seven-year period, including countless outstanding performances, but Harris questioned the timing of the goalkeeper's arrival from Crystal Palace, a few months into the 1973-74 season. Ray Goddard, popular with players and fans alike, had made the green number one jersey his own over the previous five years and, out of the blue, was shocked and dismayed to be replaced.

"It was more the manner in which the change of goalkeeper was handled," said Paul. "I remember it very clearly. We were all sitting on the coach waiting to go to training, there was a little delay and we're thinking, 'what's going on?'. Then, all of a sudden, the door opens and in walks John Jackson. Everyone on the bus, including Ray, went quiet. No-one said a word.

"John was obviously a great goalkeeper but I thought the timing was wrong and it had a very bad effect on us. I don't know who did and didn't know that 'Jacko' would be signing for us but the majority of us had no inkling that it was about to happen.

"Ray was a great keeper in his own right and I can't remember him ever letting the club down."

Like Goddard, Harris knew that his Orient days were numbered. He started to pick up a series of injuries which stalled his career.

"For me, from '73 onwards was my downfall. My knees and ankles started to play up and still trouble me today – more so than ever," Paul confirmed.

After 110 senior appearances for his local club, Harris moved to Swansea City in July, 1975 – despite being offered another contract by Orient.

"I was a bit despondent because of the injuries I was getting and decided to try and start afresh elsewhere. It was a big move going to Wales having spent my whole life in and around London. But I had two terrific seasons there until injuries forced me onto the sidelines.

"The cartilage operations I'd had were taking their toll and I became slower than I already was. I played every match of the first season but never played again. I didn't see the point of lingering on in the Fourth Division. I'd started a business which was doing well, so I decided to concentrate on that.

"Then one day, this chap turned up on the doorstep and said: 'I'm Lyn Davies, manager of Bridgend, and I want you to play for me'. I said: 'No thanks, I've packed up' but he suggested we went for a drink and have a chat. At first I turned him down but he wouldn't take no for an answer and contacted me on three more occasions. And on the final time, I gave in and agreed to play.

"I have to admit that I had a great year playing in the Welsh League – we won the title and got into what is now the equivalent of the National League. I only played for the one season because I'd already decided to return to London. But then I got a call from Johnny Boyle whom I knew from my playing days at Orient.

"He had just become manager of Dartford and asked me to sign for them. Again, I said 'no' but he kept on, so I told him I was signing for Enfield, which was a lie but I said it just to try and deter him. But he wouldn't be deterred – he said: 'Don't sign for them, come and see me'. So I did and of course, I ended up signing for Dartford.

> **"I love the Orient. My dad died soon after I turned pro but what the club did for me at that time was fantastic and I will never ever forget it. It was a mega-blow when he died but the funeral procession passed the ground and everyone at the club turned out all clad in red to pay their respects, which was fantastic."**

"On paper, we were the best side in the league bar none but in fact, it was the worst side that I'd ever played in. 'Boylers' got the sack after six months and I followed soon after, so I finally decided that was it, my playing days had finished.

"I don't even know whether Dartford stayed up or went down, I never even looked! All I checked on was that they continued to send my money to me, because I'd got a two-year contract. It was the easiest money I'd ever earned and by sacking me they did me a lot of favours, because I was skint at that time."

Knee problems and floating bones in an ankle finally dictated that Paul would have to finally end his playing days. He embarked upon a career as a black-cab driver and also in chiropody. In fact, he came back to Brisbane Road to work as the club's consultant chiropodist.

"I love the Orient. My dad died soon after I turned pro but what the club did for me at that time was fantastic and I will never ever forget it. It was a mega-blow when he died but the funeral procession passed the ground and everyone at the club turned out all clad in red to pay their respects, which was fantastic.

"I've got very fond memories of my time at Orient. It has a great reputation as a family club and, happily, that tradition carries on today."

Interview: Paul Hiscock & Martin Smith

Phil the power

Born: Battersea, London, January 6, 1952
Usual position: Central defender Orient Career: 1971-78
Orient Appearances: League 255, FA Cup 24, League Cup 16
Orient Goals: League 9, FA Cup 2, League Cup 1

IF any former player can truly empathise with fans about the rollercoaster of emotions we've all been through, none will understand it better than Phil Hoadley.

The popular centre-back has first-hand experience of the agony and the ecstasy. From goal-scoring Cup legend to conceding the penalty that denied Orient a place at the top table of the English game, the Battersea boy has been there, done that and thrown away the T-shirt.

Hero to villain? No, in this instance it's just a cliché. No-one would be deranged enough to ever describe this heart-on-the-sleeve talismanic leader as a villain, because he did so much good for the club over his six years and 295 league and Cup games at Brisbane Road to ever warrant such an insult.

Lured away from Crystal Palace as a 19-year-old by his old Selhurst Park coach George Petchey in October, 1971, Hoadley's name became inextricably enshrined in O's folklore just four months later when his spectacular long-range strike inspired one of the greatest comebacks in the club's history.

> **"What made it all the more special for me was that my family were watching from the main stand. My dad, Fred, who has since died, was there. He was about to roll another fag just as I scored, so when everyone jumped up from their seats he spilt his tin of tobacco and my missus, Mandy, was covered in it!"**

Orient were on the ropes, still reeling from two early Chelsea blows, in their home FA Cup fifth round tie when his 30-yard goal in first-half injury-time breathed new life into the 'minnows'. Mickey Bullock and Barrie Fairbrother grabbed the late goals that completed a sensational 3-2 victory but Hoadley's wonder-strike was by far the pick of the five and proved the catalyst for the bedlam that followed.

"It has to be my best-ever goal, simply for its importance. I must admit, though, it has to be the worst goal celebration I've ever seen – as my grandchildren are quick to tell me when they see it on YouTube," says Phil, who is rarely short of a self-deprecating quip or one-liner.

"We were Orient and we weren't supposed to beat Chelsea, were we? We're talking here about a very good Chelsea side. They had won a European trophy the year before. You go out there thinking, 'we'll have a crack at this' but then when you go two down you think 'bugger!' Anyway, I was pushing up on the right by that stage of the game and when the ball came out to me from their penalty area, I just whacked it. It wasn't a case of deliberately aiming for the top left-hand corner of the net – I just wanted to hit the target. And it went in. I think it broke Peter Bonetti's hand on the way. No, I'm only joking!

"Coming as it did just before half-time, my goal at least gave us a chance. George Petchey made that point to us in the dressing room. He said: 'One more and you are right back in this'. He kept our heads up and we went out for the second-half with some belief.

"When you faced a strong side like Chelsea were in those days, it would be like playing Barcelona or Manchester City today. They had quality players – Peter Osgood, Alan Hudson, Charlie Cooke and Stevie Kember, who I'd played with at Crystal Palace.

"What made it all the more special for me was that my family were watching from the main stand. My dad, Fred, who has since died, was there. He was about to roll another fag just as I scored, so when everyone jumped up from their seats he spilt his tin of tobacco and my missus, Mandy, was covered in it!

"It still haunts me to this day. I can't put my head on the pillow without thinking about what happened that night. As players, you forget most things but it's a day that is always in the back of my mind."

"When I look at video footage from the game now, it makes me realise that we were a better team than perhaps even we thought we were at the time. We had some good players – Dennis Rofe for one.

"After the game, the players tried to get into the Coach and Horses. But we were told it was shut, so we went in the pub via the back door and when we got inside it was absolutely packed. The fans were coming up to us and going: 'All right, boys, we beat the Chelsea, eh!' It was lovely. That was a typical Orient thing, like one, big family together."

Fast-forward two years or so and Hoadley discovered how cruel football can be. What it was like to suffer at the opposite end of the spectrum. By then he had switched from right-back and established himself in the middle of the back four. In the thick of the action.

You listen to Phil re-live that awful nightmare of the drawn game against Aston Villa in May, 1974 and his pain is tangible.

"It still haunts me to this day," he admits with typical candour. "I can't put my head on the pillow without thinking about what happened that night. As players, you forget most things but it's a day that is always in the back of my mind.

"I gave away the penalty when I took out Brian Little and Ray Graydon scored from it. I can still hear Ray Goddard telling me to 'leave it' – obviously he must have felt that he could deal with the situation himself.

"But as I saw it, Little was through on goal, one-on-one with Ray, and I thought he would dribble round him and stick the ball in the net, so I felt I had to try and do something. There's always the chance he could have missed the penalty.

"I made the tackle but missed the ball and brought him down. It was a penalty.

"I was absolutely gutted to miss out on promotion by just one point. When we

Defending in the 1972 FA Cup quarter-final against Arsenal with Peter Bennett, a fellow long-distance commuter from west London.

came out of the main entrance after the game, I think we gave the flowers we'd been presented with earlier to the supporters.

"Of course, everything gets focused on that one game but we really hadn't got too many wins in the weeks leading up to the Villa match. One more point and it would have been all so different.

"For example, I remember a match at West Bromwich Albion towards the end of the season (Apr 13) which we lost 1-0. Gerry Queen had an open goal and we were all shouting 'just put it in' but he missed – and that could have been the difference. We also had a perfectly good goal ruled out against Millwall. But that's football - you can't worry about it, because it doesn't change anything.

"I don't know whether we would have survived in the top-flight but we would have given it a damned good go. I would like to think that we could have been another Wimbledon."

PHIL explained why he was happy to follow George Petchey's exodus from SE25 to E10: "He was a big influence on me and I owe him a lot.

> **"I was on £80 a week at Orient. If I was in the reserves, the money was reduced to £60 a week. I know at one stage I wanted a £10-a-week rise and I really had to battle hard for it. When you see what players earn these days, it's laughable really."**

"It was actually Arthur Rowe who scouted me and signed me for Palace but it was George who coached and encouraged me from the day I joined them. I left school at 15, turned apprentice and George continued to work with me until the day he left to take over as Orient manager."

"As a youngster I played at right-back but I was really a utility player who could play anywhere in defence except goalkeeper. My best position, though, and the one I most preferred, was centre-half.

"George brought me to Brisbane Road and, to be honest, if it wasn't for him I wouldn't have joined Orient. Palace were in the top flight at the time but I didn't see myself getting enough first team football at Selhurst Park under Malcolm Allison, so I was happy to drop into the Second Division.

"I thought the club made a mistake by sacking George at the start of the 1977-78 season but that's football."

The chasm between what players earned in the 70s – certainly more than the average person but not a fortune – and the eye-watering figures clubs lavish – in many cases waste – on even very mediocre players today is impossible to compare. Hoadley, who was a snip for Orient at £35,000, said: "Funnily enough, I was talking to somebody the other day about the money players earn now. I went rummaging through some old papers at home and found an old contract of mine which showed I was on £80 a week at Orient. If I was in the reserves, the money was reduced to £60 a week. I know at one stage I wanted a £10-a-week rise and I really had to battle hard for it. When you see what players earn these days, it's laughable really."

Two years after Hoadley signed for Os another important recruit from Palace, goalkeeper John Jackson, followed Petchey north of the Thames for 10 grand less than what Phil cost the club. On the giant in green playing behind him, he said: "Jacko was great, a fabulous fella. He was a big, old lump and you knew that when he came out for the ball he would knock you flat. But you didn't mind, because he'd come and deal with crosses and that's all a central defender wants to know.

"Before Jacko, we had Ray Goddard – he played in the cup games against Chelsea and Arsenal in '72 – and he was another good keeper. Ray, bless him, who died the other year, was another lovely fella. When I lived at Wimbledon and he was based at Putney, he used to pick me up in his Mini and drive us to Orient."

The journey from west to east was one Hoadley regularly shared with two other team-mates.

An unusual group of players, wearing an assortment of clothing, pictured by Tony Furby during the 1975-76 season. Back row, left to right: Gerry Queen, Bobby Fisher, Bill Roffey. Middle row: Laurie Cunningham, Alan Whittle, Derek Possee, Tony Grealish. Front row: Peter Allen, Nigel Gray, Glenn Roeder and Phil Hoadley.

Captain Phil meets his Partick Thistle counterpart John Craig before the Anglo-Scottish Cup semi-final, second leg at Brisbane Road in November, 1976. Os topped their ASC group ahead of Norwich, Chelsea and Fulham, saw off Scottish Premier Leaguers Partick in the semis but were beaten 5-1 on aggregate by Nottingham Forest in the final.

"Peter Bennett – we all called him 'Les' – and Joe Mayo both became close pals of mine because I spent so much time with them travelling into training. We lived out Windsor way, in a village called Englefield Green, and used to meet up at eight o'clock and get to Leytonstone around 10.00am.

"We'd get a train from Egham to Waterloo, change, and then take the Underground to Bank, change again, get the Central Line to Leyton, and then on to the training ground. It was unbelievable and I did that for seven years.

"Sometimes we might change our routine and drive in. We'd go around the North Circular, via Hanger Lane, but that was often a nightmare and we preferred the train."

What about the three fellow central defenders he played alongside? "I probably enjoyed playing with Paul Harris – or 'Dobbin' as we knew him – the most. He wasn't the quickest but like all players at Orient then, he was genuine and gave his all. He'd put his head in where others wouldn't. We had a good understanding and we still keep in touch – he's been up to Norfolk to visit.

"Tom Walley was really a midfielder who played a bit at the back. I liked Tommy. He used to make me laugh. When we did cross-country runs, he'd go running off as fast as you like but he'd soon be knackered and come in last. He'd whack you in the stomach as his way of saying 'good morning'.

"Paul was a more natural centre-half than Tommy – Dobbin couldn't play anywhere else!

"It was probably harder for me, physically, when we played Glenn Roeder as sweeper but, then again, it was good to know that I had someone quick behind me. He was a good, young player coming through in the late 70s.

"We played four at the back with Glenn sweeping. He didn't touch the ball in a lot of games and wasn't hard enough to be a defender as such. But he was a confident lad and the first player in England I saw perform the step-over – the 'shuffle' as they called it. Glenn often seemed quite miserable but he was a good guy and everyone got on well."

Phil revealed that he also played alongside another former Orient centre-half before he left Crystal Palace. He represented South of England as a schoolboy and it was then that he combined with Tommy Taylor, while the duo later teamed up when selected for the England Youth side. "I used to do all his running for him and I think that's one reason why I probably had to retire early!" Phil joked. "By the time I went to Orient, Tommy had moved on to went to West Ham, so he obviously didn't fancy having me around again!"

A natural leader you would want alongside you in any battle, Hoadley was handed extra responsibility when he succeeded Peter Allen as captain. As well as Roeder, there were a number of other teenagers emerging in the mid-70s. Did Phil ever have to bring them in line?

"Laurie Cunningham didn't give me any cause for concern but I had to have a few words with 'Paddy' Grealish, bless him. He liked a drink and I'd say: 'Tone, you don't smell right' and 'don't do that again' – that sort of thing. And he respected what I said.

"But 'Lol' was brilliant. We would have plenty of banter. I used to give him some stick, to be honest. He told me once: 'If we (black people) take over the world, you'll be the first to go!' He also told me to sort my barnet out. But he was awful at card games.

"We had a few hard men in the team, people like Bill Roffey and Tom Walley who were prepared to kick anything that moved. But, generally speaking, if there were any problems on the pitch there were always a few players to sort things out.

"Another excellent player, who didn't get the recognition he deserved, was Ricky Heppolette. Orient signed him from Preston and he did a great job for us. I actually played with him in Hong Kong much later in our careers and he was another terrific lad.

"Terry Brisley was another unsung hero. He was a terrific team player and one of those you tended to take for granted, although you really missed him when he wasn't playing. 'Les' Bennett was good on the ball. He wasn't the quickest but he was a key part of the team and proved a really good signing from West Ham. He and Bobby Fisher were both funny guys.

"It surprised me a little just how well Ian Bowyer did in the game and the same applies to Dennis Rofe. We knew they were both good, talented players and had ability but Ian went on to forge a really outstanding career at Forest and good luck to him. Dennis worked hard at his game and did really well at Leicester after signing for them for a six-figure fee. He later played for Chelsea and Southampton.

"All the players I've mentioned in the course of this interview and a few that I haven't – people

Phil (5), Glenn Roeder (6) and Peter Bennett (11) defend a Chelsea attack during the 1978 FA Cup tie at Brisbane Road, while policemen patrol behind John Jackson's goal following yet another outbreak of crowd trouble involving the same visiting fans.

149

like Alan Whittle and Derrick Downing – helped make my days at Orient so special. They all had something about them. For instance, Gerry Queen – who was a good mate of mine – was quick but the fastest when I was at Orient was Barrie Fairbrother. He was lightning-quick."

FOUR years after Arsenal burst Os' FA Cup bubble, Phil led the side out to face the Gunners in the 1978 semi-final at Stamford Bridge. His reaction to the 3-0 defeat again underlines this good bloke's natural empathy for what the fans endured.

"As we walked off the pitch at the end I thought, 'this ain't right'. Thousands of Orient supporters were there and they must have been as gutted as us, so I got the players to come back out onto the pitch to clap them and show our appreciation."

By then, Orient were again under the management of Jimmy Bloomfield, although Phil says: "I never really got to know Jimmy very well in the relatively short time we spent together at Orient. He was poorly and away from the club a lot having treatment, so Peter Angell took charge of the team and that's when we went on our Cup run in '78.

"All the players liked Peter. When George left we urged Peter to apply for the manager's job but he didn't fancy the extra pressure. It was such a shame that both Jimmy and Peter died at an early age."

Little more than a month after suffering abject semi-final misery, Hoadley was about to make unwanted history at Orient, as the first player to exercise his right to leave the club under the new freedom of contract rule. He joined Norwich City for a fee of £110,000 fixed by a tribunal.

"The offer I received from Norwich was simply too good to refuse," he explained. "They were in the First Division, a league above Orient, they doubled my wages and also gave me a car – a Triumph Herald with an 8-track stereo and everything. I think it had a sun-roof too!

"The fact that I was the first player to move from Orient under freedom of contract led to a crazy situation, because I wasn't even allowed to train properly with the club after my contract had run out and before I'd signed for John Bond at Norwich. I joined in some of the five-a-sides at the end but not the rest of the session – it was stupid.

Phil in his final season at Orient before his historic transfer to Norwich.

"It's gone too far the other way now. If a club wants to buy a player, they don't talk to him, they speak to his agent first. The only 'agent' I had was my wife!

"The funny thing is, two days after I signed for Norwich, I returned to Orient and went out for a sherbet with all the lads. That's the way it was."

Hoadley made 89 appearances for The Canaries before going on loan to a club in Hong Kong called Eastern Athletic, where a serious knee injury ended his professional career in 1981. Phil moved into the non-league scene with Loddon, Norwich United and Holt United as manager before starting a building business and then running The Queen's Head pub in his home village of Thurlton.

> **"For me it was all about the family thing, the bonding of players and supporters. There were no big-time Charlies in our 70s' teams. Before training in the morning, I'd go and see the groundsman and sit down and have a cup of coffee and a fag with him and the other groundstaff. What players do that now?"**

"I was only about 30 when I had to retire and it was a big shock. I'd always played football as long as I could remember but I needed to work because the bills still kept coming through," he added.

In 1997 he returned to Norwich City as their 'Football in the Community' officer and has remained a friendly, familiar face on the Carrow Road scene as a popular match day host in the club's corporate hospitality lounges.

"It was 40 years ago that I moved up to Norwich and I never expected to stay in the area even after I retired. But the family became settled there, it suited us perfectly and we're still there." Phil and Mandy Hoadley, who married in June, 1972, have three grown-up children: Daniel, Tommy and Kelly; and 10 grandchildren: Millie, Bella, Libby, Freddie, Jack, Ellie, William, George, Hannah and Katie.

Final thoughts from one of Orient's finest servants: "What the game lacks now is physical contact. That's wrong, because it's a man's game. The way I used to tackle, I probably wouldn't last 10 minutes in the modern game. I look at the DVD of the Orient Cup game with Chelsea in '72 and see tackles that players like Ron 'Chopper' Harris were putting in . . . and the referee is just waving play on. These days, all you'd see are red cards.

"Players generally seemed to enjoy playing then, when there was often a smile or a wink during the game.

"As for Orient, for me it was all about the family thing, the bonding of players and supporters. There were no big-time Charlies in our 70s' teams. Before training in the morning, I'd go and see the groundsman – I can't remember his name but he was a Welshman, Tommy Walley's mate – and sit down and have a cup of coffee and a fag with him and the other groundstaff. What players do that now?

"I've played for Palace, Orient and Norwich and there was good camaraderie everywhere but when I go back to Orient, it always feels like I'm coming home. It's fantastic that so many Orient fans still remember me and *the* goal – they always mention it whenever I go back."

Interview: Tony McDonald & Paul Hiscock

Management, coaches, players and staff gather for this unusual group photo taken during the 1975-76 season.

Tommy Taylor, Henry Hughton, Bobby Fisher and Billy Jennings weight training in 1979-80.

Calm before the storm. Photographer Tony Furby captured this relaxed dressing room scene featuring Ray Goddard, Derrick Downing, Bill Roffey and skipper Peter Allen shortly before the final home game of the 1973-74 season, when Aston Villa held Os to the 1-1 draw that ultimately denied us a place in the top flight.

In safe keeping

Born: Hammersmith, London, September 5, 1942
Usual position: Goalkeeper Orient Career: 1973-79
Orient Appearances: League 223/5, FA Cup 15, League Cup 10
Orient Goals: League 226, FA Cup 19, League Cup 11

IF any Orient fan thought George Petchey was mad to sign a 31-year-old goalkeeper when he had a perfectly capable one – Ray Goddard – who was seven years younger and had plenty of football left in him, then they would be proved totally wrong.

John Jackson, once called England's best uncapped keeper, repaid his £25,000 transfer fee to Crystal Palace time and again over a six-year period in which he firmly established himself as Os' greatest number one in living memory.

In particular, his heroics 'between the sticks' during the 1978 FA Cup surge spring to mind but his main strength was his sheer dependable consistency over an admirable 18-year career that spanned a staggering 656 league matches.

'Jacko' already had 364 league appearances under his belt when Petchey plucked him from Malcolm Allison's Selhurst Park revolution in October, 1973. Palace fans have still not forgiven Big Mal for discarding Jackson – whose saves had done much to help Palace reach the top flight for the first time in 1969 and then keep them there the following season – and treating him so disrespectfully. Allison gave the green jersey to Paul Hammond but his decision to oust the cult hero backfired. Palace's loss was certainly Orient's gain.

> **"Ray Goddard was very popular with the fans and it did take a while for me to win them over. Ray and I got on really well; we had no beef with each other."**

Jackson was a bold signing by Petchey, because Ray Goddard was a long-time crowd favourite, having held down the number one jersey since taking over the gloves from Ron Willis at the start of the 1967-68 season.

"Ray was very popular with the fans and it did take a while for me to win them over," John admits. "But Ray and I got on really well; we had no beef with each other. There were a couple of other goalkeepers at the club at that time as well; Mike O'Shaughnessy was one. But we all got along OK. We all understood that if you didn't do your job properly, you'd lose your place in the side."

Jackson made his Orient debut in the 2-0 home win over Luton Town on October 20. Recalling his first impressions, he said: "The initial feeling was that they were a nice, friendly club. I was made very welcome by everybody – not just the players but all the staff members and so it was a nice atmosphere to come into. I just hoped that I could help push the club forward.

"I'd worked with George at Palace and seemed to get on OK with him, so when he contacted me about joining him at Orient, I thought 'why not?'. To be honest, it didn't take much to persuade me to move from Palace. As far as certain people at that club were concerned, my time there was finished, so I felt it was in my best interest to move on.

"Yes, I was leaving a First Division club to go down a division but knowing George as a good coach, I felt we would have a good chance of getting Orient into the top-flight.

"There wasn't a lot of difference between the facilities at the two clubs. At Palace, we always had to train at different places during the week, because we never had our own training ground. Sometimes we'd use the Crystal Palace Sports Centre, which had a running track around it. We did

Jacko with his Player of the Season award at the Sportsmans' Club, Spring Hill, Clapton after the final home game of the 1974-75 season in which he kept 19 clean sheets in an ever-present 42 league matches.

cross-country runs at Hayes in Kent and on Fridays we'd kick a ball about in a car park that had a black shale-like surface. So coming to Orient at that time was easy – they were in a similar situation."

Jackson and Petchey clearly enjoyed a mutually beneficial working relationship spanning most of their respective parallel careers.

"I spent a lot of time with George throughout my career at Palace, Orient, Millwall and then Brighton, where he asked me to do some coaching with their youth side," says John. "George was one of those people who would support a player through thick and thin provided they gave everything out on the pitch. You might be on the end of a hammering in some games but if he thought you were giving 100 per cent, he'd defend you.

"But he didn't take fools lightly. Anyone who didn't put in a shift . . . well, he'd soon sort them out. I learned a lot about coaching just from watching him. George was very shrewd and astute. His tactical nous was outstanding."

As you would expect from having spent such a long time together in football, Jackson and Petchey always worked in harmony.

"I never had any fall-outs with George. My attitude was to just go into work and get the job done. It was always just a job to me. Like all professional players, it's your living and it's not like being a fan. A fan will support the same club year after year and you see some fans who get upset because a player gets transferred and some see that player being a traitor. I could never understand that.

"If I heard fans saying that, I'd ask them what job they did and they might say: 'I'm an engineer' or something. And I always said to those fans: 'Well, if someone came in and offered to double your money, you'd go – wouldn't you?'. But they never really saw it like that; they felt your players should always stay with their club.

"But it's just a job. You might have a wife and kids to look after and because you want to do the best for them, you'll go wherever you need to achieve the best living for yourself and the family.

"George always treated me fairly in regards to my own contract; I've no complaints about that."

JOINING Os must have felt like a home from home for Jackson. "A few of my former team-mates from Palace had already moved across to Orient before I got there – people like David Payne, Phil Hoadley and Gerry Queen, and then Bill Roffey came in a week after me.

"I lived down in Hove and used to travel up by train every day with Peter Allen. So after we had finished training, we'd tend to get our skates on and catch the first train back home.

"I didn't mix a lot with the other players outside of training simply because of where I lived. I wasn't stand-offish or anything like that. A number of the boys would go out together in the afternoon after training had finished but I never did – and neither did I do that at Palace, to be honest, because I was in the same situation. I'd just dash off and get the train home; I was married with kids.

"The thing I did appreciate about living down on the Sussex coast was that if things hadn't gone well in training or whatever, I had an hour on the train to mull things over and get it out of my system before I got home to the wife (Cathrine) and three daughters (Ruth, Sarah and Amanda).

"I'm afraid a lot of the lads who lived local to clubs would walk down the street and people would start to talk to them, so the players couldn't get away from it. Fortunately, I didn't have any of that – I could just get away and clear my head.

> **"I don't think we had any dressing room cliques, despite the number of former Palace players we had at Orient. Team spirit was always good."**

"I don't think we had any dressing room cliques, despite the number of former Palace players we had at Orient. Team spirit was always good.

"George always ensured the players got together at Christmas. It was something he'd done at Palace, so it continued and we always had a good time. There was always someone who was pulling a few stunts and larking about but it was all done in good fun. There were a few jokers around the place and there was good camaraderie in the dressing room.

"When I was at Palace people like Stevie Kember, David Payne and myself were always up to tricks and I liked to wind a few players up. David was a comedian; he would often be really quiet and then come up with some prank or wisecrack and get everyone laughing. Bill Roffey was a funny guy and Peter Allen was boss-cat. He was club captain but I got on well with him and still see him now on occasions.

"I'm in a walking group down in Hove. Because I've got diabetes, it's good to do some exercise to try and keep fit, so on a Wednesday night I walk along the sea front with my group and now and again, I see Peter and his wife out walking the dog."

JACKO also approved of George Petchey's training philosophy: "When I was at Palace one of my managers, Dick Graham, who managed Orient for a while in the 60s, had been a goalkeeper with West Bromwich Albion in his playing career. He took me and Bill Glazier for coaching sessions – I was in the reserves and Bill was Palace's first team goalie.

"We worked a lot on our own game but Dick insisted that we also did all the same work the outfield players were doing. I'd say: 'Dick, why am I doing all this running? I only have to go out as far as the 18-yard line, I'm rarely going beyond that'. But he told me to get on with the running. He was a strong character, so we had to keep going.

"Later, when George was first team coach and in charge of training, he's do goalkeeping drills with us and he continued that when I came to Orient.

"But I used to do a lot of goalkeeping disciplines myself. I thought a lot about my positional play – trying to work out angles, where I should be on my six-yard line and the various positions I should be in for crosses and corners.

"Also, I would tell other players what to do both in training and in matches. Because I believed that if I got the players to do the correct things in front of me, it would make my job a lot easier.

And George encouraged me in that respect.

Fitness was hardly an issue for Jacko. He made 220 consecutive league appearances for Palace before playing 210 successive Division Two games for Orient. How does he explain his exemplary appearance record?

"Generally, I could look after myself and I suppose I was lucky that I avoided finger injuries and things like that which could have kept me out of action. I did suffer a hairline leg fracture, though, when I came to Orient and that caused me to miss a few matches.

"I actually played with the fracture for a couple of weeks without realising I had the injury. I got sent to hospital for an x-ray after one particular game but nothing showed up, although I knew something wasn't right. So I was resting all week and playing on the Saturday but eventually, I went for another X-ray and this time, it showed a hairline fracture and that caused me to miss the end of the season – the one when we so nearly got promoted.

"In those days, you earned your money playing for the first team – you'd not earn much playing for the reserves – and so it was my living and I had to ensure that I was always at the top of my game. It's different today with all the money that's around. I suppose I was lucky to keep fit. I did get a few knocks but I just tended to shrug them off. I wasn't one to go charging along to the physio, telling him I'd done this or that. Obviously, I needed to see him from time to time but I just carried on playing.

"It was a bit like how it is today . . . there aren't many keepers that get injuries that keep them out for a long period of time. Not like outfield players who are on the end of a bad tackle and do some serious damage.

"Going back to the hairline fracture injury, I couldn't even remember how I did it. My shin hurt me a bit as I came off the pitch at the end of a game and I thought that I may have been caught with a boot. We used to wear shin pads, of course, and I thought nothing more about the injury until it got progressively worse.

"No team has a right to win the league or finish in the top three, because there are so many clubs trying to achieve those places, but the way in which Villa scrapped and fought for every ball, well, that was a big surprise to me. It makes you think."

"I never wanted to give myself any excuses for not playing well. I felt that if I'd not played well, it was because I hadn't done certain things properly during a match.

"So I'd wear what I thought was my lucky shirt, a bit of superstition really, and it was so that I couldn't start blaming a bad performance on not wearing my lucky shirt. I was an honest guy and would analyse what went wrong in my performance and what I should do to put it right. If I wasn't playing well, I knew there must be a reason and I tried to eliminate all the things that could possibly be used as an excuse."

ORIENT stumbled in their quest for promotion in the spring of 1974 without their trusty custodian, who finally succumbed to the shin injury after we lost 3-1 at Luton on March 16. This incredible 210-match sequence – falling just 18 short of the club record set by legendary pre-war keeper Arthur Wood – ended an ever-present run stretching back to the first game of the 1974-75 season. His young understudy, John Smeulders, had to be content with very few low-key cup outings over a five-year period.

Jacko missed all of Os' last nine games of the '74 run-in which yielded only two victories, five draws and two defeats. In truth, the team had already run out of steam, failing to win any of its previous six league matches before Ray Goddard regained his place.

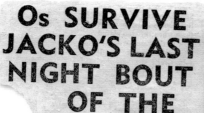

Os SURVIVE JACKO'S LAST NIGHT BOUT OF THE JITTERS

It was extremely rare for John to make the headlines for an error but a draw against Hull in May, 1977 turned out to be just enough to keep Os safe.

Glover's goal keeps them up

ORIENT 1
HULL C 1

"I RECKON Jacko had taken a bribe," joked Orient manager George Petchey nervously, laughing off the bizarre goal his veteran 'keeper had conceded ten minutes from the end of Tuesday's relegation cliffhanger with Hull City.

Jackson had allowed a speculative 40 yards lob from Hull's Paul Haigh to creep into his net after bouncing once just inside the penalty box ...

"We're staying up." Orient celebrate with the champagne after Tuesday's hard-earned point from Hull that ensures their Second Division survival.

We will never know if Jackson would have saved Ray Graydon's decisive penalty that secured Aston Villa the point that denied Os promotion on the last night of the season. It must have been agonising for John sitting on the bench having to watch us play one of the most important games in the club's history knowing there was nothing he could do to influence the outcome.

"Well, that's part and parcel of football, isn't it? But I will say this. I couldn't believe how committed Aston Villa were. It was the last game of the season for them, they hadn't got a chance of winning anything and they had no fears about relegation – they were in mid-table – so to a certain extent, you wouldn't have expected them to be playing as if they were going for promotion in the manner we were. I'm not suggesting that you'd expect them to just go through the motions but to play the way they did, as if their lives depended on the result, was very unusual.

"No team has a right to win the league or finish in the top three, because there are so many clubs trying to achieve those places, but the way in which Villa scrapped and fought for every ball, well, that was a big surprise to me. It makes you think."

Denied a second crack at top level football, John and his team-mates were also deprived of an FA Cup Final appearance at the final hurdle in 1978. Looking back at that unforgettable run in which he pulled off a string of crucial saves, especially to deny a long-range shot from Chelsea's Ian Britton in the dying moments of the goalless fifth round draw at Brisbane Road, he says: "The outstanding memory for me is playing at Stamford Bridge in the semi-final against Arsenal and they had Malcolm MacDonald at centre-forward. And he got two goals that both took wicked deflections. The first one . . . he took a shot and it was going out for a throw-in on the other side of the pitch when it flew across the box and hit poor Bill Roffey, who was tearing back to try and help out, and went into the back of the net.

"Arsenal really hadn't done much against us at that stage. Tactically, we'd got them and they were getting frustrated. So that goal gave them the advantage.

"Then MacDonald scored another deflected goal (via Glenn Roeder) and that was us done for, which was a great pity.

"But we'd had so many good performances on the way through our Cup run. We had a group of players who were at ease with each other and were happy to help one another and work hard.

159

"Tactically, we had a little bit of a different way of playing compared to other sides and we got some good results."

ASK supporters to nominate John Jackson's best-ever game in Orient colours and the chances are they will recall the FA Cup fourth round tie at Ipswich Town in January, 1979. The colossus the fans nicknamed 'Stonewall' defied everything Ipswich could throw at him in the goalless draw played on a near frozen Portman Road pitch.

Invite them to remember a rare Jacko clanger and they will cast their minds back to the final game of the 1976-77 season – Petchey's last before being sacked early the following season – when Orient needed at least a point at home to Hull City to avoid being relegated to Division Three. They achieved their task thanks to a 1-1 draw – but only after an uncharacteristic error by their normally dependable keeper 10 minutes from time, when a speculative '40-yard lob' by Paul Haigh slipped horribly through his raised hands and ended up in the net. Luckily, Allan Glover's 36th minute goal proved just enough.

Ask Os fans to name another costly Jackson blunder and they will invariably scratch their heads, lost for words.

All these years later, John admits his memory is a little bit hazy when it comes to the finer details. "I honestly couldn't say there was a single stand out game. I just wanted to do well in every match I played. I always looked upon the goalkeeper as being either the hero or the idiot. You can have 10 shots against you, play well and stop nine. But let one in that's your fault, and that's the one and only shot people remember.

"What I learned quickly was not to get on a high just because I'd played well but, then again, not to become too disheartened when things didn't go to plan."

> **"I always looked upon the goalkeeper as being either the hero or the idiot. You can have 10 shots against you, play well and stop nine. But let one in that's your fault, and that's the one and only shot people remember."**

Jackson points out that it wasn't the departure of Petchey – and the return of Jimmy Bloomfield – that prompted his own exit in the summer of 1979.

He said: "Jimmy was a nice guy, he wanted to help people and always wanted to do things right. I had no problems with Jimmy and I only left the club because he'd paid a lot of money to bring in Mervyn Day from West Ham. I couldn't see a club the size and stature of Orient paying out a lot of money for a player if he wasn't going to play in their first team, so I spoke with Jimmy about it. He said: 'Johnno, I want you to teach people about goalkeeping, including him'.

"I replied: 'You haven't spent all that money just for me to coach him. Look, because of my age I'm coming to the end of my career and I've given the club six years decent service, so I'd appreciate it if you'd allow me to join another club who might still want me for their first team'. I just thought it was in my best interests to go somewhere else and he agreed."

Orient paid West Ham £100,000 for 24-year-old Day – a club record for a keeper – and the former Chelmsford schoolboy made 170 league appearances over the next four seasons at Brisbane Road.

By a twist of irony, Jacko's last game for Orient – aged 36 – was against his former club Palace in the televised home game on May 5, 1979. The ITV cameras were in attendance to capture the south Londoners clinch the title, a point ahead of Brighton.

"I didn't realise at the time that the final game of the season would be my last for Orient, because Jimmy went and signed Day in the summer. By then, George Petchey was at Millwall, we obviously knew each other really well and he contacted me and made me an offer which I accepted."

Jackson cost the Lions a small fee of £7,500 and after 79 appearances at the old Den he moved on to Ipswich Town in August, 1981. Just one outing, against Manchester United in the top flight, was followed 12 months later by a four-game spell for Hereford United in his 40th year.

His last job in football was as youth development officer at Brighton between June, 1996 and May, 1998, while his old guv'nor George Petchey was Seagulls' assistant manager.

In conclusion, we can only acknowledge what a shrewd piece of business it was for all concerned when, in 1973, Petchey revisited his old club again and came away with one of England's finest goalkeepers. Only the successive sustained brilliance of legendary England keepers Gordon Banks, Peter Shilton and Ray Clemence prevented him from earning a full international cap.

"Going to Orient was a good move for me and I hope the club and the fans think it was also good for them. That's not for me to say – it's for them to make that judgement," says the ever-modest Jacko, who kept an astonishing 83 clean sheets for Os.

"There's nothing I can look back on and say I wish I'd done this or that differently, or wish that I could have changed anything – apart, of course, from that drawn game with Villa and the FA Cup semi-final.

"I'm glad that I played in the era I did – although I'd like the money they earn now – but there are certainly no regrets. If players can earn the money they do nowadays, then good luck to them. Today, it's all about the individual rather than the player being part of the club. It takes a lot to get players to play for each other as we did when I was playing.

"I was delighted to have played for Orient – it's tragic to see where they are now – and I have a lot of good memories of my time there. It was just a shame that I didn't bring them some success."

Interview: Paul Hiscock

SUN SOCCERCARD No 432

J. JACKSON (Orient)

JACKO'S ORIENT CLEAN SHEETS				
	LEAGUE		CUPS*	
	M	CS	M	CS
1973-74	16	5	3	0
1974-75	42	19	4	0
1975-76	42	13	2	0
1976-77	42	12	8	5
1977-78	42	11	9	4
1978-79	42	13	4	1
Totals	226	73	30	10
* FAC & LC				

JACKO'S PENALTY SAVES			
1	Oct 27, 1973	A	Oxford Utd
2	Feb 21, 1976	A	Southampton
3	Nov 8, 1976	A	Partick Thistle (ASC)
4	Mar 29, 1977	A	Nottm Forest
5	Oct 8, 1977	A	Notts County
6	Oct 29, 1977	H	Millwall

The TROUBLE with Orient

PAUL ROBERTS doesn't hesitate a second to calculate what supporting Leyton Orient has cost him down the years: "Two marriages, four jobs and about £25,000 a season since 2001."

He was sacked from one job after his boss spotted him in the crowd, wearing a high-vis jacket during a televised game at Stockport County.

Born in Leyton in July, 1963, Paul is affectionately known as 'Beefy' to his friends and it's not difficult to see why. He's big and powerful and, though living in Colchester, now earns a living providing security for wealthy Premier League footballers and celebrities in posher parts of north London – a far cry from his Leyton working class roots.

But inside that large frame beats an equally big heart that pumps out unconditional love for the Orient and which he always wears on his sleeve.

"I was born and bred at 96 Church Street, just 150 metres from the ground, where I lived with my mum. I was one of the local scallywags. At the ages of seven, eight or nine we didn't have any money and our parents couldn't afford to pay for us to go in, so our group of about half a dozen used to bunk into the ground over the wall behind the West Stand, or wherever else we could get in. We just used to try our luck.

"The first game I actually paid to watch was against Plymouth Argyle – we beat them 1-0 – in September, 1975."

One of Beef's favourite stories has former Os' boss Jimmy Bloomfield at the centre of it. He said: "One day Jimmy saw us outside the ground before a home game and as he approached in his trademark suit with the overcoat folded over one arm, he asked: 'Have you eaten, lads?' Of course we hadn't – we were a bunch of scallies from the Beaumont Road estate. Some days dinner and tea didn't exist. Anyway, we told Jimmy that we'd be bunking into the ground as usual and he just said: 'OK, come and see me afterwards and we'll have a word'. We thought, 'fair enough'.

"So after the game we went back around to the main entrance, where we met up with him again. The next thing we knew, Jimmy invited us into the main stand and gave us some leftover food from one of the lounges. We scoffed the lot. That went down very well and showed just what a great club we were.

"When I got home Mum wanted to know why I was so late. I told her I'd been with Jimmy Bloomfield and he fed us all. 'Who's he?" she asked. 'He's the manager of Orient,' I replied. 'Never heard of em,' she said. 'They play down the road, by the way,' I told her.

"For a kid to watch live football in the 70s was very inspiring, an incredible experience. It was a great time to be supporting Orient on my own manor. We were growing and rebuilding as a club again and to see us beat Chelsea and rub shoulders with the likes of Arsenal in the Cup was superb. We were most probably punching above our weight but we were still a good club, getting regular crowds of 9,000 to 10,000."

Beefy attended Sybourn Infants in Walthamstow, followed by George Mitchell School and Leyton Senior High. "At school in those days, you were either Orient, Spurs or West Ham. If you lived this side of the borough (of Waltham Forest), in Leyton or Leytonstone, you were a West Ham or Orient fan; if you came from Walthamstow or Chingford, you supported Spurs.

"Many people looked upon Orient as their second team. I was actually a 'Cockney Red' from birth – I loved Man United and in particular Bobby Charlton – but I've always been an Orient fan.

"I used to sell Orient lottery tickets from a booth on platform one at Liverpool Street station. We thought that whatever we could do to bring money in to the club was good for us."

HOOLIGANISM

WHILE many of us like to romanticise about the 'golden era of the 70s', the reality is that it was a nasty decade riddled by trouble in and around football grounds. Hooliganism was rampant on a scale that is unimaginable for supporters today who enjoy relative luxury surroundings in all-seater stadia.

Even the most low-key matches, attended by less than five-figure crowds, when nothing but pride and the league points were at stake, would be marred by outbreaks of fighting.

And if there was something important on the line, like promotion or relegation, as well as

Paul 'Beefy' Roberts in the Laurie Cunningham Bar at Leyton Orient in October, 2018.

163

The great Sir Matt Busby appeals for calm and order as trouble flares.

kicking s**t out of each other on the terraces, hundreds would clamber over perimeter walls at full-time to dance or fight on the pitch. Earlier still if you were from Millwall or Chelsea, your team was losing and you made a futile attempt to get the match abandoned.

On the worst occasions, those unfortunate supporters innocently caught up in the mayhem were carried off on stretchers to the medical room or a waiting ambulance.

At Orient in the 70s we witnessed pitch invasions, terrace battles, a bomb scare and innocent old ladies and children injured by collapsing concrete walls.

And it was a good thing that the wall did give way in 1978, or else kids at the front might have been killed as troublemakers at the back of the South Terrace surged forward in a deliberate, calculated manner. We'll come back to that very shortly . . .

The bomb threat came on the final night of the 1971-72 season, when Birmingham City beat Os 1-0 to clinch promotion and prevent Millwall from going up to the First Division for the first time. The huge crowd of 33,363 (eyewitnesses insist there were more) included several thousand Lions' fans who, in an attempt to get the game abandoned, invaded the pitch near the end of the match.

Around the same time PA announcer Keith Simpson pleaded with fans to evacuate the main stand because the club had been alerted to a possible IRA bomb under the main stand. Apparently, one device was defused, while another harmless mini 'explosion' was dismissed as a firecracker.

Supporter Ron Hudson, who runs the wonderfully nostalgic Facebook group, 'Orient FC – Remembering the 70s', recalls how fear forced his family to miss the Birmingham game. He said: "I was 10 and got to the turnstiles at the Coronation Gardens end with my dad, uncles, brother and cousins. Between them they decided it was too dangerous to go in, so we walked back over the bridge to the cars along Ruckholt Road, Eton Manner. They had no idea about the importance of the game. All they wanted to do was go and watch the Os' last match of the season."

Kevin Cowlan did watch the game and recalls: "There was an incredible atmosphere in the ground. The crowd was something like 33,000, tightly packed on all terraces, and as the match neared its conclusion, the atmosphere became quite threatening. It was evident there was a fairly large Millwall contingent in the ground and an Os win would have meant them being promoted instead of Brum.

"I was in the old West Side, at the front of the terrace, and on the final whistle I jumped over the wall and went onto the pitch to join hundreds of others to cheer our players off.

"I recall feeling quite intimidated as scuffles were breaking out all over the pitch. And then over the tannoy came the voice of PA announcer Keith Simpson asking everyone to evacuate the East Stand, as there had been a bomb warning.

"As you can imagine, it was mayhem for a while and I do remember a small 'explosion' while I was on the pitch but I think it was no more than a firecracker. The police restored order after a while.

"It was only a couple of years earlier I had stood on that same pitch applauding Terry Mancini and all the Os squad as we celebrated the Division Three championship. The two scenes were in marked contrast but I consider myself privileged to have been around then to witness some great Orient

The visit of Man United made headlines for all the wrong reasons.

teams and characters of that era."

Vincent Sheehan added: "Bob Latchford scored the winner – and help throw some Millwall fans off the pitch as they tried to get the match abandoned. Some Millwall threw a piano leg into Blues fans behind one of the goals but soon regretted it because all the older Market lads from Brum were positioned there."

Stephen Yelland: "I was there with a mate and his girlfriend. We were in the East Stand and watched the Millwall fans invade the pitch. Then, at the end, there were increasingly urgent announcements asking us all to evacuate to the pitch. We bundled over the wall on to the grass but two or three press reporters remained in their seats with a screaming Keith Simpson urging, then pleading, with them to get out of the stand. In the end, it was, as others have suggested, just a large firecracker but before that it was just a tad scary."

Os fans swarmed onto the pitch after seeing their team secure a vital point against Hull City in May, 1977.

Beefy sums it up: "They were very bad, hard times. There was a real breakdown in society, with millions of people stuck in poverty. We had three-day working weeks and power cuts – not nice when you live on the 11th floor of a tower block and no lifts work after 6.00pm. The country was in recession, there was plenty of angst about and a lot of people were just losing it, so football seemed the ideal outlet for them to vent all their pent up frustration and aggression. Three o'clock on Saturday was the time to let it all out."

INVASION OF THE RED ARMY

I WAS a 14-year-old on that hot Saturday afternoon in August, the first day of the 1974-75 season, when newly-relegated Manchester United were in town. Mighty Man United in the Second Division was big news in itself but it wasn't their 2-0 victory that made the headlines that weekend; it was the unruly behaviour of their fans, who must have made up half to three-quarters of the near 18,000 crowd. Considering the stadium capacity was considerably higher, it's safe to assume that it wasn't just holidays that accounted for the stay-aways.

The atmosphere inside and outside the ground was palpably hostile from lunch-time onwards, when long queues began to form at the turnstiles. The police were obviously on high alert, with meat wagons patrolling the surrounding streets or parked up along Brisbane Road. An already difficult task was made all the tougher for the coppers trying to distinguish between two sets of fans decked out in red and white scarves and the visiting hordes made up of London-based 'Cockney Reds' and thousands of others from the Home Counties with southern accents.

There were dozens of arrests inside the ground, one or two pitch invaders were thrown out and at one point United director, their great former manager Sir Matt Busby, stood in the directors' box and appealed for calm over the PA system.

"The Man United invasion was proper mad stuff," says Beefy. "High Road shops were boarded up from the Thursday and all the red army descended on Walthamstow on the Friday night. Then, on the day of the game, they went on a long march down to the ground – it was a sight to behold,

Players Gerry Queen, Glenn Roeder, Terry Brisley and David Payne inspect graffiti sprayed on walls outside the ground in Brisbane Road by West Ham fans in 1976 . . . and (inset) the clean-up operation outside the main entrance is underway.

One of the darkest days at Orient, when walls at both the Coronation Gardens end and in the south-west corner of the West Stand gave way as fans surged forward during the Chelsea Cup tie in 1978. Also, see opposite pic. . .

one long procession down Hoe Street and Leyton High Road, with lads carrying large cans of Watney Party Seven and fights breaking out at every pub along the way."

Angi Brown became an unwitting victim of trouble that day. She recalls: "I was selling 'Goal-time' tickets under the East Stand and the Man United supporters pushed me to the ground and stole my money."

Bill Harrison observed: "It was no surprise that at a ground that could hold 35,000 against the biggest football club in the land, only 17,000-odd turned up. That's what hooliganism did to our beautiful game."

Laurence Hoppen recalls: "I entered the ground in my usual place, the South Terrace, and was horrified to see that it had been allocated to the 'other fans from London'. I asked a steward to transfer me to the section containing Orient fans and he walked me around the perimeter of the pitch and said that I would have to leave the ground in one door and re-enter.

"That was all very well but nobody could find a key to let me out. While it eventually got resolved, I suddenly thought, 'what if there is a fire? How would the fans get out? Where are the fire engines?'.

" Not so many years later we witnessed the Valley Parade disaster, and that reminded me of the Manchester United game. Thankfully, Leyton Orient have always had a good relationship with the local fire service, whose attendance is quite visible."

As was widely expected, Manchester United made a swift return to the First Division, going back up as champions the following May, and have not returned to Brisbane Road for a league or cup game ever since. Unfortunately, Chelsea have been far more frequent visitors for all manner of fixtures, including a Anglo-Scottish Cup tie in 1976.

The skirmishes that took place on the field immediately following the final whistle of Os' famous FA Cup victory over the west Londoners in 1972 were nothing compared to the horrific scenes six years later, when the wall at the front of the South Terrace collapsed during the televised fifth round tie against the Blues. Orient chairman Brian Winston, never one to shy away from the coalface or the spotlight, rushed to aid stricken supporters, pulling old women and kids away from fallen rubble and leading them to safety. After the game he launched a blistering attack on the mindless idiots who deliberately provoked this potential disaster.

Winston said: "It was all organised. The Chelsea boys came in to the ground with hammers and coal chisels and broke the wall. The structure of the wall was weak, there is no doubt about it, but we'd had other matches with crowds of between 15,000 and 20,000 without any problems. That was the standard of facilities at grounds in those days.

"I felt a great deal of personal responsibility, because nothing like that had ever happened at Orient before. It made me realise that people went to football and believed in safety, they expected it without even thinking about it, so we had all the walls rebuilt and new crash barriers installed."

Chelsea fans had a history of demolition at Orient. On the opening day of the 1976-77 league season their jubilant fans knocked down a 30-foot stretch of concrete wall at the front of the West Stand as they celebrated their side's 1-0 victory, although this incident was more likely attributable to the weak structure than a deliberate act of vandalism.

Paul 'Beefy' Roberts refers to them as "the infamous Chelsea gits and morons". He says: "Chelsea always caused trouble at our place, as did Birmingham, Southampton and Nottingham Forest. I remember a lot of aggro in the ground when Sunderland came down here in 1975-76 and then in the latter years of the decade, between 1976 and '79, the main troublemakers were Millwall, Stoke, Spurs, Ipswich, Cardiff, Charlton and Sheffield United."

It might be easier to list the clubs whose travelling contingent didn't engage in trouble.

"It all kicked off when Hull City came down for the final game in 1977," Beef continued, "although this time it was Orient fans who caused it. Needing a result to stay up, we released the tension on the horrible Hull thugs.

"The worst away grounds for trouble were Chelsea, Millwall, Charlton, Spurs, Luton, Stoke and Birmingham. And most northern venues, especially Sunderland and Newcastle. Those were classic away days where it got very hairy.

"I went to Millwall in around 1975-77, walked all the way around the ground, over the playing fields and down into the away turnstiles, where I was applauded by their boys just for turning up. I was only aged about 12 or 13 – naive – and my mate 'Westy', who was only 10 or 11, came with me from the estate. We – ALL FIVE OF US! – stood in that massive corner at the away end of the

Amid the chaos, Orient chairman Brian Winston helps a distressed mother and child to safety.

old Den with not another Os fan in sight. And in those days, Millwall was always a nightmare, a very intimidating, scary place to go.

"Charlton was another dangerous trip, with scuffles and running battles every time before being chased all the way back to the Greenwich foot tunnel. The first time I was beaten-up at football was during a game at The Valley when I was 12 years of age. I was attacked by about 30 Neanderthal Charlton fans in their forties wearing donkey jackets. My mate's little boy was only nine and the adults beat him up, too.

"That was stupid. But that was the 70s. And even as a kid, or 'young hooligan', I never backed down. I never really felt intimidated, to be fair, you just had to take it."

Being able to hotfoot it from the away end to the sanctuary of the train or coaches before being beaten up by home fans was part and parcel of watching away games from the terraces. Ironically, you tended to feel safer and less conspicuous among larger crowds, at big stadiums such as Stamford Bridge and Old Trafford, than at much smaller grounds where there were less than 7,000 present and you stood out like a sore thumb. You would stand at one end, minding your own business, and see a rival group at the opposite end of the ground slowly manoeuvring into position, getting ready to mount their attack.

This was often the case at Brisbane Road, where it was possible to walk from the terraces at both ends along the West Side, where the Orient 'hard men' congregated. This freedom of movement didn't end until the start of the 1974-75 season, when newly installed gates at both ends of the West Enclosure blocked the mob in its tracks.

I remember standing on the open terrace behind the goal at Oxford and Swindon with my best mate at school, Dave Watts, in about 1973-74. And afterwards, the pair of us running like the wind back to the Orient supporters' coaches to avoid a good kicking. While I suppose, as young teenagers, we liked the idea of this sense of belonging to what was always only a small crew of

---

Making his Mark

EVER wondered how the re-designed Orient crest came about when it was introduced at the start of the 1977-78 season, along with the ever popular 'braces' shirt that adorns our front cover?

Earlier in the previous season the club invited supporters to enter a competition to design a new badge. And in December, 1976, local fans Mark Hodges and Clive Brown were declared joint-winners.

A product of Leyton Senior High School and living in Matlock Road, E10 at the time, Mark began watching Orient in 1968 and still attends home matches with his father Terry.

He said: "I was only 15 but thought I'd give it a go and submitted two designs – one of which was two dragons supporting a football, with 'Orient Football Club' in scroll below the badge. I was amazed to find I had won when it was announced in the Luton home programme at around Christmas time."

Orient's then chairman Brian Winston says

that he added some finishing touches to the final badge but Mark (and Clive) are the people who should be credited for the original idea.

Mark, now based in Leytonstone, explained: "My original badge had been changed slightly from my griffin dragons to the wyvern-type, and a more old fashioned football.

"I used griffins, rather than wyverns, because I wanted to retain a degree of continuity with the old badge and it also resembled the City of London coat of arms – us being a London club and all that.

"My alternative entry featured a red silhouette of the head of a griffin, with a raised talon on a football surrounded by a large black 'O'. I noticed that, about 15 years ago, the club later adopted this idea in the badge for a while – they also had a metal pin badge made reflecting this design. In fact, something very similar is now featured in the large crest that appears above what used to be the main entrance in Brisbane Road."

Mark's reward for his part in originating the club crest that Orient are still using on their match shirts, replica kits and all manner of other merchandise more than 40 years later?

"My prize was a season ticket for the rest of that 1976-77 season! I had no copyright, so haven't received any income from royalties," Mark added.

Os fans, I was too much of a coward to stand there and fight. Dave's brother, John, who was about four or five years older than us, would walk back nonchalantly back to our coach, without batting an eyelid.

Midweek away games during the bleak winter months could prove more threatening. If you didn't know your way around, it was easy to take a wrong turn in the dark recesses of those old stadiums and find yourself ambushed.

"You took your life in your hands watching Orient away. The train stations up north after games were brutal places, it felt like the whole town was coming out after you," Beefy recalls.

JEWISH CONNECTION AND RACISM

LEYTON Orient has traditionally attracted strong support from the local Jewish community. In fact, for a number of years in the late 50s and early 60s the club was run and bankrolled by wealthy rags-to-riches Jewish businessmen, well known showbiz impresarios Leslie Grade and his brother Bernard Delfont, while of course Harry Zussman was the 'larger than life' chairman during the Os' halcyon days of the 1961-62 promotion to the First Division and remained a popular and influential figure as a board director until 1981.

In his 2012 book, *Does Your Rabbi Know You're Here?,* Anthony Clavane wrote: "As Clapton Orient in the 1930s, they boasted a Jewish goalkeeper, Monty Berman, and Arnold Siegel played for them just after the war. In the 70s and 80s, when Jewish players like Mark Lazarus, Barry Silkman and Bobby Fisher graced Brisbane Road, and Brian Winston replaced Zussman as chairman, the West Stand became known as Kosher Corner. Former *Jewish Chronicle* writer Bernard Josephs remembers the section 'issuing friendly Yiddish curses to the players, unless of course they were playing a blinder'.

"Bernard Sonenfield eventually graduated from the unofficial Jewish section to the vice-presidents' lounge, joining three other East-Enders-made-good: Arnold Pinkus, who was nearly as wide as he was tall, Alf Nathan and Derek Weinrabe. At half-time, Jewish jokes would be told as salt beef sandwiches and chopped herring were served. 'I shlepped all over the country to watch them," says journalist James Masters'."

Trevor Simmons, a supporter since he was aged eight in 1972, is originally from Mill Hill in north-west London but now based in East Sussex. He said: "There wasn't much anti-semitism in football around that time, because there were only a few Jewish players. But I was brought up on Laurie Cunningham and other black players and I felt the level of racism they had to cope with was disgusting.

"Growing up as a non-religious Jewish boy in a multi-cultural society in Mill Hill, it was a real shock to hear the abuse – it's not 'banter' – thrown around and thank god we are where we are now.

"As I got older, in the late 70s I used to attend home games on my own and would stand on the East Terrace, the Coronation Gardens side of the players' tunnel. I would lead the chant of 'OR-I-ENT!' . . . and then walk away while they carried on!

"The day Chelsea came in 1978 and the wall collapsed was very upsetting. We were very lucky that nobody died.

"Orient didn't have many fighters and we were proud of that reputation.

"I chose to support Orient because it's in your blood, part of family history. My father Barry came from Clapton and he passed it down to me. He gave me the choice of Chelsea or Orient and I chose the Os.

"Yet I remember when we were a laughing stock. At school I was surrounded by kids who supported Spurs, Arsenal, Chelsea or West Ham. If you mentioned Orient, you were laughed at – and that happened right through the 70s too. We were always 'little Leyton Orient', people's second club.

"We go through it all as Orient supporters. We're the second oldest professional football club in London (behind Fulham) and now – by virtue of being in the National League – the worst! But here we are, in 2018, and all of us are as happy as Larry that we still have a club to support," Trevor added.

Trevor and Paul, who know each other from back in the day, and myself conducted a three-way conversation in the Leyton Orient Supporters' Club bar after a game early in the 2018-19 season. Beef remembers a different fan named Paul who stood out in the crowd.

"Paul Nelson, who lives down in Exeter now, was the one and only black fan among our group in the 70s. It was just brilliant going with him to away games all over the country," he recalls.

"There was a lot of racism in the crowd, even at Orient. Away fans used to give it to us in the late 70s because we had a lot of black players in the team. The West Brom thing, with Laurie Cunningham, Regis and Batson, was only glorified because they were a First Division side but at one time in the late 70s and early 80s we could've fielded six or seven black players. They got abuse but because they were *our* black players, we gave it back, so you ended up with two groups of WHITE people fighting each other over BLACK footballers!

"Where I grew up around here, among the second highest black population of London behind Brixton, there was no such thing as racism. Half the people from Leyton were black and the other half white. Some of my friends at school were black and we saw no distinction between us. It was a case of, 'you're black and I'm white, so what? . . . let's go to football'. I can call a white bloke 'a bastard' just as easily as I can a black bloke 'a bastard'. It's never been about racism. It's about what they're like as people."

I asked Beef if he considered himself to be a hooligan in his youth. "Oh yeah," he replies with barely concealed pride, before immediately correcting himself. "No, no, that's not right. Dysfunctional and horrible, yes, but not a hooligan. I just wouldn't back away from a fight. If someone wanted to beat me up, I always stood my ground even though I did take some beatings from much older men. But never, ever have I started a fight.

"As little kids in the West Side at

HOME LEAGUE ATTENDANCES

Season	Highest	Average	Lowest
1969-70	19,861 (Plymouth)	11,367	4,593 (Rotherham)
1970-71	14,746 (Charlton)	9,119	3,941 (Portsmouth)
1971-72	33,363 (Birmingham)	10,822	5,202 (Oxford)
1972-73	10,532 (Millwall)	6,443	3,887 (Hull)
1973-74	29,766 (Aston Villa)	11,783	7,216 (Bristol C)
1974-75	17,772 (Man Utd)	7,589	4,352 (Notts C)
1975-76	15,509 (Chelsea)	6,389	3,876 (Hull)
1976-77	11,456 (Chelsea)	6,222	4,062 (Bristol R)
1977-78	24,131 (Spurs)	8,365	4,426 (Mansfield)
1978-79	19,945 (C Palace)	7,323	4,340 (Oldham)
1979-80	23,885 (West Ham)	7,241	3,779 (Swansea)

STAND SEASON TICKET PRICES

	Centre (C/D/F)	Wing (A/B-G/H)	West Stand Seats
1969-70	£8 8s	£7 7s	N/A
1970-71	£12 12s	£10 10s	N/A
1971-72	15.75p/£12.60p	£12.60p/£10.50p	N/A
1972-73	£21	£15.75p	N/A
1973-74	£23	£17.30/£14.00	N/A
1974-75	£27	£20.50	N/A
1975-76	£28.80/£27.60	£22.80/£21.60	N/A
1976-77	£33.50/£31.50	£27.00/£25.00	N/A
1977-78	£43.20/40.80	£34.80/£33.60	N/A
1978-79	£51.60/48.00	£40.80/£38.40	£50.40/£38.40 (centre) £39.60/£33.60
1979-80	£51.60/48.00	£40.80/£38.40	£50.40/£38.40 (centre) £39.60/£33.60

MATCHDAY TICKET PRICES

	Centre	Wing	Terrace
1971-72		50p (NW)	
1974-75	£1.20	95p	
1975-76	£1.50	£1.20	75p
1976-77	£1.60	£1.30	80p/45p
1978-79			£1.00 (East Terrace £1.20)
1979-80			£1.00/70p (East Terrace £3.00/£2.20

Orient, we looked around and wanted to be with the older blokes like Charlie Hasler, our leader, the main man. I've got a lot of time for Charlie – he's a legend – but not some of the idiots who followed him."

Beef became the leader himself in time. He started a crew called the OTF – Orient Train Firm – who would defend Orient's honour the length and breadth of the country.

"As I said, it wasn't about starting trouble. But if someone wanted to start on us . . . well, you had to stand up for yourself. Never shy away."

Sometimes, though, some neighbourly help came in handy.

EAST LONDON SOLIDARITY AND 'FLOATING FANS'

WHEN other London clubs visited Orient in the 70s, especially Millwall and Chelsea, Orient could count on extra support from their east London neighbours from Upton Park whose Inter-City Firm cultivated a fearsome nationwide reputation and were only too pleased to supply reinforcements in times of trouble.

"In the early part of the decade, and even up to the early 80s, we always got a lot of West Ham boys at home games, so the away fans were always in for a scuffle. There was trouble at every Orient game in those days. And I mean EVERY game," continued Beefy.

"I remember when we played Ipswich at home in the FA Cup (1979) and all the West Ham fans came over to batter the Ipswich fans on the North Bank. Proper thuggery.

"As kids we'd turn around on the West Side and see older men who were West Ham ICF helping out Orient. We felt safe knowing they would be looking out for us.

"Sometimes when I was young, if Orient were playing away and West Ham were at home, I'd happily join my Hammers-supporting mates at Upton Park. But the idea of supporting two clubs and wanting them both to be successful is largely unheard of today."

And yet, historically, it's an unarguable fact that for many years Os drew a healthy size of its support from their more illustrious London neighbours, who would go along to Brisbane Road to cheer on Orient and see what the lower divisions had to offer when their team was playing outside the capital.

I fully understand how patronising it must feel to diehard Orient supporters when they see or hear West Ham, Spurs and Arsenal fans refer to Os as their 'second club' – although you don't hear it so often in these more parochial times where, for some strange reason, a lot of people feel

Smoke alarm

THERE was always a sense of pride when the TV cameras came to Brisbane Road but not for supporter Mark Palman. He explained: "I certainly remember the Texaco Cup match against Luton in August, 1974 BECAUSE it was televised.

"I was 14-years-old, standing on the Coronation Gardens terrace with a friend, and we were both having a smoke at half-time. What we were unaware of was ITV commentator Brian Moore's half-time report was shown on World of Sport. My dad, Fred, had just settled down to watch the wrestling as the camera zoomed straight in on us puffing away.

"Dad was much older than me. He had turned 50 when I was born, so we were almost two generations apart and never really had that father/son connection. He was originally from Poland and if you got on his bad side, he'd let you know it.

"When I got home from the game, my mum (Pearl) greeted me with the words: 'Your dad's really angry with you, he saw you smoking at the match'.

"Mum knew I was smoking but always warned me of the old man finding out, which is why my Saturdays at Brisbane Road were a sanctuary, where I felt I could smoke as much as I liked without any problems.

"She got all the grief from him from the moment Kent Walton introduced wrestling until I got back home to Whitechapel. I ran straight up to my bedroom, while Dad chased after me, calling me every name under the sun! He shouted through the door: 'You're not going out for the rest of the week'. But I was back out with my friends the following evening."

ashamed to admit even mild feelings for another club. Even one four or five divisions removed from their own!

But Os fans who resent their much more wealthy neighbours shouldn't forget the important role fans of those clubs played in boosting crowds at Brisbane Road over many years, admittedly during the best of times at Orient and for the bigger games. While checking the record books for the 70s and noting those near capacity crowds of 25,000-to-30,000-plus who turned out to watch Orient go up against Chelsea (twice), Arsenal, Birmingham and Aston Villa, helping to create an unforgettable atmosphere; and that more than 13,000 came along to share in the joy of the Third Division title run-in and other key games in Division Two, don't kid yourself that they were all dyed in the wool Orienteers.

And when Os were wobbling on the precipice of extinction in 1966, don't forget that it wasn't just Orient people who chucked their money into buckets and blankets to enable the club to survive.

The value of the 'floating fan' to clubs like the Os – highlighted in our table showing season-by-season average home attendances – should never be underestimated.

Hopefully, the excellent 'Football For a Fiver' initiative instigated by the club's new American owners will help to restore the days of dual support among capital teams, for the benefit of Leyton Orient.

Before he returns to the bar for another lager, the final words go to Paul Roberts: "Football has changed since I first started coming to games, it's not a working class sport anymore. But one thing that will never change is my love for Orient."

What they remember about

ORIENT IN THE 70s

WE asked supporters, including our followers on social media sites Facebook and Twitter, what immediately springs to mind when they think back to Orient in the 70s . . .

Dave Bruce: *Evening Standard* and *Evening News* classified newspapers. I remember waiting at the newsagent's when I got home from games. The *Standard* normally turned up first. Jimmy Bloomfield and George Petchey. Chants of 'You'll never take the West Side'. The programme huts at each end of the ground, where I used to buy most of my away programmes.

Davis Watson: '70 promotion team, '78 Cup run, Anglo-Scottish Cup.

In January, 1974, 45 (yes, forty-five) coachloads of fans left Brisbane Road headed to Portsmouth for the fourth round FA Cup tie played on a Sunday afternoon.

Les Coombs: "Peanuts! . . . tanner a bag."

Philip Crick: Hostile West Stand.

Steve Jenkins: A well established Division Two side, with a great youth set-up.

David Rose: Big teams – Man United, Spurs, Chelsea – getting relegated into our league. *Evening Standard* Five-a-Sides, Laurie Cunningham, Ralph Coates' combover, Mark Lazarus' lap of honour, Braces kit, Brian Winston 'getting down with the kids' (teenagers) and climbing down into the small bit of terracing by the players' tunnel for some "come on Orient" chanting (pretty sure Stephen White, Michael White and Russell Brooks were next to me at the time), a fan called Linda Thorne who stood next to the players' tunnel for every game, being on ITV's *The Big Match* on Sunday, 'Mayo and Glover' song to the tune of *Hava Nagila.*

George Sargent: My son David was mascot versus Charlton (May 3, 1979, 0-0). Gutted, because I had my camera on the wrong setting and all the photos were blurred. Once in a lifetime experience.

Dennis Barefield: Chicken and chips in the Atlanta fish shop on Leyton High Road after every match.

Nigel Gray (ex-Os defender): Getting off the coach and seeing how many supporters had followed us away to Aberdeen in the Anglo-Scottish Cup.

John Mapp: The torrential rain storm against Sunderland at home in 1970, when the players had to be taken off the pitch. The Forest FA Cup replay, when only half the game was completed on a giant puddle (rather than a pitch) and Orient wore all-white. The East Stand stamping their feet and shouting "OR-RI-ENT! (stamp, stamp stamp) OR-RI-ENT! (stamp, stamp, stamp)." The con of having to pay for a programme in your admission fee and, when going as a family, coming home with several. I must have at least six from a Christmas game against QPR. Being able to walk around the ground to change ends depending on which way Orient were attacking (always a dodgy move while going through the West Stand when at home to Millwall or Cardiff). The ironic cheers of the crowd whenever the ball got hoofed onto the East Stand roof, then rolled slowly down, only to get stuck in the guttering.

Martin Stern: Sock tags, push-and-run, the Bolton and Palace 3-0 home games in that 1973-

A Pearly King and Phil Hoadley lead out the Os before the FA Cup tie against Blackburn Rovers in January, 1978.

74 season. The most Orient fans ever at a game, 29,766 (-25 Villa fans). There have been bigger attendances but never more fans supporting the Os.

Andy Harrington: Broken-hearted pitch invasion to support the team after losing to Villa.

Ian Ochiltree: Walking round the pitch with a big tray of Wagon Wheels and crisps. Serving warm beer into plastic beakers in the West Side for scary Millwall and Cardiff fans.

Gary Phillips: Laurie Cunningham, Peter Kitchen and Joe Mayo, Phil Hoadley and Glenn Roeder, John Jackson. And Bill Roffey knocking out Wayne Entwistle.

Chris Horsford: First official Sunday games. Entry was by pre-bought programme.

Gary White: Seeing Laurie Cunningham's debut. Pure quality.

Paul Hutton: Losing 4-2 at home to Wolves and Laurie Cunningham being named Man of the Match. Drawing 1-1 with Hull at home, last game of the season, to avoid relegation and send Carlisle down (sweet revenge for '74). Playing games on a Sunday, the Pompey FA Cup trilogy, the scoreboard at the Coronation Gardens end that broke after a couple of games and was never fixed.

Russell Brooks: 45 coaches to Portsmouth for an FA Cup tie.

George Sayer: Two trains to Middlesbrough in the FA Cup.

Don Hales: Run to the FA Cup semi-final, especially overcoming Middlesbrough in the replay.

David Graham: Chelsea 1 Orient 2, FA Cup fifth round, 1978 – one of the best away days (nights) ever. And my best mate was a Blues fan.

patto lofc 65: West Ham 0 Orient 2 – Boxing Day, 1978.

Clive Ellis: Club shop on the corner of Osborne Road.

Julian Lillington: June Brown serving in the club shop on Leyton High Road. Very easy on the eye for a 10-year-old boy and his dad! Always smiling and good customer service. Made for Orient.

Bill Harrison: The most boring game ever at Brisbane Road, versus Hull City in 1975, when Os managed only 28 goals all season and finished mid-table. Not surprisingly, the game again finished 0-0. However, towards the end, the biggest cheer of the day came when an Orient supporter ran on the pitch, grabbed the match ball and then ran to the Hull City goal, where he put the ball down and shot the ball into the net. Terry Neill, Hull's manager, said in the paper the following day: "He nearly missed the target!" The pain we've had to sit through over the years, eh?

From the Independent Leyton Orient Forum

omygawd: Mark Lazarus doing a lap of honour after scoring his second in a 3-1 win against Sheffield United in 1970-71. The game was still going on!

Bill Roffey's Left Foot: The smell of Westler's burgers and stewed onions wafting in the air outside the ground. You wouldn't complain about the current burgers if you had tasted one of those. The peanut seller used to have this bizarre cry that sounded like "Orient stink".

aylesburyos: Pearly Kings and Queens in the '78 Cup run. Have they been back since?

ORIENT ON TV

IF you followed Os in the 70s, then you'll know what a rare treat it was to see our boys feature in televised matches.

Long before football was run at the behest of satellite TV's multi millions, forcing games to kick off at stupid o'clock and just about every day of the week, we happily survived on a staple diet of weekend highlights programmes shown by the only two terrestrial broadcasters, BBC and ITV.

This was a time when, apart from midweek matches, the vast majority of league and FA Cup matches were played at 3.00pm on Saturdays. Precious few were on Sundays and until the 80s, only England internationals and the FA Cup Final were shown 'live'.

Armchair viewers would be eased into the weekend with two half-hour shows on Saturday lunchtime. From 1974, BBC1 employed Bob Wilson to present *Football Focus* as part of their general *Grandstand* sports programme, while on the other side Brian Moore hosted *On The Ball* to kick-off ITV's weekly *World of Sport* show. The format was simple: previews of the main First Division games scheduled for later that afternoon, a round-up of current football themes, plus interviews with players and managers. Orient would barely get a mention unless – as in 1972 and '78 – they ruffled feathers in the FA Cup.

Sometime after 10.00pm on Saturday, with all the afternoon results known, we'd tune into BBC1's *Match of the Day,* where David Coleman (1967-73) and Jimmy Hill (1973-88) would present edited highlights of two top flight games lasting around 30 minutes each.

We had to wait until the following afternoon for ITV's hour-long football flagship show, *The Big Match,* where Brian Moore would introduce highlights from three matches selected from the independent company's regional network. London Weekend Television sent their cameras to one of the capital's First Division grounds, although there was the occasional glimpse of Orient too.

Sky and BT Sport hype their forthcoming live games up to a week in advance but, back in the day, you wouldn't know if the match you were attending had been chosen as part of the highlights package until you arrived at the ground and spotted the outside broadcast unit parked up in the street.

To the best of our knowledge, these were the televised games (excluding very brief newsreel clips) involving Orient in the 70s:

1969-70
Aug 23, 1969 Luton 3 Orient 2 (FL3) ITV
Dec 13, 1969 Brighton & H A 0 Orient 0 (FL3) ITV
Jan 17, 1970 Torquay Utd 0 Orient 1 (FL3) ITV
Mar 21, 1970 Orient 3 Stockport County 0 (FL3) BBC

1970-71
Sept 12, 1970 Orient 1 Sunderland 0 (FL2) ITV

1971-72
Feb 26, 1972 Orient 3 Chelsea 2 (FAC5) BBC
Mar 18, 1972 Orient 0 Arsenal 1 (FAC6) ITV

1972-73
Sept 16, 1972 Blackpool 1 Orient 1 (FL2) ITV
Jan 13, 1973 Orient 1 Coventry City 4 (FAC3) BBC

1973-74
Oct 20, 1973 Orient 2 Luton Town 0 (FL2) ITV
Dec 29, 1973 Orient 1 Fulham 0 (FL2) BBC
Jan 19, 1974 Orient 2 Sunderland 1 (FL 2) ITV
Feb 2, 1974 Carlisle Utd 3 Orient 0 (FL2) BBC
Apr 13, 1974 WBA 1 Orient 0 (FL2) ITV
Apr 20, 1974 Orient 1 Notts County 1 (FL2) BBC

1974-75
Aug 3, 1974 West Ham Utd 1 Orient 0 (Texaco Trophy) ITV
Aug 10, 1974 Orient 2 Luton Town 2 (Texaco Trophy) ITV
Aug 17, 1974 Orient 0 Manchester Utd 2 (FL2) ITV
Jan 4, 1975 Orient 2 Derby County 2 (FAC3) BBC
Jan 8, 1975 Derby County 2 Orient 1 (FAC3R) ITV
Mar 22, 1975 Orient 1 Aston Villa 0 (FL2) ITV

1975-76
Oct 11, 1975 Sunderland 3 Orient 1 (FL2) ITV

1976-77
Nov 20, 1976 Sheffield Utd 1 Orient 1 (FL2) ITV

1977-78
Oct 1, 1977 Orient 1 Tottenham Hotspur 1 (FL2) ITV
Feb 18, 1978 Orient 0 Chelsea 0 (FAC5) ITV
Feb 27, 1978 Chelsea 1 Orient 2 (FAC5R) ITV
Mar 11, 1978 Middlesbrough 0 Orient 0 (FAC6) ITV
Apr 8, 1978 Orient 0 Arsenal 3 (FACSF) ITV

1978-79
Aug 19, 1978 Sheffield Utd 1 Orient 2 (FL2) ITV
Dec 30, 1978 Crystal Palace 1 Orient 1 (FL2) ITV
Jan 27, 1979 Ipswich Town 0 Orient 0 (FAC4) ITV
Apr 7, 1979 Orient 3 Brighton & HA 3 (FL2) ITV
May 5, 1979 Orient 0 Crystal Palace 1 (FL2) ITV

1979-80
Mar 22, 1980 Chelsea 1 Orient 0 (FL2) ITV
Apr 12, 1980 Sunderland 1 Orient 1 (FL2) ITV
May 3, 1980 Orient 0 Leicester City 1 (FL2) ITV

'72 CUP HEROES

For a few months at the start of 1972 Orient fans were in dreamland. After seeing off Wrexham, 3-0 at home in the FA Cup third round, they went to Leicester - where their old boss Jimmy Bloomfield was now in charge - and stunned them with a 2-0 victory.

Then Chelsea, the 1970 Cup winners managed by another former Os manager in Dave Sexton, came to Brisbane Road and succumbed 3-2 to George Petchey's muddy marvels in the most dramatic fashion.

But Orient's luck ran out in the home quarter-final against Arsenal, who sneaked a 1-0 win with a contentious goal in front of another large E10 crowd.

Barrie Fairbother turns away to celebrate his last-minute, fifth round winner against Chelsea. Ian Bowyer has sunk to his knees in sheer exhaustion as Brisbane Road goes wild and Chelsea keeper Peter Bonetti is looking for answers.

ORIENT FOO
F.A. CUP 6th ROU
ORIENT
V.
ARSENAL or DE
SAT. 18th MARCH,
Admit Bearer to
TERRACE
(Windsor Road end)
50p

No 000432
BALL CLUB
ROUND
NT
LSEA
1972 K.O. 3.00 p.m.
Entrance—SOUTH WEST
Turnstile Nos.
28, 29, 30, 31, 32

WE
THREE
KINGS
OF ORIENT ARE

LUCKY, LUCKY

UNIMPRESSIVE Arsenal sneaked into the Cup
semi-final with an Alan Ball goal, which
brave little Orient still swear should never have

Orient 0
Arsenal 1

Bloomfield forgives as 'old boy' Bowyer finds killer touch

Leicester 0   Orient 2
By ALEX BANNISTER

Peter Allen tries to split Arsenal's George Graham and Frank McLintock.

By George, it was close

Born: Whitechapel, London, June 24, 1931
Orient Management Career: July 1971-August 1977
Matches in Charge: League 254, FA Cup 16, League Cup 17
LEAGUE – P 254 W 74 D 89 L 92 GF 257 GA 294 Pts 237
CUP – P 33 W 10 D 10 L13 GF 38 GA 43

George just after arriving in 1971.

GEORGE PETCHEY will forever be remembered as the 'nearly man' after his Orient team missed out on promotion to the First Division by just a single point in May, 1974. If Aston Villa's Ray Graydon hadn't equalised from the penalty spot on that agonising final night of the season in Leyton, Petchey would have emulated the feat of John Carey, who remains the only manager to have led Os into the top flight.

What will mortify Orient supporters is Petchey's suspicions, 44 years later in 2018, that not all of the club's hierarchy actually wanted the club to dine at football's top table, rubbing shoulders with giants like Arsenal, Tottenham, Liverpool and Everton, as they all too briefly did in 1962-63.

"To be honest, I always felt that Aston Villa 'cheated' and must have given their players an extra bonus for beating us," claims Petchey, who had just turned 87 when we spoke. "Carlisle went up instead of us and, I don't know that they did, but I reckon they did something to encourage Villa to play really hard to beat us. The thing that annoyed me was that quite a number of Villa players had spoken to me at different times previously, asking if they could come to Orient!

"Unfortunately, our form had dipped in the latter part of the season and that was what really cost us promotion. Also 'Jacko' (John Jackson) got injured and missed the last nine games. I think that he was a huge loss. He was a big influence to the rest of the team when he was playing, because he did on the field what I tried to do off it. He was a very big influence at the time and we missed him.

"People asked me if our players 'bottled it' in that final game with Villa but I don't think so. After all, Villa only got a draw because they scored from a penalty.

"But, you know, I'm not sure all the directors at the time even really wanted the club to get promotion – they never said this to me directly but it was suggested that they told other people as much – and that even if Orient went up, they would go straight back down again. And somebody would come along and take me to another club.

"But that's neither here nor there, because I'm not sure how much, if any, was actually true, so I can't verify any of it. But all the same, it was disappointing to hear those suggestions from someone within the club.

"I do know that I had tried to sign a player before the transfer deadline – a winger to replace (Barrie) Fairbrother because he missed more than he scored – but the directors wouldn't allow me to sign the player.

"And the player in question was Ray Graydon who, of course, came back to haunt us by scoring the penalty for Villa that cost us promotion.

"The directors weren't really ambitious about promotion. They wanted to finish the season in a good position but they didn't want us to go up. As I say, nobody actually told me that – I just got the feeling that was the situation but, to me, it was a strange attitude to have."

IN many ways the then 40-year-old Petchey was a surprise choice by the Os' board to replace Jimmy Bloomfield. According to the press, he was chosen from a short list of four that also included former Leyton Orient half-back Cyril Lea, who was progressing as a coach with Ipswich Town, former England full-back George Cohen, who coached Fulham's youth side, England Under-23s and managed at non-league Tonbridge, and Aldershot player-manager Jimmy Melia.

Petchey's playing career as a left-half spanned 400 league appearances with three London clubs – West Ham, where he appeared twice (1952-53), Queens Park Rangers (255 games, 1953-60) and Crystal Palace (143 matches, 1960-65), where he took up coaching after hanging up his boots.

Os' chairman Arthur Page declared: "I am sure we have picked the right man. Petchey was chosen because of his fine record for Crystal Palace and we feel sure that he will do well at Orient."

Although he'd earned a good reputation as a coach at Palace for a decade, assisting manager Bert Head as the south London club rose from the Fourth Division to the First and had survived among the elite for two years, Petchey had never been a manager. And as he explains, there were other tempting options worthy of serious consideration.

"I was looking to do something more than just coaching," he explained. "I had offers to go to a number of clubs, including two from abroad, but I couldn't go overseas because my kids, Carol and Stephen, were growing up. They were around 13 or 14-years-old, so to move away from where we lived in Brighton was never an option for me.

"Alec Stock phoned me and asked me to go back to Queens Park Rangers, where I'd been a player previously, but at that time it wasn't convenient for me to leave Crystal Palace. I had four cornea grafts to my eye and was sick and tired of hospitals, going to and from the ground to East Grinstead, where the hospital was, and continuous consultations about whether they should operate or not.

"At that time, I was thinking of quitting football. The wife (Molly) wanted me to give up, because she said it was hurting me. I'd been offered a business down here – running a big shop – and at other times I would have taken up the offer. But I had to face the reality that football was in my blood and that's what I really wanted to be involved with.

"Then I met Reg Briggs, an Orient director, at an FA function and he said to me: 'What are Palace going to do next year?'. And I replied: 'We will win the Cup!'. I had big ideas at Palace but he said: 'Why don't you come to Orient?'

"I think they were bottom of the league at the time and I couldn't see that my going there would make any difference. Anyway, we talked about it and he invited me to dinner at his house with my wife. We took up his invitation and had a very pleasing time. We had a very enjoyable conversation because he kept telling me how good I was!

"After that my wife said: 'It's too much travelling from where we live – you can't go there'. I thought about it . . . QPR was still in my mind, plus there were more wealthy clubs interested in me. One offer was a coaching job with Arsenal, which nearly happened. Anyway, after much thought, I decided to put my mind at rest by staying at Palace.

"Then, one day, I went out on the pitch . . . it's funny how things just happen. I'm usually very quick to make up my mind on things but I was out on the pitch taking the first team and we were working on reconstruction of the defence. Two people kept walking around, looking at what I was doing and writing things down and I thought, 'what the bloody hell are they doing here?'

"So I asked one of them and he said: 'Bert (Head) asked us to see what you are doing'. I replied: 'Well, Bert can come out and talk to me if he wants to know anything'.

"I went home and I was fuming, I thought I'll go in to Palace tomorrow and quit and get a job down here near my home. So I walked in and said to the secretary: 'Can I have my P45, please,' and he replied: 'No, you can't'. I told him I would sue them if I didn't get it and in the end he gave it to me. I didn't speak to anybody else, I didn't ask for anything. The chairman rang me and tried to get me to change my mind but Bert Head never said anything. He didn't ring me or come to see me, or ask why I wanted to go. Consequently, I quickly left.

"Then I had a problem: What do I do now? I looked at Orient but their future at the time looked a bit dim. But Reg Briggs got in touch with me again and then Arthur Page, the chairman. That was an interesting meeting, because he said: 'We like how you talk and how you work and we hope you will spend a long, long time with us here'. I thought, 'well, I don't want a long job'. My eye was still a problem – by now I'd had four grafts and a reconstruction and I knew it was never going to fully heal. I thought it might last between two and four years, so I could go to Orient for that time and see if I could help make them a better club."

Os had ended Bloomfield's final season without a win in their last 10 matches and although they still had young full-back Dennis Rofe attracting the attention of top division scouts, there was a group of ageing players the wrong side of 30.

"I was a bit surprised when I got there because the club looked a bit derelict," George recalls. "I walked into the dressing room and it was just four brick walls, so I got hold of one of the local tradesmen, who did jobs around the club, and asked him to put up some wood panelling to make it look a bit more luxurious.

"We found a training ground and maybe should have been more sensible and bought it. But at that time, nobody at the club had any money.

"As for the players, I got rid of the old regime and brought in a lot of youngsters and that is when things began to look up for the club. I knew there was no money to be spent because the club hardly offered me any! In fact, I was still on the wages I received when I was at Palace – and I stayed on the same wages all the time I was at Orient!"

Eye problems or not, Petchey didn't look far for new recruits. "The people who had taken over at Palace when I left had gone back to the old way of playing and so the old football style I enjoyed and worked with had gone. The players were just lumping the ball around, so I decided I would go back to Palace and get some of the players I had worked with there and bring them to Orient."

Veteran full-back John Sewell and Len Tompkins, both on frees, were the first of a spate of signings from Palace. They were followed a few months later by Phil Hoadley, who cost Os a new club record fee of £35,000. The record was broken again the following October when Gerry Queen left Selhurst Park to be reunited with his former boss for £50,000. And before the start of 1973-74, Petchey raided his old club for four more players – David Payne, John Jackson and Bill Roffey. The following summer Derek Possee became the eighth signed from Palace and then, in 1975, Malcolm Beason made it nine when he too followed the well trodden path from SE25 to E10.

"They were good footballers, had done well in the First Division and because they knew me and the way I liked to play football, I was able to manipulate them into joining Orient. I sold a couple of players who had been with Orient for a while and got a bit of money for them and used that money to get the players over from Palace."

To Petchey's credit, the sale of Dennis Rofe to Bloomfield's Leicester for £112,000 – a then British record for a full-back – early in the 1972-73 campaign covered the combined transfer fees paid for Hoadley, Jackson, Queen and Roffey. Of those, only Scottish forward Queen's return on investment could be questioned; the other three were superb acquisitions who went on to establish themselves as long-serving crowd favourites. At a meagre £5,000, Roffey – who went on to play 358 games over 11 years – was an absolute steal, one of the best pieces of business the club has ever done.

Ironically, Petchey admits he was peeved when Palace lured Ricky Heppolette – another club record buy, £60,000 from Preston – away from the Orient. "He went to Palace, which irritated me a bit, but he insisted he wanted to go."

What might have been . . . George at Brisbane Road in the summer of 1974.

Although Phil Hoadley took over the captaincy after Petchey left in 1977, the manager chose leaders who were already at the club when he arrived. "Peter Allen and Peter Bennett were my captains and both were good lads. Peter Bennett had a hernia problem and was out for quite a while but when he came back, he carried on doing a super job for us. He was a nice bloke – as is Peter Allen, who I still see now down where we live in Hove."

AS well as revamping the playing squad, Petchey also relieved Palace of several key backroom staff that enhanced the Orient set-up, especially at youth level where he had a major impact. He brought in a trusted mentor in Arthur Rowe, the mastermind behind Spurs' first championship-winning side – the 'push-and-run' purists – in 1950-51, in an advisory role.

After his famous deeds at White Hart Lane, Rowe had a stint as manager at Crystal Palace, where the two men, 25 years apart in age but both staunch advocates of flowing one-touch football, sang from the same hymn sheet. Rowe died in November, 1993, aged 87, but his protegé has always been grateful for his words of wisdom.

"Arthur had a great influence on me over a long period," Petchey confirmed. "I thought he could do something with us at Orient but he couldn't at first because he had to go in to hospital for about 18 months. I often went to see him. We talked about football and he told me that, in his opinion, many people got the game the wrong way round. He said that there was madness in football – getting stuck in and kicking people up in the air, which prevailed at the time. He believed that trying to play football seemed to come second behind everything else and Arthur said to me: 'You have to change that, get your teams playing the way the game should be played'.

"So I did. Arthur did come and join us at Orient (Feb, 1972) and he looked after the youth side for me. He was still ill at the time and he wasn't paid anything, so all that he did was out of the goodness of his heart. He loved the game."

NOT only did Petchey sign several players who wore Orient red with distinction over many years, probably his greatest legacy was the emphasis he placed on cultivating a youth system that produced a string of talent to benefit the senior side. Including Laurie Cunningham, the most brilliant discovery of all. The huge role Petchey played in patiently nurturing the young Cunningham to stardom should never be forgotten.

"Right from the time I first set eyes on him, I could see he was a special talent. When he first came to us, he did the same thing that he tried to do later at West Bromwich Albion, and that was to show everybody how clever he was. I cut that out of him and made him go for goal and score goals for us. And that's what he did. It made him a better player and enabled him to get by opponents quickly without being kicked up in the air, as he often used to be.

"I liked Laurie and John Chiedozie and would've loved to have kept them longer because I think we'd have gone up if we'd had both of them in the team at the same time. Brian Winston, the Orient chairman, thought he knew everything about football and wanted £60,000 for Laurie. I told him: 'No, I want to get £115,000 for him' and in the end that's what we got. But I never got any thanks or a 'well-done'. The chairman said nothing, yet he'd have sold him much cheaper.

"I remember giving Laurie his debut in the Texaco Cup at West Ham and although he was only 18, he was good even then. He had initially been at Arsenal but they didn't like him. He didn't do what they wanted, he had his own ideas. The difference in playing football and having ability is in using the ability. I looked at Laurie and thought, 'crikey, if he uses his ability, he'll be a world-beater'.

"I didn't treat Laurie any differently. In fact, everyone was treated the same irrespective of who they were or what they did. When I heard that he was going dancing in the evenings, I didn't go mad at him. I just said to him: 'What are you doing with the money you are picking up, are you saving it?' He looked at me and laughed and said: 'I'm going to buy a car'. I told him not to do that but, instead, to walk to the ground and put his money in a bank for later on.

"I did fine him a few times, because he would turn up late for training, but he was bloody stupid, he really was. I used to send Peter Angell round to his digs and Laurie would still be in bed. When asked why he wasn't at training, he'd say: 'Oh, I didn't think we trained on Mondays, Arsenal don't'. So I said to him: 'Well, you are in the wrong club, mate. You're at Orient now and we do things differently here'.

"Later in his career, I went to watch him play for Real Madrid and Laurie was just the same as he was at West Brom. He'd get the ball, beat the full-back several times and then cross to nobody, whereas if he'd been more direct and scored a couple of goals, he'd have been the world-beater I thought he could be.

"I did keep in touch with him. We always got on well and he always thought I'd done well for him – and that's the best thanks you can get from a player.

"I didn't ever see him as an orthodox player. I also tried to get him in the England side. I thought he was better than any winger we had at the time. I remember Orient played at Hereford on one occasion and Laurie was absolutely brilliant. He played just how you wanted him to play. When you looked at him then . . . well, there wasn't a player like him . . . he was brilliant.

"I always thought that John Chiedozie would be the same but I left Orient before he became established in the first team.

"The thing about Orient's youngsters was that they were paid hardly any money," Petchey revealed. "In fact, the people running the youth teams would often give them money out of their own pockets by way of a little bonus. So I put a stop to all that and put the young players on a basic wage.

"Laurie Cunningham is a great example. He came to us (after being rejected by Arsenal) for £46.00 per week and I found out that he was going to a dancing cabaret place in the West End in the evenings and picking up a £150 per night. So I must have had some persuasive powers.

"I went to watch East London Boys play West London Boys and I would have bought five or six of them and put them straight into our team, because they were better than what we had.

"John Chiedozie was one of them. I wanted John to play outside-right and Laurie outside-left, and that would have got us promotion. But the more I talked about it to the directors, they didn't seem that interested. I didn't get much help from them.

"Amongst our excellent youngsters we also had Bobby Fisher, Glenn Roeder and Tony Grealish. I went round to Tony's house on one occasion. His mum and dad ran a pub and even at a young age, Tony was a sly drinker and he used to drink in the family pub. I heard about this, so I told him that if ever I saw him and he was smelling of beer, I would kill him. That cured him at that time, although I think he got back on the booze after he left Orient."

As well as paying his respects to Arthur Rowe, Petchey also remembers the help he and the club received from a local scout called Maurice Newman. "He did a good job for us scouting the kids and, basically, he was the one who convinced me about John Chiedozie. Initially, I thought he was too small and light but he definitely had a quick burst of speed. I said to Maurice that if we could get him fit he would be some player. So Maurice was the one who talked to him and got him organised to the levels he needed to be.

"Maurice did quite well for us in that way – he could talk to kids and get a positive response from them. We sent a load of kids to Maurice for him to work with because he encouraged them to do the right things."

Petchey talked about other key members of his backroom staff . . .

"I'd played with Peter Angell at QPR. He was a good guy and did his job. I think he wanted to be appointed as assistant manager but I told him he was better off being a coach, because he had a good job in that role. If you are appointed assistant manager anywhere, people will want you to do certain things that will become more demanding. He did his best for me. I told him everything that was going on but he preferred the previous manager, Jimmy Bloomfield, to me. He'd got on really well with him. Of course, when I left Jimmy came back and Peter was happy.

"I appointed Len Cheesewright as our chief scout. He was a good bloke and worked really hard for the club, spotting a lot of youngsters. He had a good reputation, lots of contacts, he knew a lot of people and brought many good youngsters into the club.

"Another one who did a good job was Ronnie Heckman but then Ron suddenly became ill and I was very sorry when he had to leave like he did.

"I brought in Terry Long from Palace as a youth team coach because I knew he would always back me up and, in turn, he knew I'd do the same for him. We'd played football together for 10 years previously and always got on really well.

"Ernie Shepherd was already physio at the club before I joined. He was another good bloke. He worked hard but something happened between him and the chairman. I'm not too sure what occurred but he moved on.

"Eventually, we got to a stage where I would say that we had the strongest youth set-up in London. All the kids we had were good kids; they worked and battled hard and consequently they could all play. It was interesting to see how they grew up and developed in their careers.

"We had done a similar thing at Crystal Palace, pushing the youngsters into the first team. Kids like David Payne, Bill Roffey and Phil Hoadley. Phil was another one who should have played for England if he'd been more conscientious. But he didn't train hard enough when he was at Palace. When he rejoined me at Orient, he came because he knew me and knew that I wouldn't stand any nonsense.

"He did quite well for Orient and signing players like him allowed me to get rid of the big noises, as it were, who were questioning the way I wanted to take the club forward. I don't want to name names but they weren't players I wanted to have around. They would have an argument or were content to always find an excuse as to why this had happened or why that had gone wrong. Always excuses. I couldn't stand that and I found it difficult to handle some of those guys."

In his interview elsewhere in the book, Mark Lazarus makes no secret of his fall outs with Petchey. Here's the manager's view of the volatile right-winger: "I knew him from my days at QPR and Palace. He thought I didn't like him just because I worked him hard and I wouldn't take

With key members of Orient's backroom staff. From left: Ernie Shepherd (physio), Terry Long (youth coach), George, Peter Angell (coach) and Peter Barnes (secretary).

'no' for an answer. He always acted the big man but through all the years I've known him, he's never said anything to me to make me think he was against me.

"But in the end at Orient, he wrote to the chairman and said he couldn't play under me for some reason or another – I don't know what the problem was, because I never saw the letter. But the chairman came to see me and said: 'Look, Mark says he wants to go'.

So I said: 'OK, give him a free transfer and let him go'.

"I had to let a few of the players go that had been at the club before I arrived. They became a bit disruptive – people like Ian Bowyer, for example. He couldn't agree with anything or anybody, so I got rid of him.

"Also, they weren't good enough; they didn't want to take on my ideas. There were around half a dozen players aged around 29 or 30 who thought they had done it all and so they didn't always try as hard as I wanted. They would fight each other, bicker and argue. Well, I couldn't stand that. I wanted to build a good team, go out and coach and get the team playing how I wanted them to play. So I did, and we did all right, but things altered when Arthur Page resigned as chairman and Brian Winston came in."

APPOINTED to the board of directors in 1972, Brian Winston's forceful personality soon made him a prominent figure around the club, well known and highly visible to supporters whose interest he always appeared keen to represent. He succeeded Page as chairman before the start of the 1974-75 season.

But Petchey makes it clear that Winston, the man who sacked him in August, 1977, was never his cup of tea. "He was a pain in the arse and I didn't get on with him at all. In fact, I hardly spoke to him, so never got to know him.

"With Winston, it wasn't so much that he caused problems but he had this manner and air about him, as if he was the top man, the one that did everything and made all the decisions. That gave me a problem with the players, because I needed the authority to do what I needed to do with the playing side of matters. That's the way I left it and I made it plain that I was the one in charge of all the players and playing issues. And that's why they sacked me!

"Winston wanted to get rid of me because he knew I was looking to get promotion and he was frightened of that. The future had looked bright and the club were in the black financially. We were getting a decent squad of players together, there were younger players coming in and I had just signed Peter Kitchen to partner Joe Mayo. But two games into the 1977-78 season, I was sacked.

"It wasn't a surprise to me when I was dismissed because I got to know how Brian Winston worked and what his attitude was. He did one or two things I didn't like. For example, he brought a couple of pin-ups in and took them in the bath with the players while I wasn't there. I played blue murder over that. There were other things that happened that I didn't have any control over.

"I didn't have any major fall-outs with Winston but we did have quite a few harsh words over a period of time. I always say what I think, especially on football matters, and at least everyone always knew what I felt.

"I liked to play football by keeping the ball on the floor but our pitch wasn't conducive to that style. I tried to improve the condition of the pitch and that is about the only thing I got from

Winston. I told him that if he wanted to see good football, he needed to get us a better pitch. It seemed to get flooded every time it rained.

"I didn't really see a lot of the other directors. Arthur Page's son Max was a bit of a mystery. I didn't know whether he was with us or against us. Frank Harris was fair and straight and, of course, I got on well with Reg Briggs, although I think he was only there for about a year after I joined the club before he stood down from the board.

"I had a good relationship with most of them. It's like everything, though, it doesn't last and everything always has to be right for them. There was always someone, either in the boardroom or elsewhere at the club, who would be moaning about something or other. I tried to get everybody thinking positively and be united but it just didn't happen.

"So I left Orient and went to Millwall to help out their chairman, who begged me to go there and get them sorted. I only did it for a couple of years and then I gave it up because I couldn't see myself staying long at Millwall – it wasn't my type of club.

"After I left Orient I was disappointed that they sold John Chiedozie and I'd had to sell Laurie Cunningham, and there were about four other kids who they let go. We had some terrific youngsters. Apart from Chiedozie, there was Glenn Roeder, Nigel Gray, Bobby Fisher and others. I didn't really get the time to develop the team I wanted.

"But I don't look back at my time at Orient as a disappointment, though. I look back and think that had the club been running OK, then I probably wouldn't have been invited to go there and manage them anyway. I only went for the battle and I thought we were winning that. Then the chairman resigned, Brian Winston came in and that's when we started to lose it.

"Other people will have their own views of my time at Orient but I think I earned my money. When I joined Orient as manager, I was on the same money that I'd earned coaching Crystal Palace. Nobody ever gave me a rise in my time with Orient. I kept them up a couple of times, had a good Cup run (1972), nearly won promotion and we'd progressed into a good side.

"But when I asked for a rise, back came the reply: 'At the moment, we can't afford it'. So for 10 years I'd been on the same money doing a bloody good job for Palace and then a damned good job at Orient . . . all on the same wage.

"I'd have loved to earn the sort of money they do nowadays but I've no regrets.

I really haven't any. I started in football when I was 11, went to West Ham and signed as a pro at 17 on top money. Then I went in the Army for two-and-a-half years, which was a waste of time for me.

"But I was still on a good wage when I came out and resumed my pro career. At that time I was on £9 per week. I was single, had no ties, so I could do what I liked. My father was only earning £2 10 shillings a week and he was working in a brewery that made thousands of pounds. He used to envy my £9 per week.

"When I came out of National Service, I continued as a pro until I went into coaching. Football has been my life – I've enjoyed playing, coaching and managing and been my own man. So no, there are no regrets – not even with Brian Winston.

"As I said earlier, I often meet Peter Allen down here in Brighton and he's said to me on a few occasions: 'You are the best manager I ever had' and I tell him: "I'm the *only* manager you've ever had!

"Football has been a great life for me and, when I look back, although I won't say that I've been 100 percent successful, I've had enough success to please me."

Interview: Paul Hiscock

'78 CUP HEROES

HISTORY was made in the spring of 1978, when Orient reached the FA Cup semi-final for the first time. It was the most exciting period in the club's history – against the odds victories reminiscent of the sensational run six years earlier and with a couple of familiar London rivals too.

Jimmy Bloomfield's men needed replays to dispose of three First Division opponents – Norwich City, Middlesbrough and Chelsea – with a late 3-1 home win over Division Two rivals Blackburn Rovers thrown in for good measure.

After being held 0-0 at home by Chelsea in round five, not even the most optimistic fans could've imagined that two Peter Kitchen goals would sink the Blues at Stamford Bridge. Kitch and Joe Mayo – the dynamic duo who scored all nine of Os' FA Cup goals in this run between them – put Boro to the sword in the quarter-final replay at Brisbane Road to set up the mouth-watering 'Cockney Semi-Final' against Arsenal.

But just as they did back in '72, the Gunners got lucky and shot Orient's Cup dreams to pieces.

Malcolm MacDonald's wayward shot was heading wide until it deflected off Bill Roffey into the Orient goal. 'Lucky Arsenal' shattered our Wembley dreams.

34 The Daily Telegraph, Wednesday, March 15, 1978

Quick one-two by Kitchen and Mayo decisive

ORIENT HOLD ON TO REACH THEIR FIRST F A CUP SEMI-FINAL

By DONALD SAUNDERS

Orient 2   Middlesbrough 1

ORIENT, so long London's forgotten football club and currently struggling in the bottom half of the Second Division, will line up against mighty Arsenal three weeks next Saturday in their first F A Cup semi-final.

The impudent East Enders bundled Middlesbrough out of the competition, at windswept Brisbane Road last night, with an exhilarating performance that did not allow their opponents a look-in until the closing minutes.

This quarter-final replay was really settled in the first

Bloomfield is 'over moon'

Orient's manager, Jimmy

Peter Kitchen epitomises Orient's determination to reach the FA Cup semi-final for the very first time as he dashes for the ball against Middlesbrough in last night's replay.

London's night of Cup glory 🏆 **Orient goal twins make it a date with the Gunners**

BRAVO

ORIENT ...... 2 — B...

Football Association Cup Semi-Final
ARSENAL v. ORIENT
SATURDAY APRIL 8th 1978
Kick off 3 p.m.
You are advised to be in position by 2.15 p.m.
NORTH TERRACE STANDING
(Brittania Entrance C)
£2.00 Inc. VAT
This ticket is issued subject to the Rules and Regulations of the Football Association and the Football...
district...

PLEASE ENTER BY ENTRANCE U

ORIENT FOOTBALL CLUB
F.A. CUP 5TH ROUND
ORIENT v CHELSEA
Leyton Stadium
on Saturday 18th February 1978
Kick-off 3 pm
Gates open 1.30 pm
WEST ENCLOSURE
(See plan on reverse)
To be retained   £1.50 inc VAT

Middlesbrough Football & Athletic Co. Ltd.
Ayresome Park, Middlesbrough.
F.A. CUP TIE
CLIVE ROAD ENTRANCE H
at AYRESOME PARK
For Date and Kick-off Time See Press
£1.80 (Inc. VAT)   ROW G   SEAT 40
YOU ARE ADVISED TO BE IN YOUR SEAT AT LEAST 30 MINUTES BEFORE KICK-OFF THIS PORTION TO BE RETAINED
T.H.E. Green SECRETARY

ARSENAL v ORIENT SOUVENIR EDITION WITH COLOUR

Evening Standard 15p

Although left out of the side, Derek Clarke embodies Os' great team spirit by rushing onto the pitch at Stamford Bridge to embrace fifth round replay goal heroes Peter Kitchen and Joe Mayo.

Growing up fast

Born: Owerri, Nigeria, April 18, 1960
Usual position: Right-winger Orient Career: 1977-81
Orient Appearances: League 131/14, FA Cup 7, League Cup 8
Orient Goals: League 20, FA Cup 2, League Cup 1

JOHN CHIEDOZIE'S extraordinary, inspirational story of London life began in 1972, when, as a 12-year-old, he left the family home near the city of Owerri in Nigeria to join his father Julius, who had emigrated to Forest Gate some years earlier to try and make a better life for himself and his family amid civil war in their homeland.

John's elder brothers – twins Peter and Paul, and Dickson, who is two years his senior – were reunited with him in England the following year. Their parents split up when John – full name John Okechukwu ('Okay') Chiedozie – was a 10-month-old baby, at which point he lost all contact with his mother Mary for the next eight years. The four boys were brought up by their grandmother Lucy and their father's brother.

"Six of us slept in one room and as a little kid I remember humping around heavy bricks for local builders so that I could earn money to give to my grandma. She would carry me on her shoulders as she tried to sell food that she had cooked," recalled John as we chatted on the terrace at his local golf club in Barton-on-sea, Hampshire, where he has been a member for more than 25 years. He has twice won the club championship and plays off a two handicap. It's a world away from the Igboland he came from.

"Coming to England by myself at such a young age was a strange experience and very tough at times," he admits. "I went to St Bonaventure's School in Forest Gate, where a very kind English teacher – I wish I could remember her name – would take the time and trouble to help me learn to read and write during break times. It was difficult. I could hardly speak any English at first but at least

Soon after making his debut, John shoots for goal against Hereford in May, 1977.

having an elder brother (Dickson) at the same school meant I was never bullied or suffered racist abuse there.

"Dickson was a better footballer than me. In fact, before I joined Orient he had a four-week trial for Blackburn Rovers. They wanted to sign him but didn't because they realised he was more interested in socialising and girls."

Chiedozie had to get used to growing up fast and standing on his own two feet in the new family home in Earlham Grove, E7. He reveals: "After Dad moved to England and worked as an engineer at the Ford motor factory in Dagenham, he met and married another Nigerian woman. So, at the age of 13 or 14, I then had a new step-brother and step-sister to look after. I had to grow up quickly.

"Like most Nigerian parents, Dad wanted his sons to become doctors or lawyers and he never came to see me play for the school or district teams. He didn't want me to become a professional footballer. As well as the school and district teams, I also played for SM/Tate & Lyle on Sundays and,

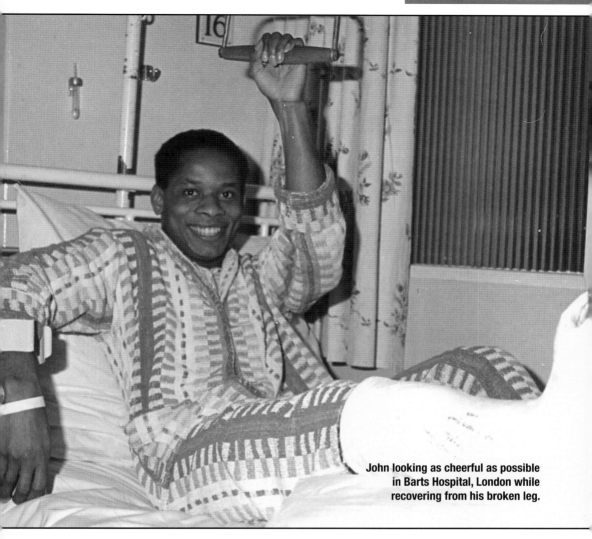

John looking as cheerful as possible in Barts Hospital, London while recovering from his broken leg.

without my father knowing, I'd sneak out the back gate when our manager came round to pick me up and take me to our matches.

While John understandably struggled academically in the classroom, he excelled at sports, especially athletics and high-jump, and of course football, too. His best 100m sprint time of 10.6 seconds, set at the age of 14, is a record that may still possibly stand at St Bon's, where future Republic of Ireland and Spurs full-back Chris Hughton was two years above John and Chris' younger brother Henry was in the same age group.

John represented his school and Newham district at football but admits he could easily have become an athlete instead. "The teacher who took us for athletics wanted me to go in that direction but I chose football," says John, whose lightning-quick pace on the right flank quickly attracted the attention of West Ham United scouts. In fact, he did sign for Hammers as an associate schoolboy and attended a number of training sessions held on the main forecourt at the Boleyn Ground.

"We trained on a concrete car park in front of the main entrance and I was always grazing my knees. Then my school friend Henry Hughton, who was training with Orient at the time, suggested I'd be better off joining them, because the Os had much better junior training facilities than West Ham.

Orient's boys trained in a gym or in a field, not on concrete, so that's why I chose them instead.

"I think George Petchey came to see me play for Newham Boys and my Sunday team. He was very keen for me to sign pro as soon as I was 17 but he was sacked soon after I got into the first team.

"We had a really good youth set-up at Orient. One year, I think 16 of us who had joined as schoolboys . . . Henry, Kevin Godfrey, Tunji Banjo, Billy Hurley and a few others, were signed as pro's."

Chiedozie left school and signed as an apprentice for Orient in the sizzling summer of 1976. One of his duties was to clean the boots of star player Laurie Cunningham, another rapid black winger who would go on to play for England and Real Madrid.

"I only had to clean his boots for four months," says John, "but Laurie always treated me well. He was respectful, very helpful and gave me advice. But it wasn't long after I arrived that they sold him to West Brom.

"After light training on Fridays, a group of us – Laurie, Kevin Godfrey, Henry Hughton, Billy Hurley, myself and sometimes Tunji Banjo – would stay behind to see who was the fastest sprinter at the club. All the other players, George Petchey and the coaches would stand around to watch us compete in three 100-yard races the length of the football field. I usually won two out of three and Laurie would often win the other one, although Kevin was quick as well. It was great fun."

Interestingly, with comparisons between Cunningham and Chiedozie inevitable, John believes they were completely different characters as players who faced sometimes extreme provocation from opponents only too ready to dish out physical punishment.

"One of the reasons they sold him is that some people at Orient thought that if the full-back kicked Laurie in the first five or 10 minutes, he would lose interest and go out of the game. But they knew that if a full-back kicked me early in the game, that was it . . . he'd had it! I would keep coming at him. I watched Laurie play at Orient and for other teams and I also took the view that he could be put off his game in this way.

"I remember Frank Lampard once having a word with me just after we'd kicked-off against West Ham. He stood right next to me and said: 'Sunshine, I hear that you're quick'.

"I said: 'Yeah, I am quick'.

"So he said: 'Well, if you go past me today, I'm gonna break your leg'.

"I said: 'But Frank, you'll have to catch me first!' And he looked at me in amazement.

"But, like other full-backs, he was just trying to psyche me out. They were told by their managers to kick me as soon as the game started. But it never affected me. At the end of the game Frank came up to me again and said: 'Well done, son'.

"I don't think the West Ham fans realised that the more they abused me, the better I played. Upton Park was the worst place for racism and Millwall was also bad. But at Upton Park they threw bananas at me.

"So on one occasion when a banana came in my direction, I picked it up, peeled the skin, ate it and then threw the skin back where it came from. Everyone at Upton Park stood up and clapped me. They never threw anything at me when I played there again.

"I never allowed a crowd to affect my performance, although I know a lot of black players who did. I think it affected Tunji Banjo a lot.

"It (racism) was bad, and it's getting better, but you'll never totally get rid of it. I never had any problems from the Orient crowd, though.

"Having spent the first 12 years of my life in Nigeria and all that I went through there with the Biafran war (1967-70) – moving from one strange village to another, having to sleep in the bush sometimes, running away from army tanks while holding on to your brothers or other relatives as tightly as possible, seeing people you knew around you being killed and fired on by rockets . . . to go through all that and get to where I am . . . well, for all I cared, they could shout at me, throw bananas and call me all the names they liked, it didn't affect me. What happened to me as a young kid made me mentally tough. That's the way I looked at it.

"I've tried to bring up my own two children (daughter Robyn and son Jordan, who was with Bournemouth as a youth and has since played for a number of non-league clubs) the right way, not by lavishing gifts on them. What I experienced growing up in Nigeria made me appreciate what I had when I came to England, being able to go to good schools and the opportunities it gave me."

Dribbling at pace in front of the West Stand during the Leicester game in September, 1978.

From the Nigerian battlefields and hostile, bigoted crowds let's return to a couple of aggressive opponents Chiedozie encountered on the football field. "The only left-back I almost retaliated again, and nearly hit, was Stuart Pearce, when I played for Notts County against Forest. If I hadn't jumped out of the way to avoid him and let the ball run past me on the halfway line, he would have broken my leg. I was just about to grab him when other players moved in and pulled me back. That's the only time I lost my temper.

"The other lunatic was Mark Dennis at Southampton. I didn't enjoy playing against him.

"The left-back I really got on well with was Kenny Sansom of Arsenal and England. He would joke and say things like: 'Don't come over my side, go and play on the other wing!' He was a good guy."

In the courageous Chiedozie, the pocket dynamo with thighs like oak trees and an even bigger heart, Petchey already had a ready-made replacement for Laurie Cunningham. One minute diminutive John was cleaning Cunningham's boots and starring for the youth team, the next he was thrown to the lions of Millwall for his senior debut, in March, 1977, just days after Cunningham had left for fame and fortune in Division One and a month before his 17th birthday.

And as if following the club's finest home-grown discovery wasn't a big enough ask, Orient added another layer of pressure when they handed Chiedozie Cunningham's number seven shirt. "Oh gawd," laughs John, "I did feel a bit nervous in the dressing room before my debut. I sat quietly in the corner thinking, 'I'm 16, what am I doing here with all these players?'. But – and this happened throughout my career – as soon as I set foot on the pitch, all the nerves just disappeared."

It was impossible for any player to get too far above themselves at homespun Orient in those days and Chiedozie didn't exactly turn heads on east London streets after he passed his driving test and bought his first car. "It was a Morris Minor and I bought it from my brother Paul, who owned a small garage, for 50 quid!

"I think my weekly wage as a pro at Orient was about £300 or £400, which did seem like a lot of money to a 17-year-old. Quite a few of the lads used to blow their earnings on expensive clothes from the West End but I only ever possessed one jacket. I suppose my attitude to money had something to do with my upbringing. Touch wood, that's why I'm still OK today. Money never changed me or the way I treated other people."

Apart from a brief fall-out during which time he had an unhappy spell in local digs, Chiedozie continued to live with his strict father at Forest Gate until his move to Notts County.

CHIEDOZIE'S blistering performances for Orient caught the eye of the England youth management, who selected him for an under-18s friendly against Norway at Fulham on November 28, 1977. Although John recalls very little of the game – "I think it was 0-0" – he still has the white England number seven shirt he wore at Craven Cottage

Despite having no further contact from the national selectors, he continued to make good progress with Orient until a broken leg sidelined him for all but the first two matches of Os' memorable FA Cup campaign in 1978. "I laid on the winner for Peter Kitchen in the third round replay at Norwich and the next night Jimmy Bloomfield asked if I'd go to Ipswich as sub for the youth team in the semi-final of the Southern Floodlit Cup. Both he and I soon wished that he hadn't.

"We were losing 1-0 with about 20 minutes left to play, so they put me on. But within a few minutes, just as I was about to put the ball in the net, I was chopped down from behind by the Ipswich goalkeeper. We scored from the penalty – but the challenge broke my right tibula, just above the ankle, and it put me out of football for six months.

"I was in hospital at Ipswich when Orient chairman Brian Winston and secretary Peter Barnes turned up and took me back to London. They put me on the back seat of Brian's car with my leg up. It was the first time I'd ever been in a Rolls-Royce or Bentley!

"It's funny when I look back now," says a giggling Chiedozie. "Where I lived in Forest Gate, my attic room was on the third floor, so they had to carry me all the way up three flights of stairs.

"Orient was a family club and they knew how to treat their players. Money has ruined so much of football today but when I played for the Os, people like Brian Winston, Jimmy Bloomfield, Peter Angell and Peter Barnes looked after me.

"I know how much Jimmy regretted asking me to play for the youth team that night. Mr Lettin, the club's surgeon, performed the operation at St Bartholomew's Hospital in London. I was in plaster from my thigh to my ankle and that injury really set me back. There weren't the same gym facilities available then to what players are given now; there wasn't the same attention paid to rehab after serious injuries. I didn't build my quad muscles back up to what they were before I broke my leg and from then on I had trouble with my knee.

"The injury didn't cause me to lose any of my pace and, also, it had nothing to do with the hamstring trouble I developed later on. That was due to my speed. I had a sciatica problem at Orient, so they gave me an epidural to cure the hamstring trouble and it worked.

"Bill Songhurst was the first qualified physio Orient had and he was very good to me during my long period of rehab."

John recovered sufficiently to start the following season and quickly regained his pre-injury form. The most satisfying of his six goals in 1978-79 was the solo effort that killed off West Ham in the 2-0 Boxing Day victory at Upton Park, where he gave left-back Paul Brush (Lampard was playing right-back that day) a torrid time.

"Jimmy Bloomfield had a big influence on me. He really knew what I had and would encourage me to go out and do what I did best. He didn't want me to cross the halfway line and go back towards our defence. Orient played to my strengths even more when they bought Stan Bowles (at the start of 1980-81). I would have to agree with those who say that Stan 'made' me as a player at Orient. What a left foot he had. And what a character.

"Bobby Fisher was another good influence on me as a player. He didn't want me to track back and help him. He'd say: 'Leave me to do my job. You get the ball and do your job going forward'. I never had to come back near our 18-yard box, like most wide-midfielders do now.

"Bill Roffey was the one who didn't like it whenever I got kicked. He was a lunatic! He would get them back for me. You had to be careful not to upset Bill in five-a-sides, though.

"Tony Grealish was another character. If ever we went out in the evening for a drink, 'Paddy' would end up on the floor. But the next morning, he was our best trainer. To see how hard he worked, up and down in midfield and on the training ground, you would never know he was a drinker.

"I'd go out but I wasn't a drinker. Instead of going to the bookies or the pub after training, I enjoyed playing golf at Hainault, where I became a junior member.

"I got on with all the players at Orient but probably got on best with Glenn Roeder. He took on the responsibility of looking after me. We were room-mates on away trips and I remember him teaching me how to make the knot in my club tie. Because I got into the first team at 16, I wasn't prepared for such things.

"If you asked me to pick a team made up of all the best players I played with, he would definitely be in it. He was always calm. The 'Roeder Shuffle', you know . . . he was like our Franz Beckenbauer. He moved on to QPR and then

Lining up a shot against Stoke in September, 1978.

Newcastle and why he wasn't capped by England, I will never know.

"I played with Ray Clemence at Tottenham but I'd put John Jackson in front of him. The way 'Jacko' performed at Ipswich in the FA Cup (Jan, 1979) was something else.

"Jacko, Bill Roffey, Tony Grealish, Joe Mayo and Ralph Coates were the main talkers in the dressing room. I liked Ralph," says John, breaking into yet another boyish chuckle. "I think of him running and the 'swish' of his hair blowing in the breeze. It was funny . . . every Christmas we used to all get together and discuss what present to buy each player. One year we got Ralph a giant plastic comb – but because he hardly had any hair, it only had two or three 'teeth' on it. We snapped the rest off before giving it to him!

"I remember they bought me a pillow once because I could fall asleep within five minutes of getting on the coach for away trips. I had a few nicknames – 'The Orient Express' and 'Chidders' being two – but the players called me 'Dozy', because I slept a lot and it rhymed with my name."

ALL top strikers rely on good service, so Chiedozie's rapier-like wing play was important to Os' twin spearhead of Joe Mayo, the tall target man who was especially strong in the air, and Peter Kitchen, who was more of a penalty box predator adept at creating chances for himself.

"People said at the time that I didn't score a lot of goals. Well, yeah, that's true but I did make a lot for others. I'd be interested to know how many 'assists' I had.

"Jimmy never told me that he expected more goals from me. It wasn't until I went to Notts County that their manager, Jimmy Sirrel, played me up front alongside Trevor Christie.

"Playing with Joe and Pete at Orient was something I appreciated, as any winger would. 'Kitch' would come short for the ball, while Joe would usually go to the far post . . . you knew where they would be. We worked on things, like movement and making the most of space, in training. I don't like to see teams playing with only one striker today and making little or no use of wingers.

Chiedozie admits, with a hint of embarrassment, that he probably should have been an even better goal provider than he was, certainly at Orient and Notts County. He reveals: "It was only years later, after I signed for Tottenham, that I looked back and realised that out of 10 crosses I put it, on average, six would reach my intended target and the other four would end up finding the same fan

After running from the halfway line, John leaves West Ham's floundering defence in his wake as he slots the ball past future Orient keeper Mervyn Day to make it 2-0 and complete one of the happiest of away days on Boxing Day, 1978.

John taking on Hammers' left-back Paul Brush, who later coached and managed Leyton Orient.

West Ham defender Tommy Taylor, who had two spells with Os, tries to keep John at bay.

behind the goal.

"The fact is, I had poor eyesight – but I didn't realise it until I signed for Spurs, a big club, where they carried out all sorts of tests on all their players. That's when they found out I was short-sighted!

"So from that day on I've always worn contact lenses or glasses. And the first time I walked out to play a game after putting them in, I couldn't believe how green the pitch was. Everything looked so much clearer and brighter. Wearing lenses probably improved my game, because my vision must have been a bit blurred before. Anyway, that's my excuse for putting four bloody crosses out of 10 into the stand behind the goal!

"But I never had my eyes tested as a kid at school, nor at Orient or Notts County."

IN the summer of 1980, just a few months after Nigeria won the African Nations Cup for the first time, Chiedozie got the call to play for his country at the age of 20. It was the start of qualification for the 1982 World Cup finals in Spain and he was among a number of new caps for the home game against Tunisia in Lagos on July 12.

Another debutant was his Orient team-mate Tunji Bango, a promising midfielder who was born at Kensington in west London and emerged from the same Os youth team as JC.

John recalls: "The trip was a real eye-opener for us both. When we turned up at Heathrow airport there were long queues at the Nigeria Airways check-in desk. Tunji and I only had a small holdall each, enough to carry our basic clothes for a couple of days, and when all the people in the queue saw us travelling light, they tried to get us to take stuff through for them. We'd be pre-warned, though, so we declined and got our boarding passes.

"Tunji – who hadn't been to Nigeria before – was in front of me as we boarded the plane and tried to find the seats that matched the numbers on our boarding tickets. When we reached our seats, we found that they were already occupied by a married couple. 'Excuse me, you are sitting in our seats', said Tunji. But the man just stared back at us in amazement and said: 'Have you every travelled Nigeria Airways before? . . . it's first come, first served here, so we sit where we like!'

"On arrival in Lagos, we were approached by a couple of police officers. They asked to look at our passports and they took an instant interest in us because we had hardly any luggage. 'You must be here on business', they suggested. Although I hadn't been back to Nigeria for about eight years, I could understand what the policemen were saying to each other. Then one said: 'Well, I have a wife and four children to feed at home, so how about you pay me some money?'

"But we refused to pay them anything and before things could get awkward, the policemen disappeared as members of the Nigerian FA and airport security arrived to greet us."

The trip was an emotional one for John, who – through his father – was able to renew contact with his long-lost mother. "I found out where she was living and went to visit her at home. It was the first time we'd seen each other since I was 10-months-old. I also took the opportunity to go and see my gran who had brought me up."

Typical of John's laid-back, self-effacing nature, he admits he can't recall how many international appearances he made or how many goals he scored (we make it nine games and two goals – in Tanzania and Guinea). "I couldn't tell you how many goals I scored or the number of appearances I made for any team I played for. I'm not one for statistics," John added.

He is certain, though, that Banjo, one of Os' most promising prospects, should have played more for club and country.

"I only really got to know Tunji when we were playing for Nigeria, because at Orient, he mixed with his own group of friends.

"He was very talented, could have gone a lot further than he did, but he didn't realise it. With Tunji, whether he performed well or not, he didn't care. I suppose he wasn't dedicated enough and that is why he didn't get in the Orient team more often.

"As a midfield player, he had it all. He could get up and down and he had the skill to go past people. I would compare him to Frank Lampard (jnr) in terms of ability."

In 2002, John was honoured with the title of Officer of the Order of Niger for his contribution to Nigerian football.

AFTER making 160 (inc sub) appearances and scoring 25 goals for Orient, Chiedozie was sold to Notts County – then newly-promoted to the top flight – for £600,000 in the summer of 1981. Os were unable to resist accepting what still remains a club record fee for their flying winger, who went on to play 111 times in the league for the Magpies (15 goals).

"Just before the Notts County team coach left our ground to go to Aston Villa for my debut game, Brian approached me and gave me a set of keys – I think Orient were playing somewhere in the Midlands area not too far from Nottingham. Parked next to his car was a brand new Ford Capri. He pointed to it and then said: 'That's yours for being so loyal to the club'. I'll never forget it.

"I believe Luton Town manager David Pleat was interested in signing me. There was also talk of me going to Man City but Orient wanted me to join Notts County. Brian said: 'You've just left one family club, so Notts County will suit you better than going to another bigger club'.

"The time was right for me to move on from Orient and I was very glad that Brian made the decision for me to go to Notts County instead of one of the big city clubs. I owe him a lot. He was a great chairman and a great person."

Before the start of the 1984-85 season, Tottenham brought Chiedozie back to London in a £375,000 transfer deal.

"I could have played for my country more than I did," reflects John, "but Tottenham didn't encourage it. Peter Shreeves, their manager, once said to me: 'You can go and play for Nigeria if you want to but if you do, you won't get back in my first team', so there were times when I was torn between club and country and really had to go along with Spurs' wishes because they were my bread and butter."

A severe back injury sustained during what should have been a routine training exercise limited Chiedozie to 53 appearances (12 goals) in four troubled years at White Hart Lane and also cost him an FA Cup winner's medal in 1987. His spine fused and was operated on by a Harley Street surgeon.

Despite fears that he would never play again, he proved medics and other doubters wrong by joining Derby County in 1988 – a "bad move, I didn't enjoy playing for Arthur Cox, a sergeant-major type figure" – before winding down his career with a handful of appearances for Chesterfield. A 1-0 defeat to Cambridge United in the 1990 Fourth Division Play-off Final was a big disappointment but at least he experienced the thrill of playing at the old Wembley as he bowed out at the age of 30.

"My knee ligaments had worn away through wear and tear, it was time to quit," said John.

Since retiring from football, he ran a successful children's indoor soft playground business for 11 years, hiring out bouncy castles and slides, in the delightful New Forest area where he still lives. He also ran football coaching schools but is now retired and spends two or three days a week in summer playing golf to a very good standard.

Throughout the football season, he keeps an eye on how his favourite former club is getting on. "The best time I had in my career was at the Os with the players they had," John concludes. "Although I played for Spurs and Notts County in the top flight, believe it or not, the first result I look for is Orient's."

Interview: Tony McDonald

On national duty . . . John and Tunji Banjo wearing Nigerian tracksuits at the Orient photo call in July, 1980.

Kitchen served up goal feast

Born: Mexborough, South Yorkshire, February 16, 1952
Usual position: Centre-forward Orient Career: 1977-79 & 1982-84
Orient Appearances: League 110/4, FA Cup 12, League Cup 5/1
Orient Goals: League 49, FA Cup 9, League Cup 2

PETER KITCHEN proved one of the best signings in Orient's history after arriving from Doncaster Rovers in July, 1977. In his first season his goal spree famously propelled Os to the FA Cup semi-finals and the last of his 29 in that memorable campaign saved the club from relegation.

Yet this glutton for goals would not be permanently enshrined in Orient folklore had a possible dream move to either of two top flight clubs who expressed interest in him materialised.

He revealed: "Ipswich Town manager Bobby Robson invited me to Portman Road for a month's trial in May, 1977," Peter explained. "Because Ipswich had completed all their league fixtures, I played in three charity games and scored two goals. I was told by their chief scout that they were very interested and that they would be putting in a bid.

"I then met with Bobby Robson. He asked me how much Doncaster would want for me and I said around £75,000 but he said was only going to offer around £25,000. I told him I didn't think they would accept that figure. Then he added: 'If I'm honest, I can't even promise you a game in the reserves, because I've got Trevor Whymark, Paul Mariner and Clive Woods in the first team'. He also had Alan Brazil, Eric Gates, plus Robbie Turner and David Geddes on loan."

"Bobby said to 'leave it with him' and he'd speak to Stan Anderson, the Doncaster manager. I

Peter signs his first Os contract in the summer of 1977 watched by manager George Petchey and secretary Peter Barnes.

returned to Doncaster and Stan called me in to say that the clubs couldn't agree a fee, so the deal had fallen through. At the time, Ipswich were second from the top in what is now the Premier League, so I was naturally gutted."

But amid The Queen's Silver Jubilee celebrations that summer, there was a club bigger than Ipswich eyeing up Kitchen before he finally completed his move to Leyton. He explained: "George Petchey wanted to sign a striker for the Os and heard I was available, so he contacted Doncaster and I understand an offer of around £30,000 was made, although fees of £40,000 and £50,000 were often quoted in the press.

"I came down to London three times while I was still considering the move, because I wasn't sure I could settle there. Now, the ridiculous thing is, I wouldn't dream of moving back up north. Anyway, on the third occasion I came down, I agreed a deal with Orient, although I only wanted a two-year contract just in case I couldn't settle.

"I'd given my word to Orient and I suppose it said a lot for the old-fashioned sense of values that my parents instilled in me that my move to Brisbane Road went ahead regardless of Spurs' interest."

"The fee was agreed, I shook hands with (Orient chairman) Brian Winston and told him that when he'd got the contract prepared, I'd sign it. I went back up to Doncaster that day to gather up all my things . . . and immediately received a phone call from Doncaster Rovers manager Stan Anderson asking if I'd signed the deal. I told him that while I hadn't actually signed anything at that stage, I'd given Orient a verbal agreement.

"He then told me that another club had come in for me and agreed to pay Doncaster the same fee as Orient. He wasn't sure whether to tell me who the club was but I said it didn't matter – I'd shaken hands on a deal with Brian Winston and given him my word.

"I was then informed the other club was . . . Tottenham Hotspur. I'd caught the eye of their manager Keith Burkinshaw and chief scout Bill Nicholson but, as I say, I'd given my word to Orient and I suppose it said a lot for the old-fashioned sense of values that my parents instilled in me that my move to Brisbane Road went ahead regardless of Spurs' interest. I never regretted signing for the Os and had a wonderful time there," said Peter, who received a £4,000 signing-on fee and a basic weekly wage of £150.

Ready for action at Brisbane Road in the new, iconic brace kit.

He forged new friendships on his first day at Orient that endure to this day. After training at Highams Park, he was going to a cafe by the railway crossing with team-mates Alan Whittle and Bill Roffey when a white van with Waltham Forest Borough Council painted on the side pulled up. The window was lowered and a rotund Cockney gentleman introduced himself to Peter with the words: "Orright, mate, you the new signing from up norf? Welcome to the Orient, mate. I'm Den, a sparky. If you need any jobs doing, give me a bell." And with that, he thrust his phone number into a bemused Kitchen's hand. Peter and life-long supporter Dennis Barefield have remained firm friends ever since.

Ipswich and Tottenham's loss would be Orient's gain, although the man who pulled off one of the club's shrewdest signings was not given the opportunity to work with his new capture for long.

"I liked the way George Petchey wanted to play football. He was a very under-stated man – it wasn't about *him*, it was all about the players. I always responded more favourably to managers who were more open-minded in their approach," says the product of Mexborough Grammar School.

"But just two games into the season he was sacked. We lost 4-1 at home to Blackpool in the second game, although it was a bit of a freak result. But because we'd also been beaten 1-0 at Luton the previous Saturday, I think there was a knee-jerk reaction by Brian Winston and his fellow directors.

"It was a bit of a difficult time for me – I'd just bought a house at Epping and hadn't even moved in. But there was nothing I could do about it."

After six years in charge, Petchey was replaced by Jimmy Bloomfield. Kitchen didn't see eye to eye with Bloomfield – more on that later – but the returning manager certainly benefited from Petchey's final purchase. When he and his wife Susan swapped their South Yorkshire roots for life in 'The Smoke', Kitch couldn't possibly envisage the enduring impact he would have in one of the most memorable seasons in O's history.

Recalling the epic 1978 FA Cup run, he said: "All the ties on the way to the semis were a challenge because we were drawn against good teams and we treated each match as an adventure. We played First Division Norwich in the third round and after a replay, nicked a 1-0 win at Carrow Road where 'Jacko' (goalkeeper John Jackson) was outstanding. It's still one of my favourite memories.

"We'd drawn at Brisbane Road and everybody had written off our chances of progressing in the replay. But I thought we were the best side at Carrow Road. As well as scoring the winning goal

Peter (10) watches Joe Mayo outjump Spurs defender Terry Naylor, while onlookers include Glenn Hoddle and Keith Osgood (5) for Tottenham and Os' Tony Grealish and Bill Roffey during the Second Division derby in October, 1977.

202

(a tap-in from five yards), my general play in that game made it one of my favourite performances."

And there was a postscript to his intended move to Ipswich which had fallen through. "Bobby Robson was at Norwich that night. Afterwards, he came up to me, shook my hand and said I'd had a great game – and then added that he'd made a mistake in not signing me.

"Then we met Blackburn Rovers at home and although we were on the back foot for 70 minutes, we got through. We had great team spirit and that counted for a lot," continued Peter, whose two goals, plus one from striker-partner Joe Mayo, sealed a 3-1 fourth round victory against their Second Division rivals.

The fifth round draw pitted Os against Chelsea at Brisbane Road, evoking fond

Receiving the Evening Standard Player of the Month award from Jimmy Bloomfield. It was in Peter's second season that he fell out with the manager.

memories of the dramatic all-London battle between the sides at the same stage of the competition five years previously. This time, there were no last-minute heroics and this time many Os fans feared the run would soon end after a 0-0 stalemate in E10. But the pessimists reckoned without the hirsute number 10 in the ever-popular 'braces' kit.

"I had the ball in the net in the game at Orient but it was disallowed (rightly so, for handball by Joe Mayo) and I remember Jacko pulled off a couple of outstanding saves. There was a hold-up during the first-half when a perimeter wall collapsed.

"But the replay at Stamford Bridge, where we came from behind to win 2-1, always stands out as a special memory – not only for me but for all Orient fans who were there. It was a special performance by the whole team."

Os' hopes of pulling off another massive Cup shock suffered a blow when left-back Bill Roffey – under pressure from Clive Walker – bizarrely looped the ball over Jackson's head and into his own net.

"Whenever the ball came to me in the first-half, I had Ron 'Chopper' Harris right at my back hacking away at me and I hardly got a kick of the ball. Till this day, I can't understand what happened at half-time. Sometimes at half-time, the manager gives everybody a kick up the backside and gees everybody up and gets a response out of them but that didn't happen at Chelsea. Jimmy Bloomfield was in hospital and Peter Angell was in charge. Peter was a very calming influence, he never shouted or got worked up about matters, and he just encouraged us to go out in the second-half and to carry on playing as we had done.

"For some reason, we seemed to up our game and grow in stature. Suddenly we started to really take the game to Chelsea. The two goals, from my point of view, were very good goals but there was this incredible belief running through the team that we weren't going to lose."

His 49th minute equaliser is right up there among the finest Orient goals ever captured by the TV cameras. Racing on to a perfectly weighted ball into the inside-forward channel from 17-year-old right-winger Kevin Godfrey, Kitchen skipped inside Harris, tying the Chelsea hard man up

Joe Mayo (9) and Kitch celebrate one of Peter's famous FA Cup goals at Chelsea.

in knots, and then danced past Mickey Droy and Ian Britton before coolly placing the ball low to keeper Peter Bonetti's left at The Shed end. It was Greavesesque in its calm, stylish execution.

Kitchen skinned Harris again to cross for Mayo but the big number nine headed against the post and Chelsea breathed a momentary sigh of relief. But in the 72nd minute, in almost a repeat of the earlier move but with roles reversed, Mayo found his fellow forward unmarked with a left-wing cross that Orient's leading marksman controlled superbly before clipping the ball beyond Bonetti from six yards.

Orient's quarter-final opponents were Middlesbrough and for the third time in four rounds, Os went away to a First Division side and emerged with a positive result. After a goalless draw at Ayresome Park, Kitchen and Mayo again did the business in a 2-1 replay victory at Brisbane Road, where Peter again earned rave reviews for a spectacular strike.

With barely five minutes played, there seemed no hint of trouble for Boro when Kitch, lurking with intent on the edge of the 18-yard box, flicked up a hopeful forward pass from Phil Hoadley. With his back to goal, he conjured a brilliant piece of improvisation, pirouetting in mid-air before hooking a right-foot volley over his shoulder and into the net via the inside of the far post at the Coronation Gardens end.

Peter reflected: "All seven of my FA Cup goals naturally gave me a lot of satisfaction but, funnily enough, although supporters thought the one I scored against Chelsea in the replay was my best effort, I actually thought the goal against Middlesbrough was better.

"We all enjoyed the increasing attention as we progressed further in the competition and looked forward to the challenge that each match brought. I got a lot of the headlines but it was a team thing. There was a lot of media exposure which the players weren't used to but we pooled all the money we got for interviews and the like. Admiral, our kit manufacturer, even sponsored our boots and all this hype was a new experience for a lot of the players."

After their fifth round victory at Chelsea, a rapid return to the same west London ground held no fears for Os, especially as Arsenal were odd-on favourites to go all the way to Wembley after brushing aside lower league opposition in Sheffield United, Wolves, Walsall and Wrexham. One optimistic Orient fan among the near 50,000 crowd unfurled a large white banner proclaiming: 'KITCHEN FRIES RICE' – a derogatory reference to Gunners' long-serving right-back, Pat Rice.

But as with their lucky draws to the semi stage, Arsenal enjoyed another huge slice of good

Looking for the knock-down . . . another example of the formidable Kitchen-Mayo partnership, this time at Tottenham in February, 1978.

fortune at the penultimate hurdle. Malcolm MacDonald's wayward right-foot effort was heading for the corner flag until it struck Bill Roffey's left arm and flew into the O's net. And in almost an action replay of the earlier unfortunate game-changer, another less than convincing MacDonald shot hit Glenn Roeder's upper left arm before also deflecting past the helpless Jackson. Who says lightning never strikes twice in the same place?

Kitchen said. "I'd always claim a goal if I could but I don't think I would have had the front to claim either of those that MacDonald did. The own goals did for us really; you couldn't give Arsenal a two-goal lead and expect to get a result. Then Graham Rix scored a third goal to put the lid on our cup run once and for all."

Two cruel moments of misfortune had denied Kitchen the ideal chance to ram Bobby Robson's decision not to sign him back down his throat, for Ipswich Town walloped West Bromwich Albion, 3-1, in the other semi-final, at Highbury, before the 'Tractor Boys' beat Arsenal, 1-0, at Wembley.

He admits: "We were perhaps a bit overawed on the day. We'd dreamed about getting to Wembley but the match proved one game too many – we just couldn't lift ourselves for that extra push. We didn't play well or do ourselves justice."

The goal machine with the Mexican moustache also recalled that the loss of speedy right-winger John Chiedozie due to a broken leg earlier in the competition proved crucial. "Without him we lacked width and he might have caused Arsenal a few problems. But we'd all enjoyed some terrific experiences in getting to the semi-finals, including the win at Stamford Bridge in the fifth round replay when nobody gave us a chance, and there were some really treasured memories along the way."

Of all the 29 league and Cup goals Peter scored in 1977-78 and his 60 overall in Orient colours, his most vital was probably his match-winner in the final game, at Cardiff City, where a 1-0 win preserved Orient's Division Two status. It was incredibly tight at the bottom, where the East Enders and Cardiff were two of seven clubs to finish on 38 points – one clear of the relegation zone.

"It came from a Phil Hoadley knock-down. I remember the ball was bouncing around in the box and, instinctively, you poke out a toe and I connected. With that, we went from second from bottom to 14th in the table, which showed that we were a decent side who were under-performing for a lot of the season."

At the end of his first season at Brisbane Road, Kitchen had etched his name in the club history books by recording the highest number of goals by an Os player in one campaign since the incomparable Tommy Johnston amassed 35 league and one FA Cup goal in 1957-58. Peter's feat – equal to the 29 scored by Ron Heckman in 1955-56 – still stands at the end of 2018, while his tally of 21 league goals in 1977-78 puts him among an elite group of only 10 Orient players who have notched 20 or more league goals in a season since Os joined The Football League in 1905-06. No wonder he was named Player of the Season.

His only disappointment at the end of a brilliant '77-78 campaign was that Blackpool's Bob Hatton netted one more league goal than him to win the Division Two Golden Boot award. How Kitch must have cursed his penalty miss against Luton Town on January 2!

Of course, no player can do it all by himself and Peter is never slow in paying tribute to his team-mates. In particular, strike-partner Joe Mayo.

"We complemented each other's style of play even though we were very different types of players. We were both very honest, intelligent and hard-working.

"Joe was a very good player – tall but very mobile and he had good control for a big man. He was also a good finisher when he got the opportunities.

"He was the most unselfish team player I ever played with. If Joe wasn't in a very good position to go for goal himself, he'd always look to lay the ball off or knock it down for others around him. He was perfect to play alongside and we developed an almost telepathic understanding of where each other was on the field.

"I believe that Joe would have scored a lot more goals if he hadn't tracked back towards our half as much as he did. Due to his obvious height, he was often the one challenging for the majority of the high balls, with me running forward to chase the flick-ons. When our wide players crossed the

Sixth round heroes Kitch and Joe Mayo pose for photographers in the jubilant Os dressing room after their goals KO'd Middlesbrough.

Scoring from the penalty spot against Sheffield United in November, 1978. Nigel Gray (5) can't bear to watch.

ball, I would often attack the near post while he would attack the far post.

"In contrast, I did most of my running off the ball, always trying to find and create space, moving along the opposition backline or coming short for the ball. I had excellent ball control and would often hold the ball up and link in with other players, or I would be running in behind defenders chasing after loose balls or flick-ons, so when you are the furthest player forward it's much harder to chase back as much.

"Joe and I are still great mates. When he came down from the Midlands to watch the Os a few years ago, he stayed over at my house where we shared several glasses of wine. He is a real character and it's always a pleasure to be in his company."

Assessing the respective merits of other regular team members of that late 70s side, Kitchen continues: "We had a tremendous team spirit and a lot of confidence in each other's ability. Players knew that if they got the ball through to me or Joe we would try and create something. We knew that if we got the ball out to 'Chidders' (John Chiedozie) on the wing, he'd take people on and do something.

"There was supreme confidence in our back four. Glenn Roeder and Phil Hoadley were two terrific players, then you had Bobby Fisher and Bill Roffey – who had a great left peg – as full-backs and Jacko in goal.

"People like Tony Grealish and Peter Allen, who was a very underrated and hard-tackling player, were terrific for us in midfield.

"The thing about Orient at that time was that there were no stars as such, everybody was doing their job and I really feel that had they bought a couple of players instead of selling, that team could have gone on and won promotion and achieved so much. But then in the summer of '78, they sold Phil Hoadley and Glenn Roeder and that's why I decided I also wanted to leave, because it showed me that the club didn't have any ambition.

"Phil and Glenn were both proven – they went on and played in the First Division (for Norwich City and QPR respectively); Bill Roffey was a very good left-back; Tony Grealish subsequently played for Brighton and West Bromwich; Chidders left to join Spurs and then there was Joe and myself. So there you had the nucleus of a terrific side, all in our mid-twenties, but everyone got sold and replaced by thirtysomethings.

"They did bring in Stan Bowles, who was still a terrific player, and Ralph Coates, who was also superb, but had they not sold quality players, then I think Orient could have had a Premier League side."

READING this book, you will easily get the impression that Jimmy Bloomfield was generally held in the highest regard by the vast majority of players that served under him in both of his spells at the helm – with just a few notable exceptions. But that doesn't make the honest opinion of Peter and co. any less valid than anyone else's.

He admits: "I didn't ever really get on well with Jimmy Bloomfield. He brought in some experienced players but, in my opinion, some were just at the club to pick up wages.

"I have to say that Jimmy was not my favourite manager, because he was ultra-cautious and defensive in his tactics. George encouraged young players, he was very good with them, and half of the team under him had come through from the youth team. So there was some really good team spirit among those players.

"He also brought in some good experienced players, like Joe Mayo, and built a really good balance between youth and experience. I believe the team was on the verge of doing something special.

"But my personal view is that Jimmy wasn't particularly interested in young players – he wanted to bring in players who were already proven. It can work in some instances at certain clubs. Jimmy brought in a lot of players who were at the tail-end of their careers and – again, this is only my opinion – I think it was the start of Orient's decline. They had a couple of seasons where they signed a lot of experienced players and paid them a lot of money but they only lasted a year or two. They were experienced but they were only going to be short-term fixes.

"So once Orient had been relegated (at the end of 1981-82), within two or three years, all the money that had been generated from the FA Cup run of '78 had been spent. From that time, they have never been able to get back into the Championship (second tier)."

Dribbling round the Sunderland keeper before scoring in January, 1978.

Asked to explain how Bloomfield's tactics affected him, Kitchen continued: "I was asked to play a deeper role when Jimmy brought Ian Moores to play alongside Joe Mayo but I never believed that was my best position. Fair do's, that was how Jimmy wanted to play but, for me, it was frustrating because I believed that we had a really good and talented side at the Orient and could afford to be a bit more adventurous in our play.

"He inherited a very good team and should have tried to keep that together, as well as bringing in a couple more quality players. Then I'm sure the club would have gone on to better things.

"I did challenge him about our style

a number of times and we had a fierce row on one particular occasion, although it was out of character for me to act like that. We started having more arguments and it became obvious that I would have to move on. So after 18 months with Orient, I put in a transfer request and got a move to Fulham.

"I know that Norwich bid £140,000 for me after we beat them during our famous Cup run of '78. And later in the season, Terry Venables offered a deal of £150,000 – £110,000 in cash and a player valued at £40,000 – to take me to Crystal Palace but Jimmy turned down both offers, asking for £250,000.

"I'd been at Doncaster Rovers for seven years and all I'd read in the papers or been told was that one club or another had made an offer for me but Doncaster were always pricing me out of the market. In the end, I had to force the issue to move away from there by refusing to sign a new contract.

"I'd only been at Orient for a short while, had scored lots of goals and now they were asking too much for me. Unfortunately, in football, you only have a limited time when you're a saleable asset. And I didn't feel that I wanted to spend another two or three years at Orient without getting the opportunity to play at a higher level."

IN February, 1979, instead of biding his time and letting his contract run down, which would have broadened his options, Kitchen jumped hastily at a move to Fulham for £150,000, a bargain fee at a time when prices were going through the roof. However, the switch from east to west London didn't work out – Peter was plagued by injuries in his second season at Craven Cottage which ended in relegation to the Third Division.

On a personal level, he was at a low ebb on and off the field. His marriage to Susan was breaking down – they were divorced two years later – and he took a dim view of manager Bobby Campbell's aggressive, blame culture approach that led to heated dressing room exchanges with players.

"Some while after I'd joined Fulham, I visited Jimmy Bloomfield to apologise for my behaviour and was very sorry when I learned of his death in April, 1983. I did go to his funeral and I remember feeling sad that we'd never got on. He had done very well for Orient in his first spell as manager but I think he was the wrong choice when he returned in 1977."

His unhappy spell at Fulham ended with a £100,000 move to Cardiff City but he'd only swapped one struggling Second Division side for another and after avoiding relegation by the skin of their teeth in his first season in South Wales, Cardiff went down at the end of his second.

The goal machine then had a short spell in Hong Kong with Happy Valley before returning to Orient – by now in the third tier – on a free transfer in December, 1982. His basic deal was £300 per week and he received a signing-on fee of £4,000. There was also a £500 goal bonus – but we'll come to that shortly.

Ken Knighton was the manager that brought Kitch back to Brisbane Road, where he received a very warm welcome for the second time. "I'd known him when he was at Sheffield Wednesday and had met him a couple of times. I had no problem with him – he put me straight back in the team and had a lot of faith in me to score goals, which I did.

"Unfortunately, Ken didn't have a particularly good time at Orient and was sacked at the end of the season. His assistant Frank Clark got his job – basically, because I don't think the club could afford to bring in anyone else. I've got mixed views about Frank. He had a great knowledge of football and his tactics were very much based on Brian Clough's philosophy. Frank had played for Brian at Nottingham Forest, where they used to play 4-4-2, try to play through midfield and get wide men to go forward from deep.

"Frank, though, was in a precarious position himself and, understandably, he was looking out for himself as much as anything else. Perhaps he saw me as a bit of threat to his own job . . . I'd gained my coaching badges during my time at Cardiff and when I returned here from Hong Kong, Brian Winston did say to me that he saw me as a future player/manager. I'm sure Frank was aware of that comment.

"He always seemed a bit wary of my achievements on the field. For example, I'd be playing well one week and then the next game, he'd substitute me or start me on the bench.

"The classic example was a game at Brentford (March 10, 1984). Although there wasn't much money at the club, I was on a goal bonus. If I scored 20, I would receive £500. I'd got a few goals that season and having started the game at Griffin Park, I scored to give us a 1-0 lead. I was playing well but then Frank substituted me at half-time. The game ended 1-1 and to this day, I can only imagine that he must have checked with the directors to see whether they could actually afford to pay me the £500 bonus if I hit my 20-goal target."

Despite starting only 26 league matches (plus three sub appearances), Peter still ended up the club's leading scorer with 12, four of them coming in the home 5-3 thriller against Millwall (April 21, 1984). It was his third – and last – Os hat-trick.

"Frank told me they were going to offer me a new contract but then a few weeks later, he said the club had changed its mind and that I would be allowed to leave at the end of the season. The following year, Orient were relegated to Division Four for the first time in their history and it rankled with me that they'd allowed me to go because I'd always enjoyed playing for the club. I was still only 32 and could have played for another two or three seasons."

IN September, 1984, Kitchen demonstrated his spirit of adventure again by heading to the USA for a three-month stint playing for the new Las Vegas Americans franchise in an indoor league.

On his return to England, he joined non-league Dagenham, where he played seven games in manager Ken Knighton's struggling Daggers side that just avoided relegation from the Alliance Premier League (equivalent of the 2018-19 National League) in 1984-85, before making his final five Football League appearances in that season for Fourth Division Chester City. The last of his 211 career league and Cup goals from 520 (plus 26 as sub) appearances, spanning 15 seasons, came at home against Aldershot on March 27, 1985.

However, that wasn't quite the last of a veritable feast of goals served up by Kitchen – author of the aptly titled *The Goal Gourmet* which he wrote with Os historian Neil Kaufman. Southern League Margate manager, Os legend Tommy Taylor, lured the then 39-year-old Kitch out of retirement in 1991-92, when his team-mates on the south coast included another Orient 'old boy' in Bill Roffey. Even after quitting competitive football, he still enjoyed turning out for Rod Stewart's Vagabonds team (1995-98) and netted a bewildering 280 goals in 228 matches for Corinthian Casuals Vets from 1990 until finally hanging up his size nine-and-a-half boots, aged 52, in 2005.

From 1991, he spent nine happy years working for Wimbledon FC's youth academy, coaching and managing their under-13s, 14s and 15s. Away from football, he worked as Operations Director for the Sencio Community Leisure Company – a sub-contractor of Sevenoaks Council – in his adopted county of Kent between 2004 and his retirement in 2009.

He resides in the Kent village of Ightham with his long-time partner Katherine Govett. Michael – Peter's son from his marriage to Susan – lives in Osaka, Japan, where he teaches English to company executives and students. Completing the family picture are Peter's three grandchildren – Alfie, Tommy and Atalie. On a sad note, Peter's other son, Darren, died at the age of 28 from a brain haemorrhage in 2003.

When Peter looks back on his goal-laden playing days, you couldn't blame him for wondering what might have been had either Ipswich or Spurs given him the chance to prove his worth at the highest level. Orient fans can only be thankful that they didn't! Although he would be the first to acknowledge that he wasn't tall for a striker and lacked pace over long distances, he had a sharpness of mind and a burst of pace over a few yards that distinguished him as one of the most prolific and accomplished forwards operating outside the top flight.

"Once I'd established myself at Doncaster, I was a prolific goalscorer for four years and I was so determined to prove I could play at a higher level. I'm sure if I had got the right move, I would have done well in a First Division side. But it didn't happen – although I must say that I loved playing for Orient during what was a successful period in my career.

"I've had a wonderful career and loved playing for Doncaster and the Os in particular," he reflects. "Over the years, I've met some lovely people at Orient. I loved the era I played in but, if I'm honest, I think I would have embraced playing now because I would have suited today's playing style. It's not the long ball knocked up – sometimes aimlessly – like it used to be. Now, the ball is often played to feet, and played in and around the box, using one-twos to open up defences, which would have suited me ideally."

Although, like most football stars of the pre-90s, he admits he was once a heavy drinker, he added: "Players are now much more aware of the importance of diet and sports science and I would have bought into that, too.

"However, I might have found the tactical side frustrating. I am disappointed when I see the ball being passed just for the sake of passing it; and teams going out simply not to lose rather than trying to win. I don't get that mindset."

It's great to see that Peter has maintained such a close affinity to the club. Apart from having a bar at the ground (he admits to slight feelings of dismay when he discovered it was a fast food outlet and not solely where alcoholic beverages were sold!) and also one of the four blocks of flats now located in each corner of the stadium named after him, he's an actively big advocate of Os' significant historical links to the Great War effort. Satisfying both his passion for travel and interest in history, Kitch has made numerous pilgrimages to northern France to visit The Somme battlefields where three of Clapton Orient's stars are buried. He wrote the foreword to Steve Jenkins' book, *They Took the Lead*, and was also a consultant to *The Greater Game* play inspired by that book and the heroics of the Os' trio cruelly killed in action.

Visit Leyton Orient on a match day and there's a good chance you will see Peter chatting amiably to supporters, although being diagnosed with Ulcerative Colitis – a degenerative disease of the colon – in March, 2000 has forced him to watch his diet and lower his wine and beer intake.

"I always used to go into the supporters' club in my playing days and have a drink and a chat with the fans and I always enjoy going back in there to see everyone. I'm always made to feel very welcome – Orient's a lovely club with some marvellous fans," Peter concluded.

Interview: Paul Hiscock & Tony McDonald

No ordinary Joe

Born: Tipton, West Midlands, May 25, 1952
Usual position: Centre-forward Orient Career: 1977-81
Orient Appearances: League 223/5, FA Cup 15, League Cup 10
Orient Goals: League 150/5, FA Cup 13, League Cup 8/1

BLACK Country-born Joe Mayo arrived at Brisbane Road shortly before the transfer deadline in March, 1977 – along with West Bromwich Albion team-mate Allan Glover – in the exchange deal that took Laurie Cunningham to the then First Division club. Os received £110,000 for their most prized asset, while paying £25,000 of it back to secure the Baggies duo.

"It wasn't easy for me to leave Albion, because the club had been my team since I was a child and I'd go along and watch them. Then, when I went on to play for them, it was a dream come true. I never wanted to leave the Hawthorns," said Joe.

"Orient had come to Albion the previous season and were unlucky not to win there. We couldn't beat them at Orient either, even though we had a really good team at that time.

"I'd been playing in the first team until I tweaked a medial ligament in my right knee and obviously I wasn't able to play. It became apparent that I wasn't going to get back into the side, so when Orient came in for me it was a big step to join them. In fact, I wasn't really mature enough to understand just how big a step it was moving to London.

"Having said that, it was probably one of the best decisions I ever made in my football career,

Jimmy Bloomfield with his two sharpshooters of 1977-78 at the end-of-season Player of the Year awards bash. Winner Peter Kitchen and runner-up Joe Mayo, although Joe collected the main award a year later.

because I loved it down there."

While Mayo went on to win the hearts of Orient fans, left-winger Glover stayed for less than a year, making 38 appearances (five goals) before moving again, this time to Third Division Brentford. But he also failed to hold down a regular place at Griffin Park and by 1980 had dropped into non-league with his home-town club Staines Town.

"When Allan was at West Brom, he was a very quiet lad and hardly spoke to anyone," recalls Joe. "I'd played alongside him in the reserves a few times. But as soon as we came to London, he seemed to develop a gift for chatting away. He came from the south, so maybe he was happy to be returning to nearer his roots.

"Allan was good to me after we agreed to move to Orient. He helped me a lot with travel arrangements, for example. When he went back to live in Staines, I thought I'd better look for a house around that area and so I moved into a place in Marlow (Bucks). What I didn't realise at the time was that it was going to take me about three hours to drive into training from home. I lived there for about nine months and then moved to Enfield, which was a lot better."

Mayo soon settled in his new surroundings and was made to feel welcome from the top hierarchy down. "I'd been associated with a lot of people before I came down to Orient; people who said that they were going to do various things and never did. But I immediately knew that Brian Winston wasn't like that. If he said that he was going to do something, then he went ahead and did it.

"Also, he had the players at heart in everything he did – they came first. Brian was one of the team, he was great. He'd come into the dressing room but he was accepted because all the players liked him." (In fact, Joe's wife Pam became secretary to the Os' chairman.)

"Brian used to sort everything out regarding contracts and he was very fair. To be honest, I used to leave it in his hands, whereas at West Brom I'd sit outside the manager's office for two or three hours and when it was my turn to go in, we'd be haggling over five quid. The way they did things at Orient was so different and I could never complain about how they treated me.

"If you get on with the staff and the fans are supportive of you, then that reflects on your performance in matches."

MAYO could hardly have wished for a better start to his Orient career in the 2-2 draw at Blackburn Rovers on March 12, 1977.

"I scored on my debut at Blackburn and until that day, I hadn't really met anybody at the club. But both Allan and I had the good fortune to score in that game. Then I came down to London to play my first home game for Orient and it was against Bolton, who were a team of kickers at that time. Everyone kept thinking that there was a jinx on the number nine shirt at Orient, because whoever wore it seemed to get injured.

"I didn't believe in all that nonsense but on my home debut I tore my medial ligament and only returned in time for the last two matches of the season."

Os retained their Second Division status by the skin of their teeth – Glover's first-half goal in the final home game against Hull City (1-1) proving enough to avoid the drop – but much better times were just around the corner.

"The following season, we had another bit of a brush with relegation (Os finished 14th) but we also got to the semi-finals of the FA Cup. Before that we played three First Division sides, all three games went to replays and we won them all. And it certainly wasn't down to luck. We deserved the victories against Norwich, Chelsea and Middlesbrough and the players learned a lot about themselves in those games.

Relegation fight in the final game of 1976-77 against Hull City. Os' scorer Allan Glover is far left while Peter Allen, Joe and Alan Whittle try to restore calm and order.

"We were good players and we all started to believe in ourselves. We'd seen some top-class players coming to play Orient and we were putting in performances twice as good as them. Our players started to think, 'you know, I think I could play in the First Division every week' – and they were probably right. That Cup run gave everyone so much more confidence."

Mayo offered an explanation for why Orient struggled to replicate their Cup success in the second tier of 1977-78: "I think the difference in our league form compared to our FA Cup exploits was the system we played. Strangely, First Division teams struggled to break us down but Second Division sides played many more long balls and that seemed more effective against us, whereas top flight teams tried to play through us.

"The Second Division sides that beat us did so by dragging Bobby Fisher – our sweeper – over to one side, then quickly switch play to the other side and we were knackered. But the likes of Norwich, Chelsea and Boro couldn't work that out.

"When we battled against relegation in the same season we had that wonderful Cup run, we always had the confidence that we'd get out of trouble. We went to Cardiff for that last game of the season needing to win to stay up but there was so much belief among the players that we would get the result we wanted.

"There was no way we believed we were going to go down. To be honest, we should have won that game by four or five, instead of 1-0, but there you are. It was still a good season, without a doubt."

The famous strike pairing of Peter Kitchen (seven) and Joe (two) scored all nine of Os' Cup goals between them in that epic '78 run. For Mayo, the 2-1 fifth round victory at Chelsea remains a special highlight.

He said: "It was an outstanding team performance and, personally, I felt I played really well. I know that 'Kitch' got all the plaudits but we had so many players who turned in superb displays. Not least Kevin Godfrey, who had just got into the side; he looked really classy that night.

"Another game that sticks out is a match with West Ham one Boxing Day (1978). My brother

John worked at the main Ford car plant in Dagenham and his mates were all West Ham supporters. They ribbed him something rotten about how they were going to walk all over the Os.

"Anyway, we went over there and beat them 2-0 and I managed to score the first goal, so our kid was absolutely over the moon. I know he was really chuffed about that. Sadly, he died some while ago but I'd never seen him as excited and enthusiastic as he was after that game. He knew that when he went back to work, he could give all his mates the flak in return for the stick he'd taken from them earlier.

"John Chiedozie ran Frank Lampard absolutely ragged in that game and, in reality, 'Chidders' should have been like that all the time. If there were quicker footballers than him, I would like to have seen them. He was a good lad as well.

"It was a smashing result – I don't know why but we always seemed to play well around Christmas.

"There was always a good atmosphere and I just loved putting on the shirt. The spirit around the place was great. Our physio Bill Songhurst always used to say to me: 'Up to five minutes to three, you took the piss out of everybody in the dressing room but then I used to come over and put your neck back in. Then I'd look at your eyes, they crossed, and out you went. But I knew you'd play well'.

"I had this ritual . . . before every home match, we'd come out on the left-hand side of the tunnel and I used to kick the wall just before going onto the pitch. Every year, they'd have to re-plaster it because I kicked it so much. I loved playing at Brisbane Road."

JOE confirms that he enjoyed great camaraderie with his team-mates. "When I was at Orient, the team spirit was second to none. But perhaps I've been very fortunate because the dressing room spirit among all the teams I've played for has been absolutely brilliant. I suppose if you're doing well, you can't wait to get into the dressing room and share the banter and good times with your colleagues.

"At Orient, the Cockney boys were probably the best piss-takers in the world. You had to grow up quickly in there just to survive, otherwise you would be the butt of all jokes. But I'd learned how to deal with all that type of thing at West Brom, so I could give plenty back whenever necessary.

"They were all good pals but I suppose I used to knock about with Kitch more than anyone else until he got transferred. Then 'Mooresy' (Ian Moores) arrived and I seemed to pair up with him a lot. We'd have some real laughs together; he was as daft as a brush. But he and Ralph Coates, who joined Orient at the same time, were probably my best mates because we all lived near to each other. I used to play a lot of golf with Mooresy, although he was probably the worst golfer in the world. I loved playing with him because it did my confidence a lot of good!

"When Chidders got in the team, the club roomed him with me on away trips but he hardly said much. I remember asking him if wanted a cup of tea and he sort of gave a muted answer, a sort of grunt. He did that a lot. On one occasion, just as I was pouring out the tea, he said: 'Milk first'. I think those were the first words I really heard him speak.

"Later, I roomed with 'Margy' (John Margerrison) but for some reason they seemed to put me with anyone who was having a bad time. I also shared with Bill Roff (Roffey) a couple of times but over the period I was at the club, I think I must have shared a room with just about everybody.

"All this dressing room spirit they talk about depends on how well you get on with people. I know Kitch went through a time after the Cup run when he wasn't very happy, he was a bit down in the dumps and wanted to get away. I've spoken to him about it since and I feel he should have

Joe picks his spot before scoring against Cardiff City in October, 1978.

stayed, had another good season with Orient and then moved on, rather than dig himself into a hole and sulk, which is basically what he did.

"And that's sad. If you're feeling like that, the players take the mickey out of you. If he'd had another season like the previous one in 1977-78, he would have been playing First Division football for the rest of his career.

"I'd like to think that I got on well with all the lads at the club and would still regard them as mates even to this day. As I said earlier, it was a big decision for me to come down South but I made so many friends and I've never regretted it for one moment. They were all lovely people at Orient."

JOE and Peter Kitchen enjoyed a great mutual respect for each other as players and remain good pals to this day. They enjoyed an on-field chemistry that was almost telepathic. As well as their thrilling Cup strikes in 1977-78, they netted 30 league goals between them – the most since the Bullock (16)-Fairbrother (14)-Queen (12) triumvirate of 1973-74 – while the rest contributed a combined total of just 13.

Joe says: "I think Kitch and I hit it off from the first match we played together. I was flicking on a few things and he was getting on the end of them. I'd always been taught that you had to make things happen rather than wait for it to fall into place. If the ball was going in a certain direction, you had to think, 'I've got to be on the end of that'. And 'Kitch' was great at doing that. He'd get on the end of corners even though he wasn't that tall.

"His reading of the game in situations around the box was just incredible. I'd played with Jeff Astle, Tony Brown and other players with fantastic credentials in the old First Division and you have to say that Kitch was on a par with them.

"The first goal he scored at Chelsea in the Cup was amazing but he'd score three or four like that in a season. Every time he collected the ball in the box, he'd do a jink and score. He was top-notch.

"I like to think that on the field, I was good at other things and 'Kitch' was good at scoring goals, which is the hardest thing in the game. Sometimes the two mould together and that's what happened with our partnership. The thing is that not all players are made the same way. My strength was that I could run all day – I weighed 12st 8lbs at my fittest – and I was happy to do all the running throughout the match.

"Some of the pitches we played on were diabolical but back then it did actually help you as a forward, because you could close people down, get a foot in and maybe win the ball. Nowadays, you'd be running around like a headless chicken because pitches are so good and players have better control of the ball.

"Looking back on my career, I played for two or three years in the West Midlands League for Dudley Town FC and it was the most physical football I ever experienced. It was rough and competitive and people would be kicking you all the time. It gave me a good grounding, though, because it made me want to play at a higher level. And after playing part-time football at that level, the one thing I always thought about professional football was that it was a bit namby-pamby. In non-league, you'd be kicking your opponents all through the game and getting plenty back but in The Football League, I used to kick a few people and rarely got anything back."

Returning to the style of football Os played under Jimmy Bloomfield, Joe says: "We used to play with a sweeper yet Kitch still got 20 goals a season. Bobby (Fisher) played the sweeper role and then Glenn (Roeder) did when they moved 'Fish' into the right-back position.

"We had some fabulous players. I played a couple of games at the back alongside Bobby and he was a far better player than people give him credit for. I also played next to Nigel (Gray) with Fish sweeping behind us, so we'd often leave the ball for him to deal with."

Joe recalled the management duo he played under throughout his five years – four full seasons – at Orient. "Jimmy Bloomfield and I used to get on fine, we'd have a laugh and a joke, but he was not in good health.

"I don't think anyone realised just what a talent Jimmy was. If we were out on the training pitch, he would take all the freekicks and wouldn't allow the session to finish until he'd scored from a freekick. The players were supposed to be practicing but at times, it was more of a session for *him*. But he was a good fella.

"His assistant, Peter Angell, had been a no-nonsense defender himself when he played (for QPR). He did a lot of coaching because Jimmy was ill a lot of the time. Peter was a good coach and had a sound tactical understanding of the game."

Tragically, Peter was on a training run with the players in Epping Forest in July, 1979, when he suffered a fatal heart attack.

"It was shocking when he died – it happened in front of the lads and I'm sure it affected our results and knocked us back a lot. I can't remember ever seeing anything like that in all my days. He just collapsed.

Joe, with Ralph Coates for company, unsettling the Notts County defence in January, 1979. Joe congratulates Ian Moores, his inferior golfing partner, after he'd also netted against Brighton.

"He was from the old school was 'Gunner'. You were expected to be fit and if he told you something once, he wasn't going to tell you again. He was of that ilk. But what a smashing bloke he was."

SUPPORTERS always warm to players who never fail to give their all. The fact that Joe, tall and rangy, also possesses an endearing personality and the ability to enjoy a laugh only enhances his popularity among the Orient faithful.

"I loved them and they were great to me," smiles Joe. "I made a number of friends, such as Dennis Barefield. He always turns up at events and talks as if he's got a mouthful of spaghetti! He was really one of Kitch's early mates but he's a good fella. I remember Jimmy Sawyer, too. He was a character.

"I've got a story about another supporter. My brother Denis was on holiday in Spain with his mates; he's was about 5' 7", only a little lad. Anyway, this guy called Steve Fullbrook, an Orient supporter, was there on his honeymoon and it was the night of our Cup quarter-final replay with Middlesbrough. Steve went into the bar where Denis and his mates were, although they didn't know one another.

"Steve started whooping and hollering and Denis asked him: 'What's up?' and he replied: 'Orient have just beaten Middlesbrough, 2-1. So Denis asked him who'd scored the goals. 'Kitchen and Mayo' came the reply, so Denis said: 'Oh, that's our kid'.

"Steve looked at Denis and asked: 'Who, Peter Kitchen?' To think he thought that Denis looked more like Kitch than me was strange. Anyway, Denis said: 'No, Joe Mayo is my brother'. Steve responded with: 'There's no way – clear off, mate. Look at the size of you, you're not his brother'."

"The upshot of their meeting in Spain is that they became good mates and Denis invited him to meet up when they got back to England, where he'd introduce Steve to me. Denis and Steve arranged for us to meet in a bar in Hackney one afternoon but Steve still wasn't ready to accept that I was Denis' brother; he still thought it was a wind-up – until I walked in! Steve couldn't believe it but they both came over, we got chatting and we've been mates ever since.

"Steve typifies Leyton Orient supporters: he's a really good lad, very down to earth and has been loyal to the club all his life.

"I won the supporters' Player of the Year award in 1978-79 but it was really more for what I'd done the previous season, when they gave it to Kitch instead. It was nice, because when fans show their appreciation of you like that, it brings a tear to your eye. It really does."

Brighton's defence looks all at sea as Joe finds space in amongst six of them to score in the 3-3 draw in April, 1979.

AFTER 177 league and Cup matches which produced 40 goals, Joe made his final Orient appearance as sub in the 1-1 League Cup draw against Millwall at Leyton on September 1, 1982.

"Paul Went had just been appointed manager when the club decided to release me. As always, Brian Winston was as honest as the day is long with me and he said: 'We've got a problem. We've made 'Wenty' manager and you two are such good mates, I know it will break his heart if you're not playing well and he's got to leave you out of the side. So, I've had a bit of a chat with a couple of clubs and I think I can get money for you'.

"Naturally, I was disappointed but I thought, 'Oh well, if that's what you think'.

"As I said, I trusted Brian but the seed had been sown in my brain that my time with Orient was up and it was time to go. So we went up to Cambridge United, where Brian saw John Docherty, their manager, and came out with the thumbs-up, which meant he'd got what he wanted for me. Then I went in to talk terms and listen to what he had to say. Afterwards, I said to John: 'I'll let you know'.

"On the way back to Orient, Brian said: 'They've offered £100,000 for you' and I replied: 'Well. I've got to go then, haven't I, for the good of the club?'

"So I did. I got a cut of the fee and started to score goals straight away. Cambridge played a very direct brand of football, with George Reilly up alongside me. Balls were dropping in front of me and I scored a few goals.

"The sad thing is, 'Wenty' only lasted a month in the manager's job and at the end of that season Orient got relegated."

After 40 senior appearances and 14 goals for Cambridge United in the second tier, Mayo spent a brief loan spell with Blackpool before linking up with Peter Kitchen again in Hong Kong with the Happy Valley club in June, 1983. Since then he ran the Plas Isa Hotel in Criccieth, north Wales for 13 years and worked as a sales rep for Imperial Tobacco.

But big Joe looks back with mainly fond memories of his time with Orient, adding: "The five years I had with them were the best five years of my career, better than anything else I experienced. Remember, as well, that I'd played for my boyhood club, the Albion, and helped to get them up and out of the Second Division – we got promoted in my first full season with them. But that achievement didn't come close to that Cup run with Orient.

What I would have loved was to have played for Orient against West Brom in the 1978 semi-final and to have seen what sort of reaction I got from the Albion players. I go back there sometimes and see some of the players from that era and they tell me they would have kicked hell out of me. It would have been interesting, so that's one of the only things I would have changed during those happy years on and off the pitch with Orient. I've got some great memories but also a few sad ones, what with Jimmy and Peter passing away.

"When you join a club, you don't know too much about them really. When I first got down to Orient, I did wonder whether I'd made the right decision but it didn't take me too long to realise it was the right one. Talking to the management and chairman, I thought, 'this is a club that is going places'.

"But the unfortunate thing was that they sold so many of their good players. I appreciate they had to do that to survive but just think if they could have kept Glenn Roeder, Phil Hoadley, John Chiedozie, Paddy Grealish and others. They were playing the best football of their careers and if they had stayed another season or two, who knows what Orient might have gone on to achieve. They all had a passion for the club."

Interview: Paul Hiscock

Bright shades of Gray

Born: Fulham, London, November 2, 1956
Usual position: Centre-half Orient Career: 1974-83
Orient Appearances: League 233, FA Cup 20/1, League Cup 8
Orient Goals: League 4, FA Cup 0, League Cup 0

IN the midst of Orient's thrilling, audacious charge to the FA Cup semi-final in 1978, Nigel Gray had other things on his mind. He decided to get married . . . and it's all Peter Kitchen's fault!

"At the start of that year my girlfriend Angie proposed to me in The Britannia pub, close to Chelsea football ground," explains Nigel, "but we didn't have a lot of money between us at the time, so to delay things a bit I told her: 'If we have a decent Cup run and I manage to earn some extra money in bonuses, maybe we can afford a wedding . . . '

"So what does 'Kitch' do? Starts banging in the goals, the silly sod!"

As everyone knows, Kitchen scored both Orient goals in the third round against Norwich City, netted twice in the fourth round win over Blackburn Rovers and then famously struck twice again at top flight Chelsea as Os pulled off a sensational victory in Fulham-born Nigel's back yard.

"So I've never forgiven 'Kitch' for scoring all those goals that took us to the semi-finals!"

Nigel and Angie were married at Fulham Registry Office – three days before Os' daunting quarter-final trip to Middlesbrough. The ceremony, followed by the reception at the Man in the Moon pub on the King's Road, was attended by team-mates Bobby Fisher, Tony Grealish, Glenn Roeder, Bill Roffey and John Smeulders.

> **"The club did look after us well. Even though we lost the semi-final to Arsenal, at the end of the season they paid for all the players and wives to go on holiday to Orlando, Florida, visiting Disney World and all the other theme parks – so that was Angie's and my honeymoon."**

We can only presume that the lads stuck to soft drinks, because the concentration and effort it took to hold First Division Boro to a goal-less draw at Ayresome Park was a considerable feat.

"I remember our skipper Phil Hoadley negotiating the players' win bonuses with chairman Brian Winston on the team coach going up to Middlesbrough. We were all on a fair amount to get beyond the quarter-final – about £500 each, if I remember rightly – because no-one really expected us to get past Middlesbrough.

"The club did look after us well. Even though we lost the semi-final to Arsenal, at the end of the season they paid for all the players and wives to go on holiday to Orlando, Florida, visiting Disney World and all the other theme parks – so that was Angie's and my honeymoon."

The couple, who celebrated their 40th anniversary earlier in 2018, live in Sutton, Surrey and have a son, Adam, and two daughters, Sophie and Emily.

Nigel speaks very highly of Winston, Orient's patriarchal figurehead who once admitted to me that he initially considered being chairman as part of an ego trip. He said: "I didn't hesitate to accept the offer (in 1974). At first, becoming chairman was an ego trip – to be in control of the club I supported as a boy was a dream I'd never had that came true.

"But then you realise that there is much more to it. I started to look at how we could improve things but the club's finances were in a dreadful mess. We had to run it as a business. You weren't

allowed to be a paid director in those days – you could only receive expenses – but I never claimed them from Orient anyway. When I left the club (in 1982) they had £400,000 in the bank."

Nigel experienced the caring side of Winston, saying: "Brian was always very keen to tie the younger lads down to longer contracts and he encouraged us to settle down, get a steady girlfriend or wife, and buy somewhere to live. I don't think he liked the idea of us going out drinking as a group.

"Some time before the Cup run Brian and his wife took Angie and me for a meal at The Dorchester Hotel on Park Lane, where he stressed the importance of settling down. Brian obviously paid for the meal. And when we bought our first place – a flat in Fulham – the club helped us out.

"I've got to say, Brian was, to me, as good as gold. You could always talk to him. He really cared about Orient and always had the players' best interests at heart.

"The last time I saw him was at Paddy Grealish's funeral (in 2013). I had trouble getting parked because there was this bloody big Bentley already taking up a lot of space. Of course, it was Brian's. We stood talking about the old times for about three-quarters-of-an-hour."

Winston recalls: "I went to Tony's funeral and introduced myself to his mother, Nora. She hugged me and said: 'You took my son to Disney World and I'm ever so grateful'. There she was, burying her son, and she came out with that – it was unbelievable."

NIGEL spent a decade with Orient as a dependable centre-half who made 262 league and Cup appearances between seasons 1974-75 and 1982-83. But as one of many talented youngsters who came up through the ranks at Brisbane Road, he spent far longer at his first club than those first team years. He has fond memories of simpler times when young players were happy even though they weren't mollycoddled like many are today.

"I played for Beaumont, a boys' team in Leyton, who supplied a lot of players to the Orient. Our

Nigel (4) receives the congratulations of Glenn Roeder (6) and Derek Possee (9), with Peter Allen (8) also in picture, after scoring against Bristol Rovers in February, 1977 – one of his four senior goals for Os.

manager Maurice Newman lived in east London but every Sunday morning he would drive all the way over to west London in his blue Commer van and pick up a few of us. As well as myself, there was Paddy, Gary Hibbs, and Dean Mooney, although he was the year above us, and then on the way we'd pick up Tony Robinson at Holloway.

"There were no seats in the back of the van, so we'd be rattling around in there while Maurice drove from one side of London to the other. Before every game, all the team would meet up at Maurice's flat, where his wife Rita would feed us and make sure we were all right. 'Anyone want a cup of tea or a sandwich?' . . . that sort of thing.

"Maurice would then drive all the players to the game in his van and, afterwards, take us west London boys all the way home, dropping each of us off in turn.

"I don't know how Maurice first heard of me – I guess he saw me playing for West London and Middlesex Schoolboys. I just got a phone call from him one day. The next thing I knew, I was asked to join Beaumont and played for them for three or four years.

> **"Maurice Newman was a really nice fella – one of Orient's unsung heroes who did a lot behind the scenes bringing youngsters to the club's attention and then taking good care of us."**

"We were a good, strong side. As well as our west London-based group, we had keeper John Smeulders, Sean Drummy and Stanley White, who were also signed by Orient. Our main rivals were Senrab, who had a few youngsters associated with Chelsea – the likes of Ray Wilkins, Johnny Sparrow and Steve Wicks.

"I'd say Maurice was in his early forties around that time. He was very quiet – until things went wrong. If he thought we had slacked off, he'd blow his top a bit, because he knew we were capable of so much better. He'd have a right pop.

"He was a really nice fella – one of Orient's unsung heroes who did a lot behind the scenes bringing youngsters to the club's attention and then taking good care of us. I never saw George Petchey or Len Cheesewright watching our games, so Maurice played an important role.

"Maurice asked me if I wanted to come over every Tuesday and Thursday to train in a gym somewhere along Leyton High Road. And it was great for me, because when I joined Orient I already knew most of the boys very well from having played with them at Beaumont.

"After leaving Orient, the next time I saw Maurice was at Paddy's funeral."

ORIENT signed Gray as an associated schoolboy, aged 14-and-a-half, in 1971 and then as an apprentice on leaving school in July, 1973. As he grew to around 6ft 2ins tall, he stood out as a dominant centre-half playing in Os' successful South-East Counties League side before quickly progressing to Midweek League action with the reserves.

After signing pro in April, 1974 he had to wait a year for his Football League debut, at home to Bolton Wanderers on April, 12, 1975 as the 18-year-old replacement for the injured Phil Hoadley. The new boy must have done OK, because the game ended goal-less and the defence kept another clean sheet on his second appearance three days later, when Gray started the 1-0 home win against Bristol City but had to leave the field injured.

"I had to mark Tom Ritchie that day but damaged my ankle in a tackle and that continued to trouble me a bit, on and off, for the rest of my career."

He had to learn the art of patience, too, because he was given only one league game the following season, in the 3-0 defeat at Plymouth Argyle on January 10.

"I would have been up against Paul Mariner, who went on to play for England, that day," he recalls.

"When George Petchey was manager, he always seemed to pick me if the opposition had a centre-forward who was over six-feet tall and needed man-to-man marking. But whenever the smaller ones were about, I got left out."

Gray's progress was interrupted, however, by a freak accident during a home reserve team game against Watford early in 1976 that caused one of his lungs to collapse.

"Tom Walley and I went up together for a high ball with one of their forwards and his elbow bashed my ribs. I went down and although I felt nothing of it, when I got up and started running around, I could hardly breathe.

"In those days, they didn't really have qualified physio," Nigel recalls. "Ernie Shepherd would show us his 'wall of death' round his bucket but that was about it, so he said: 'Just strap it up and come back in the morning'.

"So I did that, Elasto-plastered the rib and came back in for training the next morning. But as I jogged round the pitch, I couldn't get any air in my lungs, plus I'd come up in a rash thanks to the Elastoplast!

"The next morning I went to Charing Cross Hospital and they took me straight in. One of my lungs had completely deflated, so they had to insert a tube between my ribs to enable me to breathe properly.

"I made a full recovery, the lung never gave me any further problems, although most people who saw me run would probably disagree! I was never good on long runs anyway."

Gray made an unwanted slice of Orient – and football – history when he was sent-off at Brisbane Road on January 17, 1981. He was the last player to receive a red card before The FA abandoned its original trial scheme (although yellow and red cards were reintroduced at the start of the 1987-88 season).

"On the last day of the trial period, before the authorities reverted to the old totting up points system, I was sent off for fighting with Gary Stevens, Cardiff's big centre-forward. He got booked and sent-off and, because I was further away from the ref, I was sent-off after him.

"The outcome of that incident actually became a Trivial Pursuit question and the funny thing was, it came up years later while I was playing for Tooting and Mitcham and a group of us were playing the game while travelling to a match at Yeovil. To the amazement of my team-mates, I got the answer right, so that's my claim to fame in football!"

THE refreshingly self-deprecating Gray played all of the second half of the following 1976-77 season and it was very much the same story in 1977-78, although by now Jimmy Bloomfield had returned and his new sweeper system opened up exciting opportunities for the big man.

He explained: "Jimmy had Phil and me as centre-halves, with Bobby Fisher at right-back and Bill Roffey left-back, with Glenn Roeder sweeping. My role was always to mark their biggest forward, with Phil marking the smaller one. We both marked man-to-man and we could go as tight as you liked, because we knew we had Glenn behind us.

"I got on really well with Phil. He was as hard as nails and wouldn't take any prisoners. He had a great shot and was a really nice lad. But I didn't play with him for very long, because after the Cup run he left us in the summer.

"I got on very well with Glenn, too – we'd played together in the youth team throughout the early 70s in a flat back four, although he always liked to come out with the ball. He wasn't a great tackler but he always seemed to have a lot of time on the ball. He was quiet on and off the pitch but a nice lad."

Several observers, including Peter Kitchen, viewed Bloomfield tactics as conservative bordering on negative. But Gray says: "You can look at it two ways. Both full-backs would get forward and push on as often as they could, although 'Fish' was probably a bit more conservative than 'Roff'. So they would make an extra man in midfield, leaving four, or sometimes three, of us at the back when the team was attacking."

It was a tactic effective enough to outwit three First Division opponents en route to the semi-final, including Chelsea in the fifth round. The 2-1 replay victory at Stamford Bridge, where that man Kitch scored both Orient goals, not only gave many Os' fans the happiest night of their lives, it rang wedding bells for Nigel and Angie.

"You could almost see Chelsea's ground from where I grew up near Fulham Broadway. As a young kid, my father (Alan) would take me to watch Fulham one week and Chelsea the next. I trained with both clubs as a schoolboy but neither of them signed me as an apprentice.

"My brother Jeff, who is sadly no longer with us, was a Chelsea fan and a lot of our mates were, too, so they were all gutted when we knocked them out of the Cup in '78. After the game, while the rest of the Orient team headed back to east London, I met up with my brother at the main gate and then we walked about 100 yards to join a crowd of his friends at their local, The Princess Royal. I walked in with a big smile on my face. I got a bit of grief at first but they all knew me in there anyway, so there wasn't a problem. Besides, they got their own back when they beat us 7-3 (Nov 10, 1979)."

> **"I'd get the District Line train to Mile End, change to the Central Line and go two more stops to Leyton, then walk down to the ground. It was about 25 stops on the train."**

Remarkably, because he didn't have a driving licence at the time, even after becoming a regular first teamer at Orient, Gray still travelled to home games and training via public transport.

"I moved out to Southfields, which is the next borough to Fulham and just before Wimbledon. From there I'd get the District Line train to Mile End, change to the Central Line and go two more stops to Leyton, then walk down to the ground. It was about 25 stops on the train."

Try to imagine a Championship footballer today, putting himself at the mercy of the busy and unreliable Underground train network, travelling 50 stops on a round trip lasting – without any unscheduled delays – at least two hours. No, I can't visualise it happening either.

"By the time me and a few team-mates left

the ground after home games, most of the fans had already made their way home or were drinking in the local pubs, so I didn't really have any memorable one-to-one conversations with them on my journeys home," Nigel continued. "A few of us would go for a drink and unwind in The Yorkshire Grey at Stratford High Street. And I'd make my way home from there."

Alas, some six weeks after that triumphant, unforgettable night in Chelsea, there would be no repeat celebrations for Gray following Os' swift return visit to his old SW6 neighbourhood

"The semi-final was a big disappointment. The occasion got to us. I was substituted (by Tunji Banjo) in the end because I wasn't really doing anything. They put me up front to try and replicate what had worked when we came back to beat Blackburn in the fourth round. To be honest, I don't think I actually touched the ball when I was up there that night – I just made a nuisance of myself but we ended up winning 3-1.

"But the same thing wasn't going to happen against Arsenal. Willie Young and Peter Simpson weren't having any of it and they did a good marking job.

"After the game at Stamford Bridge, this time all the players went back to the hotel where we'd stayed the night before. Brian and Jimmy thanked us for our efforts in getting that far and then we all went our separate ways.

"I just felt sorry for the fans. We'd done really well to get to the semi-final but didn't give a good account of ourselves on the day. Even though they had a lot of luck with MacDonald's two goals, I didn't really think we were in the game.

"Just before the semi-final draw was made, with Ipswich, West Brom, Arsenal and ourselves in the hat, we all said that Arsenal was the one we didn't want, because it meant playing in London again. We all wanted another away day."

AFTER loan spells with Blackburn and Charlton, Nigel was recalled to Orient and made his final first team appearance on May 14, 1983, a 4-1 home win over Sheffield United as the club narrowly avoided back-to-back relegations and dropping into Division Four.

"I played under a few managers at the O's: George Petchey, Jimmy Bloomfield, Paul Went, Ken Knighton and Peter Angell, who was caretaker when Jimmy was ill. Peter did a brilliant job and I don't think he ever got all the credit he deserved. When Jimmy came out of hospital just before the semi-final, all the media focus switched back to him but it was Peter who got us there.

"I very much regret leaving the club when I did, because just a few days after Ken Knighton – who I didn't get on with – went, his assistant Frank Clark was appointed as manager, and I always got on really well with Frank."

His last pro club was Swindon Town, who loaned him out for spells at Brentford and Aldershot before he went into non-league football. "I suffered a detached retina in a collision while playing for Swindon and because of that they didn't want to re-sign me, so that's when I joined Enfield instead," Nige explained.

"They were a leading semi-pro club at the time, although I only signed for them because the former Orient club doctor – I can't remember his name but he was partially sighted and did a lot of his medical work by feel – had gone there and he suggested I join them.

"I had two really good years with Enfield. We won the Gola League (today's Vanarama National League), as it was then, in 1985-86 but it wasn't until the following year that the champions gained automatic promotion into the Football League – and we finished fourth.

"After that, I knocked around a few clubs, because I still wanted to play. I went to Wycombe Wanderers and Tooting & Mitcham and after that I started to play for my brother's team. I got a job with the Post Office and then the Met Police as a civil servant. Now I work for a cleaning company, making sure things are being done properly. I packed up playing vets' football when I was 50."

Nigel is still doing his bit to encourage youngsters to follow the same successful path he took. "I'm vice-chairman of Morden Little League, an organisation funded by donations which enables 600 kids, ranging from eight to 15, to play football every Saturday. They don't have to pay for their kit, pitch hire or anything, just bring their own boots."

Summing up, Nigel said: "I loved being a professional footballer – it's every kid's dream and I was living that dream. I thoroughly enjoyed my time in the game and particularly at the Orient, which was a smashing club.

"There were a lot of players better than me but maybe they didn't enjoy the game as much as I did. For me, it was a good time to be around. It was hard, though.

"I was tall, I could head a ball and tackle a bit. But once I got the ball, I didn't really know what to do with it, so I'd just pass to Glenn Roeder, or Tony Grealish, and let him get on with it. I made them both look good!"

"People talk about the money in the game these days but I enjoyed every moment," he added. "I was playing football, which is always better than having a normal job – it's better than working. Maybe we weren't getting as much money as some players at other clubs but that was never going to happen at Orient with the crowds they were getting and that was never an issue for me. I was getting paid for something I loved doing."

Although based in Surrey, Nigel makes a point of getting along to around half-a-dozen Leyton Orient home games a season. Typical of his very likeable, unassuming nature, he doesn't expect any special treatment and is very happy to sit among the fans and come into the Supporters' Club afterwards for a beer and a chat.

Interview: Tony McDonald

Greatest feeling . . . while John Jackson shakes the hands with officials, Nigel walks off at the end of the FA Cup fifth round victory at Chelsea knowing that he has a few celebratory beers at the local, plus his wedding, to look forward to . . .

Ray of sunshine

RAY GODDARD passed away in Spain in 2007 following a major stroke at the early age of 58 years. He was a fine, long-serving goalkeeper who is fondly remembered by Orient fans.

After being initially spotted and then released as an apprentice by Chelsea, Ray continued to progress with their west London neighbours Fulham, working his way through their youth ranks and spending long spells in the reserves, although he never made an official first team appearance for The Cottagers before moving to Orient in March, 1967, when still only 18 years-old.

Manager Dick Graham gave the blond-haired teenager his Football League debut, at home to Workington Town in the final match of the 1966-67 campaign, and Ray played his part in securing a 2-1 victory.

After vying with Ron Willis in the early weeks of the following campaign, Goddard made the keeper's jersey his own for the next six seasons. In total, he made 278 appearances for the club – the second-highest by any Orient goalie since Arthur Wood's record-breaking, pre-war haul of 373.

Jimmy Bloomfield, who had by now replaced Graham as boss, was so impressed with the keeper's level of consistency that he recommended him for an England Under-23 cap, although he was never selected.

Ray was ever-present in seasons 1970-71 and 1972-73 but the arrival of George Petchey as manager brought about an end to his first-choice claims to the position. He was upset when Petchey bought John Jackson from Crystal Palace in October, 1973 and found himself playing second fiddle to the 31-year-old shot-stopper.

Injury to Jackson, though, meant Ray made 25 starts that season, including the final nine matches of a 1973-74 campaign that saw us finish tantalisingly close to regaining a place in the top flight. In fact, Ray was 'between the sticks' and unable to save Ray Graydon's penalty that ultimately denied the Os a much-coveted place in the top three.

His disappointment at being cover for 'Jacko' mirrored the frustration reserve team keeper Steve Bowtell must have experienced throughout his years as Goddard's understudy.

After a brief loan spell at Scottish First Division Greenock Morton, which necessitated in him flying up to attend Friday training and Saturday matches, Ray joined Millwall in a £9,000 deal in November, 1974. He made 80 league appearances for the south London club that won promotion from Division Three.

But the arrival of Petchey as Lions' boss resulted in a £4,500 move to Dario Gradi's Wimbledon in February, 1978. He made 119 appearances for Dons and missed only one league game as they gained promotion from the Fourth Division in May, 1979.

The following season, he also played a defining role on the night Orient were knocked-out of the League Cup by Wimbledon, who were 5-4 penalty shootout winners after the teams had finished 2-2 at the end of extra-time. Crucially, Ray saved a penalty from Joe Mayo and then took the deciding spot-kick, sending Mervyn Day the wrong way to clinch the second round tie at Plough Lane.

It wasn't a fluke either. With retirement looming, Ray was brought back for a farewell appearance in Dons' final home game of 1980-81. Although they lost 4-2, he signed off his pro career in style by slotting a late penalty past a young Bury keeper called Neville Southall!

Ray finished his playing days with non-league Wealdstone, where he proved something of a promotion talisman yet again as the Stones won the Southern League Southern Division title and

RAY GODDARD (1949-2007)

the Southern League Cup double – the ever-present Goddard was their cup final hero with a string of fine saves in a 1-0 win at Gloucester City.

Retiring at the age of 36, he briefly joined Isthmian League strugglers Leatherhead – where he conceded seven goals on his debut against Barton Rovers – but soon moved to Spain with his wife and daughter.

IN the years prior to his sudden death on December 11, 2007, Ray and his second wife Trish ran the El Lido bar in Fuengirola on southern Spain's Costa Del Sol, where his cheery smile and happy demeanour remained as warm as the Andalucia climate.

Peter Allen was among the first to pay tribute to Ray, one of the most well-liked players to have represented the club. "I was very sad when I heard that Ray had died," said the former skipper and Os' longest-serving player. "He was a room-mate of mine when we played for Orient and I got very close to him. We were all mates in the Orient team that did particularly well in the 70s but Ray, Terry Brisley, Barrie Fairbrother and myself seemed to get on particularly well together.

"Ray was godfather to my daughter and we kept in touch long after we both moved on from the club. He was an excellent and consistent goalkeeper and turned in a string of fine performances for the team. The news of his passing has hit me very hard."

Tommy Taylor, another former colleague of Ray and member of the '70 promotion side, also expressed his sadness at his passing: "I'm totally shocked; 58 is no age, it's so sad," he said.

"Ray was a good lad and we started our careers in the Orient first team around the same time. He was a good keeper and also a nice guy off the pitch. He got on really well with everybody.

"There was a good spirit among the lads. I think that was because a lot of us were Londoners, and Ray was good company. I'm deeply saddened at this news."

Ray's first wife, Linda Edwards, posted the following online tribute: "Although we parted in 1984 we remained close friends and shared the happiness of our daughter Jaime. We were both so proud in October (2007), when Jaime got married to Keith in Cyprus and Ray gave her away, with our grandson Jake as page boy. Ray lives on in Jake, as he looks very much like him, and I hope this helps Jaime cope with the sad loss of her very much-loved dad. Keep making them laugh wherever you are, Ray."

By Paul Hiscock & Tony McDonald

OUR LAURIE

From Brisbane Road
. . . to the Bernabéu

HE enthralled 120,000 Real Madrid fans at the Bernabéu, wore the famous red jersey of Manchester United, played for Wimbledon in the FA Cup Final, became a West Bromwich Albion folk hero and, best of all, he was the first black professional footballer to represent England at any level during an era when overt racial prejudice was rife.

But to supporters of Leyton Orient, Laurie Cunningham will always be one of *ours*. A Brisbane Road legend, the most naturally gifted talent the club has ever produced.

Laurence Paul Cunningham was born on March 8, 1956 at the Whittington Hospital in Archway, north London of Jamaican descent, went to Highgate Wood Secondary School in Hornsey and played for London Schoolboys.

Arsenal had him (and future Orient team-mate Glenn Roeder) training at Highbury but didn't think it was worth the trouble nurturing the kid who needed careful handling. Laurie didn't enjoy the Arsenal coaching staff's conformity and quickly became disillusioned with the game.

That's why certain people working for Orient at the time deserve enormous credit. Chief Scout Len Cheesewright (see p250-251) was quick to recognise precocious young talent and when Arsenal dithered, he seized his opportunity.

In August, 1972, while still living at home in Finsbury Park with his mother Mavis and father Elias, first generation immigrants who arrived here separately in the late 50s, Cunningham joined Orient as an apprentice and it's no secret that Cheesewright and the coaching staff had to keep a watchful eye on the lad and constantly remind him of what was expected. Laurie's tardiness is legendary, although maybe he thought that if he didn't make it as a footballer, a career as a dancer or fashion designer were other attainable options.

Using his poise, elegance, balance and control.

In a new interview elsewhere in this book, manager George Petchey recalls the challenge of keeping Laurie on the straight and narrow. Back in 1977, soon after the player left the Os, Petchey recalled: "When I signed Laurie he was a skinny kid, very erratic in his behaviour towards football and he didn't treat life or the game very seriously."

Interviewed by Robert Oxby for the *Daily Telegraph* in 1976, Laurie admitted: "At first, I was not the sweetest person to live with. Nothing stirred me. I felt life should come along and do something for me. I was just a dreamer. It took George Petchey to show me that the only person who could make dreams come true was me."

Oxby added: "If he were not one of the most exciting prospects in British football, Cunningham, who already has a thriving menswear business, would be a professional dancer. The ballet and modern dance training he has had give obvious clues to his extraordinary talent. 'I live for dancing. It's really part of me,' Laurie said."

Soon after Laurie made his dream move to Real Madrid in the summer of 1979, I was impressed to read a Q&A interview he gave to one of the English weekly football magazines. Asked to name his biggest influence, he singled out Bob Cottingham, the patriarchal manager of Highgate North Hill, the multi-cultural Sunday afternoon boys' team Cunningham starred for.

Giving a Blackburn Rovers full-back the runaround in front of the West Side in October, 1976.

Petchey tolerated Cunningham diffidence and perceived indifference because he knew Orient had an unpolished diamond that could turn out to be a gem. But the quietly-spoken youngster wasn't flash off the field or in training. His contemporaries in the Os' dressing room remember him as a shy, almost awkward, lad.

When he wasn't practicing yoga to aid his concentration, dancing or listening to Marvin Gaye, James Brown and other jazz, blues and soul music, or hanging out with girlfriend Nikki Hare-Brown whom he met on the dance floor when they were 15, Laurie was a prominent member of the Os' youth side of 1973-74 that finished runners-up to Chelsea in the South-East Counties League (Div 1) and won the London Youth Cup. He was voted player-of-the-tournament when Orient's youngsters visited Holland for a summer tournament and he became a full professional on his 18th birthday, in March, 1974.

Petchey could have been forgiven for keeping his flying winger under wraps for as long as possible but he wasn't afraid to test him up against high calibre opposition.

The Texaco Cup was in reality little more than a series of glorified pre-season friendlies but Orient's visit to West Ham for their first group match on Saturday, August 3, 1974 attracted added interest because ITV's *The Big Match* cameras were there to capture it. The visitors suffered an honourable 1-0 defeat but the player who caught the eye was the rookie number seven on his senior debut. He showed not a hint of fear as he took on, and skinned, Hammers' vastly experienced left-back Frank Lampard, who wasn't known for taking any prisoners.

Laurie's next two senior appearances were also against First Division opposition – Luton Town (Texaco Cup) and QPR (League Cup). His Second Division debut followed 12 matches into the season, on October 12, when he replaced Barrie Fairbrother on the right wing in a 3-1 home victory against Oldham. After playing in the next two games he resumed with the reserves in the Midweek League before reappearing in the senior side more regularly in the latter stages of the campaign. He made 15 starts and appeared three times off the bench, most notably his second-half cameo in the FA Cup replay at Derby that was also televised.

He opened his scoring account in the final match of the season with an individual effort in our 2-1 win over Southampton on April 26, 1975.

A star was born.

While Cunningham was rapidly gaining experience and earning plaudits, he didn't have the luxury of being able to integrate into a side that was winning regularly. Although Petchey would not have wanted to put his young prodigy under pressure at such an early stage of his career, the fact is that Cunningham quickly became the go-to man in the team, the player to make things happen when nothing much else was happening. When Laurie received the ball at his feet, a buzz of expectation went round the ground.

He wasn't simply a provider from the flanks. His pace, drive and sinuous grace meant he created chances for others and himself out of nothing. Which meant taking on the opposition at every opportunity, running at speed while caressing the ball glued to his boot, head up, riding wild tackles that threatened to puncture holes in his sinewy calves unprotected by shin pads that he was reluctant to wear.

He would beat defenders with a burst of pace, a drop of the shoulder or a magical, mazy dribble. On either flank or through the middle, right foot or left, it didn't matter to him. He even turned the taking of corners into an art form; nonchalantly crossing the ball with the *outside* of his foot. Os' fans loved him for his youthful arrogance and touch of swagger.

Our Laurie was a symbol of hope, a source of great pride.

One of the finest of his 16 goals in 86 Orient appearances came in a 4-2 home defeat by Wolves, in November, 1976. He ran on to a flick by Alan Whittle and cracked his first-time, long-range shot into the roof of the net. But the result left his team bottom of the table.

Others remember a solo effort at Stamford Bridge in April, 1976, when he collected the ball in the centre circle and left several bemused Chelsea defenders in his wake before sealing a 2-0 away win. Even referee Clive Thomas applauded his mastery.

Orient's opponents all understood Cunningham was their main threat, the one they had to try and stop. To evade the worst Second Division cloggers he displayed the suppleness and athleticism of an Olympic gold medal hurdles champion. More than once, Petchey felt compelled to substitute his most valuable asset for his own protection.

And he wasn't just up against crude opponents. At times, an equally big hindrance to the agile Cunningham were the mud-cloying pitches so prevalent of that time – and the Brisbane Road paddy field was among the worst. You see the 'carpets' they play on today and rules that have virtually eliminated tackling from the game, and it's very easy to imagine him gliding effortlessly over pristine turf.

Even on frosty surfaces, Petchey wanted to wrap his best player – who often played with socks down by his ankles – in a comfort blanket. Explaining why he removed Laurie from the action 10 minutes from time on a treacherous top at chilly Carlisle one wintery afternoon, despite his team fighting a losing cause, he said: "With his pace he could have broken a leg. The thought was going through my mind to take him off before. Such is his value to this club that it was far better to have him off the pitch and watching."

Taking control of the situation in his penultimate home game, a 2-0 win over Bristol Rovers in February, 1977, with team-mates Nigel Gray and John Jackson looking on.

From filthy rivals who verbally and physically abused him because of his colour to dodgy pitches, Laurie had to put up with a lot. Worse of all, he had to endure the racist abuse from bigoted crowds in an era that saw the rise of the National Front and English Movement, extreme right-wing groups that subjected black players to monkey chants, cries of 'coon' and 'nigger', boos each time they touched the ball and bananas thrown from the terraces.

But I can't ever recall him retaliating and he certainly never hid on a football field. On the contrary, he wanted the ball at his feet;

that's where he did all his talking. He learned quickly that the best way to silence the ignorant was to beat their team.

Whether he enjoyed it or not, Laurie's rise from the mean streets of north London, where black kids were largely treated with contempt by the police and employers, to Second Division stardom got him noticed far beyond Leyton Stadium and the First Division scouts eyeing him up. In 1976 he was the cover story for *The Sunday Times Magazine,* posing in Os' yellow-and-blue away shirt while holding a football (although, typically, he didn't actually turn up for the pre-arranged interview with journalist Brian Glanville, who had to settle for tea and cake with Laurie's mum, Mavis!). Cunningham was also the subject of a slot on the ITV's popular children's programme *Magpie.*

But it was what he did on the field that took his career, and his life, to another level. From 33 league appearances in 1975-76, he finished his first full season as the club's top goalscorer, albeit with eight goals. And he was leading the way again in the following campaign with six from 24 matches – probably supplied most assists too – before his final game, a 2-0 home defeat by Oldham on March 5, 1977.

Outside the top flight, where clubs live on the breadline, money doesn't just talk, it screams loudly, and no-one in the Orient boardroom needed a hearing aid to appreciate what was on offer. Two days before Laurie celebrated his 21st birthday, amid growing speculation, with Norwich and West Ham mentioned as most likely suitors, Os had to accept the inevitable when he signed for West Bromwich Albion.

"He said: 'I don't want to force you into selling a player – I'll give you another 25 grand overdraft facility' – but I told him I didn't think the club should run at that level of borrowing."
Os' chairman Brian Winston

Brian Winston did the deal to sell Laurie to West Brom.

WHILE putting together the *Brisbane Road Memories* book five years ago, I interviewed at length the Orient chairman whose final decision it was to sell the club's jewel in the crown to West Brom for £110,000. Brian Winston's insightful account is worth re-telling here.

He said: "It wasn't a small fee and I thought about it very deeply. We had a situation where we owed the bank £125,000, which was our limit. We had the bank manager, a Mr Cameron, and Nat-West's area controller come down to our home game to put pressure on.

"Around this time I was in discussions with West Bromwich Albion about Laurie. I knew their chairman Bert Millichip from serving on the FA Council with him. We pushed them to get to that fee – they originally offered about 80 grand – so to pass six figures for a young black player was a very good deal back then. No-one knew which way his career would go, although he was an extraordinary boy. As well as being a talented footballer, he was a fantastic dancer.

"He went to West Brom but I offered him to Tottenham. They were co-owned by the Richardsons and I went there and said to them: 'Buy Laurie Cunningham from us, he really is going to be a great player. He lives in Tottenham and I need the money. West Brom are in for him but if you match their offer, I'd sooner he joined you'. But they wouldn't agree to it.

"I went up to West Brom with Laurie and was there when their manager Johnny Giles signed him. As part of the deal I wanted their centre-forward, Joe Mayo, and an inside-forward/midfielder Allan Glover, who had impressed George Petchey when he was at QPR. Anyhow, West Brom agreed that we could have Mayo and Glover for 15 grand – we got them down from £25k – and I distinctly remember asking Bert Millichip if he would grant me credit terms. I asked if we could pay the money in three instalments over three years.

"That morning, Mr Cameron from our bank phoned and asked why we were selling Laurie, and I told him: 'Because we need the money'. He said: 'I don't want to force you into selling a player – I'll give you another 25 grand overdraft facility' – but I told him I didn't think the club should run at that level of borrowing. Our limit at the time was just over £120k and we were using it to the max. Despite being in the Second Division – today's Championship – we were still struggling.

"So Cameron said: 'You make a decision, sell him because *you* want to sell him, not because the bank is forcing you to let him go'. That was all very nice of him but we still sold him – on *our* terms. We signed Joe and Allan and paid West Brom five grand a year over three years.

"The next day I spoke to Johnny Giles again – it was the day Laurie made his debut for them at Tottenham (March 12, 1977) – and he mentioned that he'd heard how I used to sit with Laurie for a while in the dressing room before a game, talking to him and boosting his confidence. He asked me if there was any chance of me popping over to White Hart Lane that afternoon.

"This was the same day Orient were playing at Blackburn, where Joe Mayo and Allan Glover got our goals in a 2-2 draw, but while that was happening I was at Tottenham, sitting in the dressing room talking to Laurie Cunningham. I used to say to him: 'Get the full-back booked in the first 15 minutes and you're home and dry'. He asked me what I thought was going to happen and I just told him to relax and play his own game. Johnny Giles was player-manager and I told Laurie that he would be given the freedom of the park.

"As Giles was about to start his pre-match team-talk, I got up to leave the room but he told me to stay. He literally said what I'd told Laurie a few minutes earlier, that he had freedom to go wherever he felt was right and that they would work it out on the pitch. Giles was a brilliant tactician and forever moving his players around.

"I wished Laurie good luck and went upstairs to take my seat in the directors' box, where I saw West Brom win 2-0 and Laurie set up both goals. The Richardsons gave me a look as if they were about to tear their hair out.

"We always said with Laurie that he lived life in the fast lane and he was going to die in the fast lane. He was a great guy but he needed a lot of nurturing, as did John Chiedozie. That wasn't George Petchey's forte but his assistant, Peter Angell, was brilliant at it. Talk to any player from around that time, whether they were home-grown or signed from other clubs, and you will never hear a bad word said about Peter. He was one of the nicest men I ever met in my life and he never got the credit he deserved. All the kids went to him and he did much to keep them on the straight and narrow.

"There was a lot of 'Black Power' going on in those days and we had the odd player involved in it, but that was never Laurie's scene. And neither did John Chiedozie or Tunji Banjo get involved in politics."

ALTHOUGH the £110,000 fee was considerable for the time, many observers reckoned Albion had bagged a bargain and that the former Orient star was destined for England recognition. For context, it was some £28k less than West Brom's then record fee paid to Glasgow Rangers for Willie Johnston four years earlier, while Everton had already smashed the £350,000 barrier in 1974 when signing Bob Latchford from Birmingham.

Cunningham appreciated how Giles, one of the youngest managers in the game, continued to allow him the freedom to express himself against the very best. Unfortunately, the Irishman who won almost every domestic honour with Leeds United only lasted at The Hawthorns for another couple of months before he resigned citing boardroom interference. After brief stints playing under Ronnie Allen and caretaker John Wile, it was the arrival in January 1978 of the flamboyant Ron Atkinson that thrust Cunningham into the big-time limelight.

Media-friendly Big Ron proudly boasted about his trio of black stars, Cyrille Regis, Laurie and Brendon Batson, famously branding them 'The Three Degrees' after the American soul music hit-makers, and even set up a photo-shoot involving the players and girls at The Hawthorns (in fact, West Ham, under Ron Greenwood, had already beaten WBA to this ground-breaking landmark by fielding a black trio of Clyde Best, Clive Charles and Ade Coker in a First Division game against Spurs in 1972).

West Brom and Laurie were perfectly in tune and his stirring performances soon caught the eye of Greenwood, who left Hammers in 1977 to become England manager. Cunningham marked his international debut with a milestone winner for England's under-21s against Scotland at Bramall Lane, Sheffield on April 27, 1977 and two years later became the first black player to start a competitive international, in the drab goalless draw against Wales at Wembley on May 23, 1979 (Viv Anderson of Nottingham Forest had made his England debut in a friendly earlier that season).

But when, in the summer of '79, European giants Real Madrid offered Albion almost £1million and Laurie an eye-watering five grand a week (a huge rise from £120 a week at The Hawthorns), nothing could keep him from the Spanish capital.

As the first Brit and black to play for Real Madrid, Laurie – dubbed 'The Black Pearl' or 'El Negrito' – scored twice on his debut in a 2-1 win against Valencia and helped *Los Blancos* complete the La Liga and Copa Del Rey double at the end of his first season there under Yugoslav coach Vujadin Boskov. The fact that Spanish teams were permitted only two foreign players in their squad (German midfielder Uli Stielike was the other) underlined their huge valuation of him.

Writing for *The Independent* in 2013, Ed Aarons recalled Cunningham's impact at Madrid: "Of all the legendary players to have worn the Real Madrid shirt down the years, only one has ever left the Nou Camp pitch to a standing ovation. His name was Laurie Cunningham.

On February 10, 1980, the son of a former Jamaican racehorse jockey from Holloway in north London who used to pay his numerous £1 fines for being late to training at Leyton Orient by winning dancing competitions, suddenly became one of the most famous faces in Spain.

"A dazzling display in a 2-0 victory at the home of Real's bitter rivals Barcelona was the pinnacle of a meteoric rise that had also seen Cunningham become the first black player ever to wear an England shirt (this was later corrected). To mark the 25th anniversary of the game, Madrid newspaper *AS* ran a feature with the headline 'The man who ran riot in the Nou Camp' and quoted one Barcelona fan who was there: 'It was like seeing (Johan) Cruyff but with black skin,' he said. 'That kid could do anything with a football'."

As one who has always been quick to champion Ron Greenwood's deserved reputation as one of the most inventive, far-sighted coaches of his generation, it disappoints me that having recognised Cunningham's class in giving him his England debut and awarding him six senior caps, he proceeded to overlook him in the early 80s in favour of Arsenal's Graham Rix and West Brom's Peter Barnes – ironically, the man Albion bought to replace him.

Laurie helped Real Madrid reach the 1981 European Cup Final, where they lost 1-0 to Liverpool, but there was no longer a place for his adventurous spirit in a more cautious, compact England side containing only one specialist winger. Having been omitted from the team during the Euro 80 finals in Italy, he earned his final cap in a 2-1 World Cup qualifying defeat by Romania in October, 1980.

For a player blessed with such enormous natural talent, he should have had more chances to shine on the international stage, although Real Madrid must also take a large share of the blame for this

237

by sometimes exercising their contractual rights and preventing him from joining England squads.

Apart from being shackled to the left wing and denied the freedom he'd enjoyed under George Petchey, Cunningham's 44-game stay at Santiago Bernabeu was punctuated by injuries, including three left knee operations and a broken toe, and bad press that contributed to his split from Nikki Hare-Brown. So, in April, 1983 it was a relief to be briefly reunited with Atkinson at Manchester United for a five-match loan period.

His remarkable career also included spells with Sporting Gijon, Marseille, Leicester City, Charleroi and, bizarrely, with Wimbledon's Crazy Gang – he came on as sub for the last 34 minutes of their shock 1-0 win over Liverpool in the 1988 FA Cup Final.

In his second spell with Rayo Vallecano, he helped the unfashionable Madrid club reach La Liga for the first time in its history by scoring the goal that clinched promotion.

Tragically, he never got the chance to show Real Madrid what they missed. After drinking sangria at a restaurant, it was around 4.30am on Saturday, July 15, 1989 when, on a notorious stretch of road to the north-west of Madrid, he swerved to avoid a car with a flat tyre, lost control, hit a lamp-post and rolled his Seat car over several times before being thrown from the vehicle (unlike Laurie, his passenger, American business partner Mark Latty, was wearing a seat belt and survived the accident with barely a scratch).

One of the world's truly exceptional trailblazers had died from chest and head injuries at 33 years of age.

Bobby Fisher read a eulogy to Laurie at the funeral held at Holy Trinity Church, Tottenham on August 2, 1979.

Cunningham is survived by his Spanish wife Silvia and son Sergio, who made an emotional pilgrimage to Brisbane Road one day in 2017, when no game was being played, to see just where his late father became a king.

Hero Cunningham

by DAVID HARDING

LAURIE CUNNINGHAM became Orient's hero with the winning goal five minutes after the interval at Plymouth.
Gerry Queen and Alan

Plymouth 1 Orient 2

In to fire a brilliant angled shot into the net. Argyle's revival was short-lived as Orient fought back to regain their lead five

WHEN long-in-the-tooth supporters who have been watching Leyton Orient for 50-60 years rate Laurie Cunningham as Os' greatest-ever player, certainly the most talented and exciting to watch, who are the rest of us to argue?

What he achieved in the game inspired generations of black players who followed his path to football stardom. In an interview with *Shoot!* magazine soon after joining WBA and before his first senior England call-up, he understood his responsibilities as an influential role model when he said: "If I played for England and it inspired other black lads around, that would be marvellous. There are a lot of talented black kids about and I hope they stick to it and make it. It's certainly worth all the hard work."

He certainly fulfilled that legacy.

Orient fans who were fortunate enough to see him play continue to revere Cunningham today.

And thanks to ITV's *First Among Equals* documentary in 2013, Dermot Kavanagh's excellent 2017 biography *Different Class* and other admirable initiatives to permanently honour this pioneering legend, current and future generations of supporters will also learn about the unique achievements of 'Our Laurie'.

As Orient-supporting journalist Steve Tongue put it so aptly: "It may be a while before another Os' player makes it to Real Madrid."

Or appears on the front cover of *The Sunday Times Magazine*.

By Tony McDonald

LAURIE CUNNINGHAM'S legacy lives on in his native London and around the Leyton Orient ground.

● On October 12, 2013, the Nubian Jak Community Trust (NJCT) – a commemorative plaque and sculpture scheme that highlights the historic contributions of black and minority ethnic people in Britain – unveiled a blue plaque on the main wall of the residential flats alongside the stadium in Brisbane Road. The unveiling ceremony was attended by several of Laurie's former team-mates, including Peter Allen and Phil Hoadley, plus the two other members of West Brom's

'Three Degrees', Cyrille Regis and Brendon Batson.

● In September, 2015 English Heritage erected a blue plaque on Cunningham's childhood home at 73 Lancaster Road, Stroud Green.

● In November 2017, a statue by Graham Ibbeson was unveiled in Coronation Gardens, behind what was the South Terrace in Laurie's playing days.

1 & 2 On the day of the NJCT blue plaque unveiling, Laurie's face adorned the cover of the programme for the game against MK Dons, attended by his family and friends.

3 Laurie's brother, Keith Cunningham, speaking at the blue plaque launch.

4 Brendan Batson (left) and Cyrille Regis with Nikki Hare-Brown, Laurie's former long-time girlfriend who was with him since before his Orient debut and during his early spell in Madrid.

IN paying our respects to Jimmy Bloomfield, Peter Angell, Ray Goddard and Laurie Cunningham earlier in the book, lest we forget the others who represented Orient in the 70s who have sadly passed away since leaving Orient . . .

BARRY DYSON (1942-1995)

RALPH COATES (1946-2010)

DAVE HARPER (1938-2013)

BOBBY MOSS (1952-2010)

GORDON RIDDICK (1943-2018)

PETER BRABROOK (1937-2016)

PAUL WENT (1949-2017)

IAN MOORES (1954-1998)

TONY GREALISH (1956-2013)

NICE TO SEE YOU AGAIN

1 Catching up with our heroes in more recent times . . .

It's always great to see familiar faces back at Leyton Orient and we've been lucky to be able to reminisce with quite a few ex-players in recent years. The club are always quick to mark significant anniversaries, while there's also a guaranteed warm reception awaiting our former heroes in the Supporters' Club before and after games. See how many you can recognise before checking the captions.

1 Players and staff from the 1970 Third Division title-winning squad. From left: Brian Blower (commercial manager), Mark Lazarus, Steve Bowtell, Terry Mancini, Peter Allen, Mick Jones, Dickie Plume (Oct 2012); **2** Peter Allen (2012); **3** Mark Lazarus, with Brian Blower and Paul Went behind (2012).

4 Peter Brabrook with his three England caps (2012); **4b** Peter with the Rotherham programme from the 1969-70 season. He scored in the 1-1 draw (2014); **5** Terry Mancini (2012). **6** Tommy Taylor (2013); **7** Mickey Bullock (2014); **8** Dickie Plume (2012).

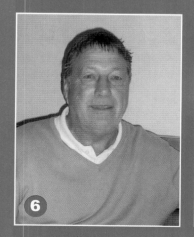

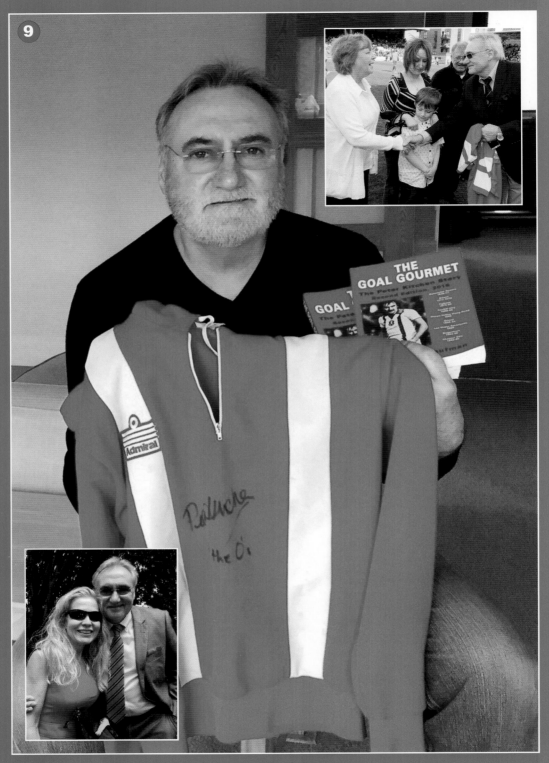

9 Peter Kitchen with his original 'Braces' hooded 1977-78 tracksuit top which he autographed and donated to the Leyton Orient Fans' Trust (LOFT) regeneration fund in June, 2017, when it was feared that the club was on the brink of bankruptcy. It fetched £350 at auction (2017). Inset: Kitch presenting Os shirts to descendants of the families of the Clapton Orient players who were killed on the Somme, about whom *The Greater Game* play was written (2016). Inset: Peter and partner Katherine at a family wedding (2016).

10 John Chiedozie with a memento from his successful early days on the wing for Os (2014); 11 Nigel Gray (2016); 12 Kevin Godfrey (2016); 13 Former chairman Brian Winston (2013).

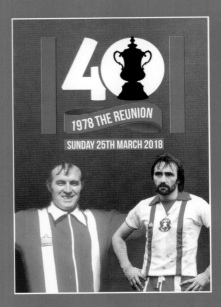

The club celebrated the 40th anniversary of the 1978 FA Cup run in style with another nostalgic reunion at the ground in March, 2018. **14** Bobby Fisher (2018); **15** Phil Hoadley wearing Os tie and badge (2018); **16** Joe Mayo (2018).

17 Supporters attending the '78 reunion were given the chance to have their photo taken with the ex-players. Here's loyal fan Caroline Burkinshaw – who still has her Orient scrapbooks from the 70s – with our happy group. Standing, left to right: Phil Hoadley, Nigel Gray, Peter Allen, David Payne, Derek Clarke, Joe Mayo. Seated: Tunji Banjo, Peter Kitchen, Caroline, Bobby Fisher (2018). Inset: Caroline pictured with the '78 cup squad at the club's 'open morning' held at Brisbane Road shortly before the semi-final. She says: "I don't remember too many other fans attending, as it was held during the week. I was 14 at the time and my dad took the morning off work to take me to it. I took my scrapbooks along and all the players looked through them and signed them for me. A memory that has always stayed with me." **18** Tunjo Banjo (2018); **19** David Payne in his Os tie (2018).

Welcome back
Barrie

20

20 Hair today, gone tomorrow! Barrie Fairbrother, the bearded wonder who crushed Chelsea, made his first return to the club in 33 years when he flew in from Australia to attend the home game against Sutton United on September 29, 2018. LOSC chairman David Dodd arranged for several of Barrie's former team-mates to join the reunion. Barry is pictured afterwards in the supporters' club clutching the 70s book whose cover he adorned. Inset: the LOSC volunteers had a special personalised card produced which fans signed before it was presented to Barrie (2018). **21** Terry Brisley and Ricky Heppolette (2018); **22** Ricky Heppolette (2018); **23** Paul Harris (2018).

Youth
Opportunities

Len Cheesewright receives a presentation on the night Leyton Orient honoured their former chief scout with a testimonial match against West Ham United in July, 2002.

THE key to survival for most clubs outside the top sphere depends on the quality of their grass roots youth set-up. It's the lifeblood of every club operating on a shoestring outside the top sphere and there was no better example of this in the 70s than Orient.

As well as using his own eyes and ears, a knowledgeable chief scout maximises the use of his network of junior club managers and school sports teachers to further help him indentify young local talent. Once the talent-spotting is done, it needs to be supported by a high level of coaching at the football club. And in this respect, Os were tremendously well served throughout the decade.

Len Cheesewright, whom George Petchey promoted from youth team manager to chief scout soon after his appointment as manager in 1971, deserves a great deal of credit for his role in shaping the flourishing conveyor belt of youngsters unearthed by the Os over many years. Given his brilliant record as a star-finder, he could be dubbed the 'Million Pound Man'.

Coaches such as Peter Angell, Ronnie Heckman, Terry Long, Jimmy Hallybone and Alan Stephenson should also be recognised for doing their bit to encourage, harness and develop that potential.

Finally, it requires a manager with the courage and vision to trust the 'kids' by picking them for the first team. Jimmy Bloomfield and Petchey both put their faith in a string of likely lads by giving them a chance to make the grade.

At Brisbane Road during the 70s, no fewer than 27 home-grown products progressed through the junior ranks and reserves to the senior side – an impressive average of more than two per season. The five given first team debuts by Petchey in 1974-75 – Tony Grealish, Laurie Cunningham, Dean Mooney, Glenn Roeder and Nigel Gray – went on to play 624 senior games for the club between them.

The combined number of appearances by all 27 graduates totals a massive 2,832 league matches, with Peter Allen taking pride of place at the top of that long list. Even though he'd started out as a junior at Tottenham, he joined Leyton Orient as an apprentice schoolboy, so we shouldn't hesitate to claim him as 'one of ours'.

In a number of cases, not only did the emergence of these young prospects save Orient money it didn't have available to spend in the transfer market, a handful ended up keeping Os solvent by generating vital profits – club record transfer fees in several instances – when they were eventually sold on to bigger clubs for a handsome profit. As can be seen from our table, four of Cheesewright's greatest finds brought more than £1million back into the club.

His most famous discovery – arguably Os' finest of all-time – was, of course, Cunningham. Within three years of making his Second Division debut on the wing, he left for West Brom in March, 1977 in a deal worth £110,000. The talented Archway-born winger, a gilt-edged product of the Beaumont academy, went on to win six full England caps and play for Real Madrid and Manchester United.

Within 18 months of Cunningham's departure, his former youth team-mate, cultured central defender-cum-sweeper Roeder, left for Queens Park Rangers in a £250,000 move. Shrewd Cheesewright got in quickly to snap-up both Cunningham and Roeder as soon as he heard a whisper that Arsenal weren't going to retain them.

He put a smile back on the face of Orient's bank manager again in August, 1981, when a £600,000 bid from Notts County for winger John Chiedozie proved irresistible. Previously under Bloomfield, both Tommy Taylor (£78,000 to West Ham United) and Dennis Rofe (£112,000 to Leicester City) were also Orient club record sales at the time of their departures – and yes, Cheesewright had a hand in bringing all three of them to Brisbane Road, too.

But it's not only Cheesewright to whom Orient owe a huge debt of gratitude. Numerous others also did much unheralded work behind the scenes to keep Os' production line well oiled, including Dave Woolley, Harry Spinner, Ken Grimes and Maurice Newman whose Beaumont FC was a prolific junior feeder club to Orient far beyond supplying Laurie Cunningham.

To put the value of the above transfer transactions into true perspective, Leyton Orient haven't spent more than £175,000 on a player since they paid that amount to Wigan Athletic for centre-back Paul Beesley almost 30 years ago, in October 1989.

HOME-GROWN PLAYERS WHO MADE THE FIRST TEAM
HERE is a list of the 27 home-produced players who appeared in at least one Second Division fixture (including sub appearances) for Os during the 70s. England youth goalkeeper, Hackney-born John Smeulders, had two first team outings against Fulham in the 1977-78 League Cup and also appeared in the Anglo-Scottish Cup.

Player	Debut	Games	Moved to	Date	Fee
Peter Allen	1965-66	432	Millwall	1978	Free
Tommy Taylor	1967-68	230	West Ham Utd	1970	£78,000
Dennis Rofe	1967-68	171	Leicester City	1972	£112,000
Barrie Fairbrother	1969-70	188	Millwall	1975	Free
Steve Bowtell	1969-70	8	Margate	1973	Free
Terry Brisley	1970-71	142	Millwall	1975	PX
Bobby Moss	1970-71	5	Colchester Utd	1972	Free
Paul Harris	1970-71	96	Swansea City	1975	Free
Peter Johnson	1971-72	5	AEK Athens	1974	Free
John Lewis	1972-73	2	Romford	1974	Free
Malcolm Linton	1972-73	19	Tampa Bay Rowdies	1975	Free
Bobby Fisher	1973-74	314	Cambridge Utd	1982	Free
Mike O'Shaugnessy	1973-74	1	Harlow Town	1975	Free
Tony Grealish	1974-75	171	Luton Town	1979	£150,000
Laurie Cunningham	1974-75	75	WBA	1977	£110,000
Dean Mooney	1974-75	22	Dulwich Hamlet	1976	Free
Glenn Roeder	1974-75	123	QPR	1978	£250,000
Nigel Gray	1974-75	233	Swindon Town	1983	Free
Gary Hibbs	1975-76	1	Aldershot	1977	Free
Terry Glynn	1976-77	2	Brentford	1977	Free
John Chiedozie	1976-77	145	Notts County	1981	£600,000
Billy Hurley	1976-77	2	Retired	1977	NA
Kevin Godfrey	1977-78	285	Brentford	1988	Free
Tunji Banjo	1977-78	27	AEL Limasol	1982	Free
Henry Hughton	1978-79	129	Crystal Palace	1982	Free
Mark Smith	1978-79	3	Tilbury	1981	Free
John Kane	1978-79	1	Rainham Town	1980	Free
Totals		2832			£1,300,000

Key: Games = League games (inc sub); PX = part-exchange
Appearances relate only to the period from 1969-70 to 1979-80 inc
Source: Leyton Orient – The Complete Record (2006)

Youth

They pulled on the jersey

ON the previous pages we highlighted the most successful youth products who experienced first team football with Orient before the end of the 70s.

This extended list includes former apprentice professionals who also played for Os' Colts teams in the South-East Counties League, as well as those who appeared for the reserves in the Midweek League and Football Combination.

A few were signed from other clubs, while some went on to graduate to the senior side in the early 80s. Several went on to become pro's at other clubs.

We believe they all deserve to be acknowledged because they managed to achieve what thousands of us can only dream of . . . they pulled on the jersey.

ABBOTT (76-77)
ABEBRESE (77-78)
AKERS (77-78)
ALCORN, Roddy (75-76)
ALLEN (76-77)
ALPAY (79-80)

BAILEY, Bill (69-70)
BAINES, John (74-75)
BALL (77-78)
BARCLAY (77-78)
BARNES (77-78)
BARR, Ron (74-75) P
BATHO (71-72)
BEASON, Malcolm (75-76) P*
BENJAMIN, Terry (75-76)
BERNET (74-75)
BINKS, Martin (69-70)
BIRKS (76-77)
BISHOP, F (76-77)
BLACKHALL, Mark (76-77)
BLYTH, John (76-77)
BOLLE, John (78-79)
BOSE (75-76)
BOTHAM, Ray (71-72) P
BOWLER, P (71-72)
BRAGG, Billy (72-73) P
BRIGHT, Kelvin (77-78)
BRIGHT, Micky (76-77) P
BROOKS, John (69-70)
BROOKS (74-75)
BROOKS, Barry (78-79)
BROOMFIELD, Bobby (74-75) P
BURT, Martin (73-74)

CANHAM (71-72)
CARENZAR, Chris (78-79)***
CAREY, Steve (75-76)
CARRIGAN, Mark (75-76)
CHEVANNES (76-77)
CLAPTON, Danny (78-79)
CLARK, Paul (73-74)
CLARKE (76-77)
CLARY, A. (69-70)
COLE, Graham (72-73) P

COLE (76-77)
COOK (72-73)
COOMBES, Ray (69-70)
COTTON, Roy (74-75) P*
CORNWELL (74-75)
COVENTRY, Steve (69-70)
CROW (71-72)
CURTIS (76-77)

DARK (77-78)
DAVIS (78-79)
DEW (72-73)
DILLON, Tommy (71-72)
DOBRAN (76-77)
DROGMAN, Chris (74-75)
DRUMMY, Sean (72-73)
DUFF (72-73)
DUFOSSE (76-77)
DUNNE (74-75)
DUNWELL, Joe (69-70)
DURRANT, Alan (69-70)

EDWARDS (71-72)
ELLIS, Laurie (71-72)
ELLIS, Philip (79-80)
EMANUEL, Terry (75-76)
EMMANUEL, David (69-70)
ERYSTHEE (78-79)
EVANS (77-78)
EVERITT, Mike (75-76) P*

FAREBROTHER (77-78)
FENWICK, Steve (79-80)
FIDGE (77-78)
FIELDING, Jeffery (79-80)
FILBY, Ian (71-72) P
FILBY, Malcolm (69-70) P
FINEMAN, Alan (73-74)
FINDLAY (77-78)
FINLAY, Steve (75-76)
FLETCHER (72-73)
FOLEY (75-76)
FOSTER, Colin (79-80)
FRANCIS (77-78)

GAMMONS (72-73)
GERRETT (79-80)
GLIBBERY (77-78)
GOFF, John (79-80)
GRANT, Gary (69-70)
GRANT, Paul (76-77)
GRAY, M (69-70)
GREALISH, Brian (74-75)

HALL (78-79)
HALLYBONE, Jimmy (78-79)
HAMILTON (71-72)
HANDLEY (78-79)
HANSBURY, Roger (78-79)****
HARPER (76-77)
HARRINGTON (77-78)
HARVEY (77-78)
HATFIELD (77-78)
HEARN, Robert (71-72)
HEMPKIN, Bob (74-75)
HENNEY, Chris (75-76) P
HILLEN, Gordon (70-71)
HOLMES, John (74-75)
HOLYOAK, Phil (78-79)
HOOK (71-72)
HUDSON, Paul (72-73)
HUDSON, Neil (77-78)
HUNT, Terry (74-75) P

JABLONSKI (72-73)
JOHNSON, Dennis (74-75)
JOHNSON, John (74-75)
JOHNSON, Stephen (75-76)
JOHNSON, Colin (75-76) P
JULIANS, Gary (75-76)

KANE, Jimmy (76-77)
KANE, Mark (77-78) P
KAYLOR, John (74-75)
KEEFE, G (69-70)
KEEN, Russell (78-79)
KEENAGHAN (77-78)
KELLY, Mark (78-79)
KIDD, Stephen (77-78)
KIDNEY (77-78)

KINGHAM, Graham (77-78)
KINGHAM, P (76-77)
KINNEAR, Chris (72-73) P
KIRTON (78-79)
KROUGH (71-72)

LAPWORTH, S (69-70)
LAW (75-76)
LAZARUS, Nicky (76-77)
LEACH, Malcolm (71-72)
LEE, John (69-70)
LEVY, Neil (75-76)
LITTLEFIELD, Martin (71-72)
LLOYD, Mark (77-78)

MADDEN, David (78-79)
MALLETT, David (Gk) (76-77)
MANKELOW, Jamie (78-79)
MANNING, Phil (69-70)
MANNING, Terry (69-70)
MASON (76-77)
MAVIN (79-80)
McCARTHY, Barry (74-75)
McCORMICK (72-73)
McFARLANE, John (79-80)
McLELLAND (69-70)
McNEIL, Mark (78-79) P
MEEKING, Nigel (78-79) P
MELIUS (77-78)
MERCER, Tony (79-80)
MERRY (79-80)
MERRIN (79-80)
MESSOM (71-72)
MILLS (74-75)
MOLES, Peter (76-77)
MOORE, Gary (76-77)
MOORE, George (75-76)
MORRIS, Ian (74-75)
MORRISON, Brian (71-72)
MOSSON, B (71-72)
MUNDY (77-78)

NAYLOR, P (71-72)
NEWMAN (79-80)
NICHOLLS (76-77)

OLEOSIE, Henry (78-79)
OSBORNE, Gary (77-78)

PAGE, Gerald (77-78)
PALMER (71-72)
PALMER (77-78)
PARSONS, Ian (74-75)
PEACOCK, Richard (69-70)
PENNYFATHER (69-70)
PIATKOWSKI, Luigi (74-75)
PLAYELL (72-73)
PORTER, Billy (74-75)
POWLEY (74-75)
PRICE, J (71-72)

RATFORD, C (77-78)
RAYMOND (77-78)
REARDON (74-75)
REDDER (72-73)
REYNOLDS, Stuart (76-77)
ROBINSON, Keith (69-70)
ROBINSON (72-73)
RODGERS (77-78)
RUGELEY (75-76)
RUTT (78-79)

SAMBRIDGE (74-75)
SANDERS (77-78)
SARGENT, Grant (78-79)
SCANES, Tony (75-76) P
SCOTT, Lloyd (77-78) P
SCRIMSHAW, Brian (69-70) P
SELLEARS (75-76)
SHORD, Jimmy (74-75)
SIANI, Brian (76-77)
SIMMONS (79-80)
SIMPSON, Michael (74-75)
SIMPSON, Tony (72-73)
SMITH, Malcolm (71-72)
SOPER, Terry (74-75)
SOUTH, John (69-70) P
SPICER, Trevor (71-72)
SPRING, Barry (71-72)
SPRINGALL, Stephen (77-78)
STAINES, David (70-71)

STAPLETON (79-80)
STEPHENSON, Alan (76-77)
STEPHENSON, David (75-76)
STOCKWELL, Barry (77-78)
STROUD, Stan (75-76)
SULLIVAN, Gerry (71-72)
SWASH, K (71-72)
SYRETT (71-72)

TAYLOR (77-78)
TEMPLEMAN, Lee (78-79)
THACKERAY, Brian (77-78)
THEODOTOU (71-72)
THOIRS, Gary (74-75)
THOMAS, Kim (74-75)
THOMAS, R (74-75)
THOMPSON (76-77)
TIPLOW (72-73)
TITLOW (74-75)
TODD, Barrington (78-79)
TOMKINS, Len (71-72) P
TONKIN (79-80)
TRICE, Stephen (69-70)
TSINDIDES (76-77)
TUCKER, Tony (72-73)
TURNER (77-78)
TUTU, Osei (72-73)
TYLER (78-79)

VINER, Steve (72-73)

WALSH, Keith (71-72)
WALTERS, Eric (75-76)
WARD, G (77-78)
WARD, J (71-72)
WAREING (71-72)
WATERFALL, Robert (79-80)
WESTERN (77-78)
WHITE, J (74-75)
WHITE, Stan (72-73)
WILLSON (72-73)
WILSON, Ricky (78-79)
WINN (76-77)
WOODCOCK, Kevin (76-77)
WOODWARD, Ian (71-72) P

* Signed from Crystal Palace
** Signed from Brentford
*** On trial from USA
**** Loan from Norwich City
***** Signed from Walthamstow Avenue

* Christian names or initials stated where known. The years in brackets denote the first season in which the player appeared. Names in bold followed by a 'P' indicate those who were signed as full professionals. We've tried to make the list as accurate as possible, based on info published in the match programme, but we apologise to anyone we've overlooked.

A youth team group from 1977-78. Standing, left to right: Tunji Banjo, Colin Johnson, Chris Henney, Gary Moore, Mark Blackhall, Jimmy Kane, David Mallett. Front: John Kane, Henry Hughton, Kevin Godfrey, Billy Hurley, John Chiedozie.

Collectibles

Orient Football Club Limited

Leyton Stadium · Brisbane Road · Leyton E10 5NE
Telephone 01-539 2223/4
Telegrams "The Orient" Leyton E10

AUTOGRAPH SHEET

SEASON 1974 / 75

Ray Goddard

Peter Allen

Tom Walley

Derrick Downing

Terry Brisley

Gerry Queen

Peter Bennett

Paul Harris

Laurie Cunningham

Malcolm Linton

Peter Angell
(Trainer)

Ernie Shepherd
(Physiotherapist)

John Jackson

John Boyle

David Payne

Phil Hoadley

Barrie Fairbrother

Mickey Bulleck

Ricky Heppolette

Bobby Fisher

Bill Roffey

Derek Possee

George Petchey
(Manager)

Terry Long
(Coach)

ORIENT FOOTBALL CLUB

ORIENT

1881

FOOTBALL CLUB

ORIENT F.C.
PLAYER OF THE YEAR
Dinner - Dance
Saturday, 21st April, 1979
at the
INGREBOURNE SUITE
LADBROKE MERCURY MOTOR INN
Southend Arterial Road, Hornchurch, Essex

ORIENT

PLEASE ENTER
BY ENTRANCE

Z

ORIENT
FOOTBALL
CLUB

FOOTBALL LEAGUE DIVISION 2

ORIENT v
WEST HAM UNITED

Leyton Stadium

on Saturday 14th April 1979
Kick-off 3 pm
Gates open 1.30 pm

SOUTH TERRACE
(See plan on reverse)

£1.00 incl VAT

To be retained

FINEST TEAS
BLENDED EXCLUSIVELY FOR
'ORIENT'
SUPPORTERS CLUB

 Orient Football Club

FOOTBALL LEAGUE DIVISION TWO

Date SAT 01/10/77 Kick-off 3.00PM

ORIENT

VERSUS

TOTTENHAM HOTSPUR

Stand NORTH WING Entrance A

Row B Seat 9 £ 1.60 Including
VAT

ROW SEAT

A 9

FOOTBALL LEAGUE—2nd DIVISION

WOLVERHAMPTON
WANDERERS
v.

ORIENT
Saturday
April 23rd 1977

KICK-OFF 3.0 P.M.

Molineux Street Stand
(Centre)

£1.60

This portion to be retained

LEAGUE APPEARANCES

		1969-70	1970-71	1971-72	1972-73	1973-74	1974-75	1975-76	1976-77	1977-78	1978-79	1979-80	Total	Sub
1	Allen	46	42	40	42	37	31 (1)	7	29	18 (3)			292	4
2	Hoadley			32	42	42	38	40	22	39			255	0
3	Fisher					4 (4)	42	36 (1)	31 (1)	42	37	42	234	6
4	Bullock	42	41 (1)	42	25 (6)	40 (1)	28	16 (2)					234	10
5	Jackson					16	42	42	42	42	42		226	0
6	Bennett		30	35	25	2	15 (1)	33 (1)	25 (2)	24	6		195	4
7	Roffey					20 (1)	6	13 (1)	34 (1)	42	39	40	194	3
8	Goddard	44	42	39	42	25							192	0
9	Fairbrother	35 (4)	31 (4)	17 (3)	24 (3)	41	23 (3)						171	17
10	Grealish						24 (1)	38	33	35 (1)	39		169	2
11	Walley			22	8 (2)	42	41	42					155	2
12	Queen				33	34 (2)	32 (2)	32	18 (3)				149	7
13	Brisley		18 (4)	25 (3)	38 (1)	38 (1)	14						133	9
14	Rofe	45	42	40	2								129	0
15	Dyson	46	41	34 (3)	8 (3)								129	6
16	Gray N.						2	1	22	22	42	37	126	0
17	Mayo								4	35 (1)	40	39	118	1
18	Heppolette				15	34	22	34	8				113	0
19	Roeder						3 (3)	20 (5)	42	42			107	8
20	Downing				38	35 (2)	27 (2)						100	4
21	Taylor T	46	11									42	99	0
22	Jones	46	41	10 (1)									97	1
23	Harris		1	42	37	2	14						96	0
24	Chiedozie								6 (9)	21	33 (3)	35 (2)	95	14
25	Mancini	38	42	10									90	0
26	Payne					34 (1)	2 (1)	19	22	11 (3)			88	5
27	Lazarus	29	32	20 (1)									81	1
28	Possee						34 (1)	21 (1)	22 (1)				77	3
29	Bowyer			42	33 (3)								75	3
30	Hughton										33	40	73	0
31	Cunningham						15 (2)	33 (1)	24				72	3
32	Coates										30	42	72	0
33	Kitchen									42	22 (1)		64	1
34	Brabrook	37	26 (2)										63	2
35	Moores										30	21 (5)	51	5
36	Whittle								31 (2)		10	6 (1)	47	3
37	Went										37	8	45	0

SEASON-BY-SEASON

		1969-70	1970-71	1971-72	1972-73	1973-74	1974-75	1975-76	1976-77	1977-78	1978-79	1979-80	Total	Sub
38	Day											42	42	0
39	Glover								16	21			37	0
40	Allder							19 4	15 3				34	7
41	Jennings											32 2	32	2
42	Arber			3	28								31	0
43	Clarke								14 1	12 3	4 2		30	6
44	Margerrison											22 2	22	2
45	Harper	19 2		1									20	2
46	Boyle					13	5						18	0
47	Banjo									3 3	13 4	1	17	7
48	Mooney						1 2	15 4					17	5
49	Parmenter	12 2		4	1								16	3
50	Godfrey									11	3 3	2 3	16	6
51	Linton				11	2	5	1					14	5
52	Riddick		13 6		1	1							13	8
53	Plume	10 5		2	1								12	6
54	Wall				10								10	0
55	Slater	9											9	0
56	Parsons										6		6	0
57	Sewell			5	2								5	2
58	Bowtell	2		3									5	0
59	Smith									1		2	3	0
60	Penfold											3	3	0
61	Moss		2 3										2	3
62	Johnson			1	2								1	2
63	Fulton				1								1	0
64	Hurley								1 1				1	1
65	Glynn								1 1				1	1
66	O'Shaughnessy					1							1	0
67	Hibbs							1					1	0
68	Gray M.										1 1		1	1
69	Lewis				2								0	2
70	Cotton							3					0	3
71	Everett								1				0	1
72	Beason								1				0	1
73	Kane										1		0	1

* Another three players appeared for the first team in Cup matches. They were: John Smeulders (2 League Cup appearances v Fulham in 1977-78); Steve Hamberger and Sean Rafter (1 League Cup appearance each in 1979-80).

LEADING GOALSCORERS

LEADING GOALSCORERS					
Season		FL	FAC	LC	Total
1969-70	Mickey Bullock	19	0	0	19
1970-71	Mark Lazarus	6	1	0	7
1971-72	Ian Bowyer	15	2	0	17
1972-73	Barrie Fairbrother	11	0	0	11
1973-74*	Mickey Bullock	16	0	2	18
1974-75	Derek Possee	7	1	0	8
1975-76	Laurie Cunningham	8	0	0	8
1976-77**	Laurie Cunningham	6	0	1	7
1977-78	Peter Kitchen	21	7	1	29
1978-79	Ian Moores	13	0	0	13
1979-80	Billy Jennings	11	2	0	13
	Joe Mayo	11	1	1	13
Barrie Fairbrother scored 19 goals (14 FL, 3 FAC, 2 LC)					
**Alan Whittle scored 7 goals (5 FL, 2 FAC)*					

ALL GOALSCORERS

1969-70
LEAGUE: 19 Bullock, 13 Fairbrother, 7 Lazarus, 6 Dyson, 4 Mancini, 3 Brabrook, Rofe, Allen, Jones, 2 Taylor, OG, 1 Plume, Parmenter.
CUPS: 1 Harper.

1970-71
LEAGUE: 6 Lazarus, 5 Bullock, 3 Riddick, Dyson, 2 Fairbrother, Allen, 1 Harper, Moss, Parmenter, Brisley, Brabrook, Jones, Mancini, OG.
CUPS: 2 Fairbrother, 1 Dyson, Lazarus.

1971-72
LEAGUE: 15 Bowyer, 11 Bullock, 9 Dyson, 5 Allen, 2 Walley, Brisley, Harris, OG, 1 Mancini, Lazarus.
CUPS: 2 Bowyer, Bullock, Fairbrother, 1 Allen, Bullock, Hoadley, Lazarus, Dyson.

Dean Mooney (9) celebrates his only first team goal at Brisbane Road, against Oxford in April, 1976. Derek Possee (11), Doug Allder and Bobby Fisher are first to congratulate him. In 1973-74, 'Deadly Dean' scored 37 goals in 41 games for the youth team.

1972-73
LEAGUE: 11 Fairbrother, 10 Riddick, 6 Downing, 5 Brisley, 4 Bullock, Bowyer, 3 Johnson, Allen, 2 Harris, 1 Bennett.
CUPS: 2 Downing, 1 Arber, Bowyer.

1973-74
LEAGUE: 16 Bullock, 14 Fairbrother, 12 Queen, 6 Heppolette, 3 Downing, 1 Roffey, Allen, Hoadley, Walley.
CUPS: 5 Fairbrother, 2 Bullock, 1 Bowyer, Queen.

1974-75
LEAGUE: 7 Possee, 4 Queen, 3 Downing, Bullock, 2 Heppolette, Grealish, Walley; 1 Brisley, Cunningham, Fairbrother, Hoadley, OG.
CUPS: 1 Possee, Fairbrother, Hoadley, Queen.

1975-76
LEAGUE: 8 Cunningham, 6 Queen, 5 Bennett, 4 OG, 3 Mooney, Possee, 2 Roeder, Heppolette, 1 Bullock, Grealish, Hoadley, Walley.
CUPS: N/A

1976-77
LEAGUE: 6 Cunningham, 5 Bennett, Whittle; 3 Hoadley, 2 Clarke, Glover, Queen, N. Gray, Roffey, Grealish, Roeder, 1 Mayo, Possee, Allen, OG.
CUPS: 2 Whittle, 1 Cunningham, Hoadley, Possee, Roffey.

1977-78
LEAGUE: 21 Kitchen, 9 Mayo, 4 Clarke, 3 Glover, 2 Chiedozie, Bennett, 1 Fisher, Roffey.
CUPS: 8 Kitchen, 1 Allen, Bennett, OG.

1978-79
LEAGUE: 13 Moores, 11 Jennings, 7 Kitchen, 6 Chiedozie, 5 Grealish, 3 Coates, 2 Hughton, Went, 1 Whittle, Banjo.
CUPS: 2 Kitchen, 1 Chiedozie, Fisher.

1979-80
LEAGUE: 11 Jennings, Mayo, 9 Coates, 5 Taylor, 3 Chiedozie, Fisher; 2 Margerrison, 1 Godfrey, Penfold, Went, Roffey.
CUPS: 2 Jennings, Mayo, Chiedozie, 1 Hughton, Margerrison, Taylor.

PLAYER OF THE YEAR AWARDS

THE first Orient Player of the Year awards were held at the end of the 'oh so close' 1973-74 season. Commercial manager Brian Blower said: "I remember starting it off and Barrie Fairbrother was a great winner, walking away with some first class prize holidays from 4S Sports Travel. There was a great response from supporters, who cast more votes than we expected."

Award winners
1973-74 Barrie Fairbrother
1974-75 John Jackson
1975-76 Tom Walley
1976-77 Glenn Roeder
1977-78 Peter Kitchen
1978-79 Joe Mayo
1979-80 Bobby Fisher

Two Player of the Year award winners, Tom Walley and Glenn Roeder.

CUP EXITS		
Season	LC	FAC
1969-70	R1	R1
1970-71	R1	R4
1971-72	R1	R6
1972-73	R2	R3
1973-74	R3	R4
1974-75	R2	R3
1975-76	R2	R3
1976-77	R3	R4
1977-78	R3	SF
1978-79	R2	R4
1979-80	R2	R4

Alan Whittle scoring one of his two in the FA Cup second replay against Darlington at White Hart Lane in January, 1977.

FINAL LEAGUE POSITION SUMMARY AT A GLANCE														
			Home					Away						
Season	Div	P	W	D	L	F	A	W	D	L	F	A	Pts	Pos
1969-70	3	46	16	5	2	43	15	9	7	7	24	21	62	1st
1970-71	2	42	5	11	5	16	15	4	5	12	13	36	34	17th
1971-72	2	42	12	4	5	32	19	2	5	14	18	42	37	17th
1972-73	2	42	11	6	4	33	18	1	6	14	16	35	36	15th
1973-74	2	42	9	8	4	28	17	6	10	5	27	25	48	4th
1974-75	2	42	8	9	4	17	16	3	11	7	11	23	42	12th
1975-76	2	42	10	6	5	21	12	3	8	10	16	27	40	13th
1976-77	2	42	4	8	9	18	23	5	8	8	19	32	34	19th
1977-78	2	42	8	11	2	30	20	2	7	12	13	29	38	14th
1978-79	2	42	11	5	5	32	18	4	5	12	19	33	40	11th
1979-80	2	42	7	9	5	29	31	5	8	8	19	23	41	14th

SECOND BEST

Stars of the 70s who played at Orient

Best of the lot: The great George Best, all alone on the Brisbane Road turf, during Fulham's visit on December 11, 1976.

IT takes two teams to produce a great football match, so having looked back at the Orient players who gave us pleasure and a million memories throughout the 70s, let's now take a quick look at the calibre of opposition that also entertained us – in LEAGUE matches only – during the period under review.

Global legends such as George Best, Bobby Moore and Peter Shilton head a stellar international cast whose presence among the opposing ranks at Brisbane Road added another layer of expectation and excitement to the match day experience.

We were also very fortunate to see, 'in the flesh', some of the classic characters of the era who played the game with a swagger – Frank Worthington, Rodney Marsh, Tony Currie and Stan Bowles (before he eventually joined Os in 1980).

Other gifted playmakers in Glenn Hoddle, Trevor Brooking; world class strikers Trevor Francis and Gary Lineker (he played in the final game of the 1979-80 season, so we're sneaking him in!) plus wing wizards Gordon Hill, Charlie Cooke and Alan Devonshire.

In compiling the following star-studded squad of past league visitors to Leyton, it underlines the depth of quality prevalent in many Division Two sides during that era, when clubs such as Spurs, Chelsea, West Ham and past European Cup winners Manchester United were forced to slum it outside the top sphere for a while. Our squad includes England internationals with more than 1,250 full caps between them.

It's fair to say that at the time these players faced the Os most were young, possibly little known, and still progressing towards stardom, or were already on the down slope of an illustrious career. Nevertheless, it's a very impressive squad from which to pick, including an abundance of seasoned internationals from all the home nations.

You could pick several completely different teams and they would all be unplayable.

Now imagine them all playing together in their prime.

And then think how much better this imaginary squad would be if we included those who appeared at our place in Cup ties: Alan Hudson (Chelsea), Charlie George (Arsenal/Derby), Alan

Hansen (Partick Thistle), Derek Dougan (Wolves), Kevin Beattie (Ipswich), Arnold Muhren (Ipswich) and Mick Mills (Ipswich).

Just for fun, why not have a go at selecting your own 'Visiting Team of the 70s' from the following:

GOALKEEPERS: Peter Shilton (Leicester City), Peter Bonetti (Chelsea), Phil Parkes (QPR/West Ham), Alex Stepney (Man Utd), Jim Montgomery (Sunderland).

FULL-BACKS: David Nish (Leicester City), Dave Clement (QPR), Viv Anderson (Nottm Forest), Ron Harris (Chelsea), Keith Newton (Burnley), Kenny Sansom (C Palace), Ray Stewart (West Ham), Frank Lampard (West Ham).

CENTRAL DEFENDERS: Bobby Moore (Fulham), Dave Watson (Sunderland), Alvin Martin (West Ham), Billy Bonds (West Ham), Chris Nicholl (Villa), Martin Buchan (Man Utd), Jim Holton (Man Utd), Mike England (Cardiff), Mark Lawrenson (Brighton), Mike Doyle (Stoke), Gary Mabbutt (Bristol R).

MIDFIELDERS: Graham Paddon (Norwich), Terry Venables (QPR), Gerry Francis (QPR), Alan Mullery (Fulham), Graeme Souness (Middlesbrough), Nobby Stiles (Middlesbrough), Martin Dobson (Burnley), Dennis Mortimer (Coventry), Bruce Rioch (Villa), Brian Little (Villa), Martin O'Neill (Nottm Forest), Asa Hartford (WBA), Peter Reid (Bolton), Brian Greenhoff (Man Utd), Colin Harvey (Sheff Wed), John McGovern (Nottm Forest), Ray Wilkins (Chelsea), Alan Ball (Soton), Steve Perryman (Spurs), Glenn Hoddle (Spurs), Howard Kendall (Stoke), Martin Peters (Norwich), Billy Bremner (Hull), Archie Gemmill (Birmingham), Trevor Brooking (West Ham), Paul Allen (West Ham).

WINGERS: Dave Thomas (Burnley), Gordon Hill (Millwall), Peter Thompson (Bolton), John Aston (Luton), John Robertson (Nottm Forest), Charlie Cooke (Chelsea), Willie Morgan (Bolton), Peter Houseman (Oxford), Terry Paine (Hereford), Kevin Sheedy (Hereford), Peter Taylor (Spurs), Vince Hilaire (C Palace), Keith Weller (Leicester), Leighton James (Burnley), Alan Devonshire (West Ham).

FORWARDS: George Best (Fulham), Rodney Marsh (QPR), Stan Bowles (QPR), Trevor Francis (Birmingham), Malcolm MacDonald (Luton), John Toshack (Cardiff/Swansea), Dennis Tueart (Sunderland), Ron Davies (Portsmouth), Stuart Pearson (Hull/Man Utd), Duncan McKenzie (Nottm Forest), Tony Brown (WBA), Lou Macari (Man Utd), Bryan Robson (Sunderland/ West Ham), Peter Osgood (Soton), Mick Channon (Soton), Wyn Davies (Blackpool), Paul Mariner (Plymouth), Peter Withe (Nottm Forest/Newcastle), Tony Woodcock (Nottm Forest), John Richards (Wolves), Alan Sunderland (Wolves), Frank Worthington (Bolton), Brian Stein (Luton), Martin Chivers (Brighton), Luther Blissett (Watford), David Cross (West Ham), Paul Goddard (QPR), Clive Allen (QPR), Gary Lineker (Leicester).

Typically calm and composed under pressure, Fulham's Bobby Moore tries to play his way out of trouble under pressure from Gerry Queen.

Choose your ex-Os

HOW about this squad of ex-Os, who all played against Orient at Brisbane Road in the 70s:

Goalkeepers: Peter Shilton (Leicester), Ray Goddard (Millwall), Peter Wells (Soton).

Full-Backs: Frank Clark (Nottm Forest), Dennis Rofe (Leicester).

Central Defenders: Terry Mancini (QPR), Paul Went (Charlton/Portsmouth), Tommy Taylor (West Ham), Alvin Martin (West Ham), Glenn Roeder (QPR).

Midfielders: Ray Wilkins (Chelsea), Terry Brisley (Millwall/Charlton), John Margerrison (Fulham), Tom Walley (Watford), Ricky Heppolette (Preston), Tony Grealish (Luton).

Wingers: Allan Glover (WBA), Derrick Downing (York).

Forwards: Harry Gregory (Charlton), Stan Bowles (QPR), Joe Mayo (WBA), Gordon Bolland (Millwall), Derek Clarke (Oxford Utd), Alan Whittle (C Palace), Ian Bowyer (Nottm Forest), Vic Halom (Oldham), Peter Kitchen (Fulham).

The 70s?

Muddy marvellous!